AF814330

Recommended by **Teachers**
Trusted by **Toppers**

All in One

SOCIOLOGY
Class 12

EVERYTHING YOU NEED TO SCORE

- Simplified Theory
- NCERT & Other Important Questions
- CBQs; MCQs, A-R, Case Based
- Board Questions Upto 2025
- Sample Question Papers

CBSE Exams 2026

Recommended by **Teachers**
Trusted by **Toppers**

All in One®

SOCIOLOGY
Class 12

EVERYTHING YOU NEED TO SCORE

- Simplified Theory
- NCERT & Other Important Questions
- CBQs; MCQs, A-R, Case Based
- Board Questions Upto 2025
- Sample Question Papers

CBSE Exams 2026

Author
Charu Tripathi

arihant
SUCCESS AND NOTHING LESS

arihant
SUCCESS AND NOTHING LESS

ARIHANT PRAKASHAN
(School Division Series)

卐 *ADMINISTRATIVE & PRODUCTION OFFICES*

Regd. Office
'Ramchhaya' 4577/15, Agarwal Road, Darya Ganj, New Delhi -110002
Tele: 011- 47630600, 43518550; Fax: 011- 23280316

卐 *Head Office*
Kalindi, TP Nagar, Meerut (UP) - 250002, Tel: 0121-7156203, 7156204

卐 *SALES & SUPPORT OFFICES*
Agra, Ahmedabad, Bengaluru, Bareilly, Chennai, Delhi, Guwahati, Hyderabad, Jaipur, Jhansi, Kolkata, Lucknow, Nagpur & Pune.

PO No : TXT-XX-XXXXXXX-X-XX

Published By Arihant Publications (India) Ltd.

For further information about the books published by Arihant, log on to www.arihantbooks.com or e-mail at info@arihantbooks.com

Follow us on

卐 *PRICE* ₹ 350.00

PRODUCTION TEAM

Publishing Managers
Mahendra Singh Rawat & Keshav Mohan

Cover Designer
Rakesh Rawat

Inner Designer
Ankit Tyagi

Project Head
Manju

Page Layouting
Lalit Chaprana

Proof Reader
Bhawna Madrey

Index *cum* Study Planner

PART A INDIAN SOCIETY

PART B CHANGE AND DEVELOPMENT IN INDIAN SOCIETY

One Book- Endless Features

to Help you Succeed

Complete Theory in Each Chapter

Each chapter has Complete, Easy to Understand and Simplified theory covering latest syllabus and NCERT Textbook. Theory is developed in such a way that it is suitable for all types of learners.

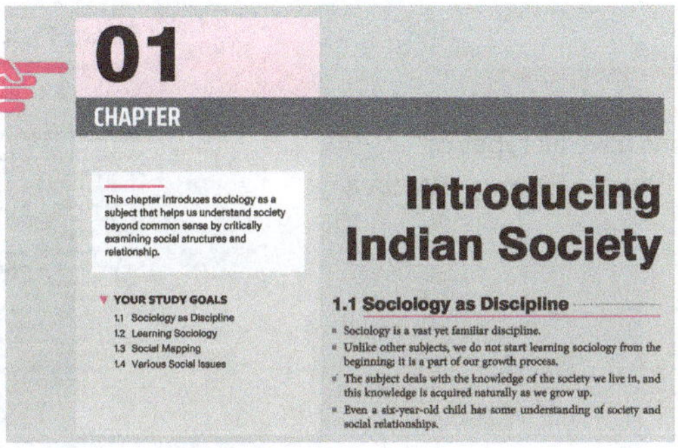

01

CHAPTER

This chapter introduces sociology as a subject that helps us understand society beyond common sense by critically examining social structures and relationship.

YOUR STUDY GOALS

1.1 Sociology as Discipline
1.2 Learning Sociology
1.3 Social Mapping
1.4 Various Social Issues

Introducing Indian Society

1.1 Sociology as Discipline

- Sociology is a vast yet familiar discipline.
- Unlike other subjects, we do not start learning sociology from the beginning; it is a part of our growth process.
- The subject deals with the knowledge of the society we live in, and this knowledge is acquired naturally as we grow up.
- Even a six-year-old child has some understanding of society and social relationships.

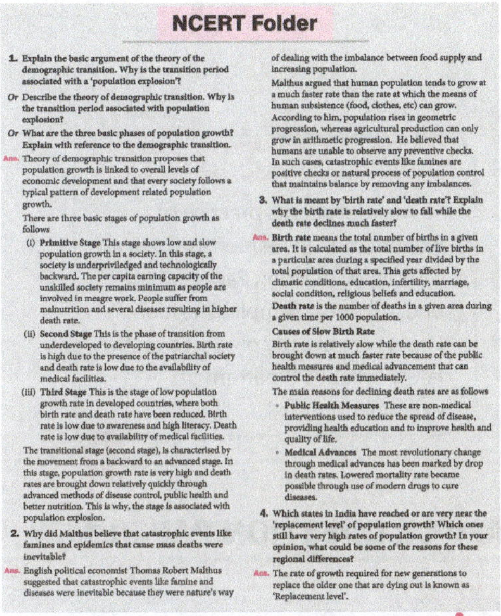

NCERT Folder

1. Explain the basic argument of the theory of the demographic transition. Why is the transition period associated with a 'population explosion'?

Or **Describe the theory of demographic transition. Why is the transition period associated with population explosion?**

Or **What are the three basic phases of population growth? Explain with reference to the demographic transition.**

Ans. Theory of demographic transition proposes that population growth is linked to overall levels of economic development and that every society follows a typical pattern of development related population growth.

There are three basic stages of population growth as follows

(i) **Primitive Stage** This stage shows low and slow population growth in a society. In this stage, a society is underpriviledged and technologically backward. The per capita earning capacity of the unskilled society remains minimum as people are involved in meagre work. People suffer from malnutrition and several diseases resulting in higher death rate.

(ii) **Second Stage** This is the phase of transition from underdeveloped to developing countries. Birth rate is high due to the presence of the patriarchal society and death rate is low due to the availability of medical facilities.

(iii) **Third Stage** This is the stage of low population growth rate in developed countries, where both birth rate and death rate have been reduced. Birth rate is low due to awareness and high literacy. Death rate is low due to availability of medical facilities.

The transitional stage (second stage), is characterised by the movement from a backward to an advanced stage. In this stage, population growth rate is very high and death rates are brought down relatively quickly through advanced methods of disease control, public health and better nutrition. This is why, the stage is associated with population explosion.

2. Why did Malthus believe that catastrophic events like famines and epidemics that cause mass deaths were inevitable?

Ans. English political economist Thomas Robert Malthus suggested that catastrophic events like famine and diseases were inevitable because they were nature's way of dealing with the imbalance between food supply and increasing population.

Malthus argued that human population tends to grow at a much faster rate than the rate at which the means of human subsistence (food, clothes, etc) can grow. According to him, population rises in geometric progression, whereas agricultural production can only grow in arithmetic progression. He believed that humans are unable to observe any preventive checks. In such cases, catastrophic events like famines are positive checks or natural process of population control that maintains balance by removing any imbalances.

3. What is meant by 'birth rate' and 'death rate'? Explain why the birth rate is relatively slow to fall while the death rate declines much faster?

Ans. Birth rate means the total number of births in a given area. It is calculated as the total number of live births in a particular area during a specified year divided by the total population of that area. This gets affected by climatic conditions, education, infertility, marriage, social condition, religious beliefs and education.

Death rate is the number of deaths in a given area during a given time per 1000 population.

Causes of Slow Birth Rate

Birth rate is relatively slow while the death rate can be brought down at much faster rate because of the public health measures and medical advancement that can control the death rate immediately.

The main reasons for declining death rates are as follows

- **Public Health Measures** These are non-medical interventions used to reduce the spread of disease, providing health education and to improve health and quality of life.
- **Medical Advances** The most revolutionary change through medical advances has been marked by drop in death rates. Lowered mortality rate became possible through use of modern drugs to cure diseases.

4. Which states in India have reached or are very near the 'replacement level' of population growth? Which ones still have very high rates of population growth? In your opinion, what could be some of the reasons for these regional differences?

Ans. The rate of growth required for new generations to replace the older one that are dying out is known as 'Replacement level'.

Quick Test 1

1. What is the quantitative data on population and economy called?
2. Name some positive checks as stated by Malthus.
3. In which essay did Malthus propose his theory of population growth?
4. What are the characteristics of population explosion?
5. What are the indicators of development?

Quick Test

A set of 4-6 Questions given in between the text, helps students to remain connected with the text while studying. They can instantly assess themselves for their understanding.

NCERT Folder

Complete explanations of all the questions of NCERT Exercises.

One Book- Endless Features

to Help you Succeed

Exam Pattern Questions

Exam Pattern Questions have all types of questions; Objective Type Questions, VSA, SA & LA Type Questions

Exam Pattern Questions

Objective Type Questions

Multiple Choice Questions (MCQs)

1. Which among the following is not the use of demographic data?
(a) Economic development
(b) Planning of policies
(c) Implementation of policies
(d) Private welfare

2. Which of the following are reasons why social statistics were important for the emergence of sociology?
I. They helped establish the existence of social phenomena.
II. They provided the foundation for the study of individual behaviours.
III. They justified the need for a systematic study of societies.
IV. They highlighted the social reasons behind demographic trends.
Codes
(a) I and III (b) II and IV
(c) I, III and IV (d) I, II, III and IV

Which of the following appropriately explains the progressions?
I. 2,4,8,16 and 2,4,6,8 respectively
II. 2,4,6,8 and 2,4,8,16 respectively
III. 3,6,12,24 and 3,6,9,12 respectively
IV. 3,6,9,12 and 3,6,12,24 respectively
Codes
(a) I and II (b) II and IV (c) I and III (d) I and IV

6. Which of the following statements is true in the scenario of high fertility rate? CBSE 2023
(a) It takes more time to reach the replacement level.
(b) It takes less time to reach the replacement level.
(c) It does not impact the replacement level.
(d) The impact on replacement level cannot be determined.

7. Which of the demographic indicators are not used to calculate total fertility rate? CBSE SQP Term I, 2021
(a) Number of live births in the reproductive age group
(b) Age specific fertility rate
(c) Sex ratio
(d) Number of women in the child-bearing age group

SELF ASSESSMENT TEST

Objective Type Questions

1. How did the development policies during the Nehruvian era affect the tribal areas?
(a) They were mainly focused on the education of tribal communities.
(b) They benefited the tribes by providing them with better infrastructure.
(c) They caused the tribes to lose their land due to the exploitation of mineral-rich areas.
(d) They had no significant impact on tribal areas.

2. The impact of development policies on tribal areas has been significant because
I. Tribals lost their land due to the exploitation of mineral-rich areas for national development projects.
II. The loss of forests, which were crucial for tribal communities, has had no long-term consequences.
III. The introduction of private property rights undermined tribal communities' collective land ownership.
IV. The development policies were designed to benefit tribal communities by improving their access to modern industries and infrastructure.
Codes
(a) I and IV (b) III and IV
(c) II and III (d) I and III

3. Which of the following statements best represent the goals of the caste system's traditional structure in Indian society?
I. Maintaining occupational hierarchy and division of labour
II. Promoting social mobility and flexibility in status
III. Preserving endogamous practices within each caste
IV. Encouraging inter-caste marriages for social unity
Codes
(a) I and III (b) II and IV
(c) I, II and IV (d) I, III and IV

4. **Assertion** (A) Endogamy is a defining feature of the caste system in India.
Reason (R) Endogamy prevents social mobility and reinforces caste-based social stratification.
(a) Both A and R are true and R is the correct explanation of A
(b) Both A and R are true, but R is not the correct explanation of A
(c) A is true, but R is false
(d) A is false, but R is true

Case Based Questions

1. Theoretically, the caste system can be understood as the combination of two sets of principles, one based on difference and separation and the other on wholism and hierarchy. Each caste is supposed to be different from - and is therefore strictly separated from - every other caste. Many of the scriptural rules of caste are thus designed to prevent the mixing of castes - rules ranging from marriage, food sharing and social interaction to occupation.

Self Assessment Test

Complete Test of chapter in Exam format.

Sample Question Papers

To make students practice of examination in real sense, there are 3 Sample Question Papers at the end. All these Sample Questions Papers are exactly prepared on the latest syllabus & pattern of examination.

SAMPLE QUESTION PAPER 1

A Highly Simulated Sample Question Paper for CBSE Class XII

SOCIOLOGY

Time : 3 hours Max. Marks : 80

General Instructions

1. The question paper is divided into **four** sections.
2. There are 35 questions in all. **All** questions are **compulsory**.
3. **Section A** includes question No. **1-16**. These are MCQ type questions. As per the question there can be one answer.
4. **Section B** includes question No. **17-25**. These are very short answer type questions carrying 2 marks each. Answer to each question should not exceed 30 words.
5. **Section C** includes question No. **26-32**. They are short answer type questions carrying 4 marks each. Answer to each question should not exceed 80 words.
6. **Section D** includes question No. **33-35**. They are long answer type questions carrying 6 marks each. Answer to each question should not exceed 200 words each. Question no. 33 is to be answered with the help of the given graphics.

Section-A

1 The proportion of person in different age group relative to the total population is known as .... (1)
(a) Sex ratio (b) Age structure
(c) Occupation structure (d) Age composition

2 **Assertion** (A) Modernisation goes hand in hand with education, mass communication, urbanisation and political participation.
Reason (R) Dominance of the cultural influences from the West changes traditions elsewhere.
In the context which one of the following is correct? (1)
(a) Both A and R are true and R is the correct explanation of A
(b) Both A and R are true, but R is not the correct explanation of A
(c) A is true, but R is false
(d) A is false, but R is true

(a) Both A and R are true and R is the correct explanation of A
(b) Both A and R are true, but R is not the correct explanation of A
(c) A is true, but R is false
(d) A is false, but R is true

4 **Assertion** (A) Tribes are pristine societies uncontaminated by civilisation.
Reason (R) Tribes should really be seen as secondary phenomena arising out of the exploitative and colonialist contact between pre-existing states and non-state groups like the tribes.
In the context which one of the following is correct? (1)
(a) Both A and R are true and R is the correct explanation of A
(b) Both A and R are true, but R is not the correct explanation of A
(c) A is true, but R is false
(d) A is false, but R is true

Latest Course *Structure*

PART A INDIAN SOCIETY — 40 Marks

UNIT 1 Introducing Indian Society
- Colonialism, Nationalism, Class and Community (Non- evaluative)

UNIT 2 The Demographic Structure of the Indian Society
- Theories and Concepts in Demography
- Rural-Urban Linkages and Divisions
- Population Policy in India

UNIT 3 Social Institutions: Continuity and Change
- Caste and the Caste System
- Tribal Communities
- Family and Kinship

UNIT 5 Patterns of Social Inequality and Exclusion
- Social Inequality and Social Exclusion
- Systems Justifying and Perpetuating Inequality - Caste, Tribe, the Other Backward Classes
- Adivasi Struggles
- The Struggle for Women's Equality and Rights
- The struggles of the Differently Abled

UNIT 6 The Challenges of Cultural Diversity
- Cultural Communities and the Nation State
- Regionalism in the Indian Context
- The Nation State and Religion Related Issues and Identities
- Communalism, Secularism and the Nation State
- State and Civil Society

UNIT 7 Suggestions for Project Work

PART B SOCIAL CHANGE AND DEVELOPMENT IN INDIA — 40 Marks

UNIT 8 Structural Change
- Understanding Colonialism, Industrialisation, Urbanisation

UNIT 9 Cultural Change
- Social Reform Movements
- Different Kinds of Social Change: Sanskritisation, Westernisation, Modernisation, Secularisation

UNIT 11 Change and Development in Rural Society

- Agrarian Structure : Caste & Class in Rural India
- Land Reforms, Green Revolution and Emerging Agrarian society
- Green Revolution and Its Social Consequences
- Transformation in Rural Society
- Circulation of Labour
- Globalisation, Liberalisation and Rural Society

UNIT 12 Change and Development in Industrial Society

- From Planned Industrialisation to Liberalisation
- How People Find Jobs
- Work Processes: How work is carried out, working conditions, home based work, Strikes and Unions

UNIT 15 Social Movements

- Concept of Social Movements
- Theories and Classification of Social Movements
- Environmental Movements
- Class-Based Movements: Workers, Peasants
- Cast-Based Movement : Dalit Movement, Backward Class/Caste, Trends in Upper Caste Responses.
- Tribal Movements
- Women's Movements in Independent India

Project Work

PART C PROJECT UNDERTAKEN DURING THE ACADEMIC YEAR AT SCHOOL LEVEL — 15 Marks

Introduction	2 Marks
Statement of Purpose	2 Marks
Research Question	2 Marks
Methodology	3 Marks
Data Analysis	4 Marks
Conclusion	2 Marks

PART D VIVA-BASED ON THE PROJECT WORK — 5 Marks

PART A INDIAN SOCIETY

01

CHAPTER

Introducing Indian Society

This chapter introduces sociology as a subject that helps us understand society beyond common sense by critically examining social structures and relationship.

▼ **YOUR STUDY GOALS**

1.1 Sociology as Discipline

- Sociology is a vast yet familiar discipline.
- Unlike other subjects, we do not start learning sociology from the beginning; it is a part of our growth process.
- The subject deals with the knowledge of the society we live in, and this knowledge is acquired naturally as we grow up.
- Even a six-year-old child has some understanding of society and social relationships.

Learn-Unlearn Sociology

- Having prior knowledge about sociology can be both an advantage and a disadvantage for learners.
- One of the biggest advantages is that students are not afraid of the subject, making it easier to learn.
- On the other hand, it is disadvantageous to have prior knowledge that can lead to misconceptions or assumptions, making it harder to learn new ideas.
- The key is to unlearn preconceived notions to better understand society.
- Unlearning is the initial stage of learning sociology.

Concept of Unlearning

- Unlearning is important because prior knowledge about society is shaped by specific viewpoints formed by the social environment we live in.
- Our opinions, beliefs and expectations are influenced by socialisation, which may not always provide a complete or unbiased perspective.
- The term 'partial' can be understood in two ways as following
  (i) Incomplete (opposite of whole).
  (ii) Biased (opposite of impartial).
- Our prior knowledge is partial, allowing us to see only part of the social reality and making it biased towards specific groups.

1.2 Learning Sociology

- Sociology addresses the problem of unlearning by offering multiple perspectives, rather than claiming to provide a complete or unbiased view of reality.
- Sociologists believe there is no single, fully unbiased viewpoint.
- Sociology teaches us to view the world from different perspectives or vantage points, each providing a partial view of reality.
- These partial views help us understand how the whole might look and what is hidden from a specific standpoint.
- The concept of **self-reflexivity**[1] is introduced by sociologists, which involves reflecting on oneself and understanding how others perceive us.
- This process of self-inspection must be critical, focusing on self-criticism rather than self-praise.

1.3 Social Mapping

- Every individual holds a unique position in society.
- Like geographical maps, the concept of a social map helps locate an individual's position within society. For example, an eighteen-year-old can be mapped within the group of young people, and further categorised by religion, language, occupation, family income, economic class, tribe, etc.
- These identities place individuals within a social map and among a web of social relationships.
- Sociology explains the types of groups, their relationships and how these groups relate to individuals in society.
- Sociology, however, goes beyond simply locating people.
- Sociologist C. Wright Mills proposed that sociology helps map the connections between **personal issues** (individual problems) and **social issues** (problems faced by large groups).

1 **Self-Reflexivity** The fact of someone being able to examine their own feelings, reactions and motives.

1.4 Various Social Issues

- Societies face many challenges that must be addressed for a well-maintained social life. Some of the issues are as follows
  - The **generation gap**[2] or friction between older and younger generations, is a common problem across societies and ages.
  - Changes in the occupational structure can lead to unemployment.
  - Disturbances in communities can lead to **communalism**[3], where one religious community oppresses another, and **casteism**,[4] which involves the exclusion of certain castes.
- These social issues are evident in daily life, as everyone is affected by class and gender differences.
- To understand these issues, we use social maps, which are initially provided through childhood socialisation.
- However, the social map given to us is often misleading.
- By abandoning this predefined map, we become free to create our own social maps.
- Since there are no readymade maps, we must learn how to draw them, and sociology teaches us how to do this

---

2 **Generation Gap** It refers to a difference of attitudes between people of different generations, leading to a lack of understanding.
3 **Communalism** Communalism is when people of different religions of communities go against one another.
4 **Casteism** It refers to a social evil that refers to discrimination based on a person's caste.

02

CHAPTER

The Demographic Structure of the Indian Society

Demography refers to the systematic study of population. The term demography originates from two Greek words demos, meaning people and graphein, meaning to describe.

▼ YOUR STUDY GOALS

2.1 Introduction to Demography
2.2 Theories and Concepts in Demography
2.3 Size and Growth of India's Population
2.4 Age structure of the Indian Population
2.5 Declining Sex Ratio in India
2.6 Literacy and its Impact
2.7 Rural-Urban Differences
2.8 Population Policy in India

▼ YOUR PRACTICE GOAL

- Objective Type Questions (46 Qs ; MCQs, A-R, Case Based Questions)
- Subjective Questions (20 VSAs, 9 SAs, 10 LAs)

2.1 Introduction of Demography

Demography involves studying trends and processes related to the population, such as changes in population size, patterns of births, deaths, migration, and population structure and composition. Demography relies on the systematic collection of data through processes of counting or enumeration.

Types of Demography

1. Formal Demography

- It focuses on the **quantitative analysis** of population changes and patterns.
- It involves mathematical methods to measure aspects like population growth, rural-urban data, etc.

2. Social Demography

- It examines the social, economic and political aspects of populations.
- It investigates the broader causes and consequences of demographic changes. It considers the role of social processes in regulating population dynamics.

Demography and Sociology

- Demography played an important role in establishing sociology as recognised subject.
- In late 1700s in Europe, two significant changes that led to this development are as following
  (i) The formation of nation-states as primary political organisation.
  (ii) The beginning of modern science of statistics.
- With these changes, the role of the modern state expanded, especially in managing public health, law and order and economic policies. This expansion required systematic and regular collection of social statistics or quantitative data about populations and economies.
- The American Census of 1790 was considered the first modern census, with European nations adopting this practice in the early 1800s.
- The *first modern census in India* were first conducted by the British Indian Government between 1867 and 1872 and 10 yearly censuses started in 1881.
- After independence, India continued this practice conducting seven decennial censuses since 1951, with the latest one in 2011.
- The Indian census is the largest demographic data collection exercise in the world.
- Social statistics or demographic data, are essential for planning and implementing state policies in areas like public health, education and economic development.
- They provide a concrete basis for sociology by offering aggregate statistics that represent large populations. Example, **Death rate** data is derived by aggregating individual deaths, but the death rate itself is a **social phenomenon** requiring social explanations.
- **Emile Durkheim** illustrated the social nature of demography through his famous study on **suicide**. He argued that suicide, although often caused by personal factors, is actually a social phenomenon that must be explained by broader social causes.
- The suicide rate reflects these social influences, making it more than just an aggregate of individual actions.

2.2 Theories and Concepts in Demography

1. The Malthusian Theory of Population Growth

- **Thomas Robert Malthus** (1766–1834), an English political economist, proposed a theory of population growth in his **Essay on Population** (1798).
  - The key features of Malthus' Theory are as follows
  - Human population tends to grow much faster than the means of subsistence (e.g. food, clothing, agricultural products). Therefore, Humanity will always be stuck in poverty because the amount of food we can grow will never be enough to keep up with the growing number of people.
  - Population growth follows a **geometric progression** (2, 4, 8, 16...), while agricultural growth follows **arithmetic progression** (i.e. like 2, 4, 6, 8, 10 etc).
  - Malthus suggested that human ability to voluntarily reduce population growth is limited. It includes preventive checks such as postponing marriage, sexual abstinence or celibacy.
  - Malthus believed that **positive checks** to population growth, such as famines and diseases were unavoidable. He argued that these events were nature's way of correcting the imbalance between the growing population and limited food supply.

Thomas Robert Malthus (1766-1834)

Criticism of Malthusian Theory

- Malthus's theory was influential for a long time. But it was later challenged by theorists who argued that economic growth could surpass economic growth.
- The Malthusian theory was criticised and rejected on the following basis
  - In the late 19th and early 20th centuries, European population growth changed dramatically with declining birth rates and controlled epidemics. Food production and living standards increased despite population growth, challenging Malthus's predictions.
  - Liberal and Marxist criticised Malthus's idea that poverty was caused by population growth. Scholars argued that unequal distribution of resources, not population growth, caused poverty. Wealthy classes lived in luxury while the majority suffered.

2. The Theory of Demographic Transition

- The Demographic Transition Theory links population growth to economic development.
- It suggests that all societies follow a typical pattern of three phases of population growth as following
  - (i) **First Stage** Low population growth due to high birth and death rates in underdeveloped societies. The net growth rate remains low because both birth and death rates are high.
  - (ii) **Second Stage** A transitional phase where societies move from underdeveloped to developing stages. Population growth is very high due to a drop in death rates while birth rates remain high.
  - (iii) **Third/Final Stage** This phase is characterised by low population growth in developed countries. Both birth and death rates are reduced significantly.

  Population Explosion this occurs when death rates are brought down quickly due to advancements in disease control, public health and better nutrition, while reproductive behaviour remains unchanged. Western Europe experienced this transition in the late 19th and early 20th centuries less developed countries are seen to be following the same pattern.
- In India, demographic transition is incomplete. Although the mortality rate has decreased, the birth rate has not been reduced proportionately, contributing to the ongoing population growth.

Common Concepts and Indicators in Demography

Demographic concepts are generally expressed in **rates** or **ratios** and are essential for understanding population dynamics. Below are key concepts explained

1. **Birth Rate** It refers to the total number of live births per 1000 people in a specific area during a given period. It is calculated by dividing the total number of live births in an area by the total population in thousands.
2. **Death Rate** It is the number of deaths per 1000 population in a given area during a specific time. It is similar to the birth rate, but focuses on mortality figures.
3. **Rate of Natural Increase** It is also called population growth rate. It is the difference between the birth rate and the death rate. When this rate is close to zero or small, the population is said to have stabilised or reached the **replacement level**[1], i.e., new generations are replacing older ones. Countries like Japan, Russia, Eastern Europe and Italy experience negative growth rates, with fertility below replacement levels.
4. **Fertility Rate** The number of live births per 1000 women in the childbearing age (usually 15 to 49 years). The fertility rates offer rough averages, not accounting for differences between age groups. It is thus called a **'Crude' rate**. For better insights, age-specific fertility rates are calculated.

1 **Replacement Level** When the difference between the birth rate and death rate is zero (or very small), then we say that the population has 'stabilised' or has reached the 'replacement level'.

5. **Infant Mortality Rate** Number of deaths of babies before one year per 1000 live births.
6. **Maternal Mortality Rate** It is the number of women who die in childbirth per 1,00,000 live births. High rates of infant and maternal mortality indicates poor healthcare facilities and backwardness while lower rates reflect development and improved medical access.
7. **Life Expectancy** The average number of years a person is expected to live, based on age-specific death rates in a given area over a period of time. It reflects the overall health standards and quality of life in a region.
8. **Sex Ratio** It refers to the number of females per 1000 males in a population. Although slightly more males are born, there are usually more females overall due to women's greater resistance to diseases and longer life expectancy. Historical norm has been 1050 females per 1000 males. However, in countries like India, China and South Korea, the sex ratio is declining due to son preference and neglect of girl children.
9. **Age Structure of the Population** It refers to the proportion of people in different age groups relative to the total population. Initially, high disease rates and poor medical facilities led to a shorter lifespan and higher infant and maternal deaths. With development, life expectancy increases, resulting in a larger proportion of people in older age groups and fewer in younger groups. This leads to the ageing of the population.
10. **Dependency Ratio** It is a measure comparing the portion of a population composed of dependents (i.e. elderly people and children who cannot work) with the population that is in the working age group (15-64 years). It is calculated by dividing the population below 15 or above 64 with the population in the 15-64 age group. The resultant ratio is represented in percentage. An increasing dependency ratio causes economic stress, especially in countries with an ageing population. This is because a small proportion of working age people have to carry the burden of providing for a large proportion of dependents.

    A falling dependency ratio, with more workers as compared to non-workers, can boost economic growth. It is referred to as the 'demographic dividend'. However, this benefit is temporary, as the working population will eventually age and become non-working.

Quick Test 1

1. What is the quantitative data on population and economy called?
2. Name some positive checks as stated by Malthus.
3. In which essay did Malthus propose his theory of population growth?
4. What are the characteristics of population explosion?
5. What are the indicators of development?

2.3 Size and Growth of India's Population

India is the second most populous country in the world, following China, with a total population of 1.21 billion (121 crores) as per the 2011 Census. However, the growth rate of India's population has shown variability over time.

India's Population Growth Rate

Historical statistics of India's population growth are as follows

- **1901-1951** A modest average growth rate of 1.33% per year.
- **1911-1921** A unique period marked by a negative growth rate of 0.03%, largely due to the influenza epidemic of 1918-19, which resulted in the deaths of approximately 12.5 million people (5% of the population).

- **1961-1981** After independence, there was a substantial increase in the growth rate, peaking at 2.2%.
- **Post-1981** The annual growth rate has decreased but remains one of the highest among developing countries.

The Global Influenza Pandemic of 1918-19

The **Spanish Flu** pandemic[2], caused by the influenza virus, significantly impacted global population dynamics. Key points include

- The pandemic affected a vast portion of the world's population, leading to an estimated 40 million deaths.
- In most recent history, two influenza pandemics emerged the 'Asian influenza' in 1957 and the 'Hong Kong influenza' in 1968, both resulting in substantial global morbidity and mortality.
- The mortality rate was approximately 2.5-5% of the human population, with around 20% of the global population infected.
- In India, about 17 million people died, accounting for 5% of the country's population at the time.
- Among the British Indian Army, nearly 22% of infected soldiers died.
- While World War I did not directly cause the flu, the crowded conditions and troop movements accelerated its spread.

Birth and Death Rates in India

The period between **1921 and 1931** illustrates the impact of demographic transition

- **Before 1931** High birth and death rates.
- **Post-1931** A sharp decline in the death rate was observed, while the birth rate saw only a slight reduction.

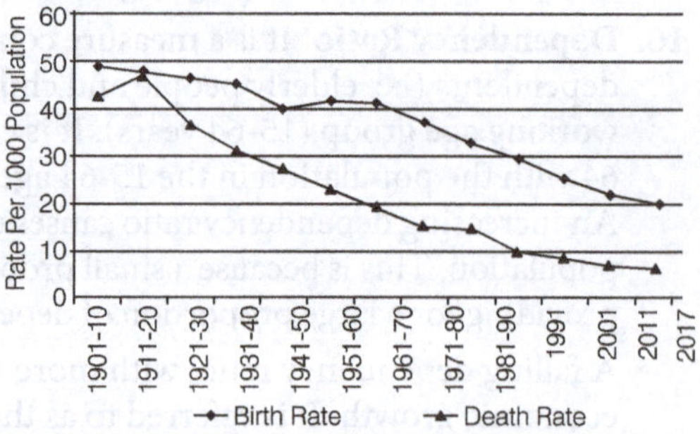

Reasons for the Decline in Death Rate

Following are the reasons for the decline in death rate

- Improved management of famines and epidemics like plague, smallpox and cholera.
- Improvements in medical treatments, mass vaccination programmes and sanitation efforts. Diseases such as malaria, tuberculosis and dysentery still pose threats, but mortality rates have decreased.
- Famines in the past were caused by poverty, malnutrition and poor rainfall. Poor transportation communication and inadequate state response worsened the situation.
- According to Amartya Sen, famines were not only due to a decline in food production, but also due to a **'failure of entitlements'**, meaning people couldn't afford or access food. Improvements in agriculture, irrigation and state relief have reduced famine deaths. However, hunger still exists in some poor areas. Initiatives like the **Mahatma Gandhi National Rural Employment Guarantee Act** aims to fight hunger in rural regions.
- Unlike the death rate, the birth rate is slow to change due to socio-cultural influences. Increased prosperity typically reduces birth rates. A decline in infant mortality, along with rising education and awareness, contributes to smaller family sizes.

Fertility Rates Across Indian States

Variations in Total Fertility Rates (TFR) across Indian states reflect these socio-cultural changes

- States with lower TFR (as of 2016)
  - Andhra Pradesh, Himachal Pradesh, Punjab, Tamil Nadu, West Bengal– TFR of **1.7**.
  - Kerala is also below replacement level and Kerala's TFR, is indicating a potential future population decline. In these states, the average woman has only 1.7 children, which is below the replacement level. This means the population will decline in future.

2 **Pandemic** It is a disease that spreads over a whole country or the whole world.

- States with higher Total Fertility Rates (TFR) in India include Bihar (3.3) followed by Madhya Pradesh (2.8), Rajasthan (2.7), and Uttar Pradesh (3.1).
- According to Sample Registration system, statistical report 2020, India's crude birth rate was 19.5, with rural areas at 21.1 and urban areas at 16.1%.
- Bihar (25.5%) and Uttar Pradesh (25.1%) have the highest birth rates. These two states will contribute to almost 50% of India's population growth by 2041, with Utter Pradesh alone accounting for 22% of the increase.

2.4 Age Structure of the Indian Population

- India's demographic profile is characterised by a predominantly young population, with the majority of Indians being youthful and the average age is lower compared to most other countries.
- The following table illustrates the age composition of India's population across different age groups from **1961 to 2026**

Year	0-14 years	15-59 years	60+ years	Total
1961	41%	53%	6%	100%
1971	42%	53%	5%	100%
1981	40%	54%	6%	100%
1991	38%	56%	7%	100%
2001	34%	59%	7%	100%
2011	29%	63%	8%	100%
2026	23%	64%	12%	100%

Key Observations

- The proportion of the population aged **0-14 years** has decreased from **42%** in 1971 to **29%** in 2011.
- The share of the **15-59 years** age group has risen from **53%** to **63%** over the same period.
- The percentage of the **60+ years** group has increased from **5%** in 1971 to an estimated **12%** by 2026.

Age Group Pyramids

Age group pyramids provide a visual representation of the population distribution across various age groups. These pyramids for the years **1961, 1981, 2001** and the projected data for **2026** depict the changes in birth and death rates, as well as life expectancy.

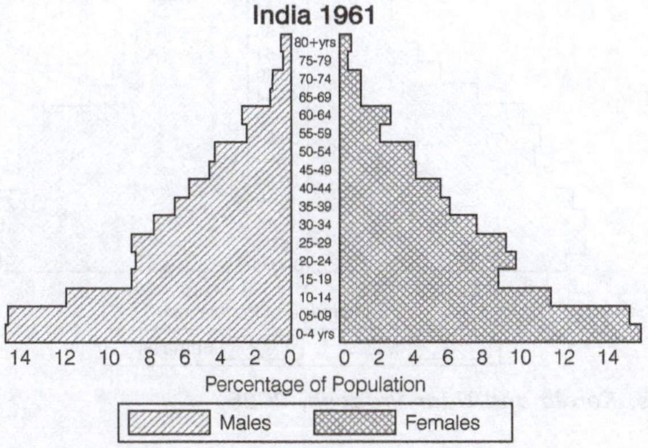

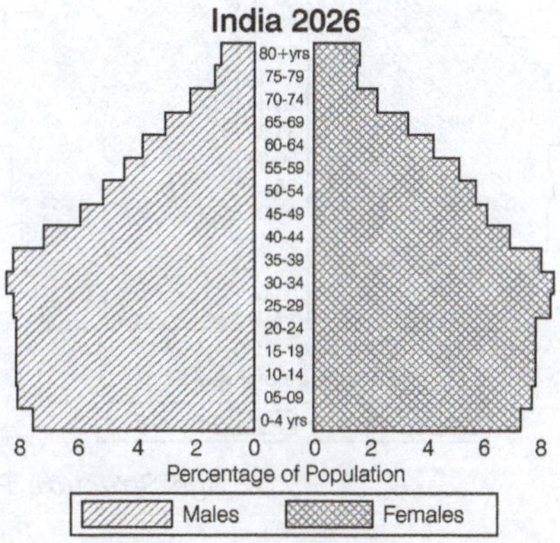

Trends in Age Pyramids

- A gradual decline in the birth rate and an increase in life expectancy are observable in the pyramids.
- As life expectancy rises, the top of the pyramid widens, indicating a growing elderly population.
- The base of the pyramid narrows due to a decrease in birth rates.
- The middle section of the pyramid expands as the total population increases, creating a bulge in the middle age group by 2026. This phenomenon is known as the **demographic dividend**.

India 1981

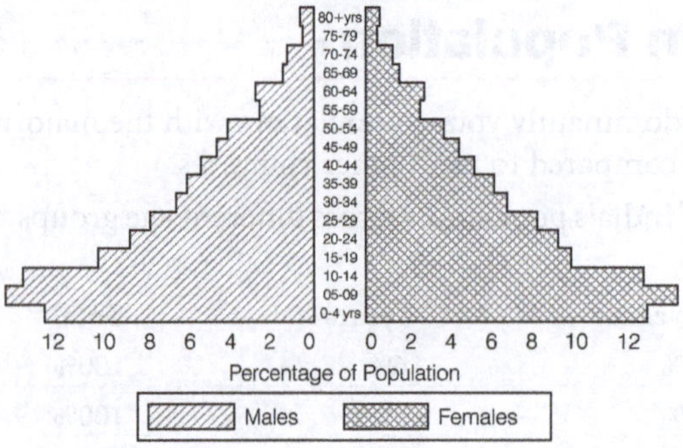

India 2001

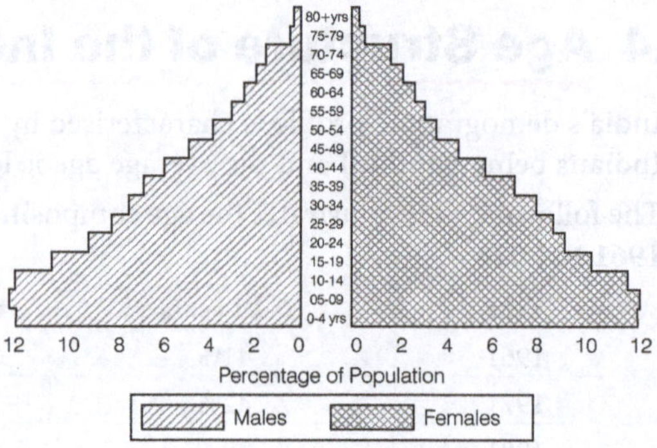

State-Oriented Pyramid

Regional Variations

- **Kerala**
  - Age structure similar to developed countries.
  - Lower proportions in younger age groups.
  - Higher proportions among the aged.
- **Uttar Pradesh**
  - High proportions in younger age groups.
  - Low proportions among the aged.

Kerala 2026

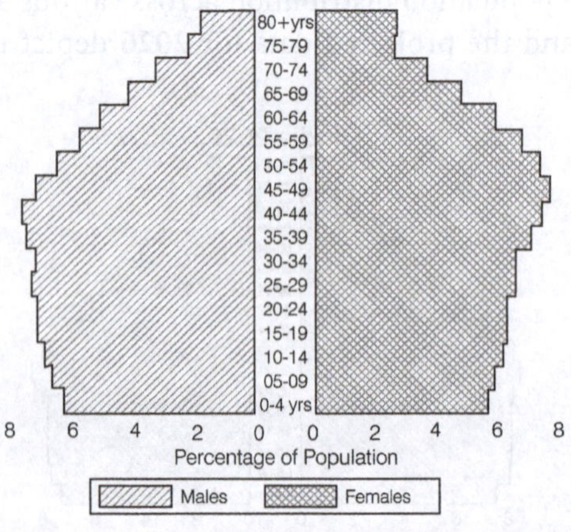

Uttar Pradesh 2026

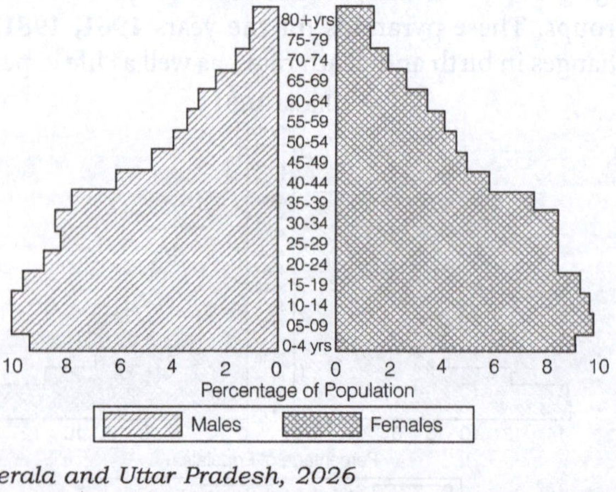

▲ *Age Structure Pyramids, Kerala and Uttar Pradesh, 2026*

Overall Scenario

- India's demographic profile is mixed. It includes states with advanced age structures (like Kerala) and those with youthful age distributions (like Uttar Pradesh).
- India's young age structure is seen as an advantage as in East Asian economies in the past decade and presently in Ireland. The demographic dividend occurs because there are more working age people and fewer elderly to support. However, this benefit is not automatic and must be used through the right policies.

Demographic Dividend Benefiting India

- India is one of the youngest countries globally. Significant bias towards younger age groups.
- In 2011, one-third of India's population was below 15 years of age. Average age in India was around 29 years in 2020.
- Comparatively, average ages are
  - 37 years in China and the United States.
  - 45 years in Western Europe.
  - 48 years in Japan.
- The 'demographic dividend' occurs when the proportion of working people in a population increases relative to those who are not working. The working age group is typically between 15 to 64 years old.
- As the age structure shifts, with more people in this working-age group, the 'dependency ratio' (the number of people not working compared to those who are) decreases, potentially fostering economic growth.
- The real challenge is understanding the dependency ratio. It's not just about the number of non-workers compared to workers, but also about how many people are unemployed or underemployed, which affects how productive the labour force can be.
- India is currently experiencing a demographic window of opportunity due to this shift. The dependency ratio, based on age, has dropped from 79 in 1970 to 64 in 2005.
- It is expected to fall further to 48 by 2025. However, by 2050, it is projected to rise again to 50 because of an increase in the elderly population.

Quick Test 2

1. Which epidemic diseases were prevalent in India during 1921?
2. What term did Amartya Sen coin in relation to famines?
3. Which Total Fertility Rate (TFR) is below the replacement level, indicating that their population will decline in the future?
4. What provides a detailed version of age-grouped data?
5. How can India benefit from the demographic dividend?

2.5 Declining Sex Ratio in India

- The sex ratio indicates gender balance in the population, expressed as the number of females per 1000 males.
- India has been experiencing a decline in the sex ratio.
- **Historical Data**
  - **1901** 972 females per 1000 males
  - **1991** 927 females per 1000 males
  - **2001** 933 females per 1000 males
  - **2011** 943 females per 1000 males

- **Sex Ratio from 1901 to 2011**

Year	Sex Ratio (All Age Groups)	Variation Over Previous Decade	Child Sex Ratio (0-6 years)	Variation Over Previous Decade
1901	972	–	–	–
1911	964	–8	–	–
1921	955	–9	–	–
1931	950	–5	–	–
1941	945	–5	–	–
1951	946	+1	–	–
1961	941	–5	976	–
1971	930	–11	964	–12
1981	934	+4	962	–2
1991	927	–7	945	–17
2001	933	+6	927	–18
2011	943	+10	919	–8

- The child sex ratio (0-6 age group) in India has sharply declined, alarming many experts. In 1991-2001, while the overall sex ratio increased, the child sex ratio dropped by 18 points, falling below the overall sex ratio for the first time.
- By 2011, the child sex ratio further decreased to 919. Nine states and UTs have a child sex ratio below 900 girls per 1,000 boys.
- Haryana has the lowest at 793, followed by Punjab, Jammu and Kashmir and others.
- Some states like West Bengal, Tamil Nadu and Kerala have ratios above 919 but still below 970.
- Arunachal Pradesh has the highest child-sex ratio of 972.

Factors for Responsible Declining Sex Ratio in India

- Demographers and sociologists have offered several reasons for the decline in the sex ratio in India. Historically, the decline in sex ratio was linked to high maternal mortality rates.
- As women faces a higher risk of death during childbirth. Improvements in nutrition, education and medical facilities have reduced maternal mortality rates. Therefore, social scientists shifted their focus to the selective treatment of girl children.
- Factors contributing to the decline in the child sex ratio include neglect of girl infants, sex selective abortions that prevent female babies from being born; and female infanticide due to religious or cultural beliefs.
- Modern medical technologies, like sonograms which were originally developed to detect health problems in the foetus, are misused to identify and abort female foetuses.
- Such practices are prevalent in prosperous regions like Maharashtra, Punjab, Haryana, Chandigarh and Delhi, indicating that poverty is not the primary cause.
- The government has enacted strict laws to combat female infanticide and sex-selective abortion.
- **Pre-natal Diagnostic Techniques** (Regulation and Prevention of Misuse) **Act** Enforced in 1996 and strengthened in 2003, imposing heavy fines and imprisonment for offenders.
- **Beti-Bachao, Beti-Padhao Campaign** was launched to improve the child sex ratio and promote awareness about the importance of girl children.

2.6 Literacy and its Impact

- Literacy is a crucial factor for empowerment. It enhances awareness of career options lead to health awareness.
- Improved literacy also contributes to participation in the knowledge economy and cultural and economic well-being.
- Significant improvements took place in literacy after independence. Almost two-thirds of the population is now got literate.

Literacy Rate in India

Year	Persons (%)	Males (%)	Females (%)	Male-Female Gap (%)
1951	18.3	27.2	8.9	18.3
1961	28.3	40.4	15.4	25.1
1971	34.5	46.0	22.0	24.0
1981	43.6	56.4	29.8	26.6
1991	52.2	64.1	39.3	24.8
2001	65.4	75.9	54.2	21.7
2011	73.0	80.9	64.6	16.3

- Literacy varies across genders, regions and social groups. Women have a literacy rate that is 16.3% lower than men, but female literacy is improving faster. This can be due to the fact that female literacy levels started from relatively low levels.
- Between 2001 and 2011, female literacy increased by 10.4%, compared to 7.6% for men.
- Overall, literacy increased by 8%, with male literacy rising by 5% and female literacy by 10%.
- Disadvantaged groups, like Scheduled Castes and Scheduled Tribes, have lower literacy rates, especially among women.
- There are also regional differences, with Kerala about to reach universal literacy and Bihar lagging behind.
- These literacy gaps are important because they lead to generational inequality, as illiterate parents struggle to ensure their children receive a good education, continuing the cycle of inequality.

Quick Test 3

1. What are the possible reasons for the decline in the child sex ratio in India?
2. How has the child sex ratio in India changed from 1991 to 2011?
3. What factors have contributed to the decline in the child sex ratio in India?
4. Why is the decline in the child sex ratio more alarming than the overall sex ratio decline?
5. How have economic prosperity and modern technology contributed to the decline in the child sex ratio in certain regions?

2.7 Rural-Urban Differences

- A large part of India's population has always lived and continues to live in rural areas.
- As of the 2011 Census, 68.8% of the population lives in rural areas, while 31.2% reside in urban areas. According to the Census of India 2011, more people still live in rural areas, but the population in urban areas has grown.
- Urban population growth has steadily increased from 11% in the early 20th century to about 28% in the 21st century.
- Modern development processes lead to a decline in the significance of agrarian rural life compared to industrial-urban life.

Agricultural Contribution

- Agriculture used to be the largest contributor to India's total economic production. Currently, it contributes about one-sixth of the Gross Domestic Product (GDP).
- Agricultural production has drastically fallen as rural populations are increasingly moving away from agriculture.
- Many rural individuals are now engaged in non-farm occupations, such as transportation services, business enterprises and craft manufacturing.

Phase of Transition

The process of urbanisation began as the mass media and communication channels became popular. The process of urbanisation can be seen in following ways

- Urban lifestyles and consumption patterns are reaching rural areas. This exposure creates new desires and aspirations for consumption among rural populations.
- Towns and cities are becoming magnets for rural populations seeking work. If employment is scarce in rural areas, individuals migrate to urban centres for job opportunities.
- Migration leads to the decline of common resources like ponds, forests and grazing lands. These resources, which previously supported landless villagers, are becoming privatised or exhausted. Villagers now have to pay for resources that were once free, increasing their hardships.
- Urban environments offer anonymity, which can benefit marginalised groups (e.g. Scheduled Castes and Scheduled Tribes) by providing protection from caste-based discrimination. It also allows socially dominant groups to engage in lower-status jobs without stigma.
- Urbanisation is accelerating, with metro cities growing fastest. India has 5,161 towns and cities housing approximately 286 million people. Over two-thirds of the urban population resides in 27 major cities with populations exceeding one million.
- Despite rapid urbanisation, rural areas continue to hold significant political power in India.

2.8 Population Policy in India

- Population dynamics significantly impact a nation's development and the health and well-being of its citizens.
- India was the first country to announce a population policy in 1952. The policy evolved into the National Family Planning Programme (NFPP).
- The key objectives of the NFPP were as follows
  - It aimed to influence the rate and pattern of population growth in socially desirable ways.
  - Slow down population growth by promoting various birth control methods.
  - To enhance health standards and raise public awareness regarding population and health issues.

Changes in Family Planning Programme

- The Family Planning Programme faced significant challenges during the National Emergency declared in 1975-76.
- The government aimed to reduce the population growth rate by implementing a forceful mass sterilisation programme. Sterilisation involves medical procedures like vasectomy (for men) and tubectomy (for women), preventing conception and childbirth.
- A large number of mostly poor individuals were forcibly sterilised. There was significant pressure on local government officials to ensure participation in sterilisation camps.
- The coercive nature of the programme led to widespread public opposition. Following the Emergency, the new government abandoned this approach.
- The National Family Planning Programme was renamed the **National Family Welfare Programme** post-Emergency. The forceful methods were discontinued.
- The programme adopted a broad set of socio-demographic objectives.
- New guidelines were established under the **National Population Policy of 2000.**
- A revised National Health Policy was introduced in 2017 with updated targets.
- Successful implementation of the programme highlighted that demographic variables are closely linked to economic, social and cultural changes.

India's Demographic Transition

- Census data indicates that population growth in India has been declining since 1991.
- **Fertility Rate** refers to the average number of children per woman. The fertility rate decreased from 3.8 in 1990 to 2.7 today (Bloom, 2011).
- Despite declining fertility and growth rates, India's population is projected to rise from 1.2 billion to an estimated 1.6 billion by 2050. This growth is attributed to **population momentum**, where a large cohort of women of reproductive age continues to drive population growth even with lower fertility rates.
- Significant drop in Crude Death Rates (CDR) and Crude Birth Rates (CBR) over the past four decades indicates progress towards a post-transitional phase.
- From 1950 to 1990, the decline in CBR was less steep compared to the decline in CDR. However, during the 1990s, the decline in CBR became steeper than that of CDR.
- The resulting annual population growth rate is now at 1.6% today.

Important Goals of National Health Policy 2017

- To raise government health expenditure as a percentage of GDP from 1.15% to 2.5% by 2025.
- To increase life expectancy at birth from 67.5 years to 70 years by 2025.
- To establish regular tracking of Disability Adjusted Life Years (DALY) Index by 2022.
- To reduce Total Fertility Rate (TFR) to 2.1 at national and sub-national levels by 2025.
- To reduce Under-Five Mortality to 23 per 1,000 live births by 2025. Lower Maternal Mortality Rate to 100 per 100,000 live births by 2020. Reduce neonatal mortality to 16 per 1,000 live births and stillbirth rate to single digits by 2025.
- **HIV/AIDS Targets** Achieve the global 90:90:90 targets for HIV/AIDS by 2020
  - 90% of people living with HIV know their status.
  - 90% of diagnosed individuals receive sustained antiretroviral therapy.
  - 90% of those on therapy achieve viral suppression.
- To maintain a cure rate of >85% in new sputum-positive TB patients and reduce new case incidence to elimination status by 2025.

- To reduce prevalence of blindness to 0.25 per 1,000 by 2025 and cut disease burden by one-third.
- To reduce premature mortality from cardiovascular diseases, cancer, diabetes or chronic respiratory diseases by 25% by 2025.
- To increase utilisation of public health facilities by 50% from current levels by 2025.
- To sustain antenatal case coverage above 90% and skilled attendance at birth above 90% by 2025.
- To ensure that >90% of newborns are fully immunised by one year of age by 2025.
- To meet the need for family planning above 90% at national and sub-national levels by 2025.
- To maintain 'controlled disease status' for 80% of known hypertensive and diabetic individuals by 2025.
- To achieve a 15% reduction in current tobacco use prevalence by 2020 and 30% by 2025.
- To reduce stunting prevalence among under-five children by 40% by 2025.
- To ensure access to safe water and sanitation for all by 2020.
- To halve the prevalence of occupational injuries among agricultural workers by 2020.
- To increase state sector health spending to >8% of their budget by 2020.
- To decrease the proportion of households facing catastrophic health expenditures by 25% by 2025.
- To ensure availability of paramedics and doctors as per Indian Public Health Standard (IPHS) in high-priority districts by 2020. Increase community health volunteer-to-population ratio as per IPHS in high-priority districts by 2025.
- To establish primary and secondary care facilities according to norms in high-priority districts by 2025. Create a district-level electronic database of health system components by 2020.

Quick Test 4

1. In which year did the computation of age-specific sex ratio begin?
2. Which state in India has the highest sex ratio?
3. According to social scientists, on what factors the declining sex ratio depends?
4. Which state in India is approaching universal literacy?
5. What event or factor marked the beginning of the process of urbanisation?
6. What is the name of India's population policy?

NCERT Folder

1. Explain the basic argument of the theory of the demographic transition. Why is the transition period associated with a 'population explosion'?

Or **Describe the theory of demographic transition. Why is the transition period associated with population explosion?**

Or **What are the three basic phases of population growth? Explain with reference to the demographic transition.**

Ans. Theory of demographic transition proposes that population growth is linked to overall levels of economic development and that every society follows a typical pattern of development related population growth.

There are three basic stages of population growth as follows

(i) **Primitive Stage** This stage shows low and slow population growth in a society. In this stage, a society is underpriviledged and technologically backward. The per capita earning capacity of the unskilled society remains minimum as people are involved in meagre work. People suffer from malnutrition and several diseases resulting in higher death rate.

(ii) **Second Stage** This is the phase of transition from underdeveloped to developing countries. Birth rate is high due to the presence of the patriarchal society and death rate is low due to the availability of medical facilities.

(iii) **Third Stage** This is the stage of low population growth rate in developed countries, where both birth rate and death rate have been reduced. Birth rate is low due to awareness and high literacy. Death rate is low due to availability of medical facilities.

The transitional stage (second stage), is characterised by the movement from a backward to an advanced stage. In this stage, population growth rate is very high and death rates are brought down relatively quickly through advanced methods of disease control, public health and better nutrition. This is why, the stage is associated with population explosion.

2. Why did Malthus believe that catastrophic events like famines and epidemics that cause mass deaths were inevitable?

Ans. English political economist Thomas Robert Malthus suggested that catastrophic events like famine and diseases were inevitable because they were nature's way of dealing with the imbalance between food supply and increasing population.

Malthus argued that human population tends to grow at a much faster rate than the rate at which the means of human subsistence (food, clothes, etc) can grow. According to him, population rises in geometric progression, whereas agricultural production can only grow in arithmetic progression. He believed that humans are unable to observe any preventive checks. In such cases, catastrophic events like famines are positive checks or natural process of population control that maintains balance by removing any imbalances.

3. What is meant by 'birth rate' and 'death rate'? Explain why the birth rate is relatively slow to fall while the death rate declines much faster?

Ans. **Birth rate** means the total number of births in a given area. It is calculated as the total number of live births in a particular area during a specified year divided by the total population of that area. This gets affected by climatic conditions, education, infertility, marriage, social condition, religious beliefs and education.

Death rate is the number of deaths in a given area during a given time per 1000 population.

Causes of Slow Birth Rate

Birth rate is relatively slow while the death rate can be brought down at much faster rate because of the public health measures and medical advancement that can control the death rate immediately.

The main reasons for declining death rates are as follows

- **Public Health Measures** These are non-medical interventions used to reduce the spread of disease, providing health education and to improve health and quality of life.
- **Medical Advances** The most revolutionary change through medical advances has been marked by drop in death rates. Lowered mortality rate became possible through use of modern drugs to cure diseases.

4. Which states in India have reached or are very near the 'replacement level' of population growth? Which ones still have very high rates of population growth? In your opinion, what could be some of the reasons for these regional differences?

Ans. The rate of growth required for new generations to replace the older one that are dying out is known as 'Replacement level'.

Some states in India like Kerala and Tamil Nadu have managed to bring down their Total Fertility Rates (TFR) meaning that they are at the replacement level. Many other states like Himachal Pradesh, West Bengal, Karnataka and Maharashtra are near to replacement levels of population growth.

But there are some states like Bihar, Madhya Pradesh, Rajasthan and Uttar Pradesh which have very high total fertility rate, means high rate of population growth.

Main reasons for these regional differences are as follows

- In India, the literacy rate is variable. The high literate state follows family planning schemes and on the other hand low literacy rate in some states leads to uncontrolled population growth.
- Social conditions such as prejudices, stereotypes and the belief that more family members mean more income is responsible for regional differences in population growth.
- Lack of understanding national interest and giving preference to individual interests over national interests.
- Variations in land forms. For example, Assam has lower population growth as it is a hilly region.

5. What is meant by 'the age structure' of the population? Why is it relevant for economic development and growth?

Ans. The age structure of the population refers to the proportion of persons in different age groups relative to the total population. The age structure changes with development, improved quality of life and improved life expectancy.

There are three age groups as follows

(i) The first, 0–14 years known as dependent group.
(ii) The second, 15–59 years known as working group.
(iii) The third, 60+ years known as elderly.

The age structure is relevant for economic development and growth in the following ways

- Dependency ratio is declining and rise in working population is a good indicator for Indian economy.
- Progress in medical sciences, public health measures and nutrition resulted into high life expectancy.
- The younger age groups in the age structure is believed to be an advantage, as India is supposed to be benefitted from a demographic dividend or demographic advantage.
- The increasing percentage of 60+ age groups reveals that life expectancy is at a rise. This indicates advancement in medical sciences, public health measure and nutrition which further indicates prosperity and development.
- With the help of the age structure, a government can review and renew its development plans.
- Age structure of the population reveals socio-cultural changes, economic and political percussions and thus, helps in review and reform planning for the wellfare of the nation as a whole.

6. What is meant by the 'sex ratio'? What are some of the implications of a declining sex ratio? Do you feel that parents still prefer to have sons rather than daughters? What, in your opinion could be some of the reasons for this preference?

Ans. The sex ratio refers to the number of females per 1000 males in a given area at a specified time period. This ratio holds an important aspect in gender balance in population.

Some of the implications of a declining sex ratio are as follows

- The phenomenon of prevailing social norms which tend to value males much more than females and leads to 'son preference' and the relative neglect of girl babies.
- Sex specific abortions that check girl babies from being born.

Yes, Indian parents prefer to have sons rather than a daughter as it is evident in the day to day media reports of foeticides, infanticides and abortions.

Some of the common reasons for the preference of male child over female are as follows

- **Socio-cultural Belief** Preference of male child due to social security for family as people believe that only male child can lead and continue the family line.
- **Lack of Awareness** The lack of general awareness about maternal mortality and differential treatment towards girl child is also the major reason for low child sex ratio.
- **Fear of Social Problems** Many parents feel that the burden of maintenance of girl child is high. Example, dowry hence prefer son over daughters.

Exam Pattern Questions

Objective Type Questions

Multiple Choice Questions (MCQs)

1. Which among the following is not the use of demographic data?

(a) Economic development
(b) Planning of policies
(c) Implementation of policies
(d) Private welfare

2. Which of the following are reasons why social statistics were important for the emergence of sociology?

I. They helped establish the existence of social phenomena.
II. They provided the foundation for the study of individual behaviours.
III. They justified the need for a systematic study of societies.
IV. They highlighted the social reasons behind demographic trends.

Codes

(a) I and III
(b) II and IV
(c) I, III and IV
(d) I, II, III and IV

3. Demographers and sociologists have offered several reasons for the decline in the sex ratio in India. Which of the following is not a reason for the decline in the sex-ratio? CBSE 2024 C

(a) Not looking after girl babies in infancy
(b) Sex-specific abortions
(c) Female infanticide
(d) Awareness

4. Consider the following codes with respect to Malthusian theory.

I. According to Malthusian theory, supply of food grains increase in geometric progression.
II. The population grows in arithmetic progression.

Which of the given code is correct? CBSE Term I, 2021

(a) Only I
(b) Only II
(c) Both I and II
(d) None of these

5. While population rises in geometric progression, agricultural production can only grow in arithmetic progression. CBSE SQP 2024

Which of the following appropriately explains the progressions?

I. 2,4,8,16 and 2,4,6,8 respectively
II. 2,4,6,8 and 2,4,8,16 respectively
III. 3,6,12,24 and 3,6,9,12 respectively
IV. 3,6,9,12 and 3,6,12,24 respectively

Codes

(a) I and II
(b) II and IV
(c) I and III
(d) I and IV

6. Which of the following statements is true in the scenario of high fertility rate? CBSE 2023

(a) It takes more time to reach the replacement level.
(b) It takes less time to reach the replacement level.
(c) It does not impact the replacement level.
(d) The impact on replacement level cannot be determined.

7. Which of the demographic indicators are not used to calculate total fertility rate? CBSE SQP Term I, 2021

(a) Number of live births in the reproductive age group
(b) Age specific fertility rate
(c) Sex ratio
(d) Number of women in the child-bearing age group

8. What is sex ratio? CBSE Term I, 2021

(a) Number of females per thousand males
(b) Number of males per thousand females
(c) Number of females per hundred males
(d) The study of population growth

9. As per the theory of Demographic Transition, which of the following statements are correct? CBSE 2025

I. Population growth is linked to overall levels of economic development.
II. Every society follows a typical pattern of development.
III. The development is related to population growth.
IV. There are four stages of population growth.

Codes

(a) I and II
(b) II and III
(c) I and III
(d) I, II and III

10. The rate of natural increase is the difference between CBSE SQP Term I, 2021

(a) Birth Rate and Maternal Mortality Rate
(b) Maternal Mortality rate and life expectancy
(c) Dependency Ratio and Death Rate
(d) Birth Rate and Death Rate

11. **India's population is projected to increase from 1.2 billion today to an estimated 1.6 billion by 2050. This happens due to** CBSE SQP Term I, 2021
(a) Population momentum
(b) Population explosion
(c) Population policy
(d) National Health Policy

12. **The live birth per one thousand person in one year in a particular area is known as** CBSE Term I, 2021
(a) Death rate (b) Birth rate
(c) Fertility rate (d) Infant mortality rate

13. **When the growth rate is 0, the population is said to have reached** CBSE SQP Term I, 2021
(a) replacement level (b) negative growth
(c) positive growth (d) high birth rate

14. **Which of the following statements is/are true regarding the role of demography in sociology?**
I. It began to develop in the latter half of the 18th century in Europe.
II. The establishment of nation-states was not a significant factor.
III. It involves the systematic collection of social statistics.
IV. Social statistics do not contribute to understanding social phenomena.

Codes
(a) I and III (b) II and IV
(c) Only III (d) I, III and IV

15. **The measure of comparing the portion of a population which is composed of dependents with the portion that is the working population is** CBSE 2023
(a) Age structure of the population
(b) Sex ratio
(c) Dependency ratio
(d) Growth rate of population

16. **Unlike the death rate, ... does not register a sharp fall because it is a socio-cultural phenomenon.** CBSE SQP Term I, 2021
(a) birth rate
(b) maternal mortality rate
(c) life expectancy
(d) dependency ratio

17. **Which of the following does not lead to population explosion?** CBSE SQP Term I, 2021
(a) Low level of economic development can lead to population explosion.
(b) It happens due to high birth rate and low death rate.
(c) It takes longer for society to alter reproductive behaviour.
(d) Reduced fertility rate

18. **Famines were a major and recurring source of increased ....** CBSE 2024 C
(a) Fertility (b) Mortality
(c) Dependency (d) Sex ratio

19. **"Famines were also a major and recurring source of increased mortality." Which of the following is not a cause of famines?** CBSE SQP 2023
(a) Continuing poverty and malnutrition in an agro-cblimatic environment
(b) Inadequate means of transport and communication
(c) Failure of entitlements
(d) Increasing birth rates

20. **Kerala is beginning to acquire an age structure like that of the developed countries. Which of the following is true in this context?** CBSE SQP Term I, 2021
(a) High birth rate and high death rate
(b) Low birth rate and low death rate
(c) High birth rate and low death rate
(d) Low birth rate and high death rate

21. **The pyramid for 2026 shows the estimated future size of the relevant age group based on the past rates of growth of each age group. Such estimates are called**
(a) Age pyramid CBSE Term I, 2021
(b) Demographic dividend
(c) Projections
(d) Rate of natural increase

22. **Which of the following factors can contribute to the decline in child sex ratio in India?**
I. Severe neglect of girl babies in infancy
II. Sex-specific abortions
III. Female infanticide
IV. Cultural beliefs supporting female infanticide

Codes
(a) I, II and III
(b) II, III and IV
(c) I and II
(d) I, II, III and IV

23. **Consider the following statements regarding the child sex ratio in India.**
I. Nine States and Union Territories in India have a child sex ratio of under 900 females per 1000 males.
II. Haryana has the highest child sex ratio in India.
III. The child sex ratio has declined more significantly than the overall sex ratio in India.

Which of the above statements is/are correct?
(a) I and II (b) I and III
(c) II and III (d) I, II and III

24. There is a close relationship between disability and poverty. Identify the option that does not hold true in this context. CBSE SQP Term I, 2021

(a) Malnutrition
(b) Frequent childbirth
(c) Inadequate immunisation
(d) High socio-economic status

25. Historically, all over the world, it has been found that there are slightly more females than males in most countries. Which of the following factors made this possible? CBSE SQP-2024

I. Women tend to outlive men at the other end of the life cycle.
II. Girl babies are more resistant to diseases than boy babies in infancy.
III. Gender-based families with preference for sons.
IV. Gender neutral behaviour.

Codes

(a) I, II and IV (b) I and III
(c) III and IV (d) I and II

Assertion–Reason Questions

Direction (Q. Nos. 26-29) Two statement are given in the question below as Assertion (A) and Reason (R). Read the statements and choose the appropriate option.

(a) Both A and R are true and R is the correct explanation of A
(b) Both A and R are true, but R is not the correct explanation of A
(c) A is true, but R is false
(d) A is false, but R is true

26. Assertion (A) The emergence of sociology and its successful establishment as an academic discipline owed a lot to demography.

Reason (R) This happened due to the rise of nation-states and the emergence of the modern science of statistics. CBSE SQP Term I, 2021

27. Assertion(A) The modern state had begun to take an active interest in the development of early forms of public health management, policing and maintenance of law and order.

Reason (R) This new and constantly expanding sphere of state activity required the systematic science of statistics. CBSE SQP 2024

28. Assertion (A) There is a close relationship between disability and poverty.

Reason (R) Malnutritioned mothers weakend by frequent child birth, inadequate immunisation programmes, accidents in overcrowded homes, all contribute to an incidence of disability among poor people that is higher. CBSE Term I, 2021

29. Assertion (A) The Population Pyramid shows a bulge in the middle age groups, due to opportunity provided by the demographic structure.

Reason (R) This is due to high birth rate in the middle age groups. CBSE SQP 2023

Case Based Questions

Read the given passages and answer the questions that follow by choosing the correct option.

30. The demographic dividend results from an increase in the proportion of workers relative to non-workers in the population. In terms of age, working population is roughly that between 15 and 64 years of age. The working age group must support itself as well as those outside this age group (i.e children and elderly people) who are unable to work and are therefore dependents. Changes in this age structure due to demographic transition lower the dependency ratio or the ratio of non-working age to working population, thus creating the potential for government growth. CBSE Term I, 2021

(i) What is demographic dividend?

(a) More dependents exist in a country
(b) Proportion of workers is more than that of non-workers.
(c) Old age proportion is more
(d) None of the above

(ii) Who are dependents?

(a) Children who are too young to earn
(b) Adults who are unemployed
(c) Aged population above 65 years
(d) Proportion of children below 14 years and aged population (64 and above)

31. Demographers and sociologists have offered several reasons for the decline in the sex ratio in India. The main health factor that affects women differently from men is childbearing. It is relevant to ask if the fall in the sex ratio may be partly due to the increased risk of death in childbirth that only women face. However, maternal mortality is supposed to decline with development, as levels of nutrition, general education and awareness, as well as, the availability of medical and communication facilities improves. Indeed, maternal mortality rates have been coming down in India even though they remain high by international standards.

(i) The main health factor that affects women differently is

(a) employment (b) education
(c) childbearing (d) nutrition

(ii) **What can be the cause of fall in sex ratio?**
(a) Increased risk of death during childbirth
(b) Lack of nutrition
(c) Lack of awareness
(d) None of the above

32. Literacy as a prerequisite to education is an instrument of empowerment. The more literate the population the greater the consciousness of career options, as well as participation in the knowledge economy. Further, literacy can lead to health awareness and fuller participation in the cultural and economic well being of the community. Literacy levels have improved considerably after independence and almost two-thirds of our population is now literate. But improvements in the literacy rate have to struggle to keep up with the rate of growth of the Indian population, which is still quite high. Enormous effort is needed to ensure the literacy of the new generations – which are only just beginning to be smaller in numbers than in the past.

(i) **Literacy levels have improved considerably after independence and almost .... of our population is now literate.**
(a) two-thirds (b) one-third
(c) half (d) one-fourth

(ii) **Literacy is considered as an instrument of......... .**
(a) accreditation (b) uncertainty
(c) exclusion (d) inclusion

33. Considered from an urban point of view, the rapid growth in urbanisation shows that the town or city has been acting as a magnet for the rural population. Those who cannot find work (or sufficient work) in the rural areas go to the city in search of work. This flow of rural-to-urban migration has also been accelerated by the continuous decline of common property resources like ponds, forests and grazing lands. These common resources enabled poor people to survive in the villages although they owned little or no land. Now, these resources have been turned into private property or they are exhausted (Ponds may run dry or no longer provide enough fish; forests may have been cut down and have vanished).

(i) **What is one of the main reasons for rural-to-urban migration in India?**
(a) Better educational opportunities in villages
(b) The decline of common property resources in rural areas
(c) Easy access to financial loans in cities
(d) Availability of free housing in urban areas

(ii) **What is one social reason for rural-to-urban migration?**
(a) The ability to buy cheaper goods in cities
(b) The chance to escape social discrimination in rural areas
(c) Access to better government services
(d) Opportunities for large-scale farming

34. It will be clear from the discussion in this chapter that population dynamics is an important matter and that it crucially affects the developmental prospects of a nation as well as the health and well being of its people. This is particularly true of developing countries who have to face special challenges in this regard. It is hardly surprising therefore that India has had an official population policy for more than a half century. In fact, India was perhaps the first country to explicitly announce such a policy in 1952.

(i) **Which country was the first to announce an official population policy?**
(a) India (b) China
(c) United States (d) Japan

(ii) **What is the name of the programme that represents India's population policy?**
(a) National Population Control Programme
(b) National Family Planning Programme
(c) National Public Health Programme
(d) National Birth Control Programme

Answers

1. (d) Private welfare
2. (c) I, III and IV
3. (d) Awareness
4. (d) None of these
5. (c) I and III
6. (b) It takes less time to reach the replacement level.
7. (c) Sex ratio
8. (a) Number of females per thousand males
9. (d) I, II and III
10. (d) Birth Rate and Death Rate
11. (a) Population momentum
12. (b) Birth rate
13. (a) replacement level
14. (a) I and III
15. (c) Dependency ratio
16. (a) birth rate
17. (d) Reduced fertility rate
18. (b) Mortality
19. (d) Increasing birth rates
20. (b) Low birth rate and low death rate
21. (c) Projections
22. (d) I, II, III, and IV
23. (b) I and III
24. (d) High socio-economic status
25. (a) I, II and IV
26. (a) Both A and R are true and R is the correct explanation of A
27. (b) Both A and R are true but R is not the correct explanation of A
28. (a) Both A and R are true and R is correct explanation of A
29. (c) A is true, but R is false
30. (i) (b) Proportion of workers in more than that of non-workers
31. (i) (c) childbearing
    (ii) (a) Increased risk of death during childbirth
32. (i) (a) two-thirds
    (ii) (a) accreditation
33. (i) (b) The decline of common property resources in rural areas
    (ii) (b) The chance to escape social discrimination in rural areas
34. (i) (a) India
    (ii) (b) National Family Planning Programme

Subjective Questions

Very Short Answer Type Questions

1. What do you mean by demography? **CBSE Diksha**

Ans. Demography is the systematic study of population. It is composed of the Greek word demos which means people and graphein meaning, describe implying the description of people.

2. In what way formal demography is different from social demography?

Ans. Formal demography is primarily concerned with the measurement and analysis of the components of population change. Social demography, on the other hand, enquires into the wider causes and consequences of population structures and change.

3. Explain the two types of demography? **CBSE 2023**

Ans. There are two types of demography

(i) **Formal** It is primarily concerned with the measurement and quantitative analysis of population growth and change, rural and urban data etc.

(ii) **Social** It focuses on the social, economic and political aspects of populations. It also enquiries into the wider causes and consequences of population structure and changes.

4. State the importance of demographic data.

Ans. Demographic data are important for a country because it aids in the following **CBSE 2019**

(i) Economic development.

(ii) Planning and implementation of state policies.

(iii) General public welfare schemes and programmes.

(iv) Identifying the demographic transition stage of a country.

5. Social demography examines the causes and effects of population trends. In this context, explain the concept of population structure? **Competency Based Que.**

Ans. By population structure theory we mean the distribution of population of country in different parts, density of population, birth and death rate, immigration, education, sex ratio, etc. In population structure, different aspects of population and features of population are studied.

6. Why did Malthus believe mass death caused by famines and epidemic were inevitable?

Ans. Malthus believed mass deaths caused by famines were inevitable because he believed that there are 'positive checks' to population growth in the form of famines and diseases. They are the natures's way for dealing with the imbalance between food supply and increasing population which humans can't control.

7. How does India benefit from a demographic dividend? **CBSE 2019**

Ans. There is a great influence of demographic dividend on the economic growth of India because the demographic dividend is the economic benefit that can arise when a population has a relatively large proportion of working age people, and effectively invests in their empowerment, education and employment.

8. Malthus's theory of population growth argued that while populations grow geometrically, the means of subsistence, particularly food production, grow only arithmetically. He believed this imbalance would lead to perpetual poverty unless population growth was controlled. However, his predictions were disproven as food production and living standards continued to rise despite population growth, particularly in Europe, where declining birth rates and better control of diseases refuted his claims. Critics also challenged his view, attributing poverty to unequal resource distribution rather than population growth.

Based on the above statement, answer the following question.

Why was Malthus's theory of population growth ultimately proven wrong?

Ans. Malthus's theory was proven wrong as advancements in agriculture and healthcare allowed food production and living standards to rise despite population growth. Additionally, declining birth rates, disease control and critiques emphasising unequal resource distribution disproved his predictions.

9. Sometimes societies can experience a 'negative growth rate'. What is 'negative growth rate'? Name any two countries that have experienced it. **CBSE 2024 C**

Ans. A 'negative growth rate' occurs when the death rate exceeds the birth rate, leading to a decrease in population size. This can happen when fertility levels fall below the replacement level. Examples of countries experiencing negative growth rates are Japan and Russia.

10. What is the 'replacement level' of population growth?

Ans. The replacement level is the rate of growth required for new generations to replace the older ones that are dying out.

11. What does high infant mortality and maternal mortality rate indicate?

Ans. High rates of infant and maternal mortality are an unambiguous indicator of backwardness and poverty.

12. What is dependency ratio? CBSE Diksha

Ans. The dependency ratio is a measure for comparing the portion of a population which is composed of dependents. Population that is out of working age group (15-64) years. It consist of children below 15 and elderly above 64 fears of age.

13. The dependency ratio is equal to the population below 15 or above 64, divided by population in the 15-64 age group. This is usually expressed as a percentage. In 2020, the average Indian was only 29 years old, compared with an average age of 37 in China and the United States, 45 in Western Europe, and 48 in Japan. What inference can you draw from this statement? CBSE SQP 2024

Ans. The statement highlights India's relatively young average age of 29, compared to countries like China, the U.S. and Japan, which have older populations. This suggests that India has a lower dependency ratio, with more people in the working-age group (15-64), potentially leading to economic growth. However, this advantage may be temporary, as the working-age population will eventually age and increase the dependency ratio.

14. Why is dependency ratio a source of economic growth and prosperity?

Ans. A falling dependency ratio can be a source of economic growth and prosperity due to the larger proportion of workers in comparison to non-workers.

15. What is meant by the age structure of the population? CBSE 2018

Ans. The age structure of the population refers to the proportion of persons in different age groups in relation to the total population. The age structure varies in response to changes in the level of development and the average life expectancy.

16. The growth rate of India in the decade 1911-21, exhibited a diverse pattern. State two reasons. CBSE SQP 2024

Ans. The growth rate of Indian in the decade 1911-21 exhibited a diverse pattern. This was due to

(i) Negative growth rate of -0.03%.

(ii) Lower growth rate was recorded due to the 1918-19 influenza epidemic which killed about 12.5 million persons of the total population of the country.

17. Define the life expectancy rate? CBSE Diksha

Ans. Life expectancy is the average number of years a person is expected to live, based on the mortality rates of a specific population. It's calculated for a specific year, country or geographic area.

18. Mention the factors responsible for the decline in the child sex ratio in India.

Ans. There are two most important factors responsible for the decline in the child sex ratio as follows

(i) Sex specific abortions that prevent girl babies from being born.

(ii) Female infanticide.

19. The rapid growth in urbanisation shows that the town or the city has been acting as a magnet for the rural population. CBSE 2024 C

Give two reasons for the above statement.

Ans. Towns and cities attract rural populations due to better job opportunities unavailable in urban areas and the decline of common property resources like ponds and forests in villages, which previously supported livelihoods, increasing rural hardships and prompting migration.

20. What is sterilisation?

Ans. Sterilisation refers to medical procedures like vasectomy (for man) and tubectomy (for woman) which prevents conception and child birth.

Short Answer Type Questions

1. Why is the study of demography essential to sociological analysis?

Ans. The social statistics or demographic data are important to sociological analysis as they help in the planning and implementation of state policies. But apart from it, social statistics also provided a strong justification for sociology. The concept of aggregate statistics or characteristics that refer to a large population offers a concrete argument for the presence of social phenomenon. For example, the data of death rate points that it is a social phenomenon that must be explained socially.

2. Despite the decline in birth rate, the growth rate of India's population is increasing. Explain the reason.

Ans. The major reasons for India's population rising despite the decline in birth rate are:

- Wide variations in the fertility rates across the states of India.

- States like Bihar, Madhya Pradesh, Rajasthan and Uttar Pradesh still have very high Total Fertility Rate (TFRs).
- Birth rate is a socio-cultural phenomenon. It gets significantly affected by the age of marriage, infertility, social and climatic conditions.
- Awareness, education and the concept of small family is yet reach to the masses.

3. Malthus's theory of population growth-outlined in his Essay on Population (1798) was a rather pessimistic one. He argued that human populations tend to grow at a much faster rate than the rate at which the means of human subsistence (especially food, but also clothing and other agriculture-based products) can grow. Therefore, humanity is condemned to live in poverty forever because the growth of agricultural production will always be overtaken by population growth.

Why Malthus was proved wrong in the productivity of agriculture? What were the factors that made agriculture more productive? **Competency Based Que.**

Ans. According to Malthus, human population growth tendency is higher in comparison to food supply and agricultural output. As a result, the positive checks of higher mortality caused by famine, disease and war were necessary to bring the number of people back in line with the capacity to feed them.

He was criticised by the historical experience of European countries. The pattern of population growth began to change in the latter half of 19th century. Birth rates had declined and outbreaks of epidemic diseases were being controlled.

Malthus was proved wrong because both food production and standards of living continued to rise despite the rapid growth of population. He failed to forecast improved technology.

The availability of natural resources such as land, soil, etc., and other inventions like the use of fertilisers, mechanisation of irrigation of land, etc., allowed farmers and others more efficient ways of growing crops.

4. What reasons are responsibile for maternal deaths in India than any other country in the world? What are the efforts of Ministry?

Ans. The major reasons for the maternal deaths are as follows
- Poverty, illiteracy and backwardness.
- Lack of medical facilities and awareness.
- Ongoing superstitions in society.

The efforts of ministry in controlling maternal deaths are
- Strengthening efforts in 264 districts that account nearly 70% of infants and maternal deaths.
- Implementation of 'Mother-Child Tracking System' which keeps a track of pregnant women.
- Ministry also ran a programme for the postnatal care and immunisation for the new born.
- Provision of enough fund per year ($ 3.5 billion) for improvement in health services and taking care of women's and children's health.

5. Highlight the main features of demographic dividend in India.

Ans. Main features of demographic dividend in India includes
- Working age of people (15 years - 64 years) is relatively large with comparison to non-workers in the total population.
- There are relatively smaller groups of dependents which need support. The working groups, thus, can easily take care of such people.
- There are also small group of young children who cannot work and are supported/dependent.
- India is facing a window of opportunity generated by the demographic dividend. It is a source of economic growth and prosperity.

6. The major epidemic diseases in the past were fevers of various sorts, plague, smallpox and cholera. But the single largest epidemic was the influenza epidemic of 1918-19, which killed about 5% of the total population of India at that time.

Differentiate between epidemic and pandemic. **CBSE 2025**

Ans.

Basis	Epidemic	Pandemic
Definition	An outbreak of a disease that spreads rapidly within a specific region or community.	A disease outbreak that spreads across multiple countries or continents, affecting a large number of people.
Geographical Spread	Limited to a particular area, city, or country.	Spreads across multiple countries or the entire world.
Example	Cholera outbreak in Bengal (19th century).	COVID-19 (2020-2022)
Impact	Affects a large population in a localised area.	Affects a much larger global population.

The Influenza Epidemic of 1918-19 was actually a pandemic, as it spread globally, affecting millions of people.

7. According to demographers and sociologists, what are the reasons for the decline in child sex ratio in India?

Ans. According to demographers and sociologists, the reasons for the decline in child sex ratio in India are as follows

- General preference against girls and preference for boys because of socio-cultural reasons.
- Severe neglect of girl babies in infancy (maternal mortality).
- Gender based abortions (female foeticide).
- Female infanticide in many parts of India.
- Misuse of highly advanced medical facilities such as sonography.

8. The Family Planning Programme suffered during the period of National Emergency. Give reasons. CBSE 2019

Ans. The Family Planning Programme suffered a setback during the years of the National Emergency (1975-76). During this time, the government tried to intensify the effort to bring down the growth rate. In order to achieve its aim, the government took the following steps

- The government introduced a coercive(forced) programme of mass sterilisation.
- Sterilisation refers to medical procedures like vasectomy for men and tubectomy for women to prevent conception and child birth. Vast numbers of mostly poor and powerless people were forcibly sterilised.
- There was massive pressure on lower level government officials (school teachers or office workers) to bring people for sterilisation in the camps.
- Due to this programme widespread popular opposition took place in the country.

9. The rapid growth in urbanisation shows that the town or the city has been acting as a magnet for the rural population. Give two reasons for the above statement. CBSE 2024

Ans. The town or city acts as a magnet for the rural population for the following reasons

(i) **Job Opportunities** Cities offer more job opportunities, especially for people who struggle to find work in rural areas. The urban economy provides diverse employment options, attracting many from villages to seek work and a steady income.

(ii) **Anonymity and Social Freedom** Cities allow individuals, especially those from oppressed or lower social backgrounds, to experience more anonymity and freedom. This can reduce the social pressures and discrimination they might face in villages, giving them a sense of security and dignity in city life.

Long Answer Type Questions

1. Explain the Malthusian Theory of population growth.

Ans. The Malthusian Theory of population growth, proposed by Thomas Robert Malthus in his *Essay on Population* (1798), suggests that human population growth tends to outpace the growth of resources necessary for survival, particularly food. The key ideas of this theory are

(i) **Population vs. Food Supply** Malthus argued that while the human population grows exponentially (in geometric progression like 2, 4, 8, 16), food production increases only arithmetically (in a linear progression like 2, 4, 6, 8). This imbalance would lead to a shortage of resources, causing widespread poverty and hardship.

(ii) **Positive and Preventive Checks**

(a) **Preventive Checks** Malthus suggested that individuals could exercise moral restraint, delay marriage, or practise celibacy to limit population growth voluntarily.

(b) **Positive Checks** When preventive measures are insufficient, Malthus theorised that nature would enforce 'positive checks' to control population, such as famines, diseases and wars, which would raise the death rate and restore balance.

(iii) **Poverty as an Outcome** According to Malthus, unchecked population growth would inevitably lead to poverty and scarcity, as resources would become insufficient to meet the needs of a rapidly growing population.

(iv) **Relevance and Criticism** While being influential, Malthus's theory has been criticised for underestimating human innovation, especially advances in agriculture and technology that have expanded resource availability and mitigated some of the dire predictions.

2. "Malthus' theory of population growth was a rather pessimistic one. It was challenged by theorists." Justify. CBSE 2023

Ans. Malthus' theory of population growth is seen as pessimistic because he believed that population would grow faster than resources like food, leading to poverty and suffering. He thought that as the population increases, food supply wouldn't keep up, causing shortages. To Malthus, natural disasters like famine and disease were necessary to control population growth.

Malthus' Theory was challenged on the following reasons

(i) **Population and Food Growth** In the late 1800s and early 1900s, European countries experienced slower population growth and better disease control. Food production increased, and living standards improved, which went against Malthus's predictions of constant shortages.

(ii) **Criticism from other Scholars** Many scholars, including liberals and Marxists, argued that poverty is due to unequal distribution of resources, not population growth. They believed that the wealthy controlled resources, leaving the majority in poverty—not because of overpopulation but because of social and economic inequalities.

3. In the context of demographic changes, explain why birth rates tend to decline more slowly than death rates. Discuss the various factors, including social, economic, and medical influences, that lead to this slow decline in birth rates. **Competency Based Que.**

Ans. In the context of demographic changes, birth rates tend to decline more slowly than death rates due to a variety of social, economic and medical factors. While death rates can fall relatively fast, especially with improvements in healthcare and sanitation, the decline in birth rates is often more gradual because it is influenced by deeper societal changes.

- One significant reason for the slower decline in birth rates is the cultural and social value placed on having children. In many societies, especially in earlier stages of development, larger families were seen as a source of labour and security, particularly in rural areas. Families with many children also served as insurance for old age when medical care and pensions were unavailable. These cultural norms take time to shift, and changing them requires broad social transformation.
- Economic factors also play a role. In agrarian societies, where children contribute to household work, there is less economic incentive to limit family size. However, as societies industrialise and urbanise, the economic cost of raising children increases, leading to a gradual shift toward smaller families.
- Medical advances, such as improved maternal and child healthcare, can significantly reduce mortality rates and make it safer for women to bear children. However, even as child survival improves, it takes time for people to adjust their family planning choices. Thus, birth rates decline more slowly due to these intertwined social, cultural and economic influences.

As a result, despite improvements in healthcare and economic conditions, birth rates tend to decline more gradually than death rates, leading to slower demographic shifts.

4. The declining Sex Ratio in India 1901-2011 is given below. **CBSE 2025**

Year	Sex Ratio all age group	Variation over previous decade	Child Sex Ratio (0-6 years)	Variation over previous decade
1901	972	–	–	–
1911	964	–8	–	–
1921	955	–9	–	–
1931	950	–5	–	–
1941	945	–5	–	–
1951	946	+1	–	–
1961	941	–5	976	–
1971	930	–11	964	–12
1981	934	+4	962	–2
1991	927	–7	945	–17
2001	933	+6	927	–18
2011	943	+10	919	–8

Based on the above data, answer the following questions.

(a) What are the reasons for the declining child sex ratio?

(b) Based on the above data, compare the data of the 20th century with that of the 21st century and state your inferences.

Ans. (a) There could be several reasons for the decline in the sex ratio some of which includes

(i) Preference for sons.

(ii) Raising women is considered a wasteful investment as they have to get married ultimately.

(iii) Girl marriage is considered a burden due to the prevalence of the dowry system.

(b) The decline in the child sex ratio at the end of the 20th century indicates gender discrimination, female foeticide and societal preference for male children. However, its rise in the 21st century indicates improved awareness, government policies like Beti Bachao Beti Padhao, stricter laws against sex-selective abortions and changing social attitudes. This trend reflects progress toward gender equality and better opportunities for girl children in society.

5. Birth and Death rate in India 1901 – 2017

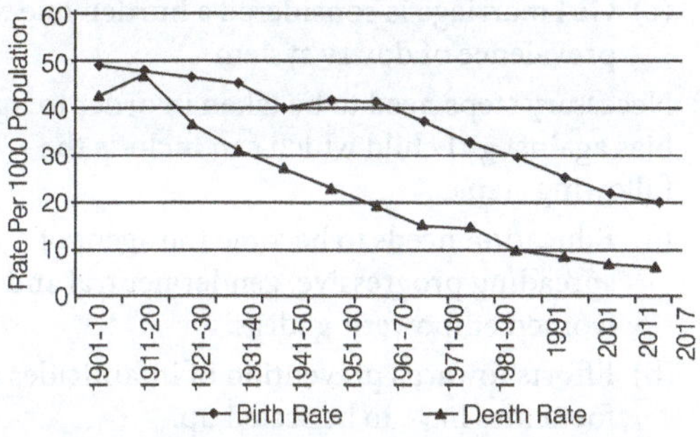

Based on the above graph, answer the following questions.

(i) **What is the relation between birth rate and death rate during the years 1911-2020?**

(ii) **Define negative growth rate.**

(iii) **Which curve declines faster? Give one reason for the same.** **CBSE 2024**

Ans. (i) The graph shows that both the birth rate and death rate in India declined from 1911 to 2020. However, the birth rate consistently remained higher than the death rate throughout this period. This gap between birth and death rates suggests that India experienced positive population growth as the number of births was greater than the number of deaths. Over time, the gap narrowed, especially as the death rate declined more sharply than the birth rate.

(ii) Negative growth rate occurs when the death rate exceeds the birth rate in a population, resulting in a decrease in the total population size over time. In this situation, the number of people dying is higher than the number of people being born, leading to a reduction in population.

(iii) The death rate curve declines faster than the birth rate curve. One reason for this rapid decline is improvements in healthcare, sanitation, and access to medical facilities, which led to a significant reduction in mortality rates. These advancements allowed for better disease control and reduced infant and maternal mortality, particularly after India's independence.

6. Age Composition of the Population of India, 1961-2026.

Year	Age Group 0-14 Year	15-59 Year	60+ Years	Total
1961	41	53	6	100
1971	42	53	5	100
1981	40	54	6	100
1991	38	56	7	100
2001	34	59	7	100
2011	29	63	8	100
2026	23	64	12	100

Based on the above table, answer the following questions. **CBSE 2024 C**

(i) **What is meant by demographic dividend?**

(ii) **Based on the data given in the above table, compare the data of the years 1961 and 2026 and state your inferences.**

(iii) **A falling dependency ratio can be a source of economic growth and prosperity. State how.**

Ans. (i) The demographic dividend refers to the economic benefit that arises when a country experiences a higher proportion of working-age individuals (15-59 years) relative to the dependent population (children and elderly). This situation occurs when birth rates decline, leading to a larger share of the population being in the workforce, thus increasing economic productivity. This demographic phase can lead to economic growth, provided there are suitable investments in education, healthcare and employment opportunities for the working-age population.

(ii) Comparing the years 1961 and 2026, we observe significant changes in India's age composition. The proportion of children (0-14 years) has decreased from 41% to 23%, while the working-age group (15-59 years) has increased from 53% to 64%. The elderly population (60+ years) has risen from 6% to 12%. These shifts reflect a decline in birth rates, an expanding workforce and an ageing population, indicating potential economic growth due to a larger working-age population but also increased support demands for the elderly.

(iii) A falling dependency ratio means a higher proportion of working-age individuals relative to dependents (children and elderly). This demographic shift can lead to increased productivity, as more people are actively contributing to the economy. It also provides a boost to savings, investments and consumption, driving economic growth and prosperity in the short-term.

7. The demographic advantage to be derived from the age structure of the population is due to the fact that India is one of the youngest countries in the world. Elaborate. **Competency Based Que.**

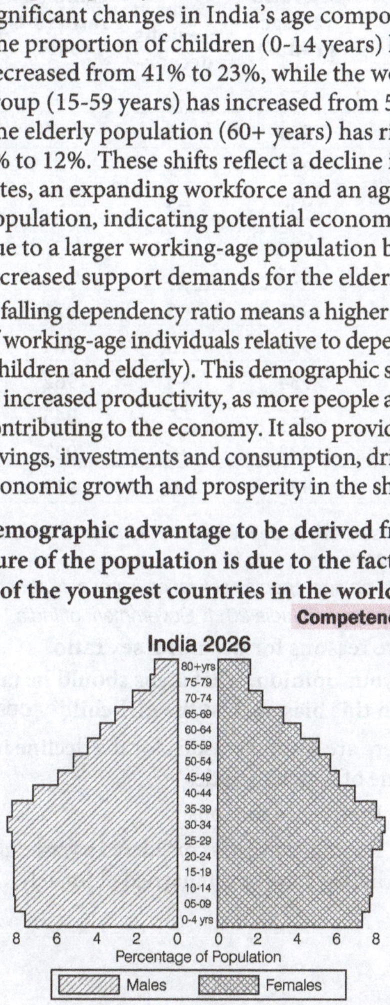

Ans. The demographic advantage or 'dividend' to be gained from the population's age structure is due to the fact that India is and will continue to be one of the world's youngest countries. In the year 2000, a third of India's population was under the age of 15. The average Indian will be 29 years old in 2020, compared to 37 years in China and the United States, 45 in Western Europe, and 48 in Japan. This means a strong and increasing labour force, which can provide unforeseen development and prosperity benefits. The 'demographic dividend' is the product of a rise in the proportion of jobs in the population compared to non- workers. In terms of age, the working population is roughly comprised of those between the ages of 15 and 64. Changes in the age structure as a result of the demographic transition reduce the 'dependency ratio' or the ratio of non-working to working-age people, allowing for growth.

8. The declining Sex Ratio in India, 1901-2011

Year	Sex ratio (all age groups)	Variation over previous decade	Child Sex ratio (0-6 years)	Variation over previous decade)
1901	972	–	–	–
1911	964	–8	–	–
1921	955	–9	–	–
1931	950	–5	–	–
1941	945	–5	–	–
1951	946	+1	–	–
1961	941	–5	976	–
1971	930	–11	964	–12
1981	934	+4	962	–2
1991	927	–7	945	–17
2001	933	+6	927	–18
2011	943	+10	919	–8

Note *The sex ratio is defined as the number of females per 1000 males*

Data on age-specific sex ratios is not available before 1961.

Source *Census of India 2011. Government of India.*

(i) Give reasons for declining sex ratio.

(ii) In your opinion, what steps should be taken to deal with this bias against the girl-child? **CBSE SQP 2023**

Ans. (i) There are several reasons for the decline in sex ratio some of which includes

(a) Preference for sons.

(b) Raising women is considered a wasteful investment as they have to get married ultimately.

(c) Girl marriage is considered a burden due to prevalence of dowry system.

(ii) Necessary steps need to be taken in order to fight the bias against girl child which can include the following steps

(a) Education needs to become the agent of spreading progressive, gender neutral and women empowering ideas.

(b) Efforts towards prevention of infanticides and foeticides have to be scaled up.

9. Answer the questions given below based on the reading of the data given in the table. **CBSE SQP 2024**

Literacy Rate in India

(Percentage of Population 7 years of Age and Above)

Year	Persons	Males	Females	Male-Female Gap in Literacy Rate
1951	18.3	27.2	8.9	18.3
1961	28.3	40.4	15.4	25.1
1971	34.5	46.0	22.0	24.0
1981	43.6	56.4	29.8	26.6
1991	52.2	64.1	39.3	24.8
2001	65.4	75.9	54.2	21.7
2011	73.0	80.9	64.6	16.3

(i) What are the different factors which determine literacy rates in our country?

(ii) How do inequalities in literacy rate lead to inequality across generations?

Ans. (i) The literacy rates in India are influenced by several factors such as

(a) **Gender** Male literacy has traditionally been higher than female literacy, though the gender gap is reducing.

(b) **Social Groups** Disadvantaged communities such as Scheduled Castes (SCs) and Scheduled Tribes (STs) have historically lower literacy rates.

(c) **Region** There is a wide disparity in literacy across regions. States like Kerala have near-universal literacy, while others like Bihar lag behind.

(d) **Economic Conditions** Poverty can limit access to education, especially for girls and marginalised communities.

(e) **Government Initiatives** Policies such as adult education programmes and mid-day meals contribute to improving literacy rates.

(ii) Inequalities in literacy contribute to intergenerational poverty. Illiterate parents often struggle to ensure quality education for their children due to limited knowledge and financial resources. As a result, children from illiterate families are more likely to have poor educational outcomes, perpetuating a cycle of poverty and limited opportunities. This gap in education perpetuates social inequality, as future generations continue to face barriers in securing better economic and social prospects.

10. **Read the given passage and answer the questions that follow.**

While urbanisation has been occurring at a rapid pace, it is the biggest cities-the metropolises-that have been growing the fastest. These metros attract migrants from the rural areas as well as from small towns. There are now 5,161 towns and cities in India, where 286 million people live. What is striking, however, is that more than two-thirds of the urban population lives in 27 big cities with million-plus populations. Clearly the larger cities in India are growing at such a rapid rate that the urban infrastructure can hardly keep pace.

(i) **Define urbanisation. What is migration of urban-rural channel?**

(ii) **What are the medium of the process of urbanisation?** **Competency Based Que.**

Ans. (i) The mechanism by which the population of cities grows and people living in rural areas internalise the urban society's lifestyle. The rapid growth of urbanisation demonstrates that the town or city has served as a draw for the rural population. Those who cannot find work (or enough work) in rural areas seek employment in the city. The continuous depletion of common property resources such as wetlands, woods and grazing lands has also increased the flow of rural-to-urban migration.

Migration of urban-rural channel refers to the movement of people from rural areas such as villages to urban areas especially the metropolis cities in search of work and better living standards.

(ii) The process of urbanisation began as the mass media and communication channels became popular.

- It bought images of urban life styles and patterns of consumptions into the rural areas.
- With urbanisation, towns and cities became the magnet for the rural population. If people do not find work in rural areas they go to the city in search of work.
- The migration accelerated the decline of common property resources like ponds, forests and grazing lands. As a result, the things that they got for free are now available for a price.

SELF ASSESSMENT TEST

Objective Type Questions

1. Which of the following statements is correct about demography?

(a) Demography is concerned with the political changes in a population.

(b) Demography focuses only on the birth rate and death rate of the population.

(c) Demography examines the structure, composition, and trends in population.

(d) Demography only studies social structures, not quantitative data.

2. The Indian census provides valuable data for

I. Understanding demographic trends at a national level.

II. Creating policies related to healthcare, education and employment.

III. Offering historical insights without having practical use today.

IV. Helping in the governance and taxation system.

Codes

(a) I and II (b) II and IV (c) I, III and IV (d) I, II and IV

3. Which of the following factors contribute to the decline in child sex ratio in India?

I. Selective female abortion

II. Low literacy rates among women

III. Preference for male child due to cultural beliefs

IV. High maternal mortality rate

Codes

(a) I and II (b) I and III (c) II and IV (d) I, III and IV

4. Which of the following sectors contribute to the decline in agricultural employment in rural areas?

I. Non-farm rural occupations

II. Urban-based business enterprises

III. Manufacturing sector

IV. IT sector

Codes

(a) I and II (b) II and III (c) I, II and III (d) I, II, III and IV

5. According to Census 2011, which state has the highest sex ratio in India?

(a) Haryana (b) Kerala (c) Arunachal Pradesh (d) Uttar Pradesh

6. Assertion (A) In India, demographic transition is not yet complete because the birth rate has not been brought down to the same extent as the mortality rate.

Reason (R) Death rates in India have declined rapidly due to better public health and nutrition, while reproductive behaviour remains largely unchanged.

(a) Both A and R are true and R is the correct explanation of A

(b) Both A and R are true, but R is not the correct explanation of A

(c) A is true, but R is false

(d) A is false, but R is true

7. Assertion (A) The theory of demographic transition suggests a uniform population growth pattern for all societies.

Reason (R) Every society experiences three basic phases of population growth based on their level of economic development.

(a) Both A and R are true and R is the correct explanation of A

(b) Both A and R are true, but R is not the correct explanation of A

(c) A is true, but R is false

(d) A is false, but R is true

Case Based Questions

1. Considered from an urban point of view, the rapid growth in urbanisation shows that the town or city has been acting as a magnet for the rural population. Those who cannot find work (or sufficient work) in the rural areas go to the city in search of work. This flow of rural-to-urban migration has also been accelerated by the continuous decline of common property resources like ponds, forests and grazing lands. These common resources enabled poor people to survive in the villages although they owned little or no land. Now, these resources have been turned into private property, or they are exhausted (Ponds may run dry or no longer provide enough fish; forests may have been cut down and have vanished...).

(i) What is the primary reason for the rapid growth of urbanisation in India?

(a) Beter infrastructure in rural areas

(b) Availability of common property resources in rural areas

(c) Rural-to-urban migration in search of work

(d) Decline in urban job opportunities

(ii) How does urban anonymity benefit people from socially dominant rural groups?

(a) It allows them to hide their wealth

(b) It offers them protection from caste discrimination

(c) It helps them gain high status jobs

(d) It allows them to live in better conditions

Very Short Answer Type Questions

1. The decline in the child sex ratio in India has been a growing concern for demographers and social activists. Despite improvements in maternal healthcare, practices such as sex-selective abortions and female infanticide continue to contribute to this issue.

   What are the primary factors responsible for the decline in the child sex ratio in India?
2. The advancement of technology, particularly ultrasound, has made it easier to determine the sex of a fetus, leading to an increase in sex-selective abortions.

   How does the misuse of modern medical technology to determine fetal sex contribute to the gender imbalance in India?
3. Write down the two methods suggested by Malthus to control the population.

Short Answer Type Questions

1. Give some main features of National Population Policy, 2017.
2. The Census of India 2011 recorded a significant drop in the child sex ratio, with the number of females per 1000 males falling to 919. Despite this decline, some states have higher sex ratios than the national average.

   How do the regional variations in the child sex ratio reflect the social and economic factors that influence gender bias in different parts of India?

Long Answer Type Questions

1. Literacy varies considerably across gender, across regions, and across social groups. As can be seen from Table 4, the literacy rate for women is 16.3% less than the literacy rate for men. However, female literacy has been rising faster than male literacy, partly because it started from relatively low levels. Female literacy rose by about 10.4 per cent between 2001 and 2011 compared to the rise in male literacy of 7.6 per cent in the same period. Literacy increased approximately 8% in total. Male literacy rose about 5% whereas female literacy rose about 10%. Again female literacy has been rising faster than male literacy.
   (a) How does literacy serve as an instrument of empowerment in a community?
   (b) What are the key factors contributing to the increase in female literacy in India between 2001 and 2011?
2. Describe with projected details on how the age group pyramid of India gives the idea of demographic dividend.
3. State how India's declining sex ratio can be curbed? What are the factors responsible for low sex ratio in India?

03

CHAPTER

A population is not just a collective of separate, unrelated individuals. It is a society made up of many interlinked communities that are sustained and regulated by social relationships and social institutions.

Social Institutions : Continuity and Change

YOUR STUDY GOALS

3.1 Caste and the Caste System
3.2 Problems of Caste in Post-Independent India
3.3 Tribal Communities
3.4 Family and Kinship

YOUR PRACTICE GOAL

- Objective Type Questions (44 Qs; MCQs, A-R, Case Based Questions)
- Subjective Questions (14 VSAs, 14 SAs, 4 LAs)

3.1 Caste and the Caste System

- In Indian society, three main institutions stand out–caste, tribe and family.
- Caste is an ancient social institution that has been part of Indian history and culture for thousands of years.
- It continues to play a central role in Indian society today, though its forms have evolved over time.
- The caste system in the past was quite different from how it functions in the present.

Caste in the Past

- The caste system is uniquely associated with the Indian subcontinent. Although it is a central aspect of Hindu society, caste distinctions have also spread to non-Hindu communities such as Muslims, Christians and Sikhs.
- The term 'caste' comes from the Portuguese word *casta*, meaning 'pure breed'. It refers to a broad institutional arrangement commonly referred to in Indian languages by two distinct terms–*varna* and *jati*.
- **Varna** It literally means 'colour,' *varna* refers to the fourfold division of society into Brahmin, Kshatriya, Vaishya and Shudra. This classification excludes a fifth category, the *Panchamas*, which included outcastes, foreigners, slaves and conquered peoples.

- **Jati** refers to species or kinds of anything. In Indian languages, **jati**[1] specifically refers to caste as an institution.
- The relationship between *varna* and *jati* has been widely debated among scholars.
- Some consider *varna* as a broad, all-India classification, while *jati* is seen as a regional or local subdivision with a complex system of castes and sub-castes that vary from region to region.

Features of the Caste System

The caste system, as we know it today, developed distinct features over time

- **Caste is determined by birth** A child inherits the caste of its parents, and this cannot be changed or chosen. However, a person can be expelled from their caste.
- **Strict marriage rules** Caste groups are endogamous, meaning marriage is restricted to members of the same caste.
- **Food rules** Caste membership prescribes specific rules about what kinds of food can be eaten and with whom food can be shared.
- **Hierarchy** Castes are arranged in a hierarchy of rank and status, and each caste has a place in the hierarchy, which can vary by region.
- **Segmental organisation** Castes are divided into sub-castes and sometimes sub-sub-castes.
- **Caste and occupation** Traditionally, caste was linked to occupation, with jobs becoming hereditary. Members of other castes were not allowed to take up certain occupations.

These features, while prescribed in ancient texts, were not always followed in practice. Still, caste remains an unequal institution where certain castes benefit while others suffer with little hope of upward mobility.

Principles of the Caste System

The caste system can be understood through two sets of principles. These are

(i) **Based on Difference and Separation** Each caste is distinct and strictly separated from others. Scriptural rules prevent caste mixing in areas such as marriage, food sharing, social interaction, and occupation.

(ii) **Based on Wholism and Hierarchy** Castes do not exist in isolation but in relation to the whole society. The system is inherently hierarchical, with each caste occupying a distinct rank.

Hierarchy of Castes

- The hierarchical order of caste is based on the distinction between purity and pollution. Purity refers to being closer to the sacred, while pollution refers to being distant from or opposed to it.
- Castes that are considered ritually pure, hold higher status, while those considered less pure hold lower status.
- Beyond ritual purity, material power—whether economic, political or military—also influences a caste's status. Historically, castes that held power tended to have higher status, while those who were defeated had lower status.
- In the past, castes were unequal but complementary and non-competing.
- Each caste had a designated place in the system and a specific occupation associated with it.
- The caste system functioned as a social division of labour with little or no mobility.

---

1 **Jati** It is a term traditionally used to describe a cohesive group of people in the Indian sub contient, like a tribe, community, clan, sub-clan or a religious sect.

Colonialism and Caste

- The period of colonial rule in India significantly impacted the caste system. Many scholars argue that the caste system, as we understand it today, is more a product of colonialism[2] than ancient Indian tradition.
- Colonial administrators, in their efforts to govern efficiently, conducted extensive surveys of the country's customs and social structures. The census, beginning in the 1860s and becoming a regular exercise by 1881, was a major tool in understanding caste. The 1901 census under Herbert Risley collected data on the social hierarchy in various regions.
- This effort to document caste status affected social perceptions of caste, as many castes sought to claim higher status, using historical or scriptural evidence. By officially counting and recording castes, the system became more rigid.
- The British administration's interest in the welfare of downtrodden castes, also known as **'depressed classes,'** led to the Government of India Act of 1935. This act gave legal recognition to lists of Scheduled Castes and Scheduled Tribes, making them eligible for special treatment. The most discriminated **untouchables** were included in Scheduled Castes.

Caste in the Present

- After India's independence in 1947, the caste system continued to exist, though its structure had evolved.
- Caste played a role in the mass mobilisations of the national movement, especially among the depressed classes.
- The efforts to organise the depressed class, specially the **untouchables**[3] began before the nationalist movement in the late 19th century.
- These initiativies came from both progressive upper caste reformers and lower caste leaders like Mahatma Jyotiba Phule, Baba Saheb Ambedkar, Ayyankali, Savitribai Phule and E.V. Ramasamy Naicker (Periyar) in different parts of India.

Ayyankali (1863-1914) | **Jotirao Govindrao Phule (1827-1890)** | **Savitri Bai Phule (1831-1897)**

- Both Mahatma Gandhi and B.R. Ambedkar protest against untouchability from the 1920 onwards. By the time of independence, there was consensus on the need to abolish caste distinctions.
- The Indian Constitution enshrined the principle of equality and aimed to abolish caste-based discrimination.
- However, caste inequalities persist and the state has been unable to fully eliminate them.

Quick Test 1

1. Which principle differentiates castes in the caste hierarchy?
2. What are the two terms in Indian languages that refer to caste?
3. How many varnas are there in the caste system?
4. What act introduced the terms 'Scheduled Castes' and 'Scheduled Tribes'?
5. Name two reformers who worked against untouchability.

---

2 **Colonialism** It is an ideology by which a country seeks to conquer and colonise or forcibly rule over another country.

3 **Untouchables** It refers to the members of the lowest castes, considered to be ritually impure to such an extent that they cause pollution by mere touch.

3.2 Problems of Caste in Post-Independent India

- The post-Independence Indian state reflected contradictions regarding the caste system and upper caste interests.
- The state was committed to abolishing caste, as mentioned in the Constitution, but was unable or unwilling to implement fundamental reforms to remove caste inequality.
- The state assumed that ignoring caste would undermine caste-based privileges, leading to its automatic abolition. For instance, in government jobs, all individuals were expected to compete on 'equal' terms, except for reservations for Scheduled Castes (SC) and Scheduled Tribes (ST).
- Development activities and the growth of private industry affected the caste system indirectly through rapid economic changes.
- Modern industries created various jobs without caste supremacy.
- Urbanisation and collective living conditions in cities made it challenging for the caste system to survive.
- Liberal ideas of individualism and meritocracy attracted modern, educated Indians, leading many to abandon extreme caste practices. However, caste system remained strong. Even in industrial jobs, like those in Mumbai's textile mills or Kolkata's jute mills, hiring often dependend on caste and kinship lines.
- Middlemen often recruited labour from their own caste and region, resulting in specific castes dominating industries. Prejudice against untouchables remained strong, even in urban areas.
- The resilience of caste was most evident in cultural and domestic aspects, particularly in marriages and politics. For example
  - **Endogamy** The practice of marrying within one's caste remained largely unchanged, with most marriages still occurring within caste boundaries. Although some flexibility exists, the boundaries between castes of similar socio-economic status remain rigid.
  - **Politics** Democratic politics in independent India is still heavily influenced by caste. Since the 1980s, caste-based political parties have emerged, making caste a decisive factor in elections.
- Sociologists, including **MN Srinivas**, have coined new concepts to understand these changes.

Sociological Concepts by MN Srinivas

- **Sanskritisation** Lower or middle castes attempt to improve their social status by adopting the practices of higher castes.
- **Dominant Caste** Castes with large populations and land rights granted by post-independence land reforms became economically and politically powerful in rural areas.
- Before these reforms, upper castes, often called absentee landlords, owned the land but didn't participate in farming, living in towns or cities instead.
- These landlords were relied on lower castes, including 'untouchables,' for farming the land. With land ownership, they gained economic power.
- Examples include Yadavs (Bihar and UP), Vokkaligas (Karnataka), Reddys and Khammas (AP), Marathas (Maharashtra), Jats (Punjab, Haryana, Western UP), Patidars (Gujarat).

Invisibility of Caste for Upper Castes

- For upper-caste urban middle and upper classes, caste became 'invisible'.
- Their caste privilege ensured access to education, professional opportunities and state-sector jobs without facing serious competition.
- They believed their success was unrelated to caste, although this privilege was not universally enjoyed by all upper-caste individuals.

Caste Visibility for SCs and STs

- For SCs and STs, caste remains a dominant part of their identity.
- Their lack of education and social capital makes caste an essential part of their identity, as it is the only thing recognised by the world.

Caste and Privilege in Modern India

- For the upper castes, especially in urban areas, caste has become less visible. This invisibility is a result of their access to education and jobs, allowing them to take advantage of opportunities provided by rapid development.
- However, caste privilege continues to benefit these groups, even though they may believe their success is not related to caste.
- For Scheduled Castes and Scheduled Tribes, caste remains a visible and central aspect of their identity, as they continue to face discrimination and lack access to the same resources as upper castes.

Quick Test 2

1. In how many categories has the Varna system been categorised?
2. What is the literal meaning of the word 'Varna'?
3. State four features of the caste system.
4. Name the three notable leaders who fought for the upliftment of lower castes.
5. What do you mean by Sanskritisation?
6. Name the dominant caste in Gujarat.

3.3 Tribal Communities

- Tribes are very old communities whose people are some of the oldest inhabitants of the Indian subcontinent.
- They did not follow a religion with a written text.
- They did not have a traditional government or political system.
- There were no clear differences in social status or rank within these communities.

▲ *A tribal village fair*

Classification of Tribal Societies

Tribes have been classified according to their 'permanent' and 'acquired' traits.

Permanent Traits

Permanent traits include region, language, physical characteristics and ecological habitat.

- The tribal population in India is widespread, with the highest concentration in central and North-Eastern regions.
- About 85% of tribal populations live in central India, stretching from Gujarat and Rajasthan to West Bengal and Odisha in the East with Madhya Pradesh, Jharkhand, Chhattisgarh and parts of Maharashtra and Andhra Pradesh.
- Out of the remaining 15%, over 11% is in the North-Eastern states and 3% in the rest of India.

- The North-Eastern states have the highest concentration of tribal's ranging more than 60% going up to 95% in states like Arunachal Pradesh, Meghalaya, Mizoram and Nagaland and over 30% in Assam.
- In the rest of the country the tribal population is less than 12% except Odisha and Madhya Pradesh.
- Tribal categorisation takes place into various divisions
  - **Language** On the basis of language, tribes are categorised into four categories. Indo-Aryan, Dravidian, Austric and Tibeto-Burman. The Indo-Aryan accounts for 1% of the population and the Dravidian accounts for 3%. The other two languages groups, Austic and Tibeto, Burman, are mainly spoken by tribal communities, with tribals accounting for all of the Austic speakers and over 80% of Tibeto-Burman speakers.
  - **Physical Racial** Concerning physical racial terms, tribes are classified under the Negrito, Australoid, Mongoloid, Dravidian and Aryan categories. The last two are shared by the majority of the Indian population.
- Tribes sizes vary in great numbers with some having 7 million people to some Andamanese islanders with only 100 people. The biggest tribes are the Gonds, Bhils, Santhals, Oraons, Minas Bodos and Mundas.
- The total population of tribes amounts to about 8.2% of the Indian population or 84 million people according to the 2001 Census which has grown to 8.6% or 104 million tribal population according to the 2011 Census Report.

Acquired Traits

- Acquired traits of tribes are categorised based on two criteria: **mode of livelihood** and **extent of incorporation** into Hindu society.
- The mode of livelihood categorises tribes into various groups, including fishermen, food gatherers and hunters, shifting cultivators, peasants, and plantation and industrial workers.
- The extent of incorporation into Hindu society classifies tribes based on their assimilation into the Hindu mainstream.
- From the perspective of the tribes, the attitude of the people towards Hinduism is crucial, differentiating between tribes that are positively inclined towards Hinduism and those that oppose it.
- From the perspective of the Hindu mainstream, tribes are viewed according to their status, with some tribes given high status and others are given low status.

Tribe-Caste Distinction

The difference between tribes and castes comes from their unique cultures. Castes are part of Hinduism and follow ideas of purity and pollution, while tribes are separate from Hinduism and organise themselves based on family and relationships. In the 1960s, scholars had a debate about whether tribes were similar to Hindu caste-based village societies or completely different.

Some scholars in the debate have noted that

- Some believed tribes were like caste societies but had fewer levels of hierarchy (less complex) and focused more on sharing resources as a community instead of individual ownership.
- Others argued that tribes were totally different because they didn't follow ideas of purity and pollution, which are key to the caste system.
- By the 1970s, scholars found problems with all the main ways of defining tribes. They showed that the common ideas used to separate tribes from peasants-like size, isolation, religion or livelihood-didn't really work.
- The discussion about the differences between castes and tribes also included many studies on how tribes became part of Hindu society over time. This happened in various ways, such as

- Indian history is often seen as a process where tribal groups were absorbed into the caste system at different levels of hierarchy as their lands were taken over and forests cleared.
- Some view this as a natural process, like how other groups are absorbed into Hinduism as sects. Others see it as exploitative.
- Early anthropologists focused on the cultural aspects of how tribes joined the mainstream. Later writers highlighted the exploitative and political side of this process.
- Many people mistakenly believe that tribes are like untouched stone-age hunting and gathering societies, but this is not true.
- Adivasis were not always oppressed; several Gond kingdoms, like Garha Mandla and Chanda, existed in Central India. Additionally, many Rajput kingdoms in Central and Western India emerged through a process of stratification.
- Adivasis historically exercised dominance over the plains through raiding and serving as local militias and occupied unique trade roles involving forest produce, salt and elephants.
- The capitalist economy's demand for forest resources, minerals and inexpensive labour has brought tribal societies into closer interaction with mainstream society.

National Development Versus Tribal Development

- The focus on development has influenced attitudes toward tribes and shaped state policies.
- National development under Nehru focused on building dams, factories and mines.
- Tribal areas, often located in mineral-rich forests, faced significant impacts from this development.
- The benefits of development came at the cost of tribal communities, who were displaced from their land for mineral exploitation and hydroelectric projects.
- Forest land taken from tribes was exploited during British rule and continues to be misused today.
- The introduction of private and ownership has negatively affected tribes, whose traditional community-based ownership is disadvantaged in this new system.
- Development has also led to heavy in-migration of non-tribals, disrupting tribal communities and culture while increasing their exploitation.
- Examples of the disadvantages faced by tribes due to development include
  - The costs and benefits from dams on the Narmada River are not shared equally among different communities and regions.
  - In Jharkhand's industrial areas, the tribal population share has decreased.
  - In Tripura, the tribal share of the population was halved in just a decade, making them a minority.
  - Similar pressures are being experienced in Arunachal Pradesh.

Tribal Identity Today

- The forced incorporation of tribes into mainstream society has significantly affected tribal culture, society and economy.
- Tribal identities are shaped by interactions rather than being based on ancient characteristics unique to tribes.
- As interactions with mainstream society became negative, many tribal identities now revolve around resistance and opposition to the non-tribal world.
- Positive outcomes of this resistance include
  - The achievement of statehood for Jharkhand and Chhattisgarh, though these states still face challenges in empowering tribal communities fully.
  - The emergence of educated middle-class communities among tribes due to reservation policies, leading to the creation of an urban professional class.

- The development of identity assertions as tribal societies become more differentiated, resulting in various bases for asserting tribal identity.

- Two main issues which led to tribal rebellion or movements are as following
  (i) Control over economic resources like land and specially forest.
  (ii) Ethnic and cultural identity.
- While these issues usually go together, they can also diverge as tribal society differentiates.
- The motivations for middle-class tribal people and poor tribal individuals to join movements may differ.

3.4 Family and Kinship

- Family is where we begin our lives and serves as a space of warmth and care, but it can also be a site of conflicts, injustice and violence.
- Family disputes are as common as stories of compassion, sacrifice and care.
- The structure of the family can be examined both as a social institution on its own and in relation to other social institutions in society.
- Families can be defined as nuclear or extended, male-headed or female-headed and can follow matrilineal or patrilineal descent.
- The internal structure of a family reflects broader societal structures, including political, economic and cultural aspects.
- Changes in family composition and structure are linked to other societal spheres. For example, men migrating from Himalayan villages can lead to the formation of women-headed families.
- Additionally, the work schedules of young parents in the software industry can result in more grandparents moving in to care for young grandchildren.
- Thus, private family life is connected to public spheres such as economic, political, cultural, and educational domains.
- Changes in society impact not only family structure but also cultural ideas, norms and values.

Nuclear and Extended Family

- A **nuclear family** consists of one set of parents and their children.
- An **extended family**, also known as a joint family, typically includes more than one family couple across two generations living together.
- The concept of an extended family is often seen as characteristic of India, but this is misleading. Extended families are limited to certain sections and regions of the community.
- According to I.P. Desai, the term 'joint family' is not native to India; the terms used for joint family in most Indian languages are merely translations of the English term.

The Diverse Forms of the Family

- Different societies exhibit diverse family forms, which can be understood through various rules.
- **Based on Residence**
  - **Matrilocal** A newly married couple resides with the woman's parents.
  - **Patrilocal** A newly married couple lives with the man's parents.
- **Based on Inheritance**
  - **Matrilineal** Property is passed from mother to daughter.
  - **Patrilineal** Property is passed from father to son.

- A **patriarchal family** structure is where men hold authority and dominance.
- A **matriarchy** is where women play a dominant role, but this concept is largely theoretical as there is little evidence of such societies.
- **Matrilineal societies** exist where women inherit property but do not control it.

Quick Test 1

1. Name two major tribes of Succession Act.
2. Which is that one tribe that has special households that make baskets?
3. What are the two criterias on which acquired traits of tribes are based?
4. Name four major tribes of India.

NCERT Folder

1. What is the role of the ideas of separation and hierarchy in the caste system?

Ans. The caste system can be understood as the combination of two sets of principles, one is based on difference and separation and the other on collectivity and hierarchy. Each caste is supposed to be different from other caste and is therefore strictly separated from every other caste.

Many of the scriptural rules of caste are thus designed to prevent the mixing of castes. Some of these are rules ranging from marriage, food sharing and social interaction to occupation. On the other hand, these different and separated castes do not have an individual existence but they can only exist in relation to a larger whole i.e. society consisting of all castes.

This societal whole or system is a hierarchical rather than egalitarian system. Each individual caste occupies not just a distinct place, but also a particular position in the social order.

The hierarchical ordering of castes is based on the distinction between purity and pollution. Castes that are considered ritually pure have high status, while those considered less pure or impure have low status. As in all societies, material power is closely associated with social status.

Castes are complementary and non-competing groups. In other words, each caste has its own place in the system which cannot be taken over by any other caste.

2. What are some of the rules that the caste system imposes? CBSE 2019

Ans. The most commonly cited defining features or rules of caste are the following

- Caste is determined by birth, a child is born into the caste of its parents. It is never a matter of choice.
- Membership in a caste involves strict rules about marriage. Caste groups are endogamous i.e. marriage is restricted to members of the group.
- Caste membership also involves rules about food and food-sharing. What kinds of food may be eaten is prescribed and who one may share food with, is also specified.
- Caste involves a system consisting of many castes arranged in a hierarchy of rank and status.
- Castes also involve sub-divisions within themselves, i.e. castes almost always have sub-castes which may also have sub-sub-castes.
- Castes were traditionally linked to occupations. A person born into a caste could only practice the occupation associated with that caste.

3. What changes did colonialism bring about in the caste system?

Or **The institution of caste underwent major changes from colonial times to the present day. Explain.**

Or **The institution of caste underwent major changes during the colonial period. Explain.** CBSE 2019

Ans. Major social institutions and specially the institution of caste underwent major changes during the colonial period. In fact, some scholars argue that what we know today as caste is a product of colonialism than of ancient Indian tradition. Some of these efforts took the shape of very methodical and intensive surveys and reports on the customs and manners of various tribes and castes all over the country.

Some of the changes in caste system are as follows

- The study of the social hierarchies and the discriminatory patterns was done exclusively by British scholars to govern India.

- They documented and crystallised the caste system which was originally fluid.
- Colonial state has an intervention of land revenue settlement and related arrangements and law to give legal recognition to the customary rights to the upper caste.
- By the end of colonial period, the administration also took a new shape in the welfare of the caste, referred as 'Depressed Class' of its time.
- In 1935, Government of India Act gave legal recognition to caste with the name of 'Schedule'. This marked the emergence of 'Schedule Caste' and 'Schedule Tribe'.

4. In what sense has caste become relatively invisible for the urban upper castes?

Ans. Caste has become relatively invisible for the urban upper caste and middle classes in contemporary India due to several factors. These groups, who have benefited the most from developmental policies, no longer perceive caste as a significant influence on their lives. Their caste status played a crucial role in securing access to education, economic resources and public sector jobs in the post-independence era, which enabled them to advance socioeconomically.

Over time, their economic and educational capital has been consolidated, allowing them to enjoy life advantages without considering caste as a determining factor. For the third generation of these groups, caste seems irrelevant, as their continued success is seen as the result of personal achievements rather than caste privileges.

As a result, caste has become a personal and private matter for them, primarily affecting religious practices or marriage, but not their public lives or careers.

5. How have tribes been classified in India?

Or **Tribes have been classified according to their permanent and acquired tracts. Explain.**

Or **'Tribe' is a modern term for communities that are very old, being among the oldest inhabitants of the sub-continent. Tribes were communities that did not practice a religion with a written text; did not have a state or political form of the normal kind and did not have sharp class divisions. In terms of positive characteristics, tribes have been classified according to certain traits. Explain the traits.** **CBSE 2024**

Ans. Tribes in India have been classified according to their 'permanent' and 'acquired' traits.

Permanent Traits

Permanent traits include region, language, physical characteristics and ecological habitat. About 85% of the tribal population lives in 'middle India'. Of the remaining 15%, over 11% is in the North-Eastern states and over 3% living in the rest of India.

- **In terms of language** tribes are categorised into four categories as Indo-Aryan, Dravidian, Austric and Tibeto-Burman. In India, about 80% tribals speak the Austric and Tibeto-Burman language, whereas only 20% tribals speak Indo Aryan and Dravidian language.
- **In physical-racial terms** tribes are classified as Negrito, Australoid, Mongoloid, Dravidian and Aryan.
- **In terms of size**, tribes range from about seven million to some Andamanese islanders who are less than a hundred persons.

The biggest tribes of India are Gonds, Bhils, Santhals, Oraons, Minas, Bodos and Mundas. The total population of tribes amounts to about 8.6%, according to the 2011 census.

Acquired Traits

Acquired traits includes criterias i.e. mode of livelihood, and extent of incorporation into Hindu society.

- **On the basis of livelihood**, tribes can be categorised into fishermen, food gatherers/hunters, shifting cultivators, peasants and plantation and industrial workers.
- **Extent of incorporation into the Hindu society**, the dominant classification of tribes is based on the extent of their assimilation in the Hindu mainstream.
- From the tribe point of view, attitude of the tribe towards Hindu mainstream is important as there are tribes that are positively inclined towards Hinduism and others who oppose it.
- From the Hindu mainstream point of view, tribes may be viewed according to their status in the Hindu society which is generally low.

6. What evidence would you offer against the view that tribes are primitive communities living isolated lives untouched by civilisation?

Or **Do you think tribes are primitive communities living isolated lives untouched by conflation? Discuss.** **CBSE 2019**

Ans. There is no reason to believe that tribes are out of contact with the rest of world or have always been the oppressed section of the society. This can be said because of the following reasons

- The presence of several Gond kingdoms in Central India such as that of Garha, Mandla or Chanda.
- Many of the Rajput kingdoms of Central and Western India emerged through a process of stratification among adivasi communities themselves.

- Adivasi often exercised dominance over the plains people through their capacity to raid them and through their services as local militias.
- They also occupied a special trade niche, trading forest produce, salts and elephants.

Evidences substantiating tribes as primitive communities

- Tribes do not have a state or political form of the normal kind.
- They have no written rules on religion.
- They are neither Hindus nor peasants.
- Primarily they are engaged in activities like food gathering, fishing, hunting, agriculture etc.
- The habitat of tribes is in dense forests and mountainous regions.

7. What are the factors behind the assertion of tribal identities today?

Or Explain the factors influencing the formation of tribal indentity today.

Ans. Forced incorporation of tribal communities into mainstream processes had its impact on tribal culture and society as much as its economy.

- Tribal identities today are formed by this interactional process rather than any primordial (original, ancient) characteristics peculiar to tribes.
- Because this interaction with the mainstream has generally been unfavourable to the tribal communities, many tribal identities today are centred on ideas of resistance and opposition to the overwhelming force of the non-tribal world.
- The positive impact of successes such as the achievement of statehood for Jharkhand and Chhattisgarh after a long struggle is moderated by continuing problems. The vicious circle of armed rebellions is provoking state response which in turn lead to further rebellions. It has taken a heavy toll on the economy, culture and society of the North-Eastern states.
- Another significant development is the gradual emergence of an educated middle class among tribal communities.
- This in conjunction with the policies of reservation is creating an urbanised professional class.
- Further due to differing visions of the tribe the reason for asserting tribal identity differs for different sects of a tribe.

8. What are some of the different forms that the family can take?

Ans. In different societies, diverse family forms are found. With regard to the rules of residence, some societies are as follows

- **Matrilocal** In this case, the newly married couple stays with the woman's parents.
- **Patrilocal** In this case, the couple lives with the man's parents.

With **regard to the rules of inheritance**, some societies are as follows

- **Matrilineal** In this, the property is passed from mother to daughter.
- **Patrilineal** In this, the property is passed from father to son.

With **regard to the dominance**, some societies are as follows

- **Patriarchal** It exists where the men exercise authority and dominance.
- **Matriarchy** It exists where the women exercise authority or dominance.

9. In what ways can changes in social structure lead to changes in family structure?

Ans. The structure of the family can be studied both as a social institution in itself and also in its relationship to other social institutions of society. The internal structure of the family is usually related to other structures of society, namely political, economic, cultural, etc.

It is to be noted here that families have different structures and these structures change. Sometimes, these changes occur accidentally, as in cases of a war or migration.

Sometimes these changes are purposely brought about as when young people decide to choose their life partner instead of letting elders decide, or same sex love or marriage is done openly in society. It is evident from these kind of changes that due to changes in cultural ideas, norms and values would affect the family structures.

10. Explain the difference between matriliny and matriarchy.

Ans. **Matriliny** Matrilineal society is also called Matriliny. In these societies, women inherit property from their mothers but do not exercise control over it. Women are not taken to be the decision makers in public affairs.

Matriarchy As in patriarchal family structure where men exercise authority and dominance, in matriarchy, women plays dominant role and exercises authority. Matriarchy is only a theoretical concept and does not have any empirical evidence i.e., there is no historical or anthropological evidence of its existence in any society.

Exam Pattern Questions

Objective Type Questions

Multiple Choice Questions (MCQs)

1. The English word Casta is actually a borrowing from the **CBSE Term I, 2021**

(a) Greek word (b) Indian word
(c) Portuguese word (d) None of these

2. Which term is applicable to foreigners, slaves and conquered people? **CBSE 2023**

(a) Panchama (b) Brahman
(c) Kshatriya (d) Jati

3. Which of the following is true regarding caste system?

(a) It is a choice.
(b) It is endogamous.
(c) It is not linked to occupations.
(d) It is based on egalitarianism.

4. Caste system imposes rules. Which of the following is incorrect in this context?

(a) Caste groups are endogamous.
(b) Caste is hierarchical system.
(c) Occupational choices are open.
(d) There are restrictions on food sharing.

5. Theoretically the caste system can be understood as the combination of two sets of principles

(a) Differences and Separation
(b) Wholism and Hierarchy
(c) Both (a) and (b)
(d) None of the above

6. Which of the following is true for 'Pure Castes'? **CBSE 2024 C**

(a) They are close to the sacred.
(b) They have a low status.
(c) They do not have material power.
(d) It is believed that they were defeated in wars.

7. How did the British try to understand the complexity of caste system? **CBSE SQP Term I, 2021**

(a) Interview
(b) Survey
(c) Participant Observation
(d) Interview and Participant Observation

8. A system in which categories of people in a society are ranked in a hierarchy.

(a) Caste (b) Prejudices
(c) Discrimination (d) Social stratification

9. Which of the following statements is not true regarding the caste system in contemporary India? **Competency Based Que.**

(a) The caste system has become invisible for the upper caste, urban middle and upper classes due to their economic success.
(b) The privileged upper caste groups believe that caste plays no part in their public lives.
(c) Scheduled castes, tribes and backward castes have seen caste become less visible in their lives.
(d) Scheduled castes, tribes and backward castes rely on caste identity as a collective asset due to a lack of inherited social capital.

10. Which of the following statements is not true with regard to colonialism and caste? **CBSE SQP 2024**

(a) All major social institutions and specially the institution of caste underwent major changes during the colonial period.
(b) All of the changes brought about by colonialism were intended or deliberate.
(c) Initially, the British administrators began by trying to understand the complexities of caste in an effort to learn how to govern the country efficiently.
(d) The 1901 Census under the direction of Herbert Risley was particularly important as it sought to collect information on the social hierarchy of caste.

11. Colonialism brought about significant changes in the institution of caste. **CBSE 2024**

Choose the correct statement related to this statement.

(a) The 1903 census was done under the direction of Herbert Risley.
(b) No information was collected on the social hierarchy of caste.
(c) The administration also took interest in the welfare of the downtrodden castes.
(d) The Government of India Act of 1950 was passed which gave legal recognition to the lists or schedules of castes and tribes marked out for special treatment by the state.

12. Castes also involve sub-divisions within themselves, i.e. Castes almost always have sub-castes and sometimes sub-castes may also have sub-sub-castes. This is referred to as a .... **CBSE 2023**

(a) Class (b) Division
(c) Kinship (d) Segmental division

13. .... is an extreme and particularly vicious aspect of the caste system that prescribes stringent social sanctions against members of castes located at the bottom of the purity-pollution scale. Which concept is being talked about here? **Competency Based Que.**

(a) Discrimination (b) Untouchability
(c) Prejudices (d) Social inequality

14. Which of the following statements best describes the impact of reservation policies on the identity of scheduled castes and backward castes? **Competency Based Que.**

(a) Reservation policies have had no impact on their caste identity.
(b) Caste identity has become less important due to economic progress.
(c) Caste has become a central aspect of their identity because of continued discrimination.
(d) They no longer face caste-based discrimination due to reservations.

15. It was in the .... and .... spheres that caste has proved strongest. **CBSE SQP Term I, 2021**

(a) economic and technical
(b) religious and technical
(c) cultural and educational
(d) cultural and domestic

16. Which of the following make the Dominant Castes dominant? **CBSE SQP 2023**

I. Small population
II. Land rights
III. Intermediate caste
IV. Decisive role in regional politics

Codes
(a) I and II (b) I and III
(c) II, III and IV (d) I and IV

17. The Government of India Act, ... gave legal recognition to the lists or schedules of castes and tribes marked out for special treatment by the State. **Competency Based Que.**

(a) 1927 (b) 1947 (c) 1953 (d) 1935

18. Which of the following statements are true regarding the role of caste in post-Independence India?

I. The Indian state was committed to abolishing caste and explicitly wrote this into the Constitution.
II. The state pushed through radical reforms that dismantled the economic basis for caste inequality.
III. The state assumed that operating in a caste-blind manner would automatically lead to the abolition of caste-based privileges.
IV. Recruitment to industrial jobs in the post-Independence era was organised along caste and kinship-based lines.

Codes
(a) I and III (b) II and IV
(c) I, III and IV (d) II, III and IV

19 Which of the following is not a correct statement about the term Jati? **CBSE Term I, 2021**

I. It is a local classification that varies from region to region.
II. It has a segmental organisation
III. Membership of Jati involves rules about food and sharing
IV. It is an all India aggregative classification

With reference to the Jati System select the correct codes
(a) I, II and IV (d) I, II and III
(c) II, III and IV (d) I and IV

20. Which of the following does the term caste in the Indian context comprise of

I. Tribes II. Varna III. Jati

(a) I and II (b) II and III
(c) I and III (d) I, II and III

21. The .... or tribes were believed to be people of the forest whose distinctive habitat in the hill and forest areas shaped their Economic, Social and Political attribute. **CBSE Term I, 2021**

(a) Nairs (b) Jana
(c) Dikus (d) Khasis

22. Societies, where women inherit property from their mothers are called **CBSE Diksha**

(a) Maternal societies (b) Matriarchal societies
(c) Matrilocal societies (d) Matrilineal societies

23. The hierarchial ordering of caste is based on the distinction between **CBSE Diksha**

(a) Role and status (b) Religion and rituals
(c) Norms and authority (d) Purity and pollution

24. Which of the following do not belong to each other? **CBSE 2024**

(a) Yadavs of Bihar and Uttar Pradesh
(b) Vokkaligas of Karnataka
(c) Jats of Punjab
(d) Khammas of Tamil Nadu

25. The interaction of the tribal communities with the mainstream has generally been on terms unfavourable for the tribals. Many tribal identities today are centred on ideas of .... to the overwhelming force of the non-tribal word. **CBSE SQP 2023**

(a) Resistance and cooperation
(b) Cooperation and opposition
(c) Resistance and opposition
(d) Movement and opposition

26. Who said Backward Hindus to the Tribal Communities among the following? CBSE Term I, 2021

(a) M.N. Srinivas (b) G.S. Ghurye
(c) A.R. Desai (d) D.P Mukherjee

27. In terms of positive characteristics, tribes have been classified according to their 'permanent' and 'acquired' traits. Which one of the following is a permanent trait? CBSE 2023

(a) Region, language
(b) Physical characteristics
(c) Ecological habitat
(d) All of the above

28. Which of the following is not a permanent trait of tribes in India? CBSE Term I, 2021

(a) Region (b) Ecological habitat
(c) Mode of livelihood (d) Language

29. The newly married couple stays with the groom's parents. Which form of family is this? CBSE SQP Term I, 2021

(a) Patrilocal (b) Neolocal
(c) Matrilocal (d) Avunculocal

30. Matrilocal and Patrilocal type of family is based on CBSE Term I, 2021

(a) Authority (b) Power
(c) Inheritance (d) Residence

31. A patriarchal family structure exists where the men exercise authority and dominance, and matriarchy where the women play a similarly dominant role. However, matriarchy – unlike patriarchy – has been a theoretical rather than an empirical concept. Which among the following is not a feature of matriarchy society? Competency Based Que.

(a) Women play a dominant role
(b) Men exercise authority
(c) Women exercise their authority
(d) None of the above

32. The .... family is often seen as symptomatic of India. CBSE SQP 2023

(a) nuclear (b) patriarchal
(c) patrilineal (d) extended

Assertion-Reason Questions

Direction (Q. Nos. 33-40) Two statement are given in the question below as Assertion (A) and Reason (R). Read the statements and choose the appropriate option.

(a) Both A and R are true and R is the correct explanation of A
(b) Both A and R are true, but R is not the correct explanation of A
(c) A is true, but R is false
(d) A is false, but R is true

33. Assertion (A) Caste groups are endogamous, i.e. marriage is restricted to members of the group.

Reason (R) Membership in a caste involves strict rules about marriage.

34. Assertion (A) India, like most societies, has been marked by acute practices of social discrimination and exclusion.

Reason (R) At different periods of history, no protest movements arose against caste, gender and religious discrimination. CBSE 2024 C

35. Assertion (A) It was in the cultural and domestic spheres that caste has proved strongest.

Reason (R) While some boundaries may have become} more flexible or porous, the borders between groups of castes of similar socio-economic status are still heavily patrolled. CBSE SQP 2024

36. Assertion (A) Sanskritisation normally presupposes either an improvement in the economic or political position of the group concerned or a higher group self-consciousness resulting from its contact with a source of the 'Great Tradition'.

Reason (R) In a highly unequal society such as India there were and still are obstacles to any easy taking over of the customs of the higher castes by the lower. CBSE SQP 2024

37. Assertion (A) Ritually highest caste – the Brahmins were subordinated to the secular power of kings and rulers belonging to the Kshatriya castes.

Reason (R) In strict scriptural terms, Brahmins were not supposed to a mass wealth.

38. Assertion (A) Tribes are pristine societies uncontaminated by civilisation.

Reason (R) Tribes should really be seen as 'secondary' phenomena arising out of the exploitative and colonialist contact between pre-existing states and non-state groups like the tribals.

39. Assertion (A) Today, barring the North-Eastern states, there are no areas of the country that are inhabited exclusively by tribal people.

Reason (R) The term Adivasi connotes political awareness and the assertion of rights. CBSE SQP 2024

40. Assertion (A) Matriarchy unlike Patriarchy has been a theoretical rather than an empirical concept.

Reason (R) There is no Historical or Anthropological evidence of matriarchy i.e. societies where women exercises dominance.

Case Based Questions

Read the given passage and answer the questions that follow by choosing the correct option.

41. Sociologists and social anthropologists coined many new concepts to try and understand these processes of change. Perhaps the most common of these are 'Sanskritisation' and 'dominant caste', both contributed by M.N. Srinivas, but discussed extensively and criticised by other scholars. Sanskritisation' refers to a process whereby members of a (usually middle or lower) caste attempt to raise their own social status by adopting the ritual, domestic and social practices of a caste (or castes) of higher status. Although this phenomenon is an old one and predates Independence and perhaps even the colonial period, it has intensified in recent times.

(i) **The process in which members of a (usually middle or lower) caste attempt to raise their own social status by adopting the ritual, domestic and social practices of a caste (or castes) of higher status is called……… .**

(a) Sanskritisation (b) Westernisation
(c) Both (a) and (b) (d) Neither (a) nor (b)

(ii) **Who coined the terms 'Sanskritisation' and 'dominant caste'?**

(a) M.N. Srinivas
(b) Mahatma Jyotiba Phule
(c) Herbert Risley
(d) Babasaheb Ambedkar

42. During the 1960s scholars debated whether tribes should be seen as one end of a continuum with castebased (Hindu) peasant society or whether they were an altogether different kind of community. Those who argued for the continuum saw tribes as not being fundamentally different from caste-peasant society, but merely less stratified (fewer levels of hierarchy) and with a more community-based rather than individual notion of resource ownership. However, opponents argued that tribes were wholly different from castes because they had no notion of purity and pollution which is central to the caste system.

(i) **According to scholars in the 1960s, how were tribes viewed in relation to caste-based peasant society?**

(a) As an entirely different kind of community
(b) As a continuum with caste-based peasant society
(c) As more stratified than caste-based societies
(d) As identical to caste-based communities

(ii) **Which of the following statements reflects the argument for a tribe-caste distinction?**

(a) Tribes are fundamentally the same as caste-based societies.
(b) Tribes have a hierarchical structure similar to caste societies.
(c) Tribes have no concept of purity and pollution, unlike caste-based societies.
(d) Tribes and castes share similar social organisation and resource ownership.

43. Tribe is a modern term for communities that are very old, being among the oldest inhabitants of the subcontinent. Tribes in India have generally been defined in terms of what they were not. Tribes were communities that did not practice a religion with a written text, did not have a state or political form of the normal kind, did not have sharp class division and most important. They did not have caste and were neither Hindus nor peasants. The term was introduced in the colonial era. In terms of positive characteristics, tribes have been classified according to their permanent and acquired traits. **CBSE Term I, 2021**

(i) **If we look at the share of tribals in the state population, then the North–Eastern States have the highest concentration with all states except ……… having concentration of more than 30%.**

(a) Nagaland
(b) Meghalaya
(c) Assam
(d) Arunachal Pradesh

(ii) **Which of the following is not a physical racial criterion for defining the tribes in India?**

(a) Austric (b) Aryan
(c) Dravidian (d) Negrito

44. The imperatives of 'development' have governed attitudes towards tribes and shaped the policies of the state. National development, particularly in the Nehruvian era, involved the building of large dams, factories and mines. Because the tribal areas were located in mineral rich and forest covered parts of the country, tribals have paid a disproportionate price for the development of the rest of Indian society. This kind of development has benefited the mainstream at the expense of the tribes. The process of dispossessing tribals of their land has occurred as a necessary byproduct of the exploitation of minerals and the utilisation of favourable sites for setting up hydroelectric power plants, many of which were in tribal areas.

(i) **How did the development policies during the Nehruvian era affect the tribal areas?**

(a) They were mainly focused on the education of tribal communities.
(b) They benefited the tribes by providing them with better infrastructure.
(c) They caused the tribes to lose their land due to the exploitation of mineral-rich areas.
(d) They had no significant impact on tribal areas.

(ii) What role did private property play in the development of tribal areas?
(a) It provided tribals with more land and resources.
(b) It had no effect on tribal land ownership.
(c) It placed tribal community-based ownership at a disadvantage.
(d) It benefited tribal communities by improving their collective ownership of land.

Answers

1. (c) Portuguese word
2. (a) Panchama
3. (b) It is endogamous.
4. (c) Occupational choices are open.
5. (c) Both (a) and (b)
6. (a) They are close to the sacred.
7. (b) Survey
8. (d) Social stratification
9. (c) Scheduled castes, tribes and backward castes have seen caste become less visible in their lives.
10. b) All of the changes brought about by colonialism were intended or deliberate.
11. (a) The 1903 census was done under the direction of Herbert Risley.
12. (d) Segmental division
13. (b) Untouchability
14. (c) Caste has become a central aspect of their identity because of continued discrimination.
15. (d) cultural and domestic
16. (c) II, III and IV
17. (d) 1935
18. (c) I, III and IV
19. (c) II, III and IV
20. (b) II and III
21. (b) Jana
22. (d) Matrilineal societies
23. (d) Purity and pollution
24. (d) Khammas of Tamil Nadu
25. (c) Resistance and opposition
26. (b) G.S. Ghurye
27. (d) All of the above
28. (c) Mode of livelihood
29. (a) Patrilocal
30. (d) Residence
31. (b) Men exercise authority
32. (d) Extended
33. (a) Both A and R are true and R is the correct explanation of A
34. (c) A is true, but R is false
35. (a) A and R are true and R is the correct explanation of A
36. (b) Both A and R are true, but R is not the correct explanation of A
37. (a) Both A and R are true and R is the correct explanation of A
38. (d) A is false, but R is true
39. (b) Both A and R are true but R is not the correct explanation of A
40. (a) Both A and R are true and R is the correct explanation of A
41. (i) (a) Sanskritisation
    (ii) (a) M.N. Srinivas
42. (i) (b) As a continuum with caste-based peasant society
    (ii) (c) Tribes have no concept of purity and pollution, unlike caste-based societies.
43. (i) (a) Nagaland
    (ii) (a) Austric
44. (i) (c) They caused the tribes to lose their land due to the exploitation of mineral-rich areas.
    (ii) (c) It placed tribal community-based ownership at a disadvantage.

Subjective Questions

Very Short Answer Type Questions

1. Define the term 'Caste'?

Ans. Caste is an ancient social institution that has been the part of Indian history and culture for thousands of years.

2. Identify the two sets of principles used to understand the caste system. Define any one set. **CBSE 2023**

Or **"Theoretically, the caste can be understood as the combination of two sets of principles." Name them and define anyone.** **CBSE 2025**

Ans. The two sets of principles used to understand the caste system are as follows

(i) Based on Difference and Separation

(ii) Based on Wholism and Hierarchy

The different and separated castes do not have an individual existence. In other words, they do not exist in isolation but can only exist in relation to the whole society that is comprised of all other castes. Further, the caste-based society is not based on equality. It is essentially hierarchical wherein each individual caste occupies a distinct place in the ordered rank.

3. Not all of the changes in social institutions brought about by the British were intended or deliberate. Give an example to justify the statement. **CBSE SQP 2023**

Ans. The given statement is true that not all of the changes that occurred in the caste system within the colonial period were deliberate or intended. It is because the British administrators initially began to understand the complexities of caste system in an effort to learn a way to efficiently govern the country. This learning included methodical and intensive surveys as well as reports on the customs and manner of the tribes and castes of the country. Intervention by the colonial states had a huge impact on the institution of caste by the land revenue system.

For example, the land revenue settlements and related arrangements as well as laws gave legal recognition to the customary caste based rights of the upper castes making them land owners in a modern sense.

4. How difference between endogamy and exogamy can be explained? **CBSE Diksha**

Ans. The meaning of endogamy is when one marries someone within one's own group or caste and the meaning of exogamy is when one marries someone outside one's own group or caste.

5. "Mahatma Gandhi worked for the upliftment of the lower caste." What are the contributions of Mahatma Gandhi for the welfare of depressed class? **Competency Based Que.**

Ans. The role of Mahatma Gandhi for the welfare of depressed class was that he advocated the abolition of untouchability and other caste restrictions. He also termed them Harijan meaning God's child. He toured and protested against the ill-treatment of lower castes.

6. What is sanskritisation?

Or **What is the meaning of sanskritisation?**

Ans. Sanskritisation refers to a process whereby members of a (usually middle or lower) caste attempt to raise their own social status by adopting the ritual, domestic and social practices of a caste (or castes) of higher status.

7. What do you mean by dominant caste?

Or **Clarify the concept of dominant caste?** **CBSE Diksha**

Ans. Dominant caste is a term used to refer to those castes which had a large population and were granted land-rights by the partial land reforms that came after independence.

8. Give two examples of dominant land-owning groups.

Ans. The two dominant land-owning groups are

(i) The Yadavas of Bihar and Uttar Pradesh

(ii) The Vokkaligas of Karnataka

9. Explain the two broad sets of issues that are most important in giving rise to tribal movements. **CBSE 2018**

Ans. Two broad sets of issues which have been most important in giving rise to tribal movements are

(i) Issues relating to control over vital economic resources like land and forests.

(ii) Issues relating to matters of ethnic-cultural identity.

10. During the 1960s, scholars debated whether tribes should be seen as one end of a continuum with caste-based (Hindu) peasant society, or whether they were an altogether different kind of community. **CBSE 2025**

Ans. The argument for distinguishing tribes from castes is based on the following factors

Distinct Cultural Identity Tribes have their own unique customs, traditions, languages, and religious practices, which are often different from the caste-based Hindu society. They follow their own forms of worship and social organisation.

Social and Economic Differences Unlike caste-based societies, which follow a hierarchical structure, tribal societies are generally egalitarian. They traditionally lived in forested or hilly areas, practicing shifting cultivation, hunting, or gathering, rather than being integrated into the settled agricultural economy of caste-based societies.

11. "Adivasi experiences of marginalisation and their sense of injustice were the mobilised to create shared Jharkandi identity." Mention the issues against which leaders of Jharkhand agitated. CBSE 2019

Ans. The issues against which the leaders of Jharkhand agitated were as following

- Acquisition of land for large irrigation projects and firing ranges.
- Survey and settlement operations, which were held up, camps closed down etc.
- Collection of loans, rent, dues which were resisted.
- Nationalisation of forest produce which they boycotted.

12. The family is linked to the political, economic, cultural and educational spheres.
Justify with the help of two examples. CBSE 2024 C

Ans. The family is connected to political, economic, cultural, and educational spheres. For example, migration can lead to more women-headed families, and work schedules may cause grandparents to move in as caregivers, influencing family structures.

13. Studies have shown how diverse forms of family are found in different societies.
With regard to the rules of inheritance, explain the two forms of family. CBSE 2024 C

Or **Studies have shown how diverse family forms are found in different societies.**
With regard to rules of residence, write two forms of family. CBSE 2024

Ans. Studies show that family structures vary across societies, particularly in terms of inheritance rules. In matrilineal societies, property is passed down from mother to daughter, while in patrilineal societies, inheritance follows the father's line, passing property to the son. These systems influence family dynamics, including the roles of men and women in decision-making.

With regards to residence family can be divided into matrilocal, where married couple live with bride's parents and patrilocal if the married couple lives with the groom's parents.

14. Distinguish between a nuclear and an extended family.

Ans. The difference between the nuclear family and the extended family is that a nuclear family refers to a single basic family unit of parents and their children, whereas the extended family refers to their relatives, as well such as grandparents, in-laws, aunts and uncles, etc.

Short Answer Type Questions

1. Caste is a discriminatory system. Elaborate. CBSE 2019

Ans. The caste system is a distinct Indian social institution that legitimises and enforces practices of discrimination against people born into particular castes. These practices of discrimination are humiliating, exclusionary and exploitative. It classified people on the basis of their occupation and hierarchy of social status.

- The privileged (and high economic status) sections of society tend to be overwhelmingly 'upper' caste while the disadvantaged (and low economic status) sections are dominated by the so called 'lower' castes.
- The proportion of population that lives in poverty or affluence differs greatly across caste groups.

2. How has casteism influenced politics?

Ans. Casteism refers to discrimination on the basis of caste. It further affects already divided castelines. It places caste interests ahead of political principles.

From its very beginning in independent India, democratic politics has been deeply influenced by caste. Its functioning has become more and more complex and hard to predict the swing of electoral results. The caste remains central to electoral politics and since the 1980s, we have also seen the emergence of strong caste-based political parties.

The situations worsens as parties compete with each other in utilising the same kind of caste calculus but does nothing or very less for the welfare of people.

3. One of the most significant yet paradoxical changes in the caste system in the contemporary period is that it has tended to become 'invisible' for the upper caste, urban middle and upper classes. Elaborate. CBSE SQP 2023

Or **Caste system in the contemporary period has tended to become invisible for the upper and middle classes but it is opposite in lower classes. Comment.**

Ans. One of the most significant changes in the caste system is that it was becoming invisible for the upper caste, urban middle and the upper classes because they have benefitted the most from the development policies. On the contrary, their caste status ensures that these groups have the economic and educational resources to take advantage of the opportunities offered by rapid development.

They were able to take advantage of the following

- The subsidised education especially professional education in science, technology, medicine and management.
- Expansion of state sector jobs in early decades after independence. Their superiority ensured that they did not face any serious competition.

As this privilege was passed to their future generations, they came to believe that their advancement was not related to caste. The matter is further complicated by the fact that such a privilege was not enjoyed by every upper caste person.

On the other hand, for the SC's and ST's, caste has been more visible eclipsing other dimensions of their identity. Because of their lack of education, social capital as well as the fact that they must face competition, they cannot lose their caste identity which is the only thing that the world recognises.

4. "The present form of caste as a social institution has been shaped very strongly by both the colonial period as well as the rapid changes that have come about in independent India. The development activity of the state and the growth of private industry affected caste indirectly through the speeding up and intensification of economic change." How has economic change affected caste? CBSE SQP 2024

Ans. Economic change has significantly influenced caste by altering traditional hierarchies and social mobility. Industrialisation and state-led development reduced the dependence on caste-based occupations, fostering opportunities across castes. Urbanisation and migration weakened the rigid boundaries of rural caste systems as people moved for jobs. Education and reservation policies enhanced access to resources for marginalised groups, challenging upper-caste dominance. However, caste remains influential in economic and political spheres, with wealth and power often reproducing inequalities, even as some mobility becomes possible.

5. "Caste plays no part in the public lives of privileged groups, while it remains central for the disadvantaged." Critically evaluate this statement. Competency Based Que.

Ans. The statement highlights contrasting roles of caste for privileged and disadvantaged groups. For privileged groups, caste seems irrelevant in public life as their inherited economic and educational advantages allow them to succeed without relying on caste identity. However, for disadvantaged groups, caste remains central due to its role in accessing opportunities and combating systemic discrimination. Reservation policies amplify this visibility, making caste a critical factor in their public lives. Thus, caste's significance depends on one's social and economic position.

6. "Scheduled Caste and Schedule Tribe, legally recognised as specific castes and tribe for special state support." How did 'Schedule Caste' and 'Schedule Tribe' come into existence? Competency Based Que.

Ans. During the colonial period, the British Government, the administration took an interest in the welfare of downtrodden castes referred to as 'Depressed Classes'.

It was the Government of India Act of 1935, which gave legal recognition to the lists or 'Schedule' of castes and tribes marked out for the special treatment by the state. This is how the terms 'Schedule Tribes' and 'Schedule Castes' came into being.

Caste at the bottom of hierarchy that suffered severe discrimination, including the 'untouchable' castes were also included in Scheduled Caste.

7. Examine the role of state's initiatives to address caste and tribe discrimination.

Ans. State's initiatives to address caste and tribe discrimination are as following

- The most important state initiative is provided by reservations. This involves the setting of reserved places or category for people of the Scheduled Castes and Scheduled Tribes in different spheres of public life. The proportion of reserved seats is equal to the percentage share of the Scheduled Castes and Scheduled Tribes in the total population.
- In addition to reservations, there have been a number of constitutional laws passed to end, prohibit and punish caste discrimination and untouchability.

8. Tribals have faced colonialism in the pre-independent India. Explain.

Or **Compare and contrast the socio- economic conditions of tribals before and after Independence.**

Ans. Tribals have faced difficulties and discrimination during the British rule. During the pre-independence period, on the political and economic front, tribal societies faced incursion of moneylenders. They also lost their land to non-tribal immigrant settlers.

Their access to forests was restricted because of the British government's policy of reservation of forests and the introduction of mining operations. In this way, their source of livelihood was snatched by the British Government.

Post-independent era, particularly the Nehruvian era, involved the building of large dams, factories and mines. The tribal areas were located in mineral rich and forest covered parts of the country. Thus, their places of dwelling was either destroyed or snatched away in the name of development. This kind of development has benefitted the mainstream at the expense of the tribes.

9. "Tribal's have paid a disproportionate price for the development of the rest of Indian society." Highlight the sources of conflict between 'national development' and 'tribal development'. CBSE 2018

Ans. Conflict between national development and tribal development

- National development in the Nehruvian era, focused on the building of large dams, factories and mines etc. As the tribal areas were rich in minerals, they paid a heavy price for the development activities, which benefitted the mainstream at the expense of the tribes.
- The displacement of tribes has been a result of setting up of dams and factories using the forested areas for various mining activities and other development work. The loss of the forests on which most tribal communities depended has been a major blow.
- The idea of private property in land, also, adversely affected the tribes. Tribes which mostly had collective community-based ownership were at a disadvantage in the new system.
  Example series of dams being built over the Narmada River.
- Many tribal regions have experienced heavy in-migration of non-tribals. This threatens to disrupt their cultures and communities.
  Example Jharkhand and Tripura.

10. In the context of identities, why did tribal societies get more and more differentiated? CBSE SQP 2023

Ans. Two broad sets of issues have been most important in giving rise to tribal movements.

- The control over vital economic resources like land and specially forests.
- Issues relating to matters of ethnic-cultural identity.

The two can often go together, but with internal differentiation of tribal society they may also diverge. The reasons why the middle classes within tribal societies may assert their tribal identity may be different from the reasons why poor and uneducated tribals join tribal movements. Ultimately, the relationship between these kinds of internal dynamics and external forces that will shape the future.

11. 'Tribe' is a modern term for communities that are very old, being among the oldest inhabitants of the sub-continent. Tribes were communities that did not practice a religion with a written text; did not have a state or political form of the normal kind and did not have sharp class divisions.

In terms of positive characteristics, tribes have been classified according to certain traits. Explain the traits. CBSE 2024 C

Ans. Tribes are classified based on permanent and acquired traits.

Permanent traits include region, language, physical characteristics and ecological habitats like hills, forests or urban areas. For example, tribes in 'Middle India' account for 85% of the tribal population and tribal languages include Austric and Tibeto-Burman.

Acquired traits focus on livelihood modes (fishing, shifting cultivation, industrial work) and the degree of assimilation into Hindu society. Assimilation varies, with some tribes integrating into the caste system while others resist it.

12. "The argument for a tribe-caste distinction was founded on an assumed cultural difference between Hindu castes, with their beliefs in purity and pollution and hierarchical integration and 'animist' tribals with their more egalitarian and kinship-based modes of social organisation."

Is this distinction between tribes and caste viable? Give reasons for your answer. Competency Based Que.

Ans. The distinction between tribes and castes is debated and not entirely viable. While caste is rooted in hierarchical integration with concepts of purity and pollution, tribes traditionally emphasise egalitarian and kinship-based social structures. However, this distinction blurs as many tribes adopted settled agriculture, integrated into caste systems through sanskritisation or became part of Hindu society at varying levels. Additionally, tribes often interacted with non-tribal communities, leading to cultural exchange and hybridisation. Thus, tribes and castes are interconnected rather than entirely distinct.

13. Some scholars have argued that there is no coherent basis for treating pristine i.e., original or pure societies uncontaminated by civilisation. The idea that tribes are like stone age hunting and gathering societies that have remained untouched by time is still common, even though this has not been true for a long time.

Based on the above passage, justify with four reasons why this idea of tribes having remained untouched is untrue. CBSE 2024

Ans. The idea that tribes remained untouched by civilisation is untrue due to several reasons as following

- **Historical Interaction** Tribes have interacted with settled communities, contributing to trade, local militias and resource exchanges.
- **Political Integration** Many tribal groups formed kingdoms, such as the Gond kingdoms or were incorporated into caste-based hierarchies through processes like sanskritisation.

- **Economic Contact** The capitalist economy brought tribes into contact with mainstream society through forest resource exploitation and labour recruitment.
- **Cultural Exchange** Continuous engagement with state and non-state groups led to hybrid identities, challenging the notion of isolation.

14. The family is linked to the political, economic, cultural and educational spheres. Justify with the help of two examples. CBSE 2024

Ans. The family is closely connected to the political, economic, cultural and educational aspects of society. Here are two examples that show this link

(i) **Economic Influence** In Himalayan villages, many men migrate for work, leaving women to head the households. This economic shift changes the family structure, leading to more female-headed families. This connection shows how economic factors like migration impact family roles and responsibilities.

(ii) **Cultural and Social Influence** In urban areas, parents working in demanding fields like the software industry often have grandparents move in to help care for their children. This cultural adjustment reflects how family roles adapt to changes in work schedules, blending private family life with broader social and economic changes.

These examples demonstrate that family structures are not isolated; they are shaped by broader economic, cultural and social factors.

Long Answer Type Questions

1. Discuss the ways that strengthened the institution of caste in India under colonial rule.

Or **The institution of caste underwent major changes during the colonial period. Explain.** CBSE 2019

Or **What changes did colonialism bring about in the caste system?** CBSE Diksha

Ans. Caste is an institution uniquely associated with the Indian sub-continent. The four varna classification is around three thousand years old.

However, the caste system stood for different things in different time periods. The present form of caste as a social institution has been shaped very strongly by the colonial period.

All major social institutions specially the institution of caste underwent major changes during the colonial period. In fact, some scholars argued that what we know today as caste is more a product of colonialism than of ancient Indian tradition.

But by far, the most important official effort to collect information on caste was through the census. The 1901 Census under the direction of Herbert Risley was particularly important, as it sought to collect information on the social hierarchy of caste. This effort had a huge impact on social perceptions of caste.

Scholars feel that this kind of direct attempt to count caste and to officially record caste status changed the institution itself.

Before this kind of intervention, caste identities had been much more fluid and less rigid but afterwards it became more complex. Further, social intervention of the colonial states had a huge impact on the institution of caste.

The land revenue settlements and related arrangements and laws served to give legal recognition to the customary (caste-based) rights of the upper castes. In addition, the Government of India Act 1935 gave special attention to the downtrodden while categorising them as SC's and ST's.

2. Sociologists and social anthropologists coined many new concepts to try and understand these processes of change. Perhaps the most common of these are 'sanskritisation' and 'dominant caste', both contributed by M.N. Srinivas, but discussed extensively and criticised by other scholars.
What is the concept of 'Dominant Caste'? Competency Based Que.

Ans. Dominant caste is a term used to refer to those castes which had a large population and were granted land rights by the partial land reforms affected after independence.

- The land reforms took away rights from the upper castes who were 'absentee landlords' in the sense that they played no part in the agricultural economy but just claimed rent. They frequently did not live in the village either, but were based in town and cities.
- The land rights were given to the next layer of claimants, those who were involved in the management of agriculture but were not themselves the cultivators.
- These intermediate castes depended on lower caste for tilling and tending the land. However, once they got land rights, they acquired considerable economic power.
- The large number of intermediate caste gave them political power in the era of electoral democracy based on universal adult franchise.

Thus, these intermediate castes became the 'dominant' castes in the country side and played a decisive role in regional politics and the agrarian economy.

3. Read the given passage and answer the questions that follow.

The precise relationship between varna and jati has been the subject of much speculation and debate among scholars. The most common interpretation is to treat varna as a broad all-India aggregative classification, while jati is taken to be a regional or local sub-classification involving a much more complex system consisting of hundreds or even thousands of castes and sub-castes.

Caste is an institution uniquely associated with the Indian sub-continent.

(i) **Define caste and explain how it emerged in Indian Subcontinent?**

(ii) **What is the difference between *Jati* and *Varna*?**

Ans. (i) Caste is a cultural institution that is special to the Indian subcontinent. Although similar social structures have been found in other parts of the world, the exact type has yet to be discovered. Despite the fact that caste is a Hindu institution, it has spread to the Indian subcontinent's main non-Hindu groups. Muslims, Christians and Sikhs are particularly affected.

'Caste' is a social institution that has been in existence for thousands of years. 'Caste', an English word is derived from a Portuguese word 'Casta', meaning pure breed. In Indian language it is referred to two distinct terms, *varna* and *jati*.

(ii) The difference between Jati and Varna are

Varna The word *varna* literally means colour, but it refers to the four fold division of society into-brahmana, kshatriya, vaishya and shudra.

Jati The word *jati* generally refers to the species or kinds of anything. In Indian languages, it is a term that refers to the institution of caste. The relationship between the terms and meaning of *Varna* and *jati* has been a subject of much discussion amongst scholars.

4. The imperatives of 'development' have influenced state policies and shaped attitudes toward tribes. Explain the relationship between national development and tribal development. Competency Based Que.

Or **Explain the impact of National Development on the tribes.** CBSE Diksha

Ans. National development is a broad concept that encompasses raising people's living standards, the per capita income, and providing social services such as education, medical care, and social services to the country's citizens. Tribal growth seeks to put together people who want to contribute to the empowerment of the country's Scheduled Tribes. The group as a whole is looking for ways to solve the problems around a holistic and all-encompassing tribal growth plan. The goal is to establish an enabling environment with equitable opportunities for education, health and livelihood, as well as to ensure the tribal community's long-term development while maintaining their distinct identities and cultures.

Large dams, factories, and mines were built as part of national growth, especially during the Nehruvian period. Tribals have paid a disproportionate price for the growth of the rest of Indian society because they live in mineral-rich and forest-covered areas of the region. The mainstream has benefited from this growth at the detriment of the tribes.

SELF ASSESSMENT TEST

Objective Type Questions

1. How did the development policies during the Nehruvian era affect the tribal areas?

(a) They were mainly focused on the education of tribal communities.

(b) They benefited the tribes by providing them with better infrastructure.

(c) They caused the tribes to lose their land due to the exploitation of mineral-rich areas.

(d) They had no significant impact on tribal areas.

2. The impact of development policies on tribal areas has been significant because

I. Tribals lost their land due to the exploitation of mineral-rich areas for national development projects.

II. The loss of forests, which were crucial for tribal communities, has had no long-term consequences.

III. The introduction of private property rights undermined tribal communities' collective land ownership.

IV. The development policies were designed to benefit tribal communities by improving their access to modern industries and infrastructure.

Codes

(a) I and IV (b) III and IV

(c) II and III (d) I and III

3. Which of the following statements best represent the goals of the caste system's traditional structure in Indian society?

I. Maintaining occupational hierarchy and division of labour

II. Promoting social mobility and flexibility in status

III. Preserving endogamous practices within each caste

IV. Encouraging inter-caste marriages for social unity

Codes

(a) I and III (b) II and IV

(c) I, II and IV (d) I, III and IV

4. **Assertion** (A) Endogamy is a defining feature of the caste system in India.

Reason (R) Endogamy prevents social mobility and reinforces caste-based social stratification.

(a) Both A and R are true and R is the correct explanation of A

(b) Both A and R are true, but R is not the correct explanation of A

(c) A is true, but R is false

(d) A is false, but R is true

Case Based Questions

1. Theoretically, the caste system can be understood as the combination of two sets of principles, one based on difference and separation and the other on wholism and hierarchy. Each caste is supposed to be different from - and is therefore strictly separated from - every other caste. Many of the scriptural rules of caste are thus designed to prevent the mixing of castes - rules ranging from marriage, food sharing and social interaction to occupation.

(i) What are the two principles on which the caste system is based?

(a) Separation and equality
(b) Difference and hierarchy
(c) Equality and unity
(d) Individuality and purity

(ii) How are castes arranged in the societal system?

(a) In a circle of equality
(b) Alphabetically
(c) In a hierarchical ladder
(d) Based on population size

Very Short Answer Type Questions

1. The caste system in India is often viewed as an enduring institution with deep historical roots. Why is the caste system regarded as a unique social institution, in the context of its role in shaping Indian society and culture over centuries?
2. Explain how the concepts of *varna* and *jati* differ and how they together form the foundation of the caste system in India.
3. In what ways did reformers like Jyotiba Phule and Ayyankali challenge the caste system?

Short Answer Type Questions

1. Explain the theoretical principles of difference and separation and wholism and hierarchy in the caste system. How do they function together?
2. "The caste system in India originated as a social and occupational structure deeply intertwined with religious beliefs. Over time, it has transformed into a political and economic framework." Illustrate the transition of caste from a religious institution to a socio-political entity.
3. "The caste system's hierarchical structure, based on ritual purity, has been reinterpreted in modern times to negotiate access to political power and resources."

   Discuss the role of reservation policies in transforming caste dynamics in India.

Long Answer Type Questions

1. Discuss the role of economic and educational capital in consolidating the privileged status of upper-caste elites over generations.
2. But by far the most important official effort to collect information on caste was through the census. First begun in the 1860s, the census became a regular ten-yearly exercise conducted by the British Indian Government from 1881 onwards. The 1901 Census under the direction of Herbert Risley was particularly important as it sought to collect information on the social hierarchy of caste i.e., the social order of precedence in particular regions, as to the position of each caste in the rank order.

   (a) Discuss how the introduction of caste-based enumeration in the census impacted the social dynamics of caste in India.

   (b) Analyse the long-term consequences of colonial caste enumeration on post-Independence Indian society.

04 CHAPTER

In the Indian society we see social inequality and exclusion are evident in everyday Indian life, with visible instances such as beggars, in the public places, child labourers and caste discrimination in schools. Violence against women and prejudice against minorities and differently abled individuals further illustrate this

YOUR STUDY GOALS

4.1 An Introduction to Social Inequality
4.2 Social Concept about Social Inequality and Exclusion
4.3 Systems Justifying and Perpetuating Inequality
4.4 Struggle for Women's Equality and Right
4.5 The Struggles of the Disabled (Differently Abled)

YOUR PRACTICE GOAL

- Objective Type Questions (31 Qs ; MCQs, A-R, Case Based Questions)
- Subjective Questions (21 VSAs, 11 SAs, 4 LAs)

Patterns of Social Inequality and Exclusion

4.1 An Introduction to Social Inequality

The commonness of social inequality can make it seem inevitable and almost natural. Some believe that such conditions are 'deserved' or 'justified,' thinking that individuals haven't tried hard enough to improve their situations.

While hard work and individual ability matter, other factors play a crucial role, leading to social inequality and exclusion. Inequality and exclusion arise from group differences, not just individual efforts.

4.2 Social Concept about Social Inequality and Exclusion

Social inequality and exclusion

- They are social phenomena that concern groups rather than individuals.
- While there is a strong link between social and economic inequality, they are primarily social issues.
- Social inequalities are systematic and structured, following definite patterns.

Social Inequality

- In a society, social resources, such as money, property, education, health and power are divided into three forms of capital as following
  - (i) **Economic Capital** Material assets and income.
  - (ii) **Cultural Capital** Educational qualifications and status.
  - (iii) **Social Capital** Networks of contacts and associations.
- These forms of capital can overlap and convert into one another. For example, wealth can enable access to higher education (cultural capital) or influential networks (social capital).
- Patterns of unequal access to social resources are commonly called social inequality.
- Social inequality may reflect innate differences but is primarily produced by societal structures.
- Sociologists use the term **social stratification** to describe the ranking of groups in a hierarchy that shapes identities, experiences and access to resources.

Key Features of Social Stratification

(i) Societal Characteristic

- Social stratification is a characteristic of society, distributing resources unequally among categories of people rather than a function of individual differences.
- In technologically primitive societies, limited production results in rudimentary stratification, while advanced societies exhibit more pronounced inequality.

(ii) Generational Persistence

- Social stratification continues across generations, often linked to family inheritance of social resources.
- A person's social position is ascribed, meaning children typically inherit their parents' social status, particularly evident in caste systems.
- Endogamy (marriage within the same caste) reinforces the ascribed nature of social inequality.

(iii) Supportive Ideology

- Social stratification is upheld by beliefs or ideologies that view it as fair or inevitable.
- For instance, the caste system is justified by notions of purity and pollution, ranking Brahmins as superior and Dalits as inferior.
- Those with greater social privileges often support stratification systems, while those at the bottom are more likely to challenge them.

Notions of Social Exclusion and Discrimination

- Social exclusion and discrimination arise not only from economic factors but also from gender, religion, ethnicity, language, caste and disability. Examples include women facing harassment or professionals from minority groups struggling to find housing.
- Everyone grows up with ideas from their community, which shape how they see their own group and others.

Key Concepts

Prejudices

- Prejudices are preconceived opinions held by one group about another, formed without direct experience or evidence, often resistant to change.
- They can be positive or negative, with negative prejudices more common.

Stereotypes

- Stereotypes are fixed characterisations applied to groups, often based on racial, ethnic or gender traits, and do not account for individual variability.
- They can be colonial creations that label entire communities with simplistic traits.

Discrimination

- Discrimination involves actual behaviours that exclude individuals from opportunities due to gender, religion, or other factors.
- Discrimination may be explained with others, more acceptable reasons instead of admiting bias. For example, someone denied a job due to their caste might be told, it was because they were less a qualified and the selection was based on merit.

Social Exclusion

- Social exclusion refers to individuals being cut off from participating fully in society, impacting access to essential goods and services.
- It is systematic and rooted in structural societal features.

Social Exclusion in India

- India experiences significant social discrimination and exclusion, affecting groups like Dalits, Adivasis (tribal communities), women, and differently-abled individuals.
- Historical context reveals that even privileged Indians faced discrimination under British colonial rule.
- Social reform movements emerged, driven by humiliation from colonial rule and inspired by ideals of democracy and justice.
- In history, movements against caste, gender and discrimination based on religion played a major role. Pertaining to these movements many legislations were passed. But, legislation alone is not able to transform society or produce lasting social change.
- A constant social campaign to create awareness and sensitivity is required to abolish them.

Groups Experiencing Inequality

- The four main groups suffering from social inequality and exclusion include
  - (i) Dalits (ex-untouchables)
  - (ii) Adivasis (tribal communities)
  - (iii) Women
  - (iv) Differently-abled individuals
- Apart from these four groups there are two more groups included in this category. These are
  - (i) **Transgender** It refers to the conversion of gender status of the body into the opposite gender by using choice or certain compulsions. By using surgical processes, male body can be converted into female body or female body into male body.
  - (ii) **Third Gender** This third gender refers to that social category of persons who are neither male nor female. The third gender of the person is based on self-understanding or made up by group choice. In India, people of the third gender have legal recognition and can nominate themself to contest in elections (Parliament/Assembly/Local Government).

Quick Test 1

1. Mention three key principles that explain social stratification.
2. What is the role of colonialism in shaping social discrimination in Indian society?
3. Name four groups that have suffered from social inequality and exclusion in India.
4. How do stereotypes contribute to prejudice in society?

4.3 Systems Justifying and Perpetuating Inequality — The Caste System as a Discriminatory System

- The caste system is a distinct Indian social institution that legitimises and enforces discriminatory practices against individuals born into specific castes.
- These practices of discrimination are characterised as humiliating, exclusionary and exploitative.
- The caste system classifies individuals by their occupation and social status.
- The **Brahmins**, the ritually highest caste, were historically not allowed to accumulate wealth and were subordinate to the secular powers of kings and rulers from the **Kshatriya** castes.
- Despite the king's high secular status and power, he was ritually subordinate to the Brahmins in religious matters.
- Historically, there was a close correlation between social status and economic status; high castes generally enjoyed high economic status, while low castes faced low economic status.
- Since the 19th century, the link between caste and occupation has become less rigid.
- Today, ritual-religious prohibitions on occupational change are less enforced, allowing individuals to change their occupations more easily.
- As the caste system has become less rigid, distinctions between castes of broadly similar social and economic status have weakened.
- Privileged sections of society, which have higher economic status, tend to be overwhelmingly upper caste.
- Disadvantaged sections, characterised by low economic status, are typically lower castes.
- The proportion of the population living in poverty or affluence varies significantly across caste groups.
- In short, despite significant changes brought about by social movements over more than a century and alterations in modes of production, the caste system continues to impact the life chances of individuals in India today as well.

Race and Caste-A Cross-Cultural Comparison

- In India, people face discrimination based on caste, while in South Africa, society is divided into a racial hierarchy.
- The **White minority** in South Africa has most of the power and wealth.
- Dutch traders settled in South Africa in the mid-17th century and by the early 19th century, their descendants moved further inland due to British colonisation.
- Political control was maintained through apartheid, which enforced racial separation.
- *Apartheid*[1] became law in 1948 and had severe effects on the Black majority. Black people were denied citizenship, land ownership and a voice in government. Everyone was classified by race and mixed marriages were banned.
- Black individuals held low-paying jobs, earning only about one-fourth of what White people earned.
- In the later part of the 20th century, millions of Black people were forcibly moved to Bantustans or homelands. These areas were very poor and lacked basic services, jobs and infrastructure.
- The Bantustans made up only 14% of South Africa's land, even though Black people made up nearly 80% of the population. This caused widespread starvation and suffering in a country rich in resources, like diamonds and minerals.
- The wealthy White minority justified their privileges by viewing Black people as inferior and used a strong military force to maintain their power. Black protestors were often jailed, tortured, or killed.
- Despite the harsh treatment, Black people fought back for many years under leaders like the African National Congress and Nelson Mandela. Their struggle led to the ANC gaining power and forming a government in 1994.
- Although the new South African Constitution bans racial discrimination, most economic resources are still controlled by White people. Helping the Black majority gain power remains a big challenge for the new society.

1 **Apartheid** It is a policy or system of discrimination on the grounds of race.

Untouchability

- **Untouchability**[2] is a harsh and extreme part of the caste system in India that enforces strict social rules against people in the lowest castes, often referred to as **untouchables**.
- These castes are seen as so 'impure' that their touch can pollute members of other castes, leading to severe punishments and forcing the so-called pure castes to perform complex rituals to purify themselves.
- In many regions of India, especially in the South, even the shadow or presence of an untouchable person is viewed as polluting.
- Untouchability is not just about avoiding physical contact; it involves a wider range of social restrictions and sanctions.
- The three main aspects of untouchability are **exclusion, humiliation** and **exploitation**. While other low castes may face some form of subordination or exploitation, the extreme exclusion experienced by untouchables is unique. For example, untouchables are often banned from sharing drinking water sources or participating in religious ceremonies, social events, and festivals.
- Untouchability is also closely linked to economic exploitation. Untouchables may be forced into unpaid labour or have their property taken away.
- Over the years, untouchables have been called many derogatory names, which are still used as insults today, even though using them is now a criminal offence.
- Mahatma Gandhi popularised the term **'Harijan'**, meaning 'children of God,' in the 1930s to replace the derogatory caste names. However, ex-untouchable communities and their leaders prefer the term 'Dalit,' which means 'downtrodden' and reflects their oppressed status.
- Although Dr Ambedkar, a key figure in the struggle for Dalit rights, did not frequently use this term, it resonates with his philosophy and the movement he led.
- The **Dalit Panthers**, a radical group formed in Western India in the 1970s, adopted the term to assert their identity and fight for their rights and dignity.

Initiatives Addressing Caste and Tribe Discrimination

- The Indian Government has had special programme for Scheduled Tribes and Scheduled Castes since before independence, with lists of these groups established in 1935 by the British Indian Government.
- After independence, these policies continued, with significant additions like including Other Backward Classes (OBCs) in the early 1990s.

Following are the key initiatives taken after independence to control caste discrimination

- **Reservations**[3] The most important state initiative attempting to compensate for past and present caste discrimination.
  - Reserved seats in State and Central legislatures (State Assemblies, Lok Sabha, Rajya Sabha).
  - Reserved jobs and seats in government services and educational institutions for Scheduled Castes and Scheduled Tribes.
  - The proportion of reserved seats corresponds to the percentage of Scheduled Castes and Tribes in the total population; however, the proportion for OBCs is determined differently.
- **Laws Against Caste Discrimination** Several laws have been enacted to prohibit and punish caste discrimination, particularly untouchability. Significant laws include
  - **Caste Disabilities Removal Act of 1850** This law prevented the restriction of citizens' rights solely based on religion or caste.

---

2 **Untouchability** It is a practice where in the so called lower caste people of the society are considered as impure and are forbidden to touch or to be touched by any member of the higher caste.

3 **Reservation** It is a policy of the government where a certain percentage of some places or seats in different public spheres are kept aside for lower or backward classes.

- **Constitution Amendment (93rd Amendment) Act of 2005** Became law on 23rd January, 2006, introducing reservations for OBCs in higher education institutions.
- **Constitution of India (1950)** Abolished untouchability (Article 17) and included reservation provisions.
- **Scheduled Castes and Scheduled Tribes (Prevention of Atrocities) Act of 1989** Revised and strengthened legal measures against violence and humiliation towards Dalits and Adivasis.

- While state actions are important, they cannot guarantee social change. People are capable of organising and advocating for justice and dignity.
- Historical struggles led by figures like Jyotiba Phule, Iyothee Das, Periyar and Ambedkar, along with contemporary organisations like the Bahujan Samaj Party and Dalit Sangharsh Samiti, show the progress of Dalit political assertion.
- Dalits have also significantly contributed to literature in several Indian languages, especially Marathi, Kannada, Tamil, Telugu and Hindi.

Quick Test 2

1. Who were considered the ritually highest caste in the caste system?
2. What is 'untouchability' in the context of the caste system?
3. What policy attempts to compensate for caste discrimination in India?
4. How did Mahatma Gandhi address the issue of untouchability?
5. Which groups were officially listed in the 'Schedules' of the Government of India Act, 1935?

The Other Backward Classes

- Apart from untouchables, there are many low-status castes facing discrimination, known as Service and Artisanal castes, which occupy lower ranks in the caste hierarchy.
- The Indian Constitution acknowledges that there may be groups beyond Scheduled Tribes and Scheduled Castes that suffer from social disadvantages.
- These groups are referred to as '*socially and educationally backward classes*,' providing a constitutional basis for **Other Backward Classes** (OBCs).
- OBCs are neither part of the upper-caste 'forward' groups nor the Dalits at the lower end of the status spectrum.
- Caste exists across major Indian religions, so members of other religions can also belong to backward castes and experience similar socio-economic challenges.
- OBCs are more diverse than Dalits or Adivasis due to this wide representation across different religions.
- The first government of independent India, led by Jawaharlal Nehru, appointed a commission for the welfare of OBCs, known as the **First Backward Classes Commission**, chaired by Kaka Kalelkar, which submitted its report in 1953.
- From the mid-1950s, OBC issues became more focused at the state level, particularly in the Southern states, which had a history of backward caste political movements dating back to the early 20th century.
- Strong social movements in the South resulted in OBC policies being implemented before discussions began in many Northern states.
- The OBC issue returned to national attention in the late 1970s with the formation of the Janata Party and the appointment of the Second Backward Classes Commission, headed by **BP Mandal**.
- In 1990, the Central Government decided to implement the long-discussed Mandal Commission report, bringing OBC issues to the forefront of national politics.
- Since the 1990s, there has been a resurgence of lower-caste movements in North India, involving both OBCs and Dalits.

- The political mobilisation of OBCs has allowed them to leverage their numbers into political influence, which was not possible before due to the neglect of earlier reports like Kalelkar and Mandal.
- There are significant disparities within the OBC category, with upper OBCs (largely landed castes) dominating rural society, while lower OBCs remain very poor and disadvantaged.
- OBCs are underrepresented in various sectors, except in landholding and political representation.
- Although upper OBCs are dominant in rural areas, urban OBCs face conditions closer to those of Scheduled Castes and Tribes rather than upper castes.

Adivasi Struggles

- The Indian Constitution recognises Scheduled Castes and Scheduled Tribes as groups that are impoverished, powerless and face social stigma.
- Adivasis, or tribal populations, are often referred to as **people of the forest,** living in hilly and forested regions and their economic, social and political attributes are shaped by these environments.
- There has been a long association between tribal groups and Hindu society, leading to a blending of tribe and caste identities.
- Migration among Adivasi populations has created complications; outside the North-Eastern states, there are no regions exclusively inhabited by tribal people, only areas with tribal people.
- Since the mid-19th century, non-tribals have moved into tribal districts in central India, while tribal people have migrated to plantations, mines, factories and other employment opportunities.
- In regions where tribal populations are concentrated, their economic and social conditions are typically much worse than those of non-tribals.
- The impoverished and exploited circumstances of Adivasis can be traced back to resource extraction patterns initiated by British colonial rule and continued by independent India's government.
- From the late 19th century, the colonial government reserved most of the forest lands for its use, cutting off Adivasis from their rights to gather produce and practise shifting cultivation.
- The colonial policy aimed to maximise timber production, stripping Adivasis of their primary means of livelihood and making their lives poorer and more insecure.
- Denied access to forests and land, Adivasis were forced to use forests illegally, facing harassment and prosecution as 'encroachers' and 'thieves,' or to migrate in search of wage labour.
- After the Independence of India in 1947Adivasis face two major issues as following
  (i) The government maintains a monopoly over forests, leading to increased exploitation.
  (ii) The policy of capital-intensive industrialisation requires minerals and power generation from Adivasi areas.
- Adivasi lands have been quickly acquired for mining and dam projects, displacing millions without proper compensation or rehabilitation.
- These policies, justified in the name of 'national development' and 'economic growth', reflect internal colonialism, subjugating Adivasis and alienating resources essential for their survival.
- Projects like the Sardar Sarovar dam on the Narmada River and the Polavaram dam on the Godavari River threaten to displace hundreds of thousands of Adivasis, increasing their destitution.
- The term Adivasi, meaning original inhabitants, emerged in the 1930s as part of the struggle against colonial intrusion and the encroachment of outsiders and moneylenders.
- Being Adivasi involves shared experiences of forest loss, land alienation and repeated displacements since independence due to 'development projects'.
- Despite facing significant challenges and marginalisation, many tribal groups continue to struggle against outsiders (referred to as dikus) and the state.
- Notable achievements of Adivasi movements in post-independence India include the establishment of statehood for Jharkhand and Chhattisgarh.

Quick Test 3

1. What were the ill-effects of apartheid law on Black people of South Africa?
2. Who was the chairman of the first Backward Classes Commission?
3. Which amendment introduced reservation for OBC?
4. Name any one dimension of untouchability.
5. What is the literal meaning of the term 'Adivasi'?

4.4 Struggle for Women's Equality and Right

- **Gender inequality**, often seen as natural due to biological and physical differences between men and women. It is recognised as a social construct rather than a biological one.
- Gender issues mirror social inequalities and exclusions, similar to caste and class, with distinct features.
- The 19th-century middle-class social reform movements brought the women's question into the spotlight, influenced by Western democratic ideals and pride in Indian traditions.
- These movements varied by region and were often led by the newly emerging, Western-educated Indian middle class.
- Key activists in the struggle for women's rights include following personalities

Raja Rammohun Roy

Raja Rammohun Roy

- He was considered a pioneer of 19th-century social reform in Bengal.
- He campaigned against the practice of sati[4] before he found the Brahmo Samaj in 1828.
- He criticised the practice of sati based on humanitarian principles, natural rights doctrines and Hindu Shastras.
- His ideas blended Western rationality with Indian traditional values.

MG Ranade

MG Ranade

- He advocated for the rights of Hindu upper-caste widows.
- He utilised writings of scholars like Bishop Joseph Butler to support his arguments.
- He authored "The Texts of the Hindu Law on the Lawfulness of the Remarriage of Widows and Vedic Authorities for Widow Marriage," which provided shastric support for widow remarriage.

Jyotiba Phule

Jyotiba Phule

- He came from a socially excluded caste, he opposed both caste and gender discrimination.
- He founded the Satyashodak Samaj, focusing on truth-seeking.
- He aimed to uplift women and untouchables through social reform.

Sir Syed Ahmed Khan

Sir Syed Ahmed Khan

- He sought to reform Muslim society using both modern Western ideas and sacred texts.
- He advocated for girls' education within the home environment.
- He proposed a curriculum that included religious education, training in household skills and child-rearing.

4 **Sati** Sati is a Hindu ritual in which a widow sacrifices her life by sitting on top of her deceased husband's funeral pyre.

Feminist Visionaries

It is often assumed that social reforms for women's rights originated solely from male reformers, and that ideas of women's equality are foreign concepts.

However, this assumption is challenged by the works of women writers such as

- **Stree Purush Tulana** (1882)
  - It was written by **Tarabai Shinde**, a Maharashtrian housewife.
  - A protest against the double standards of a male-dominated society.
  - The book highlights a case where a young Brahmin widow was sentenced to death for killing her illegitimate newborn, while no action was taken against the man responsible.
- **Sultana's Dream** (1905)
  - It is written by **Begum Rokeya Sakhawat Hossain**, a successful author in Urdu and Bengali.
  - It was considered one of the earliest examples of science fiction in India, written by a women.
  - The story depicts Sultana's dream of a magical land where gender roles are reversed.
  - Men are confined to their homes and observe purdah.
  - Women are portrayed as active scientists competing to invent devices that control clouds, regulate rain and create flying machines or air-cars.

Women Equality

- Various women's organisations emerged in India and globally to participate in the national movement for women's rights, alongside feminist visionaries.
- In **1931**, the **Karachi Session** of the Indian National Congress issued a declaration on the Fundamental Rights of Citizenship to enforce women's equality.
- Key points included in the declaration were as follows
  - All citizens are equal before the law, regardless of religion, caste, creed or sex.
  - No citizen shall face disability in public employment, positions of power, or in exercising any trade due to their religion, caste, creed or sex.
  - The right to vote is based on Universal Adult Suffrage.
  - Women shall have the right to vote, represent and hold public offices.
- In **1970**, women's issues re-emerged, shifting focus from traditional reforms (like sati, child marriage, and widow mistreatment) to modern issues such as
  - Representation of women in popular media.
  - Addressing gender inequality.
- In the **1980s**, reforming laws became a major issue, highlighting that many laws concerning women had not changed since the 19th century.
- In the **21st century**, new sites of gender injustice have emerged, including
  - The sharp decline in the child sex ratio.
  - The implicit social bias against the girl child, representing new challenges of gender inequality.

Quick Test 4

1. Which organisation was founded by Jyotiba Phule?
2. What societal aspect did social reform movements in the 1970s focus on?
3. How did Raja Rammohun Roy justify his campaign against sati?
4. Mention one early feminist work written by a woman in India.
5. How did Sir Syed Ahmed Khan view education for women?

4.5 The Struggles of the Disabled (Differently Abled)

- The differently abled are not 'disabled', only because they are physically or mentally 'impaired' but also because society is built in a manner that doesn't cater to their needs.
- It is important to think about 'disabled', because the public perception of disabled needs to be questioned.

Features of Disabled

- The common features central to public perception of disability worldwide include
  - Disability is often seen as a biological condition.
  - The problems faced by disabled individuals are believed to stem solely from their impairment.
  - The disabled people are often viewed as victims.
  - The disability is linked with the individual's self-perception.
  - It is assumed that disabled individuals need help.
- In India, terms like 'disabled,' 'handicap,' 'crippled,' 'blind,' and 'deaf' are often used interchangeably.
- The common perception of disability in India is linked to past karma (actions), implying that it is a form of retribution with no relief.
- Cultural views in India often consider disability a personal characteristic, specific to the individual.
- The term 'disabled' challenges these assumptions, emphasising that society renders individuals disabled through barriers, rather than their biological conditions alone.
- Some terms like 'mentally challenged,' 'visually impaired' and 'physically impaired' have replaced more negative terms like 'retarded,' 'crippled', or 'lame'.
- This shift in language reflects a change in understanding, acknowledging that societal structures, not just biological differences, contribute to the experience of disability.

Disability and Poverty

- The social construction of disability has another important dimension—its close relationship with poverty.
- Factors such as malnutrition, frequent childbirth, inadequate immunisation programmes and accidents in overcrowded homes contribute to a higher incidence of disability, particularly among the poor.
- Disability can exacerbate poverty by increasing isolation and creating additional economic strain, affecting both the individual and their family.
- Recently, disabled individuals themselves have played a vital role in raising awareness about the need to rethink how society views disability.
- Historically, the education system has marginalised the issue of disability, maintaining separate streams for disabled students and others, reflecting the absence of disability recognition in broader educational discourse.
- However, today, there is more learning and awareness related to disability, moving toward inclusion within education.

Approach Adopted for the Disabled in Census 2011

- During **Census 2011**, information on disability was collected during the Population Enumeration phase through a 'Household Schedule'. Questions related to **Disability** were asked for every person in the household.
- Enumerators were instructed to consult the disabled person in the household directly, in addition to the main respondent, for accurate information.
- All types of households, including National, Institutional and Private Households, were covered.
- The finalisation of questions on disability involved field trials, extensive discussions with civil society organisations and the nodal ministry and a pre-test across rural and urban areas in every state.
- Key considerations for question design included simple and easy-to-understand terminology, data relevance for policy-makers, and ensuring that all disabilities listed in the Persons with Disabilities Act, 1995 and the National Trust Act, 1999 were addressed.
- A filter question was added to identify the disability status of individuals.
- In Census 2011, information was collected on eight types of disabilities, compared to five in Census 2001.
- The placement of the disability question was moved forward in the schedule to improve visibility and response accuracy.
- Special efforts were made to enhance coverage, which included extensive training for enumerators and publicity measures to raise awareness.

- Caste, tribe, gender and disability are institutions that generate and perpetuate inequalities and exclusion in society. However, they also inspire struggles against these inequalities.
- Historically, social sciences have been dominated by ideas of class, race and gender to explain inequality. The focus on caste, tribe and disability as complex categories is relatively recent.
- There are still marginalised groups that require more attention, such as those defined by religion or by a combination of religion and caste, gender and religion, caste and region, as highlighted in the Sachar Committee Report on the Muslim community.

Concern of Education for Disabled Children

- In a country where half of the children aged 5-14 are out of school, there is limited space for children with disabilities, especially if segregated schooling is promoted.
- Although legislation may attempt to make education available to every disabled child, many parents-particularly in rural areas-do not see education as leading to autonomy for their disabled child.
- In rural areas, parents might prioritise improved agricultural facilities or easier access to water over formal education.
- In urban slums, parents expect education to be linked to the world of work, aiming to improve their child's basic quality of life rather than only providing academic knowledge.

Quick Test 5

1. Define the term 'Gender'.
2. Which was the first women's issue to receive public attention?
3. Who was the founder of 'Brahmo Samaj'?
4. Who wrote Stree Purush Tulana?
5. Which social reformer founded Satyashodak Samaj?

NCERT Folder

1. **How is social inequality different from the inequality of individual?**

Ans. Individual inequality refers to destructiveness and variations among individuals in their psychological and physical characteristics.

Social inequality refers to a social system where some people are getting opportunity to make use of the resources and others are not. Some people are at a higher level in terms of wealth, education, health and status while others are at the lowest level.

2. **What are some of the features of social stratification?**

Ans. The three key features that explains social stratification are as follows

(i) Social stratification is a characteristic of society, not simply a function of individual differences. It is a society-wide system that unequally distributes social resources among categories of people.

(ii) Social stratification persists over generations. It is closely linked to the family and to the inheritance of social resources from one generation to next. The ascribed aspect of social inequality is reinforced by the practice of endogamy.

(iii) Social stratification is supported by patterns of belief or ideology. No system of social stratification is likely to persist over generations unless it is widely viewed as being either fair or inevitable.

3. **How would you distinguish prejudice from other kinds of opinion or belief?**

Ans. Prejudice refers to pre-thought opinions or attitudes held by members of one group towards another. Prejudice may be either positive or negative. A prejudiced person's pre-thought views are generally based on hearsay or what is heard from others, rather than on direct evidence. This word is generally used for negative pre-judgements.

On the other hand, an opinion or belief is a judgement about someone or something, not necessarily based on fact and knowledge.

4. **What is social exclusion?** **CBSE 2019**

Ans. Social exclusion refers to the combined result of depriviation and discrimination which prevent individuals or groups from participating wholly in the economic, social and political life of the society in which they live.

- It is the outcome of social processes and institutions rather than individual action.
- It refers to ways in which individuals may become cut off from full involvement in the wider society.
- It focuses on a broad range of factors that prevent individuals or groups from having opportunities open to the majority of the population. It is not accidental but systematic and it is the result of structural features of society. Social exclusion is involuntary i.e. exclusion is practiced regardless of the wishes of those who are excluded.

5. **What is the relationship between caste and economic inequality today?**

Ans. In today's scenario of hierarchy of caste system, each caste has a specific place and social status. There has been a close correlation between social or caste status and economic status. The high castes were almost invariably of high economic status.

However, in the 19th century the link between caste and occupation had become less rigid. At the macro line, things have not changed much. The difference between the privileged (a high economic status) sections of society and disadvantaged (a low economic status) sections still persists.

6. **What is untouchability?**

Ans. Untouchability is an extreme aspect of the caste system where members of certains castes are considered as untouchable by upper castes. The three main dimensions of untouchability i.e. exclusion, humiliation-subordination and exploitation are equally important in defining the phenomenon of untouchability.

Untouchables/Dalits experience untouchability in different ways. They are prohibited from sharing drinking water sources or participating in collective religious worship, social ceremonies and festivals. Untouchability is associated with economic exploitation of various kinds, most commonly through the imposition of forced, unpaid (or under-paid) labour or the confiscation of property.

7. **Describe some of the policies designed to address caste inequality.**

Ans. In India, because of massive discrimination practised against lower castes, special provisions have been made for them. At the state level, there are special programmes for Scheduled Tribes (ST) and Scheduled Castes (SC). The OBCs have also been added to this special provisions.

Some laws passed to end, prohibit and punish caste discrimination were

- Caste Disabilities Removal Act of 1850, abolished all laws affecting the rights of persons converting to another religion or caste. It allowed entry of Dalit to government schools.
- Constitution Amendment (93rd Amendment) Act of 2005, for introducing reservation for OBCs in institutions of higher education.
- Scheduled Castes and Scheduled Tribes (Prevention of Atrocities) Act of 1989, to abolish untouchability (Article 17) and introduced reservation provisions.
- 1989 Prevention of Atrocities Act 1989 revised and strengthened the legal provisions against Dalits and Adivasis.

8. How are the Other Backward Castes different from the Dalits (or Schedule Castes)?

Ans. Other Backward Castes (OBCs) are different from the Dalits or Scheduled Castes (SCs) in the following ways

- OBCs are not any particular group like SCs and STs but individuals from all communities whose standard of living is below poverty line.
- OBCs have been scheduled in Constitution of India through 93rd Amendment, 2006 and these classes are recognised since the early 1990s.
- Such is not is case of SCs and STs who have been recognised by Government of India Act, 1935 during colonial India.
- There is a tough procedure for OBC candidate to establish themself in this category while SCs and STs and unconditionally recognised.
- The proportion of reserved seats is equal to the percentage share of the Scheduled Castes and Tribes in the total population but for OBCs this proportion is decided differently.

9. What are the major issues of concern to Adivasis today? CBSE SQP 2023

Ans. Major issues of concern to Adivasis today are as follows

- Development plans during post-independence period had displaced Adivasis from their natural habitat i.e. forests, but nothing has been done so far for their rehabilitation.
- The so called traders and industrialists have trickily usurped their lands, increased the trend of consumption among them, but being resourceless they find themselves in helpless position.
- Adivasi population in India is widely dispersed. They are mainly concentrated in North-Eastern states like Tripura, Meghalaya and Nagaland. Being so dispersed, they cannot organise themselves properly.
- Being dispersed population, it is also difficult to collect proper data and implement schemes for their development.
- Economic and social conditions of the Adivasis in North-Eastern states is much worse than those of other-tribals.
- The projects like Sardar Sarovar dam on the river Narmada in Western India and the Polavaram dam on the river Godavari in Andhra Pradesh are in progress and it is estimated that several lakh Adivasis are going to lost their habitat and source of survival. Economic liberalisation policies have made it easier for corporate firms to acquire large areas of land by displacing Adivasis.

10. What are the major issues taken up by the women's movement over its history?

Ans. There are no biological reasons that can explain the amount of discrimination in public sphere against women. Scholars and social reformers have shown that the inequalities between men and women are social rather than natural. The women's question became prominent in the 19th Century.

Some of the major issues taken by the women's movement by some social reformers are as following

- **Raja Rammohun Roy's** attempts to reform society, religion and status of women in Bengal brought attention to women's issues. He undertook the campaign against *Sati* which was the first women's issue to receive public attention.
- **Jyotiba Phule** founded the Satyashodak Samaj with its primary emphasis on truth seeking. Phule's first practical social reform efforts were to aid the two groups considered lowest in traditional Brahmin culture i.e women and untouchables.
- **Sir Syed Ahmed Khan** made efforts to reform Muslim society. He wanted girls to be educated, but within the boundaries of their homes. He stood for women's education but sought for a curriculum that included instruction in religious principles, training in arts of housekeeping and handicrafts and rearing of children.
- **Tarabai Shinde,** a Maharashtrian housewife wrote Stree Purush Tulana as a protest against the double standards of a male dominated society.
- Women's issues aggressively surfaced in 1970s. The burning issues were rape of women in police custody, dowry murders and gender injustice, etc.

11. In what sense can one say that disability is as much a social as a physical thing?

Ans. The differently abled are not 'disabled' only because they are physically or mentally 'impaired' but also because society is built in such a manner that doesn't cater to their needs.

Some common features central to the public perception of 'disability' all over the world are as follows

- Disability is understood as a biological event.
- Whenever, a disabled person is confronted with problems, it is believed that the problems originate due to his/her impairment.
- The disabled person is seen as a victim.
- Disability is supposed to be linked with the disabled individual's self-perception.
- The idea of disability suggests that they are in need of help.

Exam Pattern Questions

Objective Type Questions

Multiple Choice Questions (MCQs)

1. A construction worker's daily routine involves working long hours doing back-breaking tasks, but they remain in poverty.

What is the main reason they are unable to improve their life chances?

(a) Lack of hard work
(b) Social inequality and exclusion
(c) Poor financial planning
(d) Natural talent differences

2. Which of the following is the form of capital?

I. Economic capital **II. Cultural capital**
III. Social capital

Codes
(a) I and II (b) II and III
(c) I, II and III (d) I and III

3. Person from a well-off family can afford expensive higher education. Someone with influential relatives and friends may through access to good advice, recommendations or information manage to get a well-paid job. CBSE SQP 2023

Which of the following is true in the given context?

I. There are multiple forms of capital.
II. Different forms of capital cannot be converted into the other.
III. The forms of capital overlap.

Codes
(a) I is false (b) I and II are true
(c) I and III are true (d) I, II and III are true

4. Stereotypes fix whole group into single .... group. CBSE Term I, 2021

(a) homogeneous (b) heterogeneous
(c) broad (d) diverse

5. Which of the following is not true for stereotypes? CBSE SQP 2024

(a) In a country such as India, many of these stereotypes are partly colonial creations.
(b) They are flexible characterisations of a group of people.
(c) Stereotypes are often applied to ethnic and racial groups and to women.
(d) Prejudices are often grounded in stereotypes.

6. Which of the following is true regarding discrimination?

(a) In order for a person to discriminate, he or she must hold prejudicial attitudes.
(b) Discrimination is an action.
(c) Discrimination is not a form of racism.
(d) None of the above

7. The person who is refused a job because of his/her caste may be told that he/she was less qualified than others and the selection was done purely on merit. This is an example of CBSE SQP 2023

(a) Discrimination (b) Social stratification
(c) Egalitarianism (d) Stereotype

8. The ways in which individuals may become cut off full involvement in the wider society is known as CBSE Term I, 2021

(a) Social Inclusion (b) Social Inequality
(c) Social Exclusion (d) Social Stratification

9. Which of the following groups are highlighted as facing significant social inequality and exclusion?

I. Dalits II. Adivasis
III. Women IV. Urban elite

Codes
(a) I, II and III (b) II, III and IV
(c) I, III and IV (d) All of these

10. Which of the following is not a reason for social exclusion?
(a) Gender (b) Religion
(c) Individual intelligence (d) Caste

11. Which of the following statements is true about social exclusion and discrimination?
(a) Discrimination is only based on economic resources.
(b) Prejudices are always positive and help in community development.
(c) Prejudice can be based on factors like gender, religion, ethnicity and disability.
(d) Discrimination is always openly expressed and easy to prove.

12. People do not face discrimination and exclusion on the basis of CBSE SQP Term I, 2021
(a) caste (b) class (c) gender (d) family system

13. Which of the following statements is incorrect?
(a) Social exclusion is accidental and results from individual actions.
(b) Legislation alone can bring lasting social change.
(c) Protest movements have been crucial in challenging caste, gender and religious discrimination.
(d) Social exclusion affects access to essential goods and services like education, health and transportation.

14. Which of the following features is not an element of the policy of Apartheid? CBSE 2023
(a) Denial of ownership of land
(b) Denial of South African citizenship
(c) Permission for mixed marriages
(d) Denial of formal voice in government

15. Which of the following is/are true regarding the caste system in India?

I. The caste system historically classified people based on occupation and social status.
II. Ritual-religious prohibitions on occupational change are strictly imposed today.
III. The correlation between caste and economic status is weaker in modern times compared to the past.
IV. Caste distinctions remain significant at the macro level despite social and economic changes.

Codes
(a) I and III (b) I, III and IV
(c) II and IV (d) I, II, III and IV

16. Which of the following statements is not true about the caste system in India?
(a) The caste system historically linked social status with economic status.
(b) The caste system is completely abolished and has no influence in modern India.
(c) Despite changes, the correlation between caste and economic status remains strong.
(d) The caste system involved rigid occupational roles, with limited social mobility.

17. The service and artisanal castes who occupied the lower rungs of the caste hierarchy are referred to as CBSE SQP Term I, 2021
(a) Dalit (b) Scheduled Tribes
(c) Bohras (d) OBCs

18. Which of the following is not true about untouchability?
(a) It is associated with exclusion, humiliation-subordination and exploitation.
(b) Untouchability affects only the low castes, such as Scheduled Tribes.
(c) Untouchables are considered impure and are avoided in some regions.
(d) The term 'Harijan' was coined by Mahatma Gandhi to counter derogatory caste names.

19. Identify which of the following is not a main dimension of untouchability.
(a) Exclusion (b) Humiliation-subordination
(c) Economic independence (d) Exploitation

20. The city offers anonymity which is an important reason for rural to urban migration. Who enjoys this anonymity?

I. Poorer sections of the socially dominant rural groups
II. Scheduled Castes and Scheduled Tribes
III. Women
IV. Children

Codes
(a) I and II (b) II and III
(c) I and IV (d) I and III

21. Who was the founder of Satyashodak Samaj having its primary emphasis on truth seeking? CBSE Term I, 2021
(a) Raja Rammohun Roy (b) Jyotiba Phule
(c) M.G. Ranade (d) Dayanand Saraswati

22. When Raja Rammohun Roy campaigned against Sati and formed the Brahmo Samaj, defenders of Sati formed Dharma Sabha and petitioned the British not to legislate against Sati. CBSE 2024 C

Which of the following movement does it highlight?
(a) New Social Movement (b) Social Change
(c) Counter Movement (d) Revolutionary Movement

23. Stree Purush Tulana, was written as a protest against the double standards of a male dominated society. The author of this book was CBSE SQP Term I, 2021

(a) Tarabai Shinde
(b) Savitri Phule
(c) Annie Beasant
(d) Anita Ghai

24. We are disabled by buildings that are not designed to admit us and this in turn leads to a range of further disablements regarding our education, our chances of gaining employment, our social lives and so on. The disablement lies in the construction of society, not in the physical condition of the individual.

Which among the following is/are common features central to 'disability' all over the world?

(a) Disability is understood as a biological given.
(b) The disabled person is seen as a victim.
(c) Disability is supposed to be linked with the disabled individual's self perception.
(d) All of the above

Assertion-Reason Questions

Direction (Q. Nos. 25-27) Two statement are given in the question below as Assertion (A) and Reason (R). Read the statements and choose the appropriate option.

(a) Both A and R are true and R is the correct explanation of A
(b) Both A and R are true, but R is not the correct explanation of A
(c) A is true, but R is false
(d) A is false, but R is true

25. Assertion (A) For most of us who are born and live in India, social inequality and exclusion no longer are facts of our lives.

Reason (R) The everydayness of social inequality and exclusion often make them appear inevitable, almost natural. CBSE SQP 2024

26. Assertion (A) Prejudices refer to pre-conceived opinions or attitudes held by members of one group towards another.

Reason (R) An opinion is formed in advance of any familiarity with the subject, before considering any available evidence. CBSE 2024

27. Assertion (A) No social group howsoever weak or oppressed is only a victim.

Reason (R) Human beings are always capable of organising and acting on their own - often against very heavy odds-to struggle for justice and dignity. CBSE SQP 2024

Case Based Questions

Read the passage given below and answer the questions that follow by choosing the correct option.

28. Social stratification is supported by patterns of belief, or ideology. No system of social stratification is likely to persist over generations unless it is widely viewed as being either fair or inevitable. The caste system, for example, is justified in terms of the opposition of purity and pollution, with the Brahmins designated as the most superior and Dalits as the most inferior by virtue of their birth and occupation. Not everyone, though, thinks of a system of inequality as legitimate. Typically, people with the greatest social privileges express the strongest support for systems of stratification such as caste and race.

(i) The caste system, is justified in terms of the opposition of purity and pollution, with the ...... designated as the most superior and .... as the most inferior by virtue of their birth and occupation.

(a) Brahmins, Dalits (b) Dalits, Brahmins
(c) Jains, Banias (d) Banias, Jains

(ii) .... refer to pre-conceived opinions or attitudes held by members of one group towards another.

(a) Inclusion (b) Prejudices
(c) Incentive (d) Monarchy

29. The caste system classified people by their occupation and status. Every caste was associated with an occupation, which meant that persons born into a particular caste were also 'born into' the occupation associated with their caste – they had no choice. Moreover and perhaps more importantly, each caste also had a specific place in the hierarchy of social status, so that, roughly speaking, not only were occupational categories ranked by social status, but there could be a further ranking within each broad occupational category. In strict scriptural terms, social and economic status were supposed to be sharply separated.

(i) Classification of caste system was on the basis of ....

(a) occupation (b) status
(c) Both (a) and (b) (d) Neither (a) nor (b)

(ii) .... refers to that social category of persons who are neither male nor female.

(a) Third gender (b) Second gender
(c) Homosexual (d) Bisexual

30. Strictly speaking, the 'untouchable' castes are outside the caste hierarchy – they are considered to be so 'impure' that their mere touch severely pollutes members of all other castes, bringing terrible punishment for the former and forcing the latter to perform elaborate purification rituals. In fact, notions of 'distance pollution' existed in many regions of India (particularly in the south) such that even the mere presence or the shadow of an 'untouchable' person is considered polluting. **CBSE SQP Term I, 2021**

(i) Despite the limited literal meaning of the word, the institution of 'untouchability' refers not just to the avoidance or prohibition of physical contact but to a much broader set of social sanctions. Which of the following is not such a sanction?
(a) Prohibition from sharing drinking water sources
(b) Participating in collective religious worship
(c) Wearing clean clothes
(d) Imposition of gestures of deference

(ii) The names used to refer to untouchables are all almost always
(a) derogatory
(b) respectful
(c) neutral
(d) loaded with a positive charge

(iii) As per the understanding of distance pollution from the given passage, which of the following qualify as sources of distance pollution?
I. Mere presence
II. Shadow
III. Pollution associated with women during menstruation.
IV. Ceremonial pollution associated with death.
Codes
(a) I and II (b) II and III
(c) III and IV (d) I and IV

31. What is the matter dear? She said affectionately
"I feel somewhat awkward" I said in a rather apologising tone "as being a purdahnishin woman. I am not accustomed to walking about unveiled".
"You need not be afraid of coming across a man here. This is lady land, free from sin and harm."
I became very curious to know where the men were. I met more than a hundred women while walking there but not a single man.
Where are the men? I asked her. In their proper place, where they ought to be
Pray let me know what you mean by their proper places".
Oh I see my mistake you cannot know our customs, as you were never here before. We shot our men indoors".
"Just as we are kept in the Zenana? Exactly so."
"How funny" I burst in to a laugh. Sister Sara laughed too. **CBSE Term I, 2021**

(i) Identify the author of the passage.
(a) Mahatma Gandhi
(b) Tarabhai Shinde
(c) Raja Rani Verma
(d) Rokeya Sakhawat Hossain

(ii) The above passage is a
(a) novel
(b) poetry
(c) short story
(d) film

(iii) In which year Sultan's Dream published?
(a) 1805 (b) 1905
(c) 1925 (d) 1945

32. Social inequality and exclusion are facts of life. Social inequality and exclusion are social because they are not about individuals but about groups. In every society, some people have a greater share of valued resources - money, property, education, health and power - than others. People often face discrimination and exclusion because of their gender, religion, ethnicity, language, caste and disability. **CBSE 2025**

(i) Social inequality and exclusion are facts of life because.
I. This everydayness of social inequality and exclusion often makes them appear inevitable, almost natural.
II. We often think of them as being 'deserved' or 'justified' in some sense.
III. These are natural which can be changed.
IV. The poor and marginalised are not blamed for their own plight.
Which of the above statements are correct?
Codes
(a) I and II
(b) I and III
(c) I and IV
(d) II and III

(ii) Which of the following statements is not true related to Exclusion of Dalits? **CBSE 2025**
(a) The institution of untouchability does not refer to the avoidance or prohibition of physical contact.
(b) Untouchability refers to a much broader set of social sanctions.
(c) Untouchable castes are outside the caste hierarchy.
(d) They are considered to be so impure that their mere touch severely pollutes members of all other castes.

Answers

1. (b) Social inequality and exclusion
2. (c) I, II and III
3. (c) I and III are true
4. (b) heterogeneous
5. (b) They are flexible characterisations of a group of people.
6. (b) Discrimination is an action.
7. (a) discrimination
8. (c) Social Exclusion
9. (a) I, II and III
10. (c) Individual intelligence
11. (c) Prejudice can be based on factors like gender, religion, ethnicity and disability.
12. (d) family system
13. (a) Social exclusion is accidental and results from individual actions.
14. (c) Permission for mixed marriages
15. (b) I, III and IV
16. (b) The caste system is completely abolished and has no influence in modern India.
17. (d) OBCs
18. (b) Untouchability affects only the low castes, such as Scheduled Tribes.
19. (c) Economic independence
20. (a) I and II
21. (b) Jyotiba Phule
22. (c) Counter Movement
23. (a) Tarabai Shinde
24. (d) All of the above
25. (d) A is false, but R is true
26. (a) Both A and R are true and R is the correct explanation of A
27. (a) A and R are true and R is the correct explanation of A
28. (i) (a) Brahmins, Dalits
    (ii) (b) Prejudices
29. (i) (c) Both (a) and (b)
    (ii) (a) Third gender
30. (i) (c) Wearing clean clothes
    (ii) (a) derogatory
    (iii) (a) I and II
31. (i) (d) Rokeya Sakhawat Hossain
    (ii) (c) short story
    (iii) (d) 1945
32. (i) (a) I and II
    (ii) (a) The institution of untouchability does not refer to the avoidance or prohibition of physical contact.

Subjective Questions

Very Short Answer Type Questions

1. The caste system is a distinct Indian social institution that legitimises and enforces practices of discrimination against people born into particular castes. These practices of discrimination are humiliating, exclusionary and exploitative. Which social institution create and sustain patterns of inequality and exclusion.

Which social institutions create and sustain patterns of inequality and exclusion?

Ans. The social institutions which create and sustain patterns of inequality and exclusion are family, caste, tribe and the market.

2. This everydayness of social inequality and exclusion often make them appear inevitable, almost natural. If we do sometimes recognise that inequality and exclusion are not inevitable, we often think of them as being 'deserved' or 'justified' in some sense. What do you mean by social inequality?

What do you mean by social inequality?

Competency Based Que.

Ans. Patterns of unequal access to social resources are commonly called social inequality. By and large social inequality is not the outcome of innate or natural differences between people, but is produced by the society within.

3. What is social about social inequality?

Ans. Social inequalities are social because they are not about individuals but about groups. They are social in the sense, that they are not only economic but also systematic and structured.

4. What are the three forms of capital on which social inequality is based?

Ans. The three forms of capital on which social inequality is based are

(i) **Economic Capital** It can be divided in the form of material assets and income.

(ii) **Cultural Capital** It consists of educational capital and status.

(iii) **Social Capital** It is in the form of networks of contacts and social associations.

5. Social stratification is a society-wide system that unequally distributes social resources.
Explain the constituents of social resources.

Ans. The constituents of social resources are money, property, education, health, power etc.

6. What do you mean by the term 'social stratification'? Competency Based Que.

Ans. Sociologists use the term social stratification to refer to a system by which categories of people in a society are ranked in a hierarchy.

7. What are prejudices?

Ans. Prejudices refer to pre-conceived opinions or attitudes held by members of one group towards another. The word literally means pre-judgement.

8. Prejudice can be either positive or negative. Support the statement with suitable examples. CBSE SQP 2024

Ans. Prejudice can be positive, such as favouring one's own caste or group, assuming them to be superior without evidence. It can also be negative, like assuming people from another religion are untrustworthy. Both forms are based on pre-judgment rather than actual experience.

9. Discrimination can be very hard to prove because it may not be open or explicitly stated. Support the statement with suitable examples. CBSE SQP 2024

Ans. Discrimination is often hidden behind justifiable reasons. For instance, a qualified candidate might be denied a job due to caste or gender but told it was based on merit. Similarly, housing discrimination may occur under the pretext of 'availability' rather than prejudice.

10. Explain the term apartheid?

Ans. Apartheid was a political and social system in South Africa while it was under white minority rule. This policy governed the relations between South Africa's White minority and non-white majority and sanctioned racial segregation and political and economic discrimination against non-whites.

11. What are the various reasons of social exclusions and discrimination in the society?

Ans. The reason of social exclusion and discrimination in the society are economic resources, gender, religion, ethnicity, language, caste and disability.

12. Not all of the changes in social institutions brought about by the British were intended or deliberate. Give an example to justify the statement. CBSE SQP 2023

Ans. The given statement is true that not all of the changes that occurred in the caste system within the colonial period were deliberate or intended. It is because the British administrators initially began to understand the complexities of caste system in an effort to learn a way to efficiently govern the country. This learning included methodical and intensive surveys as well as reports on the customs and manner of the tribes and castes of the country.

For example, the land revenue settlements and related arrangements as well as laws gave legal recognition to the customary caste based rights of the upper castes making them land owners in a modern sense.

13. Cite the most important initiative of the state for compensating caste discrimination.

Ans. The most important state initiative to compensate for past and present discrimination is the one popularly known as Reservations, which involved the setting aside of some places or seats for members of SCs and STs in different spheres of public life.

14. The economic and social conditions of adivasis in India have been historically shaped by resource extraction policies initiated during British colonial rule and continued after independence. Despite their longstanding association with forest areas, the adivasis have faced exploitation and marginalisation.

Ans. Adivasis in India faced exploitation due to colonial and post-independence resource extraction policies. The British reserved forest lands for timber production, depriving them of their livelihood. Post-independence, industrialisation further displaced adivasis from their lands for mining and dam projects, worsening their socio-economic conditions.

15. "What is the matter, dear?" She said affectionately. "I feel somewhat awkward," I said, in a rather apologising tone, "as being a purdahnishin woman I am not accustomed to walking about unveiled." "You need not be afraid of coming across a man here. This is Lady land, free from sin and harm..."
Following abstract is taken from Sultana of my dreams. What is special about this book? Competency Based Que.

Ans. Begum Rokeya Sakhawat Hossain wrote Sultana's Dream to test her abilities in English. This remarkable short story is probably the earliest example of science fiction writing in India and among the first by a woman author anywhere in the world.

16. What are the two criteria used for defining the OBCs?

Ans. Caste rank and occupation are the main criteria by which Other Backward Classes (OBCs) are considered backward. The OBCs are above the so called Untouchable groups and below the Brahman, Kshatriya and Vaishya castes.

17. What does the term 'Adivasi' mean?

Ans. The term 'Adivasi' connotes political awareness and the assertion of rights. Literally meaning 'original inhabitants', the term was coined in the 1930's as part of the struggle against the intrusion by the colonial government and outside settlers and moneylenders.

18. Who established Satyashodak Samaj and why?

Ans. Jyotiba Phule denounced the injustice of the caste system and scorned its rules of purity and pollution in 1873. He founded the Satyashodak Samaj (truth seekers society) which was devoted to securing human rights and social justice for low caste people.

19. Why Tarabai Shinde wrote, Stree Purush Tulana?

Ans. Tarabai Shinde wrote 'Stree Purush Tulana' as a protest against society to focus on the double standards of a male dominated society.

20. Begum Rokeya Sakhawat Hossain was born in a well-to-do Bengali Muslim family and was lucky to have a husband who was very liberal in outlook and encouraged her education first in Urdu and later in Bengali and English. She was already a successful author in Urdu and Bengali when she wrote Sultana's Dream to test her abilities in English. Why was Sultana's Dream considered a remarkable short story, in context of struggle for women's equality and rights? CBSE SQP 2024

Ans. Sultana's Dream was remarkable because it envisioned a society where gender roles were reversed-men were confined to the home and women were leading scientists and innovators. This early feminist vision challenged traditional norms and highlighted women's potential, advocating for gender equality and women's rights in a male-dominated world.

21. What are the two common features of the public perception of disability worldwide?

Ans. The two common features of the public perception of disability worldwide are

(i) Disability is understood as a biological event.

(ii) The disabled person is seen as victim.

Short Answer Type Questions

1. What does social exclusion mean? Why is it involuntary?

Ans. Social exclusion refers to the systematic ways in which individuals or groups are marginalised and denied full participation in society. It goes beyond economic deprivation, encompassing barriers to essential services like education, healthcare and justice. Social exclusion is involuntary because it results from structural inequalities embedded in societal norms and institutions, not from individual choice. Factors like caste, gender, religion and disability perpetuate these barriers, making it difficult for excluded groups to access opportunities available to the majority.

2. Explain the key principles that help in social stratification. CBSE 2019

Ans. The key principles that explain social stratification are as follow

- **Characteristic of Society** Social stratification is not based on individual differences alone; it's a system within society that unequally distributes resources among groups. In simpler societies, there is less stratification because little surplus is produced. However, in advanced societies where there is a surplus, resources are distributed unequally among different social groups.
- **Inherited Across Generations** Social stratification often passes from one generation to the next. A person's social status is usually inherited from their parents. In systems like the caste system, children usually follow their parents' occupation, and endogamy (marriage within the same caste) reinforces these divisions.
- **Supported by Beliefs and Ideology** Social stratification is sustained by shared beliefs that make it seem fair or inevitable. For instance, the caste system is supported by the belief in purity and pollution, which ranks castes as higher or lower. Those at the top of the hierarchy tend to support these systems, while those who face discrimination are more likely to oppose them.

3. What is social stratification? Explain the key principles of social stratification. CBSE 2024 C

Ans. Social stratification refers to the hierarchical ranking of categories of people in society, influencing their access to resources and opportunities. Key principles of social stratification include

- It is a characteristic of society, not individual differences, distributing resources unequally.
- It persists across generations, with children inheriting their parents' social position.
- It is supported by ideologies, where the system is often seen as legitimate, particularly by those at the top of the hierarchy.

Social stratification is influenced by factors like caste, class and gender, shaping identity and experiences.

4. Differentiate between stereotypes and discrimination. CBSE 2024 C

Ans. **Stereotypes** are fixed, oversimplified beliefs about a group, often based on preconceived notions and do not acknowledge individual variation. They can be positive or negative and are typically resistant to change.

Discrimination, on the other hand, refers to actual behaviour or actions that treat individuals or groups unfairly, such as denying someone a job based on gender, caste or religion. Unlike stereotypes, discrimination is a practice that actively excludes or disadvantages others and may be disguised as merit-based or justified by other reasons.

5. Untouchability is an extreme and vicious aspect of the caste system. Explain the various dimensions of untouchability. CBSE 2019

Ans. The three main dimensions of untouchability are exclusion, humiliation-subordination and exploitation

(i) **Subordination and Exploitation** Untouchability is almost always associated with economic exploitation of various kinds, most commonly through the imposition of forced, unpaid under paid labour or the confiscation of property.

(ii) **Exclusion** Dalits experience forms of exclusion that are unique and not practised against other groups – for instance, being prohibited from sharing drinking water sources or participating in collective religious worship, social ceremonies and festivals.

6. Examine the role of states initiatives to address caste and tribe discrimination.

Ans. Some of the initiatives after independence were as follows

- Reservations of seats in the State and Central legislatures (i.e. State Assemblies, Lok Sabha and Rajya Sabha), reservation of jobs in government service across all departments and public sector companies and reservation of seats in educational institutions for Scheduled Castes and Scheduled Tribes. The proportion of reserved seats is equal to the percentage share of the Scheduled Castes and Tribes in the total population.
- In addition to reservations, there have been a number of laws passed to end, prohibit and punish caste discrimination, specially untouchability.
- The 93rd Amendment is for introducing reservation for the Other Backward Classes in institutions of higher education, while the 1850 Act was used to allow entry of Dalits to government schools.
- The Prevention of Atrocities Act 1989 revised and strengthened the legal provisions punishing acts of violence or humiliation against Dalits and Adivasis.

7. OBCs are a much more diverse group than Dalits and Adivasis. Explain. Competency Based Que.

Ans. There were a large group of castes that were of low status and were also subjected to varying levels of discrimination but were not untouchables. These were the service and artisanal caste who occupied lower level in caste hierarchy.

The OBCs are defined negatively, they are neither part of the forward castes at the upper end of the status nor of the Dalits at the lower level. But since, caste has entered all the major Indian religions and is not confined to Hinduism alone, there are also members of other religions who belong to backward castes.

They share the same traditional occupational identification and similar or worse socio-economic status. For these reasons, the OBCs are a much more diverse group than Dalits or Adivasis.

8. The women's question arose in modern India as part of the nineteenth century middle class social reform movements. The nature of these movements varied from region to region.
Explain any two social reform movements that addressed the women's question. CBSE 2024

Ans. Two social movements that addressed women's question are as follows

(i) Raja Rammohun Roy's attempts to reform society, religion and the status of women can be taken as the starting point of nineteenth century social reform in Bengal. Roy undertook the campaign against 'sati' which was the first women's issue to receive public attention. Rammohun Roy's ideas represented a curious mixture of Western rationality and an assertion of Indian traditionality. He attacked the practice of sati on the basis of both appeals to humanitarian and natural rights doctrines as well as Hindu shastras.

(ii) The widow remarriage movement in the Bombay Presidency where Ranade was one of the leading reformers, is the second movement. The deplorable and unjust treatment of the Hindu upper caste widows was a major issue taken up. M.G. Ranade's writings entitled the 'The Texts of the Hindu Law on the Lawfulness of the Remarriage of Widows and Vedic Authorities for Widow Marriage' elaborated the shastric sanction for remarriage of widows.

9. "What marked these 19th century social reform attempts was the modern context and mix of ideas?" Interpret the given statement. CBSE 2019

Ans. The statement reflects how 19th-century social reform movements in India were influenced by the modern context and a combination of ideas. Reformers like Raja

Rammohun Roy, M.G. Ranade, Jyotiba Phule and Sir Syed Ahmed Khan sought to address pressing social issues by drawing on both traditional Indian values and modern Western principles.

For example, Roy's campaign against sati was based on humanitarian ideals as well as Hindu scriptures, showcasing a blend of reason and religious tradition.

- Ranade advocated widow remarriage by combining shastric authority with modern moral philosophy.
- Reformers like Phule also addressed caste and gender discrimination, emphasising inclusivity through innovative approaches.

This blend of modernity and tradition reflected a response to the challenges posed by colonial rule and the introduction of democratic ideals. It signified a shift towards broader goals of equality and justice, with reforms rooted in both cultural pride and global principles.

10. State the declarations of the Karachi Session of the Indian National Congress which committed itself to women's equality. CBSE 2019

Ans. The Karachi Session of the Indian National Congress declared-Fundamental Rights of Citizenship in Indian whereby it committed itself to women's equality.

- All citizens are equal before the law, irrespective of religion, caste, creed or sex.
- No disability attaches to any citizen, by reason of his or her religion, caste, creed or sex, in regard to public employment, office of power or honour and in the exercise of any trade or calling.
- The franchise shall be on the basis of Universal Adult Suffrage.
- Woman shall have the right to vote, to represent and the right to hold public offices.

11. Mention some of the common features central to the public perception of 'disability' all over the world. CBSE 2024

Ans. Various common features central to the public perception of 'disability' all over the world are as follows

- Disability is understood as a biological given.
- Whenever a disabled person is confronted with problems, it is taken for granted that the problems originate from her/his impairment.
- The disabled person is seen as a victim. Disability is supposed to be linked with the disabled individual's self-perception.
- The very idea of disability suggests that they are in need of help.

Like other reformers, Sir Syed Ahmed Khan combined modern Western ideas with teachings from sacred texts in his efforts to reform Muslim society. He advocated for girls' education but preferred it to take place within the confines of their homes.

Long Answer Type Questions

1. Elaborate on state and non-state initiatives addressing caste and tribal discrimination. CBSE SQP 2023

Ans. There have been several state and non-state initiatives to address the caste and tribal discriminations. Some of them are as follows

State Initiatives

- The constitution has special provisions and programmes aimed at the social and economic upliftment of 'Schedule Tribes' and 'Schedule Castes'.
- The state's policy of reservation aims at reserving some seats in public educational institutional and workspaces so as to ensure their representation. The 93rd Amendment Act, brought Other Backward Classes under the purview of reservation.
- The Caste Disabilities Removal Act, 1850 disallowed the curtailment of rights of citizen on the basis of religion and caste.
- Article 17 of the Indian Constitution abolished untouchability and introduced the Scheduled Castes and Scheduled Tribes (Prevention of Atrocities) Act, 1989.

Non-State Initiatives

- Leaders and educationists such as Periyar, Jyotiba Phule, Savitri Phule, Babasaheb Ambedkar, Iyothee thass led social reform movements aimed at increasing education, literacy and access of the so-called low castes and women.
- Ambedkar called for a complete annihilation of caste and believed that only a complete wiping out of the rigid social system can ensure and overall development of the country.

2. What is meant by Other Backward Class? What are its problems?

Ans. Other Backward Class is that class of majority of Indian society which became weak due to social, religious, economic and geographical factors.

Some of the problems of Other Backward Classes are as follows

- **Problem of Landless Farmers** Most of the parts of India are under the control of higher castes. OBC people of villages are landless farmers and they have to work on land of other people. They are exploited by their owners and mainly depend upon the wishes of their owners.

- **Problem of Selection of Occupation** Members of these groups are generally backward from social, educational and economic point of view. That is why problem of selection of occupation remains there in front of them.
- **Problem of Salary** One of the main problems of these people is that they hardly get enough salary at exact time. These people generally work in the fields of people of higher castes and hardly get any cash payment for their work. Their owners give them grains instead of salary which hardly fulfill their needs.
- **Problem of Education** One of the other problems of these people is that they are illiterate. Their children are unable to get education due to poverty because of which their children remain illiterate and remain economically backward.
- **Problem of Indebtedness** One of the main problems of these people is the problem of indebtedness. Generally, these people are very poor because of which they take loan at the time of birth, death, marriage, etc.

Moneylenders charge very high interest from them on loans. People not only have to repay the loan themselves but also leave the burden for their children to repay.

3. How far did the status of women improve in the contemporary India? Give examples to support your answer.

Ans. The question of women's issues became central in the 19th century. Scholar and social reformers have shown that the inequalities between men and women are social rather than natural. The series of changes that took place changed or improved the status of women.

Some of the examples are as follows

(i) In the 19th century reform movements, the emphasis had been on the backward aspects of tradition like *sati*, child marriage or the ill treatment of widows.

(ii) Two decades after independence, i.e. in the 1970's, the emphasis was on modern issues such as, rape of women in police custody, dowry murders, the representation of women in popular media and gendered consequences of unequal development.

(iii) In the 21st century, new sites of gender injustice are emerging such as declining sex ratio, fall in girl child sex ratio, social bias against girl child, etc.

However, the condition of women in contemporary India has changed leaps and bound in comparison with the past. The government formulated laws and policies such as Anti-Dowry Act, one-third reservation of seats in local bodies, Beti Bachao Beti Padhao, LADLI, etc., to empower women.

4. Read the passage and answer the following questions.

In India labels such as 'disability', 'handicap', 'crippled', blind' and 'deaf' are used synonymously. Often these terms are hurled at people as insults. In a culture that looks up to bodily 'perfection', all deviations from the 'perfect body' signify abnormality, defect and distortion. Labels such as bechara (poor thing) accentuate the victim status for the disabled person. The roots of such attitudes lie in the cultural conception that views an impaired body as a result of fate. Destiny is seen as the culprit and disabled people are the victims. The common perception views disability as retribution for past karma (actions) from which there can be no reprieve. The dominant cultural construction in India therefore looks at disability as essentially a characteristic of the individual. The popular images in mythology portray the disabled in an extremely negative fashion.

(i) Why in India labels such as disability 'handicap' etc. used for differently-abled people?

(ii) How these words replaced in the modern times?

Ans. (i) Disability is regarded as a natural occurrence. When a disabled person is faced with difficulties, it is assumed that the difficulties are due to her or his disability. The disabled individual is seen as a victim. Disability is thought to be related to an impaired person's self-perception. The word 'disability' implies that they are in need of assistance.

Some of the reasons for using these labels for differently-abled people are

- The roots of such attitudes lie in the cultural conception that views an impaired body as a result of fate. Destiny is seen as the culprit and disabled people are the victims.
- The common perception view disability as result for past *karma* (actions) from which there can be no reprieve.

(ii) Terms such as mentally challenged, visually impaired and physically impaired replaced the negative terms such as retarded, crippled or lame.

SELF ASSESSMENT TEST

Objective Type Questions

1. What significant change occurred in post-apartheid South Africa regarding race?

(a) Economic capital is now equally distributed

(b) Racial discrimination was banned

(c) The Black majority gained political power but still faced economic struggles

(d) Black people were moved to more affluent areas

2. Which of the following statements about untouchability is True?

(a) It only involves physical avoidance of contact.

(b) It includes exclusion, subordination, and economic exploitation.

(c) Untouchability is practiced uniformly across India.

(d) The term 'Harijan' was used to intensify caste-based discrimination.

3. Which practice is unique to untouchability compared to other low castes?

(a) Sharing drinking water sources

(b) Participation in religious festivals

(c) Severe forms of exclusion

(d) Equal economic opportunities

4. Put the following statements in the correct order.

I. The shadow of an 'untouchable' person was considered polluting in some regions.

II. Untouchability is a pan-Indian phenomenon but varies across regions.

III. The institution of untouchability refers to a broader set of social sanctions.

IV. Untouchability is associated with exclusion, humiliation-subordination and exploitation.

Codes

(a) III, IV, I and II

(b) I, III, IV and II

(c) IV, II, III and I

(d) II, I, III and IV

Case Based Questions

1. It is important to emphasise that the three main dimensions of untouchability - namely, exclusion, humiliation-subordination and exploitation - are all equally important in defining the phenomenon. Although other (i.e., 'touchable') low castes are also subjected to subordination and exploitation to some degree, they do not suffer the extreme forms of exclusion reserved for 'untouchables.' Dalits experience forms of exclusion that are unique and not practised against other groups - for instance, being prohibited from sharing drinking water sources or participating in collective religious worship, social ceremonies and festivals.

(i) What are the three main dimensions that define the phenomenon of untouchability?

(a) Economic exploitation, political dominance and cultural assimilation

(b) Exclusion, humiliation-subordination and exploitation

(c) Discrimination, equality, and forced migration

(d) Religious worship, education and wealth distribution

(ii) How is untouchability associated with economic exploitation?
(a) Through lack of employment opportunities
(b) By restricting access to markets
(c) Through forced, unpaid or underpaid labour
(d) By denying access to government schemes

Very Short Answer Type Questions

1. Social inequality refers to unequal access to valued resources such as money, education and social connections, which are divided into economic, cultural and social capital. These forms of capital often overlap and can be converted into one another. For instance, a well-off family may use their economic capital to provide expensive education (cultural capital), leading to better job opportunities. How does the overlapping nature of these forms of capital contribute to maintaining social inequality?
2. Social stratification distributes resources unequally among social categories, regardless of individual abilities. Support this statement with suitable examples.
3. Prejudices are often grounded in stereotypes that classify entire groups with fixed characteristics, ignoring individual and contextual differences. Why do such stereotypes persist and what are the consequences of their widespread acceptance in a society like India?'
4. Name the social reformers of 19th century, who fought for women's right.

Short Answer Type Questions

1. Explain with examples the concept of social exclusion and its various dimensions.
2. Mention some features of social stratification.
3. Untouchability in India is characterised by exclusion, humiliation-subordination and exploitation. While other low castes face some degree of subordination, Dalits experience unique forms of exclusion, such as being barred from sharing drinking water sources or participating in collective social ceremonies.
   Illustrate how these practices have evolved over time and the role of legal and social reforms in addressing untouchability.
4. The Indian state has implemented various measures to address caste discrimination, including reservations in legislatures, government jobs and educational institutions. Laws such as the Caste Disabilities Removal Act of 1850 and the 93rd Constitutional Amendment of 2005 have played key roles in ensuring access to education for disadvantaged communities. Elaborate on how these initiatives have evolved over time and their impact on reducing caste-based inequalities.

Long Answer Type Questions

1. Compare the concepts of 'untouchability' and 'untouchable' communities with those of 'third gender'. How does society treat these groups differently?
2. What are the major issues taken up by the women's movement over its history?
3. Explain common features of disability all over the world.
4. Discuss the role played by the social reformers against the discrimination in the society.
5. Discuss the role of key leaders like Jyotiba Phule, Iyothee thass, Periyar and Dr. B.R. Ambedkar in shaping the pre-Independence Dalit struggles.

05

CHAPTER

The Challenges of Cultural Diversity

The term 'diversity' highlights differences among people rather than focusing on inequalities. India is a country of immense cultural diversity, where various social groups and communities coexist. Communities in India are defined by cultural markers such as language, religion, sect, race and caste.

YOUR STUDY GOALS

5.1 Introduction
5.2 Cultural Communities and the Nation-State
5.3 Communities, Nations and Nation States
5.4 Regionalism in the Indian Context
5.5 The Nation-State and Religious Issues and Identities
5.6 Relative Size and Distribution of Religious Minorites
5.7 Communalism, Secularism and Nation State
5.8 State and Civil Society

YOUR PRACTICE GOAL

- Objective Type Questions (35 Qs ; MCQs, A-R, Case Based Questions)
- Subjective Questions (34 VSAs, 12 SAs, 7 LAs)

5.1 Introduction

Cultural identities hold significant power and can evoke strong emotions, leading to the mobilisation of large groups. Cultural differences, when combined with economic and social inequalities, further complicate the situation. Efforts to address the inequalities or injustices faced by one community may provoke opposition from other communities. The situation can worsen when scarce resources, such as river water, jobs or government funds need to be shared among communities.

5.2 Cultural Communities and the Nation-State

The Importance of Community Identity

- Every human being requires a stable sense of identity to navigate the world effectively.
- Throughout life, individuals seek answers to questions such as "Who am I?" and "How am I different from others?"
- These questions are answered through the process of socialisation, where families and communities teach us how to live in society.
- Socialisation involves ongoing dialogue, negotiation and sometimes struggle with others, including parents, family, kin group and community.
- The community to which we belong provides us with the language and cultural values that help us understand the world and support our sense of self-identity.

Ascriptive Identity

- Our community identity is based on birth and belonging, not on qualifications or accomplishments.
- We don't choose which family, community or country we are born into; this is called 'Ascriptive identity'.
- Ascriptive identity means individuals are defined by their birth circumstances and not by personal choice.
- People feel secure and satisfied in belonging to communities they are born into, even if membership is accidental.
- Ascriptive identities are often hard to leave; even if we reject them, others may continue to define us by those identities.
- Emotional attachment to community identity is strong because it is accidental, unconditional and inescapable.
- Community ties through family, kinship, caste, ethnicity, language, region, or religion give meaning to our identity.
- People often react emotionally or violently to perceived threats to their community identity.
- Ascriptive identity is universal, as everyone has a motherland, mother tongue, family or faith.
- While there may be exceptions, most individuals are deeply committed and loyal to their ascriptive identities.

Identity Conflict

- Some people may not strongly be committed to one aspect of their identity, but this commitment is potentially available to most people.
- Conflicts involving communities, such as nation, language, religion or caste, are difficult to manage due to strong attachments.
- Each side in the conflict views the other as a hated enemy, leading to an exaggeration of their own virtues and the other's vices.
- In situations like war, patriots on both sides see the other as the aggressor and believe that God and truth are on their side.
- People often struggle to realise that both sides are creating reversed mirror images of each other, with similar emotions and perceptions.

5.3 Communities, Nations and Nation States

- A nation is a large-scale community, often referred to as a 'Community of Communities.'
- Members of a nation share the desire to be part of the same political community, aspiring for political unity and forming a state.
- A state is defined as a set of political-legal institutions that control a particular geographical territory and its people.
- Max Weber defined the state as an entity that successfully claims a monopoly of legitimate force in a specific territory.

Understanding the Concept of Nation and Nation-State

- Nations are based on shared cultural, historical and political institutions such as religion, language, ethnicity and regional culture.
- However, not all nations share common features like language or religion, and many such elements exist across nations without forming a unified nation.
- There is no fixed distinction between communities such as ethnic, religious or regional, as any community can potentially form a nation.

- Nations that have a state of their own are called **Nation-states.**
- In recent times, the concept of 'one nation, one state' has become prominent, though historically, states often represented multiple nations. For example, the Soviet Union recognised over 100 internal nationalities.
- People constituting a nation may be citizens of different states, as seen with Jamaicans, where more live outside Jamaica than within.
- Dual citizenship laws allow individuals to be citizens of two states, such as Jewish Americans who may hold citizenship in both Israel and the USA.
- Defining a nation is challenging, but it can be understood as a community that has successfully acquired a state.
- In the modern era, democracy and nationalism are the dominant sources of political legitimacy, where 'the nation' justifies the state and 'the people' are the source of legitimacy.
- There is no fixed relationship between the nation-state and the various communities it represents.
- Many states have historically been suspicious of cultural diversity and have attempted to eliminate it.
- However, successful examples like India show that strong nation-states can exist without homogenising different community identities.

Threatened by Community Identities, States Try to Eliminate Cultural Diversity

- Historically, states have tried to establish and enhance their political legitimacy through nation building strategies. They sought to secure the loyalty and obedience of their citizens through policies of assimilation or integration.
- Attaining these objectives was not easy, especially in a context of cultural diversity where citizens, in addition to their identifications with their country, might also feel a strong sense of identity with their community - ethnic, religious, linguistic and so on.
- Most states feared that the recognition of such differences would lead to social fragmentation and prevent the creation of a harmonious society. In addition, accommodating these differences is politically challenging, so many states have resorted to either suppressing these diverse identities or ignoring them on the political domain.
- **Policies of assimilation** often involving outright suppression of the identities of ethnic, religious or linguistic groups - try to erode the cultural differences between groups.
- **Policies of integration** seek to assert a single national identity by attempting to eliminate ethnonational and cultural differences from the public and political arena, while allowing them in the private domain. Both sets of policies assume a singular national identity.
- Assimilationist and integrationist strategies try to establish singular national identities through various interventions like

  Centralising all power to forums where the dominant group constitutes a majority and eliminating the autonomy of local or minority groups.

  Imposing a unified legal and judicial system based on the dominant group's traditions and abolishing alternative systems used by other groups.

  Adopting the dominant group's language as the only official 'national' language and making its use mandatory in all public institutions.

  Promotion of the dominant group's language and culture through national institutions including state-controlled media and educational institutions

  Adoption of state symbols celebrating the dominant group's history, heroes and culture, reflected in such things as choice of national holidays or naming of streets etc.

  Seizure of lands, forests and fisheries from minority groups and indigenous people and declaring them national resources.

Assimilationist and Integrationist Policies

- Assimilationist policies aim to persuade, encourage or force all citizens to adopt a uniform set of cultural values and norms, largely those of the dominant social group.
- Non-dominant or subordinate groups are expected or required to give up their cultural values and adopt the prescribed ones.
- Challenges of cultural diversity arise when integrationist policies promote a common national pattern in the public sphere while relegating non-national cultures to the private sphere.
- There is a risk of treating the dominant group's culture as the national culture in integrationist approaches.
- Community identities, like language, religion and ethnicity, may or may not lead to nation formation, but existing states often view them as dangerous rivals.
- States generally favour a single, homogenous national identity to control and manage diversity.
- Suppressing cultural diversity can alienate minority or subordinated communities and intensify their identities.
- Allowing cultural diversity is beneficial from both practical and principled viewpoints.

Cultural Diversity and the Indian Nation-State

- Cultural diversity in the Indian Nation-State is vast, with a population of about 1.21 billion people, according to the 2011 Census of India.
- India has about 1,632 different languages and dialects, with 22 languages officially recognised under the 8th Schedule of the Constitution.
- About 80% of the population are Hindus, who are diverse in beliefs, practices and regionally specific.
- Muslims comprise 14.2% of the population, making India the world's second-largest Muslim country.
- Other religious communities include Christians (2.3%), Sikhs (1.7%), Buddhists (0.7%) and Jains (0.4%).
- India does not follow either the assimilationist or integrationist model in its relationship with community identities.
- Although there are calls for an assimilationist model from some sections of the dominant Hindu community, India has ruled out such a model.
- While national integration is a key theme in state policy, India has not been strictly integrationist.
- The Indian Constitution declares the state to be secular, but religion, language and other factors remain in the public sphere, with communities clearly recognised by the state.
- India serves as an example of a 'state-nation', though it still faces challenges common to nation-states.

National Unity With Cultural Diversity : Building a Democratic 'State-Nation'

- An alternative to the nation-state is the 'state nation', in this various 'nation' like ethnic, religious, linguistic or indigenous identities co-exist peacefully and cooperatively in a single state polity.
- Citizens can find the institutional and political space to identify with both their country and their other cultural identities, to build their trust in common institutions and to participate in and support democratic politics.
- Modern India is facing a grave challenge to its constitutional commitment to multiple and complementary identities with the rise of groups that seek to impose a singular Hindu identity on the country.
- India's constitutional design recognised and responded to distinct group claims and enabled the polity to hold together despite enormous regional, linguistic and cultural diversity.
- India's democratic performance is impressive when compared to wealthier democracies, demonstrating a commitment to pluralism, institutional accommodation and conflict resolution.
- Building a multicultural democracy is the shortcomings of historical nation-building exercises and of the benefits of multiple and complementary identities.
- Successful strategies to build 'state-nations' can and do accommodate diversity constructively by crafting responsive policies of cultural recognition. They are effective solutions for ensuring the longer terms objectives of political stability and social harmony.

Quick Test 1

1. What are the factors that shape community identity?
2. What is the policy of assimilation?
3. Which community is marked as a large-scale community?
4. Through which strategy did the state establish their political legitimacy?
5. Define the term 'state-nation'.

5.4 Regionalism in the Indian Context

- Regionalism is a strong feeling of pride or loyalty that people have towards their regions, often including a desire for self-governance.
- In India, regionalism is rooted in the country's diversity of languages, cultures, tribes and religions.
- Regionalism is encouraged by the geographical concentration of these identity markers and a sense of regional deprivation.
- Indian federalism has been a means of accommodating regional sentiments.

Indian States

- After independence, India continued with the British-Indian administrative structure, which divided the country into large provinces called presidencies.
- Mumbai, Bombay and Calcutta were the major presidencies and all three cities have since changed their names.
- These presidencies were large, multi-ethnic and multilingual provinces that formed the major administrative units of a semi-federal state called the **Union of India**.

Language

- Language, along with regional and tribal identity, has been a powerful force for the formation of ethno-national identity in India.
- Not all linguistic communities have been granted statehood.
- Language diversity was not the prime reason in the creation of states like Chhattisgarh, Jharkhand and Uttaranchal in 2005.
- A combination of factors such as tribal identity, language, regional deprivation and ecology contributed to intense regionalism, leading to statehood.
- India currently has 28 States and 8 Union Territories within its nation-state.

Linguistic States Helped Strengthen Indian Unity

- The Report of the States Reorganisation Commission (SRC), implemented on 1st November, 1956, transformed the political and institutional life of India.
- In the 1920s, the Indian National Congress was reconstituted on linguistic lines, creating provincial units based on language (e.g., one for Marathi speakers, another for Oriya speakers).
- Leaders like Gandhi promised that the new nation would be based on provinces organised by language after gaining freedom.
- However, following India's independence in 1947, the Congress hesitated to fulfill this promise due to fears of further partition based on intense loyalty and language, following the trauma of partition related to faith.
- Some Congress leaders supported redrawing the map of India along linguistic lines, leading to vigorous movements among Marathi and Kannada speakers across various political regimes.

- The most militant protests arose from the large community of Telugu speakers. In October, 1953, Potti Sriramulu, a former Gandhian, died after a fast unto death, which sparked violent protests and ultimately led to the creation of Andhra Pradesh.
- The SRC was formed in response to these movements and officially recognised the principle of linguistic states in 1956.
- Initially, many, including Prime Minister Jawaharlal Nehru, feared that language-based states might lead to further division, but the opposite occurred; linguistic states have helped strengthen Indian unity.
- It has become consistent for people to identify as both Kannadiga and Indian, Bengali and Indian, Tamil and Indian, Gujarati and Indian.

The Challenges of linguistic Diversity

- While linguistic states may sometimes have disputes, these are not as severe as they could have been.
- In 1956, as the SRC redrew India's map along linguistic lines, Ceylon (now Sri Lanka) proclaimed Sinhala as the sole official language despite Tamil protests, leading to significant tensions.
- A left-wing Sinhala MP warned against this chauvinism, stating, 'One language, two nations' and 'Two languages, one nation'.
- The civil war in Sri Lanka, which began in 1983, partly stemmed from the denial of rights to the Tamil minority by the Sinhala majority.
- In 1971, Pakistan was divided because the Punjabi and Urdu speakers in the West did not respect the sentiments of the Bengali speakers in the East.
- The formation of linguistic states in India helped it avoid a similar fate; ignoring language community aspirations could have led to 'One language, fourteen or fifteen nations'.

Constitutional Provisions

- Constitutional provisions define the powers of the States and the Centre, including exclusive responsibilities for either entity and a concurrent list where both can operate.
- The State Legislatures determine the composition of the Rajya Sabha, the upper house of Parliament.
- Various periodic committees and commissions, like the Finance Commission established every ten years, oversee Centre-State relations, particularly in sharing tax revenues. The GST Council includes state members.
- Each Five-Year Plan involves detailed State plans prepared by the State Planning Commissions of each state.

Quick Test 2

1. What are the three major presidencies in India?
2. In which presidency are Marathi, Gujarati, Kannada and Konkani speaking people found?
3. Which states were formed in the year 2000?
4. What divides the power of the states and the centre in India?

5.5 The Nation-State and Religious Issues and Identities

- Issues related to cultural diversity in India primarily stem from religious communities and religion-based identities.
- These issues can be categorised into two groups: the secularism-communalism set and the minority-majority set.
- The secularism-communalism set addresses the state's relationship with religion and the political groups that use religion as their primary identity.
- The minority-majority set deals with how the state treats various religious, ethnic or other communities that differ in numbers or social, economic and political power.

Minority Rights and Nation Building

- Indian nationalism is characterised by an inclusive and democratic vision.
- Inclusivity acknowledges the diversity and plurality of Indian society.
- Democracy aims to eliminate discrimination and exclusion, fostering a just and equitable society.
- Influential figures like Mahatma Gandhi and Rabindranath Tagore have commented on the importance of humanism and the dangers of exclusive nationalism.

Inclusive Nationalism

- To be effective, the principles of inclusive nationalism must be embedded in the Constitution.
- There is a tendency for the dominant group to equate their culture, language or religion with the nation-state.
- A strong and democratic nation requires constitutional provisions to ensure the rights of all groups, particularly minority groups.
- The term 'minority' in sociology goes beyond mere numerical distinction; it often indicates a sense of relative disadvantage.
- Privileged groups, like extremely wealthy individuals, are typically not classified as minorities unless qualified (e.g., 'privileged minority').
- When 'minority' is used without qualification, it usually refers to a relatively small but disadvantaged group.
- A sociological perspective on minorities emphasises group solidarity, a sense of togetherness and belonging.
- Statistical minorities, such as left-handed individuals or those born on 29th February, do not constitute sociological minorities due to the absence of collective identity.
- Anomalous instances can occur where a minority group is disadvantaged in one sense but not in another; for example, religious minorities like Parsis or Sikhs may be economically well-off but culturally disadvantaged due to their small numbers compared to Hindus.
- Religious or cultural minorities require special protection due to the demographic dominance of the majority.
- During the struggle against British colonialism, Indian nationalists recognised the importance of respecting India's diversity.
- The phrase 'unity in diversity' encapsulates the plural and diverse nature of Indian society.
- Discussions on minority and cultural rights have been integral to deliberations within the Indian National Congress and are reflected in the Indian Constitution.
- The Constitution's framers understood that a strong, united nation could only be built when all groups had the freedom to practise their religion and develop their culture and language.
- Dr. B.R. Ambedkar, the chief architect of the Indian Constitution, emphasised this necessity during the Constituent Assembly discussions.

Dr. Bhimrao Ramji Ambedkar (1891-1956)

- In the last three decades, the non-recognition of the rights of different groups within a country has led to significant challenges for national unity.
- A key issue leading to the formation of Bangladesh was the Pakistani state's refusal to recognise the cultural and linguistic rights of the Bengali people.
- The imposition of Sinhalese as a national language significantly contributed to the ethnic conflict in Sri Lanka.
- Forcibly imposing a language or religion on any group in India can weaken national unity, which relies on the recognition of differences.
- Indian nationalism acknowledges this diversity, and the Indian Constitution supports it through various articles.

Constitutional Provisions

- **Article 29**
    - Any section of citizens in India with a distinct language, script or culture has the right to conserve it.
    - No citizen can be denied admission to any educational institution maintained by the state or receiving state funds based solely on religion, race, caste or language.
- **Article 30**
    - All minorities, based on religion or language, have the right to establish and administer educational institutions of their choice.
    - The state cannot discriminate against any educational institution based on the management by a minority, whether religious or linguistic.

Minorities in Nations-States

- Minorities exist in all nation-states, and most have a dominant social group that may be cultural, ethnic, racial or religious.
- There is no nation-state in the world that is composed entirely of a single homogeneous cultural group.
- Even countries previously viewed as homogenous (e.g. Iceland, Sweden or South Korea) have been affected by modern capitalism, colonialism and large-scale migration, resulting in a plurality of groups.
- Today, even the smallest states contain minorities in various forms, whether religious, ethnic, linguistic or racial.

5.6 Relative Size and Distribution of Religious Minorities

- Hindus constitute an overwhelming majority in India, numbering about 966 million, which accounts for 80% of the total population, according to the 2011 Census.
- The Hindu population is approximately four times larger than the combined population of all other minority religions and about six times larger than the largest minority group, the Muslims.
- It is important to note that Hindus are not a homogeneous group; they are divided by caste.
- All major religions in India, including Islam, also have their own internal divisions.

Muslim Population

- Muslims are the largest religious minority in India, numbering 172 million, or 14.2% of the population in 2011.
- They are distributed across the country but constitute a majority in Jammu and Kashmir.
- Significant populations of Muslims are also found in West Bengal, Uttar Pradesh, Kerala, Andhra Pradesh, Karnataka and Rajasthan.

Christian Population

- Christians make up around 2.3% of the population, totaling 27.8 million.
- They are distributed throughout India, with sizeable communities in the North-Eastern and Southern states.
- The three states with Christian majorities are all in the North-East
  (i) Nagaland 88% (ii) Mizoram 87% (iii) Meghalaya 74%
- Significant proportions of Christians are also found in Goa (25%) and Kerala (18.4%).

Sikh Population

- Sikhs constitute 1.7% of the population, numbering 21 million.
- While they are scattered across the country, they are primarily concentrated in Punjab, where they constitute a majority (58%).

Other Religious Groups

- Other small religious groups include
  - Buddhists : 8 million (0.7%)
  - Jains : 4.5 million (0.4%)
  - Other Religions and Persuasions : Under 8 million (0.7%)
- The highest proportion of Buddhists is found in
  - Sikkim : 27%
  - Arunachal Pradesh : 12%
- Among larger states, Maharashtra has the highest share of Buddhists at 6%.
- The highest concentrations of Jains are located in
  - Maharashtra : 1.3%
  - Delhi and Gujarat : Nearly 1% each.

5.7 Communalism, Secularism and the Nation State

Communalism

- Communalism is an aggressive form of patriotism based on religious identity. It is characterised by a belief that one's own religious group is the only legitimate entity, often viewing other groups as inferior or illegitimate.
- The term **'chauvinism'** refers to an attitude where one's own group is seen as superior, leading to the exclusion and condemnation of others. Communalism embodies this attitude, making it a political ideology intertwined with religion.

Politics vs. Religion

- While communalists may be intensely engaged with religion, communalism is primarily a political phenomenon rather than a purely religious one.
- A communalist may not necessarily be devout, and devout believers may not stick to communalist views.
- The defining feature is the political identity tied to religion and an aggressive stance against those with differing identities.
- Communalism asserts that religious identity supersedes all other identities, such as socio-economic status, caste or political beliefs.
- It has been a significant source of tension and violence in India, historically rooted in colonial policies of 'divide and rule.'
- India has a rich tradition of religious pluralism, evident in the peaceful coexistence and syncretism among various faiths, as illustrated by the Bhakti and Sufi movements.
- History offers examples of both conflict and harmony, highlighting the potential for unity in diversity.

Secularism

- Secularism involves the separation of the state from religious institutions. In the Western context, it often refers to the separation of church and state, emerging alongside modernity and scientific rationality.
- In India, secularism encompasses the Western definition but also includes additional dimensions.
- A secular state or individual does not favour any particular religion, promoting equal respect for all religions.
- Secularism stands in contrast to religious chauvinism but does not necessarily imply hostility towards religion itself.
- The Indian secular state recognises public holidays for festivals from all religions, demonstrating its commitment to pluralism.
- Controversies have been created due to the Indian state's dual commitment to secularism and minority protection creates tensions.
- Opponents argue that protecting minorities under secularism can lead to favouritism or appeasement for electoral support.
- Supporters counter that without such protections, secularism risks becoming a tool for imposing majority values on minorities.

Quick Test 3

1. What are the potential dangers of an authoritarian state?
2. What are the primary issues related to cultural diversity in India?
3. What are the challenges and opportunities for minority groups in India?
4. What is casteism?

5.8 State and Civil Society

- The state is a crucial institution for managing cultural diversity in a nation.
- The state operates somewhat independently of the nation and its people.
- The state structure comprises the legislature, bureaucracy, judiciary, armed forces, police and other arms of state.
- With all these components, the state has the potential to become authoritarian.

Authoritarian State

- An authoritarian state is one where people lack a voice, and those in power are not accountable to anyone.
- This type of state opposes a democratic state.
- Authoritarian states often limit or abolish civil liberties, including freedom of speech, freedom of the press, freedom of political activity, the right to protection from wrongful authority and the right to due processes of the law.
- Even outside of authoritarianism, state institutions may become unable or unwilling to respond to the people's needs due to corruption, inefficiency or lack of resources.
- In this context, non-state actors and institutions become important, as they can monitor the state, protest against injustices or supplement state efforts.

Civil Society

- **Civil society**[1] is the non-state and non-market segment of the public domain where individuals voluntarily create institutions and organisations.
- It represents the sphere of active citizenship, where individuals address social issues, influence the state, pursue collective interests, or seek support for various causes.
- Civil society consists of voluntary associations, organisations or institutions formed by groups of citizens.
- Examples of these voluntary organisations include political parties, media institutions, trade unions, NGOs, religious organisations and other collective entities.
- Inclusion in civil society requires that the organisation should not be state-controlled and also not be a purely commercial profit-making organisation.
- Civil society organisations engage in advocacy and lobbying with national and international agencies and actively participate in various movements.
- The issues addressed by civil society range from tribal struggles for land rights, urban governance devolution, campaigns against violence and rehabilitation of those displaced by developmental projects.
- Civil liberties organisations are vital in monitoring the state and ensuring it adheres to the law.
- The media, especially its visual and electronic segments, has also taken a more active role.
- A significant recent initiative is the campaign for the Right to Information, which began with an agitation in rural Rajasthan for the release of information on government funds for village development.
- This campaign grew into a nationwide movement, leading to the government passing a law formally recognising citizens' right to information.
- Such examples highlight the critical importance of civil society in ensuring that the state remains accountable to the nation and its people.

The Right To Information Act

- The Right to Information Act 2005 is a law enacted by the Parliament of India that grants Indians access to government records.
- Under this act, any person can request information from a 'Public authority', which is expected to respond quickly or within thirty days.
- The act mandates that every public authority must computerise their records for wider dissemination and proactively publish certain categories of information, reducing the need for citizens to formally request information.
- The law was passed by Parliament on 15th June, 2005 and came into effect on 13th October, 2005.
- Prior to this act, information disclosure in India was limited by the Official Secrets Act of 1923 and various other special laws, which the RTI Act now overrides.
- The act specifies that citizens have the right to
  - Request any information.
  - Take copies of documents.
  - Inspect documents, works, and records.
    - Take certified samples of materials of work.
    - Obtain information in various formats, including printouts, floppies, tapes and cassettes.

1 **Civil Society** It is the aggregate of non-government organisations and institutions that works for the interests and will of citizens.

Quick Test 4

1. What is the role of the state in managing cultural diversity?
2. What are the potential problems with an authoritarian state?
3. What is civil society?
4. What are some examples of civil society organisations?
5. What are some of the issues that civil society organisations address?
6. What is the importance of civil society in ensuring that the state is accountable to the nation and its people?

NCERT Folder

1. What is meant by cultural diversity? Why is India considered to be a very culturally diverse country?

Ans. The term 'diversity' implies differences rather than inequalities. When we say that India is a nation of great cultural diversity, we mean that there are many different types of social groups and communities living together. Cultural diversity is a concept that believes that the society is made up of many different groups having differences in–language, culture, religion system of beliefs and practices.

Due to following reasons India is considered to be a very culturally diverse country

- India has a population of about 1.21 billion plus people speaking about 1,632 different languages and dialects.
- Twenty Two of these languages have been officially recognised in 8th Schedule of the Constitution.
- In terms of religion, about 80% of the population are Hindus. They are divided by caste and language.
- About 14.2% of the population are Muslims, which makes India the 3rd largest Muslim country after Indonesia and Pakistan.
- The other major religious communities are Christians (2.3%), Sikhs (1.7%), Buddhists (0.7%) and Jains (0.4%).

2. What is community identity and how is it formed?

Ans. Community provides us with the language and the cultural values through which we conceive the world and anchor our self identity.

Formation of Community Identity

Community identity is based on accident of birth and belonging rather than on some form of acquired qualifications or accomplishments. These kinds of identities are called ascriptive i.e. they are determined by birth and individual's choice is not involved. People feel a deep sense of security and satisfaction in belonging to communities.

Expanding and overlapping circles of communities (family, kinship, caste, ethnicity, language, region or religion) give meaning to our world and give us a sense of identity. That is why people often react emotionally or even violently whenever there is a perceived threat to their community identity.

Ascriptive identities and community feeling are universal. Everyone has a motherland, a mother tongue, a family and a faith.

Because of this, it is very hard to deal with the conflicts that involve our communities (whether of nation, language, religion, caste or region) are very hard to deal with. Each side in the conflict thinks of the other-side as a hated enemy and there is a tendency to exaggerate the righteousness of ones own side as well as the immorality of the other side.

3. Why is it difficult to define the nation? How are nation and state related in modern society?

Ans. A nation is a peculiar sort of community that is easy to describe but hard to define. Many specific nations are founded on the basis of common cultural, historical and political institutions like a shared religion, language, ethnicity, history or regional culture which can be described. But it is hard to define the features and characteristics that a nation owns. Nations are communities that have a state of their own.

In modern times, there has been a one-to-one bond or relation between nation and state. It wasn't true of the past that a single state could represent a single nation or every nation must have its own state. For example, Soviet Union explicitly recognised that the people it governed were of different nations.

Also, people constituting a nation may actually be citizens or residents of different states. For example, there are more Jamaicans living outside Jamaica than in Jamaica. Dual citizenship could also be a possibility which allow citizens of a particular state to simultaneously be citizens of another state. For example, Jewish Americans may be citizens of Israel as well as the USA.

Thus, nation is a community that has been able to acquire a state of its own. It is also seen that states are finding it more and more necessary to claim that they represent a nation. A feature of the modern era is the establishment of democracy and nationalism as dominant sources of political legitimacy.

4. Why are states often suspicious of cultural diversity?

Ans. Historically States have tried to establish their political legitimacy through nation-building strategies. They try to secure the loyalty and obedience of their citizens through policies of assimilation or integration.

This is because most states have generally been suspicious of cultural diversity and have tried to reduce or eliminate it.

The states fear that the recognition of varied culturally diverse identities such as language, ethnicity, religion will lead to social fragmentation and prevent the creation of a harmonious society.

Also, apart from the fear of fragmentation, accommodating these differences is politically challenging. Thus, so many states have resorted to either suppressing these identities or ignoring them in the political domain.

5. What is regionalism? What factors is it usually based on?

Ans. Regionalism is a strong feeling of pride or loyalty that people have towards their regions including a desire to govern themselves.

Regionalism in India is based on the following factors

- Regionalism in India is rooted in India's diversity of languages, cultures, tribes and religions.
- It is encouraged by the geographical concentration of these identity markers in particular regions and fuelled by a sense of regional deprivation.
- Indian federalism has been a means of accommodating these regional sentiments. After independence, the Indian state continued with the British-Indian arrangement dividing India into large provinces called presidencies.
- Soon after Independence and the adoption of the Constitution, all these units of the colonial era had to be reorganised into ethno-linguistic states within the Indian union in response to strong popular agitations.
- Language coupled with regional and tribal identity has provided the most powerful instrument for the formation of ethno-national identity in India.

6. In your opinion, has the linguistic reorganisation of states helped or harmed India? **CBSE 2019**

Ans. In my opinion, the linguistic reorganisation has helped in strengthening the unity in India.

Prime Minister Jawaharlal Nehru feared that states based on language might encourage a further sub-division of India. Far from undermining Indian unity, linguistic states have helped strengthen it.

In India, language coupled with regional and tribal identity has provided the most powerful instrument for the formation of ethno-national identity in India. Language ensures better communication and results in more effective administration.

However, this does not mean that all linguistic communities have got statehood. For example, in the creation of three new states in 2000, namely Chhattisgarh, Uttarakhand and Jharkhand, language did not play a prominent role.

7. What is a minority? Why do minorities need protection from the state?

Ans. Minority refers to a small group of people whithin a community or country, differing from the main population in race, religion, language or political belief. Minorities need protection due to following reasons

- Religious or cultural minority groups need special protection because of the demographic dominance of majority. These groups are politically vulnerable. They face the risk that the majority community will capture political power and use the state machinery to their religious or cultural institutions, suppress ultimately forcing them to abandon their identity.
- The protection of minorities requires that they should be given special consideration in a context where the normal working of the political system places them at a disadvantage *vis-a-vis* the majority.
- This leads to the claim of favouritism. But supporters would state that without this protection, secularism can turn into an excuse for imposing majority community's values and norms on minorities.
- Minorities are small in number so their political rights may be overshadowed by the majorities. There can be prejudice and discrimination for the political dominance in favour of the majorities. So minorities may feel neglected.

8. What is communalism?

Ans. Communalism is an aggressive political ideology linked to religion. Communal means something related to a community or collectivity as different from an individual. It is important to emphasise that communalism is about politics and not about religion. There is no necessary relationship between personal faith and communalism.

One of the characteristic features of communalism is its claim that religious identity overrides everything else. Communalism is an important issue in India because it has been a repeated source of tension and violence.

9. What are the different senses in which secularism has been understood in India?

Ans. The different senses in which secularism has been understood in India are as following

- In the Western context, secularism implies separation of church and state. This implies the progressive retreat of religion from public life, as it was converted from a mandatory obligation to a voluntary personal practice.
- The Indian meanings of secular and secularism imply that state does not favour any religion. This implies equal respect for all religions rather than separation or distancing the religion practiced by the majority from the minority.
- Secularisation was related to the arrival of modernity and the rise of science and rationality as alternatives to religious ways of understanding the world. One difficult issue that arises from this is the tension between the Western sense of state maintaining distance from religion and the Indian sense of the state giving equal respect to all religions.

10. What is the relevance of civil society organisations today?

Ans. Civil society is the name given to the broad arena which lies beyond the private domain of the family, but outside the domain of both state and market.

- Civil society is a non-state and non-market part of the public domain in which individuals get together voluntarily to create institutions and organisations.
- It is a sphere of active citizenship, individuals take up social issues, try to influence the state or make demands on it, pursue their collective interests or seek support for a variety of causes.
- It includes political parties, media institutions, trade unions, NGOs, religious organisations and other kinds of collective entities.

The main criteria for inclusion in civil society are that the organisation should not be state controlled and it should not be a purely profit-making organisation. Today, the activists of civil society organisations have a wide range of issues including advocacy and lobbying activity with national and international agencies as well as active participation in various movements.

The issues taken up range from tribal struggles for land rights, devolution of urban governance, campaigns against rape and violence against women, primary education reform, etc. Media has also started to play an important role in the civil society initiatives. Among the most significant recent initiatives, is the campaign for the Right to Information.

Exam Pattern Questions

Objective Type Questions

Multiple Choice Questions (MCQs)

1. Cultural diversity can present tough challenges. Which of the following is not a reason for the same? **CBSE SQP Term I, 2021**

(a) It can arouse intense passions.
(b) It can often mobilise large numbers of people.
(c) Cultural identities are not significant.
(d) Cultural differences are accompanied by economic and social inequalities.

2. Everyone has a motherland, a mother tongue, a family and a faith. This signifies an important feature of community identify, that is **CBSE Term I, 2021**

(a) achieved (b) conditional
(c) localised (d) universal

3. Activities which are determined by the accidents of birth and do not involve any choice on the part of the individuals concerned are known as

(a) Descriptive (b) Subjective
(c) Ascriptive (d) None of these

4. Which of the following factors is not responsible for generating plurality of groups?

(a) Large-scale migration
(b) Modern capitalism
(c) Colonialism
(d) Assimilation and Integration

5. Historically, states have tried to establish and enhance their political legitimacy through nation-building strategies. They sought to secure ... the loyalty and obedience of their citizens through policies of assimilation or integration. Attaining these objectives was not easy, especially in a context of cultural diversity where citizens, in addition to their identifications with their country, might also feel a strong sense of identity with their community – ethnic, religious, linguistic and so on. **CBSE SQP 2023**

Two nation building strategies used were

(a) Assimilation and Integration
(b) Assimilation and Sanskritisation
(c) Integration and Sanskritisation
(d) Westernisation and Sanskritisation

6. To assert a single national identity by attempting to eliminate ethno-national and cultural differences from the public and political arena will be considered as a/an policy. **CBSE 2023**

(a) Assimilationist (b) Dominant group
(c) State (d) Diversity

7. Which of the following is not true for a community conflict? **CBSE SQP 2024**

(a) Communities become reversed mirror images of each other in a community conflict.
(b) People often react emotionally in case of any perceived threat to their community identity.
(c) Community identities provide a sense of security and satisfaction to its members.
(d) Community conflicts can be resolved easily.

8. How many languages are recognised officially in 8th Schedule of Constitution?

(a) Twenty Two (b) Ten
(c) Eleven (d) Fifteen

9. Which policy promote or encourage all citizens to adopt a uniform set of cultural values and norms?

(a) Integrationist (b) Assimilation
(c) Community Identity (d) None of these

10. What criterion is used to define minority in the sociological sense?

(a) Privilege
(b) Only numerical distinction
(c) Solidarity due to experience of disadvantage
(d) Individualism

11. Parsis or Sikhs are examples of anomalous minority groups because of which of the following reasons?

(a) They are religious minorities and economically well-off.
(b) They are not politically vulnerable.
(c) They do not need any special protection because of their demographic dominance.
(d) They do not face any risk from majority community.

12. The cheif architect of the Indian Constitution is **CBSE Diksha**

(a) Pandit Jawaharlal Nehru (b) Dr. BR Ambedkar
(c) Mahatma Gandhi (d) Rajendra Prasad

13. **In everyday language, the word 'communalism' refers to aggressive chauvinism based on religious identity. Chauvinism itself is an attitude that sees one's own group as the only legitimate or worthy group, with other groups being seen – by definition – as inferior, illegitimate and opposed.**

Choose the incorrect statement about communalism from the given code. CBSE SQP Term I, 2021

I. Communalism is about politics not about religion.

II. It cultivates an aggressive political identity.

III. It is a recurrent source of tension and violence.

IV. A communalist is always a devout person.

Codes

(a) I, II and III are false
(b) Only IV is false
(c) Both II and III are false
(d) All are false

14. **When religious identity overrides everything else it leads to** CBSE Term I, 2021

(a) secularism (b) communalism
(c) nation-state (d) diversity

15. **A nation is a peculiar sort of community. Choose the incorrect statement about the nation.** CBSE 2023

(a) Hard to describe
(b) Hard to define
(c) Based on shared religion, language, culture
(d) It is a community of communities

16. **.............. states often limit or abolish civil liberties.** CBSE SQP Term I, 2021

(a) Authoritarian
(b) Democratic
(c) Civil Society
(d) Libertarian

17. **Power whose basis is the threat or application of punishment. Choose from the following.**

(a) Charismatic authority
(b) Traditional authority
(c) Authority
(d) Force

18. **Soviet Union explicitly recognised that the peoples it governed were of different 'nations'; the population of 'non-resident' Jamaicans exceeds that of 'resident' Jamaicans; Jewish Americans may be citizens of Israel as well as the USA; which of the following do the given examples signify?**

(a) Nations are easy to define and hard to describe.
(b) States are difficult to define.
(c) Nations are easy to describe and hard to define.
(d) States cannot be described.

19. **Choose from the following the correct statement regarding 'A Nation'.**

(a) Nation is a community that is easy to define and hard to describe.
(b) Nation is a community that is easy to describe and hard to define.
(c) Nation is a community that is easy to understand and hard to describe.
(d) Nation is a community that has easy approach but is hard to define.

20. **Which of the following statements accurately describes the role of civil society in a democratic state?**

(a) Civil society is only concerned with profit-making activities and does not engage in political or social issues.
(b) Civil society consists of state controlled organisations that have no influence over government policies.
(c) Civil society involves voluntary associations, organisations, and institutions that work to influence the state, protect civil liberties and address social issues.
(d) Civil society only works within the private domain of family and does not interact with public authorities.

21. **Cultural diversity can often be perceived as a source of threat to states because** CBSE SQP 2024

I. states see all forms of community identity as dangerous rivals.

II. control is difficult in case of heterogeneous identities.

III. Suppressing cultural diversity can be very costly in terms of the subdued community.

IV. community identities cannot act as the basis of nation-formation.

Codes

(a) I and IV (b) III and IV
(c) I, II and III (d) I, II, III and IV

22. **Indian people had a brief experience of which rule during the emergency enforced between June 1976 and January 1977?** CBSE Term I, 2021

(a) Democratic (b) Authoritarian rule
(c) Colonial (d) None of these

23. **Which of the following is the major issue that challenges the diversity of India?**

I. Regionalism **II. Communalism**

III. Casteism

Codes

(a) I and II (b) I, II and III
(c) I and III (d) II and III

Assertion-Reason Questions

Direction (Q. Nos. 24-31) Two statement are given in the question below as Assertion (A) and Reason (R). Read the statements and choose the appropriate option.

(a) Both A and R are true and R is the correct explanation of A
(b) Both A and R are true, but R is not the correct explanation of A
(c) A is true, but R is false
(d) A is false, but R is true

24. **Assertion** (A) Cultural diversity can present tough challenges.
Reason (R) Cultural diversity is not linked to economic and social inequalities. **CBSE 2024 C**

25. **Assertion** (A) There is absorption of different tribal groups into caste Hindu society at varying levels of the hierarchy.
Reason (R) Tribal lands were colonised and the forests cut down. **CBSE 2025**

26. **Assertion** (A) In Indian Nationalism, the dominant trend was marked by an inclusive and democratic vision.
Reason (R) It was democratic because it recognised Diversity and Plurality. **CBSE Term I, 2021**

27. **Assertion** (A) Respecting regional sentiments is not just a matter of creating states.
Reason (R) This has to be backed up with an institutional structure that ensures their viability as relatively autonomous units within a larger federal structure. **CBSE 2024**

28. **Assertion** (A) Cultural diversity can present tough challenges.
Reason (R) Cultural diversity is not linked to economic and social inequalities. **CBSE 2024**

29. **Assertion** (A) Respecting regional sentiments is not just a matter of creating states.
Reason (R) This has to be backed up with an institutional structure that ensures their viability as relatively autonomous units within a larger federal structure. **CBSE 2024 C**

30. **Assertion** (A) Diversity emphasises differences rather than inequalities.
Reason (R) Cultural diversity can present tough challenges. **CBSE 2024**

31. **Assertion** (A) The separation of religious and political authority marked a major turning point in the social history of the west.
Reason (R) This separation was related to the process of secularisation or the progressive retreat of religion from public life, as it was converted from a mandatory obligation to a voluntary personal practice. **CBSE 2024**

Case Based Questions

Read the given passages and answer the questions that follow by choosing the correct option.

32. Another set of complications is created by the tension between the Indian state's simultaneous commitment to secularism as well as the protection of minorities. The protection of minorities requires that they be given special consideration in a context where the normal working of the political system places them at a disadvantage vis-à-vis the majority community. But providing such protection immediately invites the accusation of favouritism or 'appeasement' of minorities. Opponents argue that secularism of this sort is only an excuse to favour the minorities in return for their votes or other kinds of support. Supporters argue that without such special protection, secularism can turn into an excuse for imposing the majority community's values and norms on the minorities. **CBSE SQP Term I, 2021**

(i) As per the given passage, which of the following is true for India?
(a) It follows the Western definition of secularism
(b) It has nothing to do with the Western definition of secularism
(c) It uses the Western meaning of secularism and also involves other meanings
(d) Religion is not at all associated with political power

(ii) The complication mentioned in the passage is not due to
(a) difficulty created by the tension between the Western sense of the state maintaining a distance from all religions and the Indian sense of the state giving equal respect to all religions
(b) perceived need to protect the minorities
(c) accusation of favouritism
(d) authoritarian state

(iii) Which of the following does not convey the meaning of secularisation?
(a) Progressive retreat of religion from public life
(b) Rise of science and rationality
(c) Conversion of religion to mandatory obligation as opposed to voluntary practice
(d) Decline in the influence of religion

33. The notion of minority group is widely used in Sociology and is more than a merely numerical distinction– it usually involves some sense of relative disadvantage. Thus privileged minorities such as extremely wealthy people are not referred to as minorities. If they are the term is qualified in some way as in the Phrase Privileged minority. When minority is used without qualification it implies a relatively small but also disadvantaged group. The Sociological sense of minority also implies that the members of the minority forms a collectivity that is they have strong sense of group solidarity a feeling of togetherness.

CBSE Term I, 2021

(i) .... such as extremely wealthy people are not referred to as minorities.

(a) Religious minorities (b) Numerical minorities
(c) Linguistic minorities (d) Privileged minorities

(ii) Statistical minorities are not minorities in the Sociological sense because they do not form a

(a) collectivity (b) identity
(c) group (d) society

(iii) When minority is used without qualification, it generally implies a relatively small but also .... group.

(a) advantaged (b) disadvantaged
(c) privileged (d) diverse

34. Secularism is among the most complex terms in social and political theory. In the western context the main sense of these terms has to do with the separation of church and state. A secular person or state is one that does not favour any particular religion over others. Secularism in this sense is the opposite of religious chauvinism and it need not necessarily imply hostility to religion as such. In terms of the state-religion relationship, this sense of secularism implies equal respect for all religions, rather than separation or distancing. Secularisation in turn was related to the arrival of modernity and the rise of science and rationality as alternatives to religious ways of understanding the world.

(i) Choose the correct option regarding secularism.

I. Secularism is a concept of political theory and does not involve any social aspect.
II. A secular person does not favour any particular religion.
III. Secularism implies equal respect for all religions.

Codes

(a) Only I (b) I and III
(c) II and III (d) None of these

(ii) Choose from the following the main focus of Secularism.

I. Strong religious belief
II. Rationality
III. Rise of science
IV. Modernity

Codes

(a) I and II (b) I, II and III
(c) II, III and IV (d) I, III and IV

35. Language coupled with regional and tribal identity - and not religion - has therefore provided the most powerful instrument for the formation of ethnonational identity in India. However, this does not mean that all linguistic communities have got statehood. For instance, in the creation of three new states in 2000, namely Chhattisgarh, Uttaranchal and Jharkhand, language did not play a prominent role. Rather, a combination of ethnicity based on tribal identity, language, regional deprivation and ecology provided the basis for intense regionalism resulting in statehood. Currently there are 28 States (federal units) and 8 Union territories (centrally administered) within the Indian nation-state.

(i) As per the given passage which of the following is incorrect regarding language diversity.

(a) It is coupled with regional and tribal identity.
(b) It is a powerful instrument for the formation of ethnonational identity in India.
(c) Language played an important role during the division of states in 2000.
(d) Language is one of the factors in regionalism.

(ii) the states that got established during 2000 were?

(a) Uttaranchal, Chhattisgarh and Jammu
(b) Chhattisgarh, Jharkhand and Uttar Pradesh
(c) Maharashtra, Uttaranchal and Jharkhand
(d) Jharkhand, Uttaranchal and Chhattisgarh

(iii) Choose from the following the features of Linguistic Diversity.

I. Tribal identity and regional identity
II. Statehood
III. Symbol of ethnonationalism

Codes

(a) I and II (b) Only III
(c) III and I (d) None of these

36. The socialisation process involves a continuous dialogue, negotiation and even struggle against significant others (those directly involved in our lives) like our parents, family, kin group and our community. Our community provides us the language (our mother tongue) and the cultural values through which we comprehend the world. It also anchors our self-identity.

CBSE 2025

(i) Which of the following statements is incorrect?

(a) We don't have to do anything to be born into a community.
(b) No one has any choice about which family they are born into.
(c) No one has any choice about which country they are born into.
(d) These types of identities are acquired.

(ii) Community conflicts are hard to deal with because
I. each side in the conflict thinks of the other side as a hated enemy.
II. there is a tendency to exaggerate the virtues of one's own side.
III. there is a tendency not to exaggerate the vices of the other side.
IV. in such conflicts, they are constructing matching but reversed mirror images of each other.

Which of the above statements are correct?
Codes
(a) I, III and IV (b) I, II and III
(c) I, II and IV (c) II, III and IV

Answers

1. (c) Cultural identities are not significant.
2. (d) universal
3. (c) Ascriptive
4. (d) Assimilation and Integration
5. (a) Assimilation and Integration
6. (a) Assimilationist
7. (d) Community conflicts can be resolved easily.
8. (a) Twenty Two
9. (b) Assimilation
10. (c) Solidarity due to experience of disadvantage
11. (a) They are religious minorities and economically well-off.
12. (b) Dr. BR Ambedkar
13. (b) Only IV is false
14. (b) communalism
15. (a) Hard to describe
16. (a) Authoritarian
17. (d) Force
18. (c) Nations are easy to describe and hard to define.
19. (b) Nation is a community that is easy to describe and hard to define.
20. (c) Civil society involves voluntary associations, organisations and institutions that work to influence the state, protect civil liberties and address social issues.
21. (c) I, II and III
22. (b) Authoritarian rule
23. (b) I, II and III
24. (c) A is true, but R is false
25. (b) Both A and R are true, but R is not the correct explanation of A
26. (a) Both A and R are true and R is the correct explanation of A
27. (a) Both A and R are true and R is the correct explanation of A
28. (c) A is true, but R is false
29. (a) Both A and R are true and R is the correct explanation of A
30. (b) Both A and R are true, but R is not the correct explanation of A
31. (a) Both A and R are true and R is the correct explanation of A
32. (i) (c) It uses the Western meaning of secularism and also involves other meanings
(ii) (d) authoritarian state
(iii) (c) Conversion of religion to mandatory obligation as opposed to voluntary practice
33. (i) (d) Privileged minorities
(ii) (a) collectivity
(iii) (b) disadvantaged
34. (i) (c) II and III
(ii) (c) II, III and IV
35. (i) (c) Language played an important role during the division of states in 2000.
(ii) (d) Jharkhand, Uttaranchal and Chhattisgarh
(iii) (a) I and II
36. (i) (d) These types of identities are acquired.
(ii) (c) I, II and IV

Subjective Questions

Very Short Answer Type Questions

1. "Every human being needs a sense of stable identity to operate in this world. Questions like — Who am I? How am I different from others? How do others understand and comprehend me? What goals and aspirations should I have? – constantly crop up in our life right from childhood."

How are these questions answered? CBSE SQP 2023

Ans. These questions will be answered depending on the nature of our socialisation.

Socialisation is the process of continuous dialogue, negotiation and even struggle against such as set societal norms, values and institutions.

Socialisation builds our social understanding and build our relationship with the rest of the world. We view the world on the basis of the values we have grown up practicing or learning.

2. What are the two significant features of 'ascriptive' identity?

Ans. Two significant features of ascriptive identity are as follows

(i) They are determined by the accidents of birth and do not involve any choice on the part of the individuals concerned.

(ii) They are universal and applicable to most of the cases.

3. What do you understand by ascriptive identities? CBSE 2019

Ans. Community identity is based on birth and 'belonging' rather than on some form of acquired qualifications or 'accomplishment'. It is what we 'are' rather than what we have 'become'. We don't have to do anything to be born into community. No one has any choice about which family or community or country they are born into. These kinds of identities are called ascriptive identities.

4. Write any two features of community identity. CBSE 2024

Ans. The two features of community identity are as follows

(i) **Ascription** Community identities are often assigned at birth based on factors like religion, ethnicity, or region, making them difficult to change or reject.

(ii) **Collective Recognition** These identities are recognised and affirmed by both the individuals within the community and others outside it, ensuring belonging.

5. What policies should be adopted in a multicultural nation to build a feeling of unity in diversity?

Ans. The policies that should be adopted are

- Enduring democracies can be established in politics that are multicultural.
- Explicit efforts are required to end the cultural exclusion of diverse groups and build multiple and complementary identities.

6. What is a nation-state?

Ans. A nation-state is a type of state that reflects both the political entity of a state and the cultural entity of a nation.

7. Why India is not a full-fledged integrationist nation?

Ans. India is not an integrationist nation because the Constitution of India declares the state to be a secular state, but religion, language and other such factors are not removed from public sphere.

8. What is the aim of the policy that promotes assimilation.

Ans. The policies that promote assimilation are aimed at persuading, encouraging of forcing all citizens to adopt a uniform set of cultural values and norms. These values and norms are usually entirely or largely those of the dominant social group.

9. In terms of the nation-states relationship with community identities, the Indian case fits neither the assimilationist nor the integrationist model. What do policies of assimilation aim at? CBSE 2024 C

Ans. Assimilation policies aim to merge different cultural or ethnic groups into a single, dominant national culture. This often involves encouraging minority groups to adopt the customs, language, and values of the majority, eliminating distinct group identities in favor of uniformity.

10. What is the difference between assimilationist and integrationist policies? CBSE SQP 2023

Ans. **Assimilationist Policies** Policies that promote assimilation are aimed at persuading, encouraging or forcing all citizens to adopt a uniform set of cultural values and norms. These values and norms are largely those of the dominant social group. Other, non-dominant or sub-ordinate groups in society are expected or required to give up their own cultural values and adopt the prescribed one.

Integrationist Policies Policies promoting integration are different in style, but not in overall objective, they insist that the public culture be restricted to a common national pattern, while all 'non-national' cultures are to be relegated to the private sphere. In this case too, there is the danger of the dominant group's culture being treated as 'national' culture.

11. What are the most powerful instruments for the formation of ethno-national identity?

Ans. Language coupled with regional and tribal identity has provided the most powerful instrument for the formation of ethno-national identity.

12. State some features of an authoritarian state.

Ans. The features of an authoritarian state are as follows

- It is a state in which people have no voice and those in power are not accountable to anyone.
- It often limits or abolishes civil liberties like freedom of speech, freedom of press, freedom of political activity, etc.

13. Membership in our families or religious or regional communities is without preconditions, and yet it is total. In fact, most ascriptive identities are very hard to shake off; even if we choose to disown them, others may continue to identify us by those very markers of belonging.

Based on the above passage, answer the following question.

Why are community identities hard to shake off? **CBSE 2024 C**

Ans. Community identities are hard to shake off because they are deeply ingrained and often ascriptive, meaning they are assigned without our choice. Even if we try to disown them, others continue to see us through these markers of belonging, making them hard to escape.

14. State how did the people of India assert their support for a secular Constitution and state?

Ans. Ever since independence, the people of India, through their direct participation and election verdicts have repeatedly asserted their support for a secular Constitution and state.

15. Cite one of the most important characteristic features of a modern era state.

Ans. One of the most important characteristic features of a modern era state is the establishment of democracy and nationalism as dominant sources of political legitimacy.

16. State is indeed a very crucial institution when it comes to the management of cultural diversity in a nation. How? **CBSE SQP 2023**

Ans. State plays a very crucial role in the management of cultural diversity in the following ways

(i) Collective efforts led by the state need to be made in order to end cultural exclusion of diverse groups.

(ii) State must be able to build multiple and complementary identities.

(iii) Responsive policies provide a framework and structure to build a nation based on a diversity and unity.

17. States are often doubtful of cultural diversity. State two reasons for the given statement. **CBSE 2023**

Ans. States are often doubtful of cultural diversity due to the following reasons

(i) **Political Fragmentation** When a state comprises diverse ethnic, linguistic or cultural groups, there may be challenges in creating a sense of nation identity or unity. This can create tensions and conflicts between different groups within the state.

(ii) **Fear of Separatism** In some cases, states may be doubtful of cultural diversity due to the fear that certain groups may demand greater autonomy or even independence, leading to the breakup of the state.

18. 'The desire for political unity usually expresses itself as the aspiration to form a state. Describe the term 'state'.

Ans. State refers to an abstract entity consisting of a set of politico-legal institutions claiming control over a particular territory and the people living in it.
Max Weber stated that a state is a body that successfully claims a monopoly of legitimate force in a particular territory.

19. State why cultural diversity can present tough challenges?

Ans. Cultural diversity may lead to intense passions and this can often lead to mobilisation of large number of people and sometimes this diversity is accompanied by economic and social inequalities.

20. "In Indian nationalism, the dominant trend was marked by an inclusive and a democratic vision." What do you understand by the words inclusive and democrative in this statement?

Ans. In this statement, the word inclusive is addressed because Indian nationalism recognised diversity and plurality.

The word democratic is addressed because Indian nationalism sought to do away with discrimination and exclusion and bring forth a just and equitable society.

21. People constituting a nation may actually be citizens or residents of different states. **CBSE SQP 2024**

Ans. People in a nation may live in different states or regions, but they share a common identity and legal status as citizens. Despite geographical differences, they are united by nationality, cultural ties, and shared values that define their nation.

22. What is regionalism in the Indian context. **CBSE 2024**

Ans. In the Indian context, regionalism refers to the loyalty or allegiance to a particular region, often based on shared language, culture, or economic interests. It can lead to demands for political autonomy or greater regional rights, sometimes causing tension with national unity.

23. Identify the religious diversity found in India. **CBSE 2019**

Ans. The religious diversity found in India is given below

- Hindus
- Muslims
- Christians
- Sikhs
- Buddhists
- Jains

24. "Language along with regional and tribal identity has been a powerful force for the formation of ethno. national identity in India". What inference can be drawn from the given statement?

Ans. Language plays a very important role in maintaining national unity. A common medium of communication encourages interaction among the masses. Through a common language, people of different regions can share their views effectively, hence forth removing regionalism for votes.

25. What rights does the Right to Information give to citizens?

Ans. The Right to Information Act specifies that citizens have a right to

- Request any information.
- Take copies of documents.
- Inspect documents, works and record.
- Take certified samples of materials of work.

26. Who are privileged minorities?

Ans. Privileged minorities are a special group of minorities for whom some special provisions have been made or a special qualification is attached to a specific minority group.

27. State any two constitutional provisions meant to protect minority rights.

Ans. The two constitutional provisions meant to protect minority rights are as following

(i) Any section of the citizens residing in the territory of Indian or any part there of having a distinct language, script or culture of its own shall have the right to conserve the same.

(ii) No citizen shall be denied admission into any educational institution maintained by the state or received out of state funds on grounds of religion, race, caste or language.

28. How are 'privileged' minorities politically vulnerable?

Or **How are minorities politically vulnerable?** **CBSE 2019**

Ans. In democratic politics, it is possible to convert a numerical majority into political power through elections due to which privileged minorities, regardless of their social and economic position are politically vulnerable.

29. Give an example of an anomalous instance with regard to minority groups. **CBSE SQP 2024**

Ans. An example of an anomalous instance with regard to minority groups is the case of the Indian Muslim community. Despite being a minority, they have often been subject to discrimination and exclusion, which contradicts the ideal of equal treatment for all citizens.

30. Give reasons why minorities politically vulnerable?

Ans. Minorities are vulnerable in following ways

- It is always possible to convert a numerical majority into political power through elections.
- Religious or cultural minorities regardless of their economic or social position – are politically vulnerable.
- Forced to abandon their distinctive identity.

31. What is meant by secularisation?

Ans. Secularisation is the progressive retreat of religion from public life when it is converted from a mandatory obligation to a voluntary personal practice. It was related to the arrival of modernity and the rise of science and rationality as alternatives to religious ways of understanding the world.

32. Secularism in this sense is the opposite of religious chauvinism and it need not necessarily imply hostility to religion as such. Secularism implies equal respect for all religions, rather than separation or distancing.

How is Indian context of secularism different from the Western form of secularism?

Ans. In the Western context the main sense of these terms has to do with the separation of church and state. The separation of religious and political authority marked a major turning point in the social history of the West. This separation was related to the process of 'secularisation' or the progressive retreat of religion from public life, as it was converted from a mandatory obligation to a voluntary personal practice.

33. In what way communalism is different from communal?

Ans. Communalism means aggressive chauvinism based on religious identity whereas communal means something related to community or collectivity as different from an individual.

34. What are the main criteria for inclusion in civil society?

Ans. The main criteria for inclusion in civil society is that the organisation should not be state controlled and it should not be a purely profit-making entity.

Short Answer Type Questions

1. What are community identities? Why are they important?

Ans. Community identity is based on birth and belonging rather than on some form of acquired qualifications of accomplishment. It is what we are rather than what we have become.

Our community provides us the language (our mother tongue) and the cultural values through which we comprehend the world.

It also secures our self-identity. It is because of this accidental, unconditional and yet almost inescapable belonging that we can often be so emotionally attached to our community identity. Expanding and overlapping circles of community ties (family, kinship, caste, ethnicity, language, region or religion) give meaning to our world and give us a sense of identity of who we are. That is why people often react emotionally or even violently whenever there is a perceived threat to their community identity.

A scriptive identities and community feeling are universal. Everyone has a motherland, a mother tongue, a family and a faith and we are all equally committed and loyal to our respective identities.

2. In terms of the nation-states relationship with community identities, the Indian case fits neither the assimilationist nor the integrationist model. What do policies of assimilation aim at? **CBSE 2024**

Ans. Policies of assimilation aim to blend or merge diverse cultural and ethnic groups into a single, unified national identity. In this approach, people from different backgrounds are encouraged to adopt the language, customs, and values of the dominant group, often reducing the visibility of their own unique identities. The goal is to create a uniform culture and minimise differences within the population, ultimately promoting a single, cohesive national identity over individual community identities.

3. "An alternative to the nation-state, then, is the 'state nation', where various 'nations'- be they ethnic, religious, linguistic or indigenous identities- can co-exist peacefully and cooperatively in a single state polity." What factors are required to build enduring state-nations? **CBSE SQP 2024**

Ans. To build enduring state-nations, it is important to have policies that recognise and respect cultural diversity. These policies should encourage the coexistence of different ethnic, religious, linguistic, and indigenous groups within the same country. Efforts must be made to ensure that no group feels excluded, and citizens should be able to identify with both their country and their cultural identity. Creating trust in common institutions, supporting democratic values, and resolving conflicts peacefully are also essential for long-term stability and social harmony in multicultural societies.

4. Could the RTI be a means of forcing the state to respond to the people of India? Elaborate.

Ans. Certainly, the Right to Information (RTI) Act can force the state to respond to the people of India. The RTI Act was passed by Parliament on 15th June, 2005. This act had given Indians access to government records. Under the terms of the RTI Act, any person may request information from 'a public authority' (a body of goverment or instrumentality of state) which is expected to reply as soon as possible or within 30 days. The RTI Act also requires the public authority or authorities to computerise the records for wider dissemination and to publish certain categories of information so that the citizens of India require minimum resourse to request for information formally.

The Right to Information Act specifies that citizens have right to

- Request any information.
- Take copies of documents.
- Inspect documents, works and records.
- Take certified samples of materials of work.

5. Why does cultural diversity present tough challenges?

Or **"Cultural Diversity can present tough challenges." Support the statement with suitable examples.** **CBSE 2025**

Ans. The term diversity emphasises on differences rather than inequalities which means that there are many different types of social groups and communities. These communities are defined by cultural markers such as language, religion, sect, race or caste. When these diverse communities are part of a larger entity like a nation, then difficulties may be created by competition or conflict between them. These difficulties arise from the fact that cultural identities are very powerful, as they can arouse intense passions and are often able to mobilise large numbers of people. This is why, cultural diversity can present tough challenges.

6. "Encouraging cultural diversity is good policy from the practical and principled point of view." Justify the statement using India's case as a nation-state.

Ans. Nations are communities that have a state of their own, that is why the two are joined to form the term nation-state. The Indian nation-state is socially and culturally one of the most diverse countries of the world. This diverse population speak different languages.

In terms of religion, the population is diverse with Hindu, Muslim, Sikh, Christian, etc. The Constitution declares the state to be a secular state, but religion, language and other such factors are not removed from the public sphere.

In fact, these communities are explicitly recognised by the state. By international standards, very strong constitutional protection is offered to minority religion, the tribal population, Scheduled Caste population linguistic minorities, etc. Therefore, comparative surveys of long-standing democracies show that India has been very cohesive, despite its diversity.

7. Religious and cultural minorities need special protection because of demographic dominance of the majority. There is a wide distribution of religious minorities in India. Elaborate this distribution.

Ans. Following are the distribution of religions minorities in India

- Hindus constitute a major part in India, they are about 966 million and account for about 80% of the total population according to 2011 Census.
- Second majority is of Muslims, they are numbered 172 million and are (14.2%) of the population in 2011.
- Majority of Muslims are constituted in Jammu and Kashmir, West Bengal, Uttar Pradesh, Andhra Pradesh.
- Christian constitute around (2.3%) of the population. Three major Christian states are Nagaland, Mizoram and Meghalaya.
- Sikhs constitute (1.7%) of the population, there are other small religious also like–Buddhism (0.7%) and Jains (0.4%).

8. Sociologists use the term 'Social Stratification' to refer to a system by which categories of people in a society are ranked in a hierarchy. How does Social Stratification persist over generations? **CBSE 2025**

Ans. Social stratification continues over generations due to structural and cultural factors that maintain inequalities in wealth, power and social status.

(i) **Inheritance of Wealth and Property** Economic disparities persist because wealth and assets are passed down within families, ensuring that privileged groups remain dominant.

(ii) **Access to Education** Children from higher social classes receive better educational opportunities, leading to better jobs and reinforcing class divisions.

(iii) **Socialisation and Cultural Norms** Families teach social values that sustain stratification, such as caste identity, racial superiority or class consciousness.

(iv) **Occupational Continuity** Professions often run in families, as access to certain jobs is influenced by family networks and social capital.

(v) **Discriminatory Practices** Social barriers like caste discrimination, racial segregation, and gender bias prevent mobility, which keeps social stratification intact across generations.

9. Regionalism in India is believed to be a negative facts. Explain why?

Ans. Regionalism is when people of a particular region believe that their region is neglected by the government. Lack of balanced regional growth gives rise to regionalism.

Regionalism creates problems in India as it leads to protests and agitations by the people of the underdeveloped regions. People feel that they are discriminated and greatly neglected by the State or Central Government.

This disrupts the normal peace and unity of the country and often results in mass-movements. The creation of Jharkhand and Uttarakhand are due to the imbalances of regional development. Thus regionalism results in the disintegration of a region or an area.

10. How regionalism could be reduced?

Ans. Regionalism could be reduced with the help of following initiatives

- Government should give equal grants to all the regions, states and adequate help according to demands of that region.
- Government should not give preference to any particular region over the other regions to prevent the sense of inferiority among the people of other regions.
- Literacy rate of the country should be increased and people should be motivated to get higher education so that the educated people put country before the region.
- People of the country should be provided with more and more opportunities of employment so that people hardly care about regionalism.

11. Explain how secularism is understood in the Indian and Western contexts.

Ans. **Secularism in Indian Context** In the Indian context, secularism or the word secular refers to a state that does not favour the religious beliefs and practices of any particular religion or sect over others. In everyday language, secular is considered opposite of communal. It implies equal respect of all religions rather than separation or distancing. For example, the secular Indian state declares public holidays to mark the festivals of all religions.

Secularism in Western Context It is the progressive retreat of religion from public life. It is a result of arrival of modernity and the rise of reasons and rational thinking. Thus, it promotes a new way of understanding. Presently secularism in India also includes the Western understanding of secularism also.

12. What is meant by communalism in the Indian context? Why has it been a recurrent source of tension and violence?

Ans. The word communalism in Indian context refers to aggressive chauvinism based on religious identity. Chauvinism is an attitude that sees one's group as the only legitimate or worthy group, with other groups being seen as inferior, illegitimate and opposed.

Communalism is an aggressive political ideology linked to religion. It is important to emphasise that communalism is about politics, not about religion. Communalists cultivate an aggressive political identity linked to religion, and are prepared to condemn or attack everyone who does not share their identity.

Communalism is an especially important issue in India because it has been a recurrent source of tension and violence. During communal riots, people become faceless members of their respective communities. They are willing to kill, rape, and loot members of other communities in order to redeem their pride. A commonly cited justification is to avenge the deaths or dishonour suffered by their co-religionists elsewhere or even in the distant past. No region has been wholly exempt from communal violence of one kind or another.

Long Answer Type Questions

1. How can India be made a state nation instead of a nation-state? Discuss.

Ans. An examination of the events that took place after independence makes it clear that India had to choose state nation instead of nation-state. The British had left behind them, three giant presidencies including other small presidencies, a number of princely states and a number of provincial states. These were all scattered and disorganised on the basis of ascriptive identities i.e. language, caste, ethinicity, culture, religion, etc.

Multilingual Presidencies

Mumbai and Madras presidencies were multi-lingual states *viz.* Marathi, Gujarati, Kannada and Konkani speaking people in Mumbai Presidency while Tamil, Telugu, Kanada and Malayalam speaking people in Madras Presidency.

These provinces and princely states had soon raised their claims 'for their reorganisation on linguistic basis. In these circumstances, Government of India had to constitute State Reorganisation Commission and accepted its report on their reorganisation. Thus, India had to establish its federal government in which states were given the status of federal units.

Recent case studies and analysis demonstrate that enduring democracies can be established that are multicultural. Such democracies can be established only when cultural exclusion of diverse groups is ended and multiple and complementary identities are built.

The UNDP Human Development Report, 2004 states that modern India is facing a grave challenge to its constitutional commitment to multiple and complementary identities.

This report says that Hindus are willing to impose their single identity on other people.

It says that flaws have been found in nation-states and state-nation can only cure this situation. The report says national unity and cultural diversity can be maintained by opting for this assumption.

2. A nation is a peculiar sort of community that is easy to describe but hard to define. Why? **CBSE 2024**

Ans. A nation is a unique kind of community that is easy to describe but difficult to define because it is based on complex and varied factors. While describing a nation, we can mention things like shared culture, history, language, and values. These are common characteristics that most people agree upon when talking about a nation. However, defining a nation is much harder because these factors do not apply in the same way to every group of people.

A nation can exist without having clear boundaries, a common language, or even a shared religion. For example, some nations may have multiple languages and cultures within their boundaries. Others may have people from different backgrounds and beliefs but still feel a strong sense of unity. This diversity makes it hard to define a nation in a simple way.

The concept of a nation goes beyond just physical or cultural characteristics. It includes emotional bonds, shared experiences, and a sense of belonging. This emotional connection can differ from person to person, making it difficult to create one single definition that fits every nation. Thus, while we can describe the idea of a nation easily, its exact definition varies depending on the context and individual perspectives.

3. Read the given passage and answer the questions that follow.

Historically, states have tried to establish and enhance their political legitimacy through nation-building strategies. They sought to secure ... the loyalty and obedience of their citizens through policies of assimilation or integration. Attaining these objectives was not easy, especially in a context of cultural diversity where citizens, in addition to their identifications with their country, might also feel a strong sense of identity with their community – ethnic, religious, linguistic and so on. Most states feared that the recognition of such difference would lead to social fragmentation and prevent the creation of a harmonious society. In short, such identity politics was considered a threat to state unity. In addition, accommodating these differences is politically challenging, so many states have resorted to either suppressing these diverse identities or ignoring them on the political domain.

(a) **In your opinion, which type of policy is best in this regard-those based on assimilation, on integration or other kinds? Give reasons for your answer.**

(b) **Why do most states fear cultural diversity?**

Ans. (a) Assimilation policies, which often include outright repression of racial, religious, or linguistic identities, aim to reduce cultural disparities between communities. Integration policies aim to establish a common national identity by seeking to eradicate ethno-national and cultural distinctions from the public and political spheres while enabling them to exist in the private sphere. Both sets of policies are based on the assumption of a single national identity.

The best policy in this regard should be based on assimilation and integration as they sought to secure the loyalty and obedience of their citizens and can use the fissiparous elements.

(b) Most states fear cultural diversity because citizens do not only have their identification with their country but also feel a strong sense of identity with there community, ethnic, religious, linguistic and so on. The recognition of such differences would lead to social fragmentation and prevent the creation of a harmonious society.

4. Explain the reasons of unity in diversity in Indian society.

Ans. The reasons of unity in diversity in Indian society are as following

Geographical Factors India is a country full of diversities from the geographical point of view. World's highest mountains, Himalayas are in Northern India. Rivers like Sindhu, Ganga, Yamuna and Brahmaputra form the largest plain of India. India has certain places where a lot of rain falls and has the driest area as well i.e. Thar Desert. It has both fertile as well as barren land.

Social Factors In social diversity, we can see different forms of marriage, which is one of the basic institutions of the society. Some castes have the custom of fraternal polyandry and some groups like Muslims have the custom of polygamy. Joint family and nuclear family express social diversity.

Religious Factors People following different religions such as Hinduism, Islam, Buddhism, Jainism, Sikhism, etc. have been living in India since the ages. There are 3000 castes in Hindus and 94 castes as Muslims. In the same way, Christians are divided into Protestants and Catholics, Buddhists in Hinayanas and Mahayanas and Jains are divided into Digambars and Shwetambars.

Linguistic Factors India is a multilingual society where 22 languages were sanctioned by the Indian Constitution. Hindi became the national language and English was sanctioned as the official language. Most of the Indians speak, understand, write and read Hindi language. South Indian people generally use Dravidian language and North Indian people use Indo-Aryan language.

5. Membership in our families or religious or regional communities is without preconditions, and yet it is total. In fact, most ascriptive identities are very hard to shake off; even if we choose to disown them, others may continue to identify us by those very markers of belonging. Based on the above passage, answer the following question. **CBSE 2024**

Why are community identities hard to shake off?

Ans. Community identities are hard to shake off because they are based on factors like birth, family, language, region, or religion, which are deeply rooted and often inescapable aspects of our lives.

These ascriptive identities are assigned at birth and do not require any qualifications or accomplishments. Even if individuals try to disown or separate from these identities, society continues to recognise and associate them with these markers of belonging.

Additionally, there is a strong emotional attachment to these identities because they provide a sense of security, meaning and belonging.

The unconditional and accidental nature of these identities often leads people to react emotionally, sometimes even strongly, when they feel their community identity is under threat. This universal nature of community identities reinforces the bond, making them challenging to remove or ignore.

6. Civil Society makes the state accountable to the Nation and its people. Explain with reference to the RTI Act.

***Or* The Civil Society has been instrumental in taking many significant initiatives, the most recent being the campaign for the Right to Information. Discuss the initiative and its source.** CBSE 2025

Ans. Civil society is the non-state and non-market part of the public domain in which individuals get together voluntarily to create institutions and organisations. It is the sphere of active citizenship where, individuals take up social issues, try to influence the state or make demands on it, pursue their collective interests or seek support for a variety of causes.

It consists of voluntary associations, organisations or institutions formed by groups of citizen. It includes political parties, media institutions, trade unions, non-governmental organisations, religious organisations, etc. The main criteria for inculsion in civil society are that organisation should not be state. Controlled and it should not be a purely commercial profit-making entity.

The Right to Information Act, 2005 is a law enacted by the Parliament of India gives Indians an access to Government records. Under the terms of the Act, any person may request information from a public authority, is expected to reply expeditiously or within thirty days.

The Act also requires every public authority to computerise their records for wide dissemination and to proactively publish certain categories of information so that the citizens need minimum recourse to request for information formally minimum recourse to request for information formally.

This law was passed by Parliament on 15th June, 2005. The Act specifies that citizens have a right to

- Request any information
- Take copies of documents
- Inspect documents, works and records
- Take certified samples of materials of work
- Obtain information in form of printouts, diskettes, floppies, tapes, video cassettes or in any other electronic mode or through printouts.
- Civil liberties organisations have been keeping a watch on the state and forcing it to obey the law.

7. Discuss the role of civil society in the state. CBSE 2024

Ans. Civil society plays a crucial role in shaping the state and ensuring a balanced, fair society. It consists of organisations and groups that work outside the government, such as Non-Governmental Organisations (NGOs), community groups, and social movements. These organisations help create awareness on important issues, support social welfare and promote human rights. They act as a bridge between the government and the people, ensuring that the needs and concerns of the public are heard.

By holding the government accountable, civil society ensures transparency and helps prevent corruption. It provides a platform for citizens to express their opinions and demand better policies. Civil society groups are also key in raising awareness on various issues like education, health, the environment and justice, which may be overlooked by the state.

Furthermore, civil society can influence government decisions by mobilising public opinion and pushing for change through peaceful protests, petitions, or lobbying efforts. These actions ensure that the government remains responsive to the needs of its people. In this way, civil society is essential for promoting democracy, protecting human rights and ensuring that the state serves the interests of its citizens.

SELF ASSESSMENT TEST

Objective Types Questions

1. Which of the following is true about state?

(a) State is an abstract entity.

(b) State consists of a set of political-legal institutions.

(c) State claims a control over the particular territory and the people living in.

(d) All of the above

2. The old Bombay state was a multilingual state of which languages?

(a) Marathi and Gujarati (b) Kannada and Konkani

(c) Telugu and Malyalam (d) Both (a) and (b)

3. Community Identity is a significant concept in understanding individual belonging because

I. it is based on ascription, where membership is determined by birth and not personal achievement.

II. people feel a strong emotional attachment to their community, often regardless of personal choice.

III. cultural diversity within communities is often suppressed by states to maintain a singular national identity.

IV. communities, unlike professions, do not require any demonstrated skill or competence to be part of them.

Codes

(a) I and IV (b) II and III (c) I, III and IV (d) II, III and IV

4. Which of the following statements is true about nations and states?

(a) Nations and states are always the same entity.

(b) A nation-state always represents a single cultural identity.

(c) Nations may exist without having a state of their own.

(d) States do not have any claim over legitimate force in their territories.

5. Which of the following best describes the term 'state-nation'?

I. A political entity where various cultural identities coexist peacefully.

II. A state that promotes a singular cultural identity.

III. A nation that lacks a centralised state.

IV. A model that supports the erasure of cultural differences.

Codes

(a) I and II (b) I and III (c) II and IV (d) I and IV

6. **Assertion** (A) India has a diverse cultural identity that influences its national policies.

Reason (R) The Indian Constitution recognises multiple identities and accommodates them in governance.

(a) Both A and R are true and R is the correct explanation of A

(b) Both A and R are true, but R is not the correct explanation of A

(c) A is true, but R is false

(d) A is false, but R is true

7. Which of the following statements accurately reflects India's approach to regionalism?

I. Regionalism is solely based on linguistic identity.

II. Indian federalism accommodates regional sentiments.

III. Regional deprivation has no influence on regionalism.

IV. Regional identities can lead to a desire for self-governance.

Codes

(a) I and II (b) II and IV (c) I and III (d) III and IV

8. **Assertion** (A) The States Reorganisation Commission (SRC) aimed to reorganise Indian states based on linguistic lines.

Reason (R) The SRC's implementation strengthened Indian unity by promoting cultural homogenisation.

(a) Both A and R are true and R is the correct explanation of A

(b) Both A and R are true, but R is not the correct explanation of A

(c) A is true, but R is false

(d) A is false, but R is true

Case Based Questions

1. The Indian nation-state is socially and culturally one of the most diverse countries of the world. It has a population of about 1.21 billion people, according to Census of India 2011, currently the second largest– and soon to become the largest–national population in the world. These billion-plus people speak about 1,632 different languages and dialects. As many as twenty two of these languages have been officially recognised and placed under the 8th Schedule of the Constitution, thus guaranteeing their legal status. In terms of religion, about 80% of the population are Hindus, who in turn are regionally specific, plural in beliefs and practices and divided by castes and languages.

(i) Which of the following statements is true about the religious diversity in India?

(a) Hinduism is followed by over 90% of the population in India.

(b) India is the second-largest Muslim country in the world.

(c) Christianity makes up the largest religious group in India.

(d) Sikhism is the second-largest religion in India.

(ii) What does the diversity in India's population suggest about its social and cultural structure?

(a) It is a homogenous society with similar cultural practices.

(b) It is one of the most socially and culturally diverse nations in the world.

(c) The population speaks only a few major languages.

(d) Religion is uniformly followed across the country.

Very Short Answer Type Questions

1. In everyday language, the word 'communalism' refers to aggressive chauvinism based on religious identity. Communalism is an aggressive political ideology linked to religion and is a peculiarly South Asian concept, differing from the neutral English meaning of 'communal'. The Indian Constitution also ensures rights for minorities to conserve their distinct culture and establish educational institutions.

What inference can you draw from this statement?

2. The Right to Information Act, passed in 2005, grants citizens access to government records, ensuring transparency and accountability. It overrides previous laws that restricted information access, such as the Official Secrets Act of 1923.

What impact did the Right to Information Act have on government transparency, and why was it a significant step towards ensuring accountability in India?

3. Civil society in India plays a crucial role in holding the state accountable by organising movements and advocating for social issues. Civil society includes non-governmental organisations, media, and political parties, among others. How does civil society contribute to ensuring that the state remains accountable to its people?

4. While colonial rule exacerbated communal tensions in India through its divide-and-rule policies, pre-colonial conflicts also existed. Despite this, India has a long tradition of religious pluralism and syncretism, seen in movements like Bhakti and Sufism.

In what ways does India's history of religious pluralism challenge the notion of communalism?

Short Answer Type Questions

1. Mention the differences between policy of assimilation and policy of integration.

2. India does not have a full-fledged integrationist national unity. Explain.

3. Secularism is a complex term, with meanings varying across cultures. In the Western context, it refers to the separation of religion and state, while in India, secularism means equal respect for all religions without favoring any particular one. However, this concept has led to debates over the protection of minorities and accusations of 'appeasement'.

Why is the concept of secularism in India considered complex, especially in the context of protecting minorities and avoiding accusations of favouritism?

4. Communalism is an aggressive political ideology linked to religion, often marked by an attitude of chauvinism, where one's own religious group is seen as superior to others. This has led to significant tensions and violence in India, despite a rich history of religious pluralism and peaceful coexistence.

Why has communalism been a recurrent source of tension and violence in India?

Long Answer Type Questions

1. The notion of minority groups is widely used in sociology and is more than a merely numerical distinction - it usually involves some sense of relative disadvantage. Thus, privileged minorities such as extremely wealthy people are not usually referred to as minorities; if they are, the term is qualified in some way, as in the phrase 'privileged minority'. When minority is used without qualification, it generally implies a relatively small but also disadvantaged group. The sociological sense of minority also implies that the members of the minority form a collectivity - that is, they have a strong sense of group solidarity, a feeling of togetherness and belonging.

(a) What does the sociological concept of a minority group involve, beyond just numerical distinction?

(b) Why are groups like left handed people or those born on 29th February not considered minorities in the sociological sense?

2. What is minority group? Why do minorites need protection from the state?

3. What is regionalism? Discuss the main causes of regionalism.

4. Define cultural diversity. Why are states suspicious of cultural diversity?

5. State the background of emergence of RTI. Mention the provisions of RTI Act.

PART B
CHANGE AND DEVELOPMENT IN INDIAN SOCIETY

01 CHAPTER

Structural Change

Structural change involves a transition or change in the structure of society, including changes in social institutions and their governing rules. These structural changes are long-lasting and permanent.

YOUR STUDY GOALS

1.1 Introduction
1.2 Colonialism
1.3 Industrialisation
1.4 Urbanisation

YOUR PRACTICE GOAL

- Objective Type Questions (22 Qs ; MCQs A-R, Case Based Questions)
- Subjective Questions (26 VSAs, 14 SAs, 8 LAs)

1.1 Introduction

India has a long and rich history and understanding its colonial experience is important for comprehending its modern society. Colonialism brought many structural changes to Indian society. Structural changes refer to changes in social relations and social institutions. Industrialisation and urbanisation are examples of the political, economic and social changes brought about by colonialism in India.

1.2 Colonialism

- Colonialism is defined as the establishment of rule and control by one country over another.
- India experienced rule by various foreign and native rulers, but it was the British who established colonial rule.
- There is a significant difference between pre-capitalist and capitalist empires.
- Pre-capitalist rulers benefited by taking tributes or parts of economic surplus from conquered areas.
- In contrast, capitalist empires altered the economic systems of their colonies to maximise profits and exploit resources.

Colonial Experience for Understanding Modern India

- Understanding modern India requires an understanding of its past, particularly its colonial history.
- Many modern ideas and institutions were introduced to India through colonialism, which were often contradictory and conflicting.
- For example, Indians during colonial times learned about Western liberalism and freedom, while living under a colonial regime that denied them liberty.
- Such contradictions influenced the structural and cultural changes in modern India.
- Colonial rule had a profound impact on Indian society in various aspects, including railways, industries, postal systems and social, cultural, economic and political dimensions.

Use of English

- The use of the English language as a result of colonialism had a complex and **paradoxical**[1] impact in India.
- English is not used very widely across the country, yet there is now a body of literary works by Indian authors in English.
- Knowledge of English has provided Indians with an advantage in the **global market**[2].
- However, proficiency in English remains a symbol of privilege, often associated with social prestige and status.
- Traditionally marginalised groups, such as Dalits, may find that learning English can help diminish the significance of their caste status.
- Housewives and students who are proficient in English can access better job opportunities, such as working as online scorers in Business Process Outsourcing (BPO) companies.
- Additionally, housewives are taking roles as teachers, evaluating English essays written by non-English speaking students from other parts of Asia.

Quick Test 1

1. Give two examples of the political economic and social change brought by colonial rule in India.
2. Name two aspects of Indian society where colonial rule had profound impact.
3. Give any one use of English language in India.

1.3 Industrialisation

- **Industrialisation**[3] refers to the emergence of machine production that relies on inanimate power resources like steam or electricity.
- In an industrial society, a large section of the population is employed in factories or offices rather than in agriculture. However, the nature of industrialisation in India was not the same due to colonial rule.
- **Urbanisation**[4] is often associated with industrialisation, although they do not always occur simultaneously. For instance, in Britain in 1800, only 20 per cent of the population lived in towns or cities with more than 10,000 inhabitants.
- By 1900, this proportion had increased to 74 per cent. The capital city, London, grew from a population of about 1.1 million in 1800 to over 7 million by the 20th century, establishing itself as a significant manufacturing, commercial and financial centre of the British Empire.

1 **Paradoxical** It is a self-contradictory system.
2 **Global Market** It involves planning, producing, placing and promoting business products of services in the worldwide market.
3 **Industrialisation** It is the growth and development of industries in the country.
4 **Urbanisation** It is conversion of small sized villages or towns into large sized cities and towns.

Impact of Industrialisation in India

- The number of industries owned and run by Indians decreased, leading to **de-industrialisation**[5] due to competition from machine-made clothes from Manchester.
- There was a decline in old urban centres.
- Traditional exports of cotton and silk from India decreased due to competition from Manchester.
- Cities such as Surat and Masulipatnam declined, while Bombay and Madras grew.
- Towns like Thanjavur, Dhaka and Murshidabad lost their courts, artisans, and nobility.
- Urban luxury manufacturers, like high-quality silk and cotton from Dhaka and Murshidabad, collapsed due to declining indigenous court demand and external market reliance. Village crafts survived longer, mainly in regions outside Eastern India, where British influence was deepest.

Negative Impact of British Industrial Policy

- The import of cheap British machine-made goods significantly impacted village industries.
- High agricultural product prices forced many artisans to leave their professions and take up agriculture, as reported by the 1911 Census.
- No genuine middle class emerged due to a lack of economic well-being in India.
- Zamindars became exploitative landowners and educated graduates remained unemployed job seekers.
- Demand for high-quality silks and cottons in both domestic and international markets declined.

Role of Cities

- Cities played a major role in the economic system of empires. Coastal cities like Mumbai, Kolkata and Chennai were favoured for their ability to easily export primary goods and import manufactured goods.
- Colonial cities served as crucial links between the economic centres in Britain and the colonised margins in India.
- Cities were a clear example of global capitalism. In British India, cities like Bombay, Calcutta and Madras became key trade hubs.
- By 1900, Bombay handled most of India's raw cotton exports, Calcutta shipped jute to Dundee and Madras exported coffee, sugar, dyes and cotton to Britain.
- Urbanisation during colonial times led to old cities declining and new colonial cities emerging. For instance, Kolkata started in 1690 when Job Charnock leased three villages by the Hugli River for trade. By 1698, Fort William was built with a large open area (the Maidan) for defense, becoming the city's center.

The Tea Plantations

- The tea industry began in India in 1851 and serves as an example of how the British exploited Indian people and resources. Most tea gardens were located in Assam, where the British used unfair methods to hire and retain labourers.
- Labourers faced harsh living and working conditions as British planters acted on their behalf. While managers lived luxurious lives in large bungalows maintained by labourers, the workers endured unjust contracts and unfavourable conditions.
- Labourers were often recruited from distant regions under the provisions of the Transport of Native Labourers Act of 1863, which was amended in 1865, 1870 and 1873. The labour system in Assam's tea industry was indentured, (workers were contracted for several years.)
- The government supported planters by imposing penal sanctions for labourers who failed to fulfill their contracts.

---

5 **De-industrialisation** It is the decline of industries in ancient established industrial areas.

Industrialisation in Independent India

- Post-independence industrial policies were greatly influenced by the economic exploitation experienced during colonial rule. The Swadeshi Movement historically promoted national economic interests.
- For Indian planners, rapid industrialisation was viewed as a pathway to growth and social equity. The development of heavy and machine-making industries, along with the expansion of the public sector and a large cooperative sector, were deemed vital.
- Giant steel plants, dams and power plants were constructed in various locations, including Bokaro, Bhilai, and Durgapur.

1.4 Urbanisation

- Urbanisation is the process where more people move to cities and towns, leading to their growth and development. It involves changes in lifestyles, infrastructure and economic activities.
- Urbanisation during the colonial period led to the decline of some earlier urban centres and the rise of new colonial cities. For instance, Kolkata was developed in the 1690s as a trading post. In 1698, Fort William was established for defensive purposes, creating a large open area around the fort for military activities.
- The European style of town planning served as a model for South Asian cities. This model included spacious bungalows, well-planned streets, clubs for social gatherings and open spaces.

Urbanisation in Independent India

The process of urbanisation increased significantly after independence, with many villages experiencing urban influences. The impact of urbanisation varied based on the relationship between a village and the nearby city or town.

Sociologist MSA Rao identifies following three situations regarding urban impact

(i) **Migration for Employment** In some villages, many residents have migrated to larger cities or overseas for job opportunities. They have built fashionable houses in their villages, invested in land and industry and contributed to establishing educational institutions and trusts.

(ii) **Proximity to Industrial Towns** Some villages located near industrial towns may experience friction between native residents and immigrants who move in for work.

(iii) **Growth of Metropolitan Areas** In the case of expanding metropolitan areas, many villages get absorbed, with their land repurposed for urban development.

Major cities like Mumbai, Delhi, Kolkata, Chennai, Hyderabad, Bengaluru, Pune, Kanpur and Nagpur have experienced significant rates of urbanisation in the post-independence period.

Quick Test 2

1. In industrial society where are large sections of people employed?
2. Which traditional export declined due to Manchester competition?
3. What role did cities play in the economic system of empires?
4. Name the act which was passed in 1863.
5. Name any two cities which experienced a high rate of urbanisation in the post-independence period.

NCERT Folder

1. How has colonialism impacted our lives? You can either focus on one aspect like culture or politics or tract them together.

Ans. Colonialism means the establishment of rule and control by one country over another. Britishers established their colonial rule over India and impacted the social structure and culture of India. Every policy was geared towards the strengthening and expansion of British capitalism. The colonialism affected our lives culturally, politically and more or less combining the two. Due to mobility and exposure to modern Western thoughts people started thinking about freedom, liberty and human rights which provided basis for Indian freedom movement. Colonialism also had social influences particularly on the emerging middle class i.e. on their lifestyle, eating habits, language and clothing.

On the other hand, in terms of political impact of colonisalism on Indian society it becomes visible through national movement, political system, parliamentary and legal system, education system etc. Thus, by and large the whole political structure changed due to the colonial impact.

2. Industrialisation and urbanisation are linked processes. Discuss.

Or **Urbanisation and industrialisation is a linked process. Justify.**

Ans. **Industrialisation** refers to the emergence of machine based production on the use of inanimate power resources like steam or electricity.

Urbanisation is the process in which the villages or towns are transformed into towns or cities, where more people are engaged in industries and services rather than primary activities.

The two processes of industrialisation are inter-related to each other. Both strengthen and reinforce each other, in following ways

- With the increase in modernisation and industrialisation, urbanisation increases. More and more people leave primary activities and engage in secondary or tertiary activities.
- The improvement in technology leads to the improvement in production process. As a result, small industries are changed into big industries.
- With more industrial labour, the purchasing power of people increases and they invest their money in education, entertainment, sports, clubs, etc. Many civic facilities are made available to the residents in the towns and cities.
- Migration from rural area to urban area increases the industrial activity and urbanisation process. In this process, the facilities of transport and communication increase and they further increase the process of urbanisation.

Hence, industrialisation and urbanisation are linked to each other.

Exam Pattern Questions

Objective Type Questions

Multiple Choice Questions (MCQs)

1. Our parliamentary, legal and educational system are based on which model?

(a) American model (b) British model
(c) Indigenous model (d) French model

2. Which of the following statements is incorrect? Competency Based Que.

(a) Colonialism introduced deep and far-reaching changes to India's social and economic systems.
(b) Pre-capitalist empire-building involved pillaging without interfering with the economic base of subjugated areas.
(c) British colonialism did not impact land ownership laws or agricultural practices in India.
(d) The rise of nationalism is connected to the idea that colonised people have a right to sovereignty.

3. Which rulers were benefited by taking away the tribute or economic surplus from the people of subjugated area?

(a) Capitalists (b) Socialists
(c) Pre-capitalists (d) Colonialists

4. The impact of British colonialism on India was deeply rooted in capitalist interests. What was the main economic goal of British colonial policies in India? Competency Based Que.

(a) To develop India's local industries
(b) To ensure maximum profit for British capitalism
(c) To support Indian agriculture and trade
(d) To establish independent local governments

5. Which of the following statements is true for the tea plantations established by the British in India? CBSE SQP 2024

(a) The colonial administrators were clear that the measures taken on the plantation for labourers was different vis-à-vis the planters.
(b) Coolies lived a comfortable life on the tea plantations.
(c) Planters and coolies had a cordial relationship.
(d) Colonial administration stuck to democratic norms.

6. Sometimes cities may also be preferred by people for social reasons.
Which of the following is not a reason? CBSE 2024

(a) Cities offer relative anonymity.
(b) Urban life involves interaction with strangers.
(c) Continuous decline in common property resources like ponds, forests and grazing lands.
(d) The poorer sections of the socially dominant rural groups do not engage in low status work in cities.

7. MSA Rao explained how many types of impact on villages by urbanisation in India?

(a) One (b) Three
(c) Four (d) Five

8. Which of the following was the primary consequence of British industrialisation on India's traditional industries? Competency Based Que.

(a) Increase in cotton and silk manufacturing
(b) Decline of traditional exports and industries
(c) Boost in agricultural productivity
(d) Rise of industrial workers in rural areas

9. Arrange the following events related to British industrialisation in India in the correct sequence. Competency Based Que.

I. Establishment of factories and industries
II. Decline of cities like Surat and Masulipatnam
III. Importation of European goods
IV. British takeover of Indian states

Codes
(a) IV, III, I and II
(b) I, II, IV and III
(c) III, IV, I and II
(d) II, I, IV and III

10. While urbanisation has been occurring at a rapid pace, it is the biggest cities - the metropolises - that have been growing the fastest.
Which of the following statements related to urbanisation is not true? CBSE 2025

(a) These metros attract migrants from the rural areas as well as from small towns.
(b) The larger cities in India are not growing at such a rapid rate.
(c) Urban infrastructure can hardly keep pace.
(d) With the mass media's primary focus on these cities, the public face of India is becoming more and more urban rather than rural.

11. The tea industry in India exemplifies which type of labour practice during colonial times? Competency Based Que.

(a) Self-sustained labour market
(b) Voluntary migration for work
(c) Coercive and exploitative labour practices
(d) Modern unionised labour

12. In …………, an English merchant named Job Charnock arranged to lease three villages (named Kolikata, Gobindapur, and Sutanuti) by the river Hugli in order to set up a trading post. In 1698, Fort William was established by the river for defensive purposes and a large open area was cleared around the fort for military engagements.

(a) 1960 (b) 1900
(c) 1690 (d) 1950

13. Which of the following is true for a model of South Asian colonial city? CBSE 2023

(a) Recreational facilities were not available
(b) Unplanned streets
(c) Civic amenities were accessible in the European towns of the South Asian colonial city
(d) Cramped bungalows

14. Which of the following statement is correct about industrialisation? Competency Based Que.

I. British industrialisation led to deindustrialisation in some sectors.
II. Traditional exports of cotton and silk manufactures from India declined in the face of Manchester competition.
III. Industrialisation refers to the emergence of machine production and use of inanimate power resources.

Codes
(a) I and II (b) II and III
(c) I and III (d) I, II and III

15. **Which among the following states lost their courts after British took over Indian States?** Competency Based Que.

I. Dhaka II. Murshidabad
III. Thanjavur

Codes

(a) I and II (b) I and III
(c) II and III (d) I, II and III

Assertion–Reason Questions

Direction (Q. Nos. 16-20) Two statement are given in the question below as Assertion (A) and Reason (R). Read the statements and choose the appropriate option.

(a) Both A and R are true and R is the correct explanation of A
(b) Both A and R are true, but R is not the correct explanation of A
(c) A is true, but R is false
(d) A is false, but R is true

16. **Assertion** (A) The principle of nationalism assumes that any set of people have a right to be free and exercise sovereign power. It is an important part of the rise of democratic ideas.

Reason (R) Nation states are closely associated with the rise of nationalism.

17. **Assertion** (A) For Indian nationalists the issue of economic exploitation under colonial rule was a central issue.

Reason (R) Indian nationalists saw rapid industrialisation of the economy as the path towards both growth and social equity.

18. **Assertion** (A) The laws of a colonised country did not have to stick to the democratic norms that the British back home had to follow in Britain.

Reason (R) The colonial administrators were clear that harsh measures were taken against the labourers to make sure they benefitted the planters.

19. **Assertion** (A) When the British took over Indian states, towns like Thanjavur, Dhaka and Murshidabad lost their courts.

Reason (R) British industrialisation led to deindustrialisation in some sectors and the decline of old urban centres. CBSE 2024

20. **Assertion** (A) What marked capitalism from the very beginning was its dynamism, its potential to grow, expand, innovate, and use technology and labour in the best possible way.

Reason (R) Capitalism is an economic system organised to accumulate profits within a market system. CBSE 2024

Case Based Questions

Read the passage given below and answer the questions that follow by choosing the correct option.

21. **How were labourers recruited?**

Tea industry began in India in 1851. Most of the tea gardens were situated in Assam. In 1903, the industry employed 4,79,000 permanent and 93,000 temporary employees. Since Assam was sparsely populated and the tea plantations were often located on uninhabited hillsides, bulk of the sorely needed labour had to be imported from other provinces. But to bring thousands of people every year from their far-off homes into strange lands, possessing an unhealthy climate and infected with strange fevers, required the provision of financial and other incentives, which the tea-planters of Assam were unwilling to offer. Instead, they had recourse to fraud and coercion; and they persuaded the government to aid and abet them in this unholy task by passing penal laws. ...The recruitment of labourers for tea gardens of Assam was carried on for years mostly by contractors under the provisions of the Transport of Native Labourers Act (No. III) of 1863 of Bengal as amended in 1865, 1870 and 1873.

(i) The government helped the planters by providing for .... in case of non-fulfillment of the contract by the labourers.

(a) penal sanction (b) reward
(c) appreciation (d) incentive

(ii) The tea industry was established in India in ....

(a) 1871 (b) 1851 (c) 1861 (d) 1852

(iii) In which of the following states most of the tea farms are situated?

(a) Tamil Nadu (b) Kerala
(c) Assam (d) West Bengal

(iv) "They persuaded the government to aid." Which of the following governments is talked about in given lines?

(a) Indian Government
(b) British Government
(c) French Government
(d) State Government of Assam

22. **How did the planters live?**

Parbatpuri had always been an important offloading and loading point. The doughty British managers and their men always came down from the estate surrounding Parbatpuri when a steamer docked there. In spite of the inaccessibility of the gardens, they had lived lives of luxury. Huge, sprawling bungalows, set on sturdy wooden stilts to protect the inmates from wild animals, were surrounded by velvety lawns and jewel bright flower beds...They had trained a large number of malis, bawarchis and bearers to serve them to perfection. Their wide verandahed houses gleamed and glistened under the ministrations of this army of liveried servants. Of course, everything from scouring powder to self-raising flour, from saftey pins to silverware, from delicate Nottingham lace tablecloths to bath salts, had come up the river on the steamers. Indeed, even the large cast-iron bathtubs that were invitingly placed in huge bathrooms, tubs which were filled every morning by busy bistiwallahs carrying buckets up from the bungalow's well, had been brought up *via* steamer.

(i) ………… had always been an important offloading and loading point.

(a) Assam (b) Parbatpuri
(c) Bengal (d) Chhattisgarh

(ii) Which of the following lived the lives of luxury?

(a) Residents of Parbatpuri
(b) British managers
(c) Both (a) and (b)
(d) None of these

(iii) To serve them, the managers have trained

(a) bawarchis (b) bearers
(c) malis (d) All of these

(iv) What was main mode of transportation in Parbatpuri?

(a) Railways
(b) Roadways
(c) Waterways
(d) None of the above

Answers

1. (b) British model
2. (c) British colonialism did not impact land ownership laws or agricultural practices in India.
3. (c) Pre-capitalists
4. (b) To ensure maximum profit for British capitalism
5. (a) The colonial administrators were clear that the measures taken on the plantation for labourers was different vis-à-vis the planters.
6. (b) Urban life involves interaction with strangers.
7. (b) Three
8. (b) Decline of traditional exports and industries
9. (a) IV, III, I, II
10. (b) The larger cities in India are not growing at such a rapid rate.
11. (c) Coercive and exploitative labour practices
12. (c) 1690
13. (c) Civic amenities were accessible in the European towns of the South Asian colonial city
14. (d) I, II and III
15. (d) I, II and III
16. (b) Both A and R are true, but R is not the correct explanation of A
17. (a) Both A and R are true and R is the correct explanation of A
18. (a) Both A and R are true and R is the correct explanation of A
19. (a) Both A and R are true and R is the correct explanation of A
20. (a) Both A and R are true and R is the correct explanation of A
21. (i) (a) penal sanction (ii) (b) 1851 (iii) (c) Assam (iv) (b) British Government
22. (i) (b) Parbatpuri (ii) (b) British managers (iii) (d) All of these (iv) (c) Waterways

Subjective Questions

Very Short Answer Type Questions

1. India has a long and rich history and understanding its colonial experience is important for comprehending its modern society. Colonialism brought many changes structural changes in society.

Based on the above passage answer the following question.

What do you understand by structural change?

Ans. Changes which occur in our social relations and social institutions are known as structural changes. For example, changes occur in family, marriage, etc. are a part of structural change.

2. What is colonialism? Give one example.

Ans. Colonialism simply means the establishment of rule and control by one country over another.
For example, Britishers established its colonial rule in India.

3. Mention any two structural changes brought about by colonialism.

Ans. Two structural changes brought about by colonialism are as follows
(i) Our parliamentary and legal system is based on British model.
(ii) Lots of migration of people and labour took place in India.

4. What efforts were put in by colonialism for the smooth functioning of its rule?

Ans. Colonialism introduced wide range of changes in the field of legislation, culture or architecture to facilitate smooth rule in India.

5. Colonialism led to considerable movement of people. Give examples.

Ans. Colonialism led to movement of people from one part to another inside the country, as well as overseas. People moved from present Jharkhand to Assam to work on tea plantations and professionals also moved to different places in search of better jobs.

6. Why coastal cities were favoured by the colonial rulers?

Ans. Coastal cities were favoured by the colonial rulers because from here primary commodities and raw materials could be easily exported. At the same time, cheap manufactured goods could be imported in these cities such as Mumbai, Kolkata and Chennai.

7. How is colonialism different from earlier forms of conquest?

Ans. Colonialism was different from earlier forms of conquest because it brought far-reaching and deep changes in the society. It also interferred with the economic base of the country.

8. What is capitalism?

Ans. Capitalism is an economic system in which the means of production are privately owned and organised to accumulate profits within a market system. Capitalism from the very beginning was marked by its dynamism, its potential to grow, expand, innovate use technology and labour to ensure greatest profit.

9. Capitalism is marked by its global nature and dynamism. Explain the basic features of capitalism? **Competency Based Que.**

Ans. The basic features of capitalism are as follows
- It ensures the greatest profit and benefit to the capitalists.
- It changes the way of production and distribution of goods takes place.
- It changes the economic base of the country.

10. The principle of nationalism emerged as a key gorve during the modern era. What does the principle of nationalism assume?

Ans. The principle of nationalism assumes that any set of people have a right to be free and exercise sovereign power.

11. The impact of English language has been many sided and paradoxical in India. Give reasons. **CBSE 2019**

Or **With the help of four examples, show how the impact of the English language has been many sided and paradoxical in India.** **CBSE 2024**

Or **How has English language impacted our society** **CBSE 2019**

Ans. The impact of English language has been many sided and paradoxical in India.
Some of the examples are as follows
(i) English is not only widely used in India but we now have an impressive body of literary writings by Indians in English.
(ii) This knowledge of English has given Indians an edge in the global market.
(iii) On the contrary, English continues to be a mark of privilege. Not knowing English is a disadvantage that tells in the job market.
(iv) However, for those who were traditionally deprived of access to formal education such as the Dalits, knowledge of English may open doors of opportunities that were formerly closed.

12. What does industrialisation refers to?

Ans. Industrialisation refers to the emergence of machine production, based on the use of inanimate power resources like steam or electricity.

13. What were the effects of British industrialisation on Indian industries?

Ans. British industrialisation led to de-industrialisation in some sectors such as cotton and silk textiles. It also led to the decline of cities such as Surat and Masulipatnam and Indian village industries were also affected adversely.

14. "For Indian nationalists, the issue of economic exploitation under colonial rule was a central issue."

How did Indian nationalists promote industrialisation in the early years of independence? **CBSE 2022 Term II**

Ans. On the basis of massive steel, dams and power plants, Indian nationalists pushed for industrialisation. The nationalists believed that industrialisation would be facilitated by the expansion of the public sector and sizable cooperative sectors.

15. How were labourers recruited in tea industry?

Ans. The labourers were recruited in tea industry under the Transport of Native Labourers Act, 1863 with fraud and coercion by the contractors. The government penalised the labourers for violating the contract.

16. Discuss briefly that tea plantation industry in India was governed by the colonial interest. **CBSE 2019**

Ans. The British Government official report show how the colonial government often used unfair means to hire and forcibly keep labourers and it clearly acted on behalf of the British planters. So, through these aspects we get a glimpse of what life was for tea planters in this industry.

17. By contrast, a prime feature of industrial societies today is that a large majority of the employed population work in factories, offices or shops rather than agriculture. Over 90 per cent of people in the West live in towns and cities, where most jobs are to be found and new job opportunities are created.

Based on the above passage answer the following question. What are the important characteristics of an industrial society?

Ans. An industrial society is characterised by machine-based production, technological advancements and urbanisation. The large majority of people are engaged in secondary or tertiary activities such as factories, offices or shops rather than agriculture.

18. Urbanisation and industrialisation is a linked process. Justify.

Ans. Industrialisation refers to the emergence of machine based production and factory system and urbanisation refers to the transformation of village or towns into bigger towns or cities. Both the processes of urbanisation and industrialisation are related to each other as with increase in industrialisation, urbanisation also increases.

19. In India the impact of the very same British industrialisation led to de-industrialisation in some sectors and decline of old urban centres. What do you mean by de-industrialisation?

Ans. It refers to the decline of industries in ancient established industrial areas. It also refers to decreasing investment, production and destruction of industries due to various reasons.

20. How did de-industrialisation take place in the colonial India. **CBSE 2019**

Ans. De-industrialisation took place in India in following ways

- The nature of industrialisation was not same in colonial India as compared to Britain. The traditional exports of cotton and silk manufacturers from India declined in the face of Manchester competition.
- Small scale manufacturers and native industries were all closed because of the competition from the West. Many village artisans abandoned their hereditary craft and moved to agriculture.

21. Which cities were developed by the British in India and why?

Ans. British developed cities such as Calcutta, Madras and Bombay. India's raw cotton was shipped through Bombay, Calcutta exported jute to Dundee, while Madras sent coffee, sugar, indigo dyes and cotton to Britain. These cities served the purpose of import and export of goods.

22. What were the products exported from sea ports by the colonial government?

Ans. Raw cotton was shipped through Bombay, Calcutta exported jute and Madras exported coffee, sugar, indigo dyes and cotton to Britain.

23. A model of the South Asian colonial city

The European town...had spacious bungalows, elegant apartment houses, planned streets, trees on both sides of the street,...clubs for afternoon and evening get togethers...The open space was reserved for...Western recreational facilities, such as race and golf courses, soccer and cricket. When domestic water supply, electric connections, and sewage links were available or technically possible, the European town residents utilised them fully, whereas their use was quite restricted to the native town.

Read the source and answer the following question. Did the model of the South Asian colonial city cater to the needs of the natives? Give a reason for your answer. **CBSE SQP Term II, 2021**

Ans. No, the model of the South Asian colonial city did not cater to the needs of the natives.

When domestic water supply, electric connections, and sewage links were available or technically possible, the European town residents utilised them fully, whereas their use was quite restricted to the native town.

24. What is urbanisation?

Ans. Urbanisation is a process of migration of population from rural areas and smaller towns to bigger towns and cities on a large scale due to social, economic and political causes.

25. Read the source and answer the question (Sarkar: 1983:29) CBSE 2022 Term II

Urban luxury manufactures like the high quality silks and cottons of Dacca or Murshidabad must have been hit first by the almost simultaneous collapse of indigeneous court demand and the external market on which these had largely depended. Village crafts in the interior and particularly, in regions other than Eastern India where British penetration was earliest and deepest, probably survived much longer, coming to be seriously affected only with the spread of railways.

When British took over states and towns of India, some of them lost their courts, artisans and court gentry. Give any one reason.

Ans. When the British took over Indian states, towns like Thanjavur, Dhaka and Murshidabad lost their courts and therefore, some of their artisans and court gentry. From the end of the 19th century, with the installation of mechanised factory industries, some towns became much more heavily populated.

26. Urbanisation and industrialisation are often linked, but this was not always the case in India. Give two reasons explaining why industrialisation in India did not always lead to urbanisation.

Ans. Industrialisation in India did not always lead to urbanisation due to the following reasons

(i) **De-industrialisation** British policies led to the decline of traditional industries, reducing urban growth.

(ii) **Agricultural Shift** The introduction of industrialisation often resulted in more people moving to agriculture rather than cities, limiting urbanisation despite industrial growth.

Short Answer Type Questions

1. How are capitalism and colonialism linked? CBSE SQP 2023

Ans. Capitalism and colonialism are linked because British colonialism was based on a capitalist system which directly interfered to ensure greatest profit and benefit to British capitalism. Every policy was aimed at strengthening and expanding of British capitalism.

Capitalism is an economic system in which the means of production are privately owned and organised to accumulate profits within a market system.

Western colonialism was inextricably connected to the growth of Western capitalism that became dominant economic system.

This had lasting impact on the way capitalism developed in a colonised country like India.

2. There are vital differences between empire building of pre-capitalist times and that of capitalist times. Give reasons. CBSE 2019

Ans. **Empire Building of Pre-Capitalist Times**

- Outright pillage, continuous flow of tribute benefited the pre-capitalist conquerors and did not interfere with the economic base.
- They simply took the tribute that was skimmed off the economic surplus that was produced traditionally in the subjugated areas.

Empire Building of Capitalist Times (British Colonialism)

- Directly interfered to ensure greatest profit and benefit to British capitalism.
- Every policy was geared towards the strengthening and expansion of British capitalism. For instance, it changed the very laws of the land.
- It meddled with the manufacturing sector and altering the way production and distribution of goods took place.

3. How did the advent of colonialism in India produce a major upheaval in the economy? CBSE 2019

Ans. The advent of colonialism in India produced a major upheaval in the economy in the following ways

- The advent of colonialism in India produced disruptions in production, trade and agriculture. For example, cheap manufactured textiles from England completely destroyed the handloom industry and made the weavers jobless.
- Before being colonised by the British, India was a major supplier of manufactured goods to the world market, but after colonialism, India became a source of raw materials and agriculture and a consumer of manufactured goods.
- With the colonialism, the expansion of market economy in India provided new opportunities to some merchant communities, which were able to improve their position by re-orienting themselves to changing economic circumstances.

4. How is colonialism different from earlier forms of conquests? In what ways did it affect Indian society?

Ans. Colonialism is different from earlier forms of conquest or domination in the following ways

(i) The pre-capitalist conquerors benefited from their domination by taking away the tribute or part of economic surplus from the people of subjugated areas.

(ii) Colonialism means the establishment of rule by one country over other. It is the ideology by which a country seeks to conquer and colonise another. The colony becomes a subordinate part of the coloniser's country and is extremely exploited in different ways for the colonising (imperial) country's gain.

(iii) Colonialism affects the Indian society as it started a new wave of exploitation of country's resources.

(iv) Colonialism introduced a wide aray of changes in every sphere. These changes took place in two ways i.e. deliberate and intended.

5. The practice of colonialism and the principle of nationalism are contradictory. Why?

Ans. The practice of colonialism and the basic principles of nationalism are opposite to each other. Nationalism assumes that a particular group of people have a right to be free and exercise sovereign power. On the other hand, colonialism is the control of one country by another.

The contradictory nature of nationalism and colonialism can be described as

- The nationalism gives rise to freedom and democratic rights, while colonialism tries to suppress the liberty of colonised people.
- British colonial masters strengthened their capitalistic tendencies and colonial interests without caring for the welfare of colonised people. While colonialism changes the economic system of colonised people to extract maximum profit and gain.
- Nationalism promotes the economic development and industrialisation of one's own country, while colonialism tries to de-industrialise the colonies in order to promote its own colonial interests.
- Nationalism advocates the sovereignty of its own people, while colonialism denies it.

6. To facilitate the smooth functioning of its rule, colonialism introduced a wide array of changes in every sphere. Name and explain the changes in any two spheres. CBSE 2024 C

Ans. Colonialism brought significant changes in the **legal** and **economic** spheres.

Legally, it introduced new laws like land ownership reforms and Forest Acts, restricting pastoralists' access to traditional grazing areas. These laws often favoured British interests, altering existing systems.

Economically, colonialism disrupted traditional production methods by interfering in agriculture and manufacturing. Crops were chosen based on British needs, like tea plantations replacing forests. This exploitation aimed to strengthen British capitalism, ensuring maximum profit while significantly impacting India's economy and livelihoods. These changes were deliberate and far -reaching.

7. British colonialism is still a complex part of our lives. How? CBSE 2024

Ans. British colonialism continues to intricately shape our lives today through its deep-rooted influences on various aspects of society. From language and cultural practices to economic structures and political systems, its legacy persists. Social hierarchies and inequalities often stem from colonial oppression, while efforts to reclaim indigenous identities reflect ongoing struggles. Environmental degradation resulting from resource exploitation further underscores its impact. Understanding and addressing these complexities are essential for fostering equitable and just societies in the aftermath of colonialism.

8. What was the vision of the Indian nationalists to promote industrialisation in independent India? Explain.

Ans. Indian nationalists responded to the negative impact of the British colonialism in India. They witnessed the process of de-industrialisation and economic exploitation of Indian economy. Indian artisans and weavers became jobless.

The Indian leaders, therefore saw rapid industrialisation as a path to realise growth and social equity in India. They developed heavy and machine -making industries and also expanded the activities of public sector in industrialisation and development.

Besides, a large cooperative sector was also considered important for the economy. Giant steel plants, dams and power stations in various parts of country, e.g. Bhakra Nangal Dam were constructed.
The Swadeshi Movement launched by the nationalists of India strengthened the national economy and modern ideas inspired the people to eradicate poverty and underdevelopment.

9. How were labourers recruited and appointed by the colonial administration in the tea gardens? CBSE 2023

Ans. The workers worked under unjust contract and unfavourable conditions. The workers were recruited from far off places. The recruitment of labourers for tea gardens was carried out under the provisions of the Transport of Native Labourers Act of 1863 of Bengal as amended in 1865, 1870 and 1873. The labour system in Assamese tea industry was that of indenture i.e. the labourers were under contract for a number of years.

10. How did the planters in the tea plantations live? CBSE 2023

Ans. Tea gardens were mostly situated in Assam. Britishers used unfair means to hire and forcibly keep labourers, harsh measures were taken against labourers, living and working conditions were very poor as the Britishers acted on behalf of the planters. The workers worked under unjust contract and unfavourable conditions.

11. Industrialisation in the West is associated with the growth of a middle class. Discuss the Indian experience of the growth of this middle class. CBSE SQP 2024

Ans. In India, the growth of a middle class was shaped by colonialism, but it differed from the Western experience. Unlike the West, where industrialisation created a new middle class, India's middle class emerged through colonial policies such as land ownership and English education. However, these alternatives were disconnected from agricultural productivity and traditional Indian culture. The colonial system failed to create a truly independent middle class, with many zamindars becoming landowners and graduates seeking jobs in the colonial administration, rather than fostering self-sustained economic growth.

12. Which cities were developed by the British in India and Why? CBSE 2019

Ans. Cities had a key role in the economic systems of empires. Coastal cities such as Mumbai, Kolkata and Chennai were favoured by Britishers. From here primary commodities could be easily exported and manufactured goods could be cheaply imported. Colonial cities were the prime link between the economic centre and core in Britain and periphery or margins in colonised India. In British India for example, Bombay was planned and re-developed as three-quarters of India's raw cotton were shipped through the city. Calcutta exported jute to dundee while Madras sent coffee, sugar, indigo dyes and cotton to Britain.

13. What role did cities play in the economic system of empires?

Ans. Cities played a central role in the economic system of the empire in the following ways

- Coastal cities like Mumbai, Kolkata and Chennai were favoured as from here primary goods could be easily exported and manufactured goods could be cheaply imported.
- Colonial cities were the primary link between the economic centre or core centres in Britain and periphery or margins in colonised India.
- Cities were concerte expression of global capitalism. For example, Bombay during British India was planned and re-developed so that by 1900 over three-quarters of India's raw cotton were shipped through the city.
- Cities were also important as a trading post, for defensive purposes and for military engagements.
- Thus, cities strengthened the colonial and capitalistic economic system.

14. Urbanisation and Industrialisation are linked processes. Explain. CBSE 2024 C

Ans. Urbanisation and industrialisation are closely linked, as industrialisation drives the growth of cities by creating new job opportunities in factories, offices and shops. In Britain, industrialisation led to the migration of people from rural areas to urban centers, such as London, which expanded rapidly. However, in colonial India, industrialisation under British rule disrupted traditional industries, leading to de-industrialisation and the decline of cities like Dhaka and Murshidabad. At the same time, new colonial cities like Kolkata and Mumbai emerged as export hubs for raw materials, reflecting the interconnectedness of urbanisation and industrial growth.

Long Answer Type Questions

1. Explain the structural changes seen in the period of colonialism.

Or **Colonialism introduced a wide range of change in every sphere be it legal or cultural or architectural. Justify the statement with examples.**

Ans. British colonialism brought about wide range of changes in the society. The contradiction between the modern and liberal ideas of the West and their absence in colonised India brought many social changes. Almost every aspect of human life was affected in India.

Some of the areas in which the influence of colonialism can be seen are as following

- **Law System** Our legal and police system is based on the British model. Beside, Britishers brought laws such as Forest Acts and Transport of Native Labourers Act which affected the lives of pastoralists, labourers and people in general.
- **Architecture** It was also influenced by the Britishers. They developed towns in India which had spacious bungalows, elegant apartment houses, planned streets and trees on both the houses of the street.
- **Culture** It is a way of life and British colonialism has deeply affected the Indian cultural life. English language is widely used in India and it is a doorway to various opportunities. Roadside eateries and canteens also have bread omlette and cutlets in their menu. We are also habitual to drive on the left side of the road like British.
- **Education** Our education system is mostly based on the British model. India also has a great number of literary writings in English.
- **Political System** Our parliamentary system functions more or less similar to that of British. Our Constitution also has influence of British system.

2. Explain three different ways in which the Indian economy changed after the advent of colonialism.

Ans. British colonialism in India was inseparably connected with capitalism. Maximising the profit and gain became the main motive of the Britishers. They tried every mean to change Indian economy, so as to serve their own colonial interests.

Some of the ways in which the Indian economy changed after the advent of colonialism are as following

(i) **De-industrialisation** British industrialisation led to de-industrialisation of Indian industries in some sectors of Indian economy. Traditional exports of cotton and silk products manufactured from India witnessed decline severely. Besides, huge import of cheap European manufactured goods destroyed the village industries.

(ii) **Decline of Urban Centres** Many urban centres declined in India due to coming of the Britishers. The cities like Surat and Masulipatnam were declined. Towns like Thanjavur, Dhaka and Murhidabad lost their courts and as a result, they also lost their artisans and court nobility.

(iii) **Emergence of New Cities** The Britishers favoured the coastal cities of Mumbai, Kolkata and Chennai in order to fulfill their colonial interests. They made these cities as centres to export the primary goods and import the manufactured goods. These cities became the centre of trade, commerce and capitalism.

3. What is industrialisation? How did British industrialisation lead to de industrialisation and urbanisation in India?

Or **"In India, the impact of the very same British industrialisation led to de-industrialisation in some sectors."** **CBSE 2025**

Identify the impacts on the basis of the above statement.

Ans. Industrialisation refers to the emergence of machine production, based on the use of inanimate power resources like steam or electricity. British industrialisation brought about radical changes in the Indian economy.

There were changes not only in the field of economy but also in other aspects of Indian society.

De-industrialisation and urbanisation are the two important changes that were also the products of British industrialisation in India. They are discussed below

De-industrialisation

- Some sectors of Indian economy underwent de-industrialisation due to industrial policies of the Britishers in India. Indian silk and cotton fabrics could not compete with the Manchester products. Therefore, there was a heavy blow to the domestic as well as international market of Indian cotton and silk textiles. Thus, these industries were adversely affected.
- Similarly, the village industries were more or less destroyed, as their products could not compete with the cheap imports of the machine made goods from Europe.

Urbanisation

- British industrial policy in India led to the decline of many towns and cities but at the same time, it also facilitated urbanisation in some parts of India. Since, the main purpose of Britishers were to earn maximum gain and benefit, they developed the coastal cities like Chennai, Mumbai and Kolkata to facilitate different types of exports and imports.
- Besides, they also developed Fort William for the defence purpose. They also developed towns and cities which had spacious bungalows, apartment houses and well planned streets and recreational facilities.

4. In what ways colonialism has brought about a social, economic and political influence on Indian society to promote urbanisation?

Ans. British colonialism brought changes in almost all the spheres of Indian society. It also promoted urbanisation in India through social, economic and political influence in the following ways

- **Economic** Colonial cities developed by Britishers, especially the coastal cities such as Mumbai, Kolkata and Chennai facilitated the process of urbanisation in India. These cities became the centre of trade and commercial activities. There was also change in the cropping pattern and production and distribution of goods. Due to installation of mechanised industries, a few towns became much more heavily populated.
- **Social** Colonialism led to introduction of English language in India. English continues to be a mark of privilege and a means to better opportunities and jobs. It also changed the whole spectrum in day-to-day life particularly in the urban society.
  There was also large scale migration of government employees and professionals like doctors and lawyers to various parts of the country. It carried with it new ideas and ways of life.
- **Political** Our political system, legal system and police system are based on British model. These new systems gave new shape to traditional policy and laws. They also created new professionals mainly in towns and cities to enforce new laws and political ideas.

5. Colonialism in India introduced a wide array of change in every sphere. Explain. **Competency Based Que.**

Ans. Colonialism in India introduced a wide array of changes in every sphere be it legal, cultural or architectural it was done to facilitate. Smooth functioning of its rule. Some of the changes that took place were deliberate while some were unintended.

We saw how Western education was introduced to create Indians who would manage British colonialism. Instead it led to the growth of a nationalist and anti-colonial unconsciousness. This magnitude and depth of the structural changes that colonialism unleashed can be better grasped if they understood basic features of capitalism.

Capitalism is an economic system in which means of production are privately owned and organised to accumulate profits within a market system.

Capitalism in the West emerged out of complex process of European exploration of the rest of the world, its plunder of wealth and resources and an unprecedented growth of science and technology, its harnessing to industries and agriculture. Capitalism was marked by its dynamism its potential to grow, expand, innovate using technology and labour in a way that best assured greatest profit. Western colonialism was totally connected to the growth of Western capitalism. This had a lasting impact on the way capitalism developed in a colonised country like India.

6. "Sometimes the city may be preferred for social reasons." Enumerate these social reasons.

Ans. Sometimes the city may be preferred for social reasons. Following are the reasons why cities are preferred

Cities played a key role in the economic system of empires. Coastal cities like Mumbai, Kolkata and Chennai were preferred because they made it easy to export raw materials and import manufactured goods at low cost.

Colonial cities connected the economic centres in Britain with the regions in colonised India.

These cities became symbols of global capitalism. For instance, British planners redeveloped Bombay and by 1900, it handled more than three-quarters of India's cotton exports.

Urbanisation under colonial rule caused some older cities to decline while new colonial cities emerged. Kolkata was one of these new centres.Additionally, cities were important as trading posts and for military defence.

7. Sociologist MSA Rao describes three different situations of urban impact in India. Describe each of the three situations. **Competency Based Que.**

Ans. In Independence period, India has witnessed lot of urbanisation and villages which have been subjected to different kinds of urban influences. Urbanisation is a process in which more and more people opt for urban life and live in cities. In this phenomenon, the villages or small towns are gradually transformed into bigger towns or cities.

Sociologist MSA Rao describes three situations under which a village experiences the urban impact in India. These three situations are as following

(i) In this situation, lot of people migrate from villages to far off cities or overseas towns. They send money to their natal villages. Besides, they invest money on land and industry and donate for educational institutions. They build fashionable houses at their villages and have invested on land and industry.

(ii) Some villages are situated near the industrial town (e.g. Bhilai). Demand for houses and the market inside the village increases but at times it lead to hatred between immigrants and native population.

(iii) Growth of metropolitan cities do have influence over the rural areas or villages. Some villages are completely absorbed in the process of expansion of these cities. On the other hand, some villages lose their uninhabited land for urban development.

8. (i) What is urbanisation? What does the chart show in relation to percentage share of urban population?

Population Selected Metropolitan Cities (Urban Agglomerations)

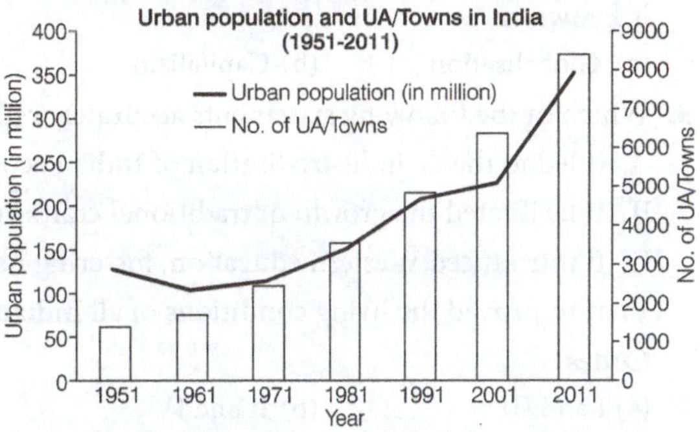

(ii) What does the industrialisation and urbanisation imply?

Ans. (i) The mechanism by which the urban population grows and people living in rural areas internalise the urban society's way of life is known as Urbanisation.

According to the graph given above, India's urban population and the number of UA/ Towns are growing.

The per cent share of the urban population is growing, the urban population's decennial growth rate is declining. In 1951, 2,843 towns housed 17.29 per cent of India's population or 62.44 million inhabitants. In 2011, 7,935 towns housed 31.16 per cent of India's population or 377.10 million inhabitants.

(ii) The decennial growth rate of the urban population, on the other hand, displayed a downward trend from 1981 to 2001, then reversed and showed a modest rise in 2011. The urban population grew at a decennial rate of 41.42 per cent in 1951 and 31.80 per cent in 2011. For the first time since independence, urban areas have seen a greater growth in population than rural areas. This is due to a dramatic drop in the rate of Growth in rural areas, although the rate of growth in urban areas remains nearly constant. Industrialisation and urbanisation imply changes not just in production systems, technological innovations, density of settlements but also 'a way of life'.

SELF ASSESSMENT TEST

Objective Type Questions

1. Which of the following statement is appropriate regarding industrialisation in India during the colonial period?

(a) There was sudden move of workers to the new industries in the initial period.

(b) The initial impact was more people moving into agriculture.

(c) Industrialisation took place in same way as it happened in Britain.

(d) The British policies favoured native tea planters.

2. The emergence of machine production based on the inanimate power resources like steam and electricity is known as

(a) Globalisation (b) Capitalism (c) Colonialism (d) Industrialisation

3. Which of the following statements accurately reflects the impact of British colonialism on Indian society?

I. It led to the de industrialisation of Indian economies.

II. It facilitated the growth of traditional crafts and industries.

III. It introduced Western education, fostering nationalist sentiments.

IV. It improved the living conditions of all Indian citizens.

Codes

(a) I and III (b) II and IV (c) I and II (d) I, III and IV

4. Assertion (A) Industrialisation in India under British rule led to significant urbanisation.

Reason (R) The colonial policies facilitated the growth of new urban centres while causing the decline of traditional ones.

(a) Both A and R are true and R is the correct explanation of A

(b) Both A and R are true, but R is not the correct explanation of A

(c) A is true, but R is false

(d) A is false, but R is true

5. Assertion (A) The introduction of the Forest Acts during British rule adversely affected pastoralist communities in India.

Reason (R) The Forest Acts restricted access to traditional grazing lands, impacting their livelihoods.

(a) Both A and R are true and R is the correct explanation of A

(b) Both A and R are true, but R is not the correct explanation of A

(c) A is true, but R is false

(d) A is false, but R is true

Very Short Answer Type Questions

1. The impact of British industrialisation in India led to the growth of certain cities while the decline of others. Name any two cities that grew during this period. What was the primary factor behind the growth of these cities?

2. Studies have shown how industrialisation has led to different social and economic changes in various societies. With reference to India, how did the impact of British industrialisation affect traditional industries and urban centres?

3. In India, traditional industries declined due to British industrialisation. Give two examples of industries or towns that were affected by this change.

4. What do you mean by nationalism?

Case Based Questions

1. Sociological writings in India have often discussed both the contradictory and unintended consequences of colonialism. Comparisons have been made between the industrialisation in the West and the growth of a Western middle class with that of the Indian experience. It also shows how industrialisation is not just about new machine based production but also a story of the growth of new social groups in society and new social relationships. In other words it is about changes in the Indian social structure. Cities had a key role in the economic system of empires. Coastal cities such as Mumbai, Kolkata and Chennai were favoured. From here primary commodities could be easily exported and manufactured goods could be cheaply imported.

(i) Which of the following statements best describes the impact of colonialism on India's industrialisation?

(a) Colonialism led to the rapid growth of indigenous industries in India.

(b) British industrialisation caused the decline of traditional industries in India.

(c) Colonialism had no impact on India's social structure.

(d) The introduction of Western industries helped strengthen India's local craft traditions.

(ii) What was the role of Indian cities like Bombay, Calcutta and Madras in the global capitalist system during the colonial period?

(a) They were centers of self-sustained local economies.

(b) They were involved in the export of raw materials and import of finished goods.

(c) They operated independently from British influence in trade.

(d) They were centers of luxury goods production for local consumption.

Short Answer Type Questions

1. Give two negative impacts of British industrial policy.

2. Analyse the impact of industrialisation in independent India.

3. Colonialism also led to considerable movement of people. Explain.

Long Answer Type Questions

1. Colonialism also led to considerable movement of people. It led to movement of people from one part to another within India. For instance people from present day Jharkhand moved to Assam to work on the tea plantations. A newly emerging middle class particularly from the British Presidency regions of Bengal and Madras moved as government employees and professionals like doctors and lawyers moved to different parts of the country. People were carted in ships from India to work on other colonised lands in distant Asia, Africa and Americas. Many died on their way. Most could never return. Today many of their descendents are known as people of Indian origin.

(a) What were some of the key reasons for the movement of people within India during the colonial period?

(b) How did the migration of Indian workers to other colonies during colonial rule impact their lives and the regions they moved to?

2. What were the different ways in which the villages in independent India came under the urban influences? Explain.

3. Explain industrialisation and urbanisation as a process of structural change in independent India.

02

CHAPTER

Cultural Change

Cultural change refers to internal and external factors leading to changes in cultural patterns within societies. It encompasses changes in customs, traditions, beliefs, lifestyles and behaviours.

YOUR STUDY GOALS

YOUR PRACTICE GOAL

- Objective Type Questions (21 Qs ; MCQs A-R, Case Based Questions)
- Subjective Questions (20 VSAs, 17 SAs, 6 LAs)

2.1 Social Reform Movements in 19th and 20th Century

Sociologists view culture as socially established norms or patterns of behaviour. The efforts of 19th-century social reformers and 20th-century nationalists aimed at addressing discrimination and transforming cultural practices through processes such as **sanskritisation**[1], modernisation, **secularisation**[2] and westernisation. Social reform movements in 19th-century India challenged colonial society. Nationalists aimed to change social practices that discriminated against women and lower castes.

Major social evils included practices like Sati, child marriage, caste discrimination, untouchability, purdah system, social inequalities and illiteracy. Reform movements emerged among all Indian communities, with some reformers supporting government regulations.

1 **Sanskritisation** It is the process through which the low castes or other groups take over the custom, belief and way of life of the high caste people.

2 **Secularisation** It is a process of decline in the influence of religion in society.

Nature of Social Reforms

- The social reforms of the 19th century blended modernity with traditional ideas.
- They represented a combination of modern liberal concepts from the West and a rediscovery of traditional Indian values.
- The movements aimed to purify and redefine Indian civilisation in alignment with European ideals of rationalism, monotheism and individualism.

Aspects of Social Reforms/Changes

Sociologist Satish Saberwal identified three aspects of social change that occurred in colonial India as following

(i) Modes of Communication

- New technologies like the printing press, telegraph and later the microphone facilitated rapid communication of ideas.
- The movement of people and goods through steamships and railways also contributed to the spread of new ideas.
- For example
  - Social reformers from Punjab and Bengal communicated with their counterparts in Madras and Maharashtra.
  - Keshav Chandra Sen from Bengal visited Madras in 1864.
  - Christian missionaries reached areas like Nagaland, Mizoram and Meghalaya.
  - Pandita Ramabai travelled extensively across the country.

(ii) Forms of Organisation

- Modern social organisations were formed, such as Brahmo Samaj in Bengal, Arya Samaj in Punjab and the All India Muslim Ladies Conference (Anjuman-E-Khawatn-E-Islam) in 1914.
- Reformers held public meetings and used newspapers and magazines to share their ideas with peoples.
- Translations of significant works, such as the Marathi translation of Vidyasagar's 'Indu Prakash' by Vishnu Shastri in 1868, were also common.

(iii) Nature of Ideas

- New ideas around liberalism, freedom, cultural pride, homemaking, marriage and roles for women emerged during the colonial period.
- Education, especially female education, gained importance. The value of female education was supported by both modern and traditional arguments.
- Jotiba Phule established the first school for women in Pune.

Different Opinions of Social Reformers

- The necessity of modernity was recognised, but the preservation of ancient heritage was also emphasised.
- Leaders like Jotiba Phule celebrated the glory of the pre-Aryan era, while Bal Gangadhar Tilak revered the Aryan period.
- Some reformers focused on issues faced by upper caste and middle-class individuals, while others addressed the struggles of marginalised castes.
- There were differing views on social evils; some thought they were due to a loss of true sprit of Hinduism, while others believed these issues were part of the religion itself.
- The Brahmo Samaj opposed the practice of Sati, while the orthodox Hindu community in Bengal established Dharma Sabha to counter British interpretations of sacred texts.

- Debates over polygamy[3] and the purdah system were prevalent among Muslim reformers. Organisations like the All India Muslim Ladies Conference and journals like Tahsib-e-Niswan opposed polygamy, while orthodox supporters upheld it.
- The 19th-century reform movements initiated a period of questioning, reinterpretation and intellectual and social growth.

Quick Test 1

1. What were some of the social evils addressed by 19th-century reform movements in India?
2. How did modern technologies help social reformers spread their ideas?
3. Which organisation was founded in 1914 to address Muslim women's issues?
4. Who opposed the practice of sati in Bengal?

2.2 Socio-Cultural Changes in India

- Changes in India can be understood through the processes of sanskritisation, modernisation[4], secularisation and westernisation.
- Sanskritisation existed before colonial rule, while the other three processes emerged in response to colonial changes.
- These processes often coexist and overlap in various situations, reflecting the complexities of Indian society and many non-Western countries.

Sanskritisation

- The term sanskritisation was coined by M.N. Srinivas and refers to the process by which a low caste, tribe, or group adopts the customs, rituals, beliefs, and lifestyles of a higher caste, especially a 'twice-born' (dwija) caste.
- This process allows individuals to improve their social status following the customs of higher-ranking groups in the social hierarchy.
- Sanskritisation typically happens when individuals or groups gain more wealth or political power.
- However, India's deep social inequalities often make it difficult for lower castes to fully adopt the customer's of higher castes.
- Traditionally dominant castes often punish lower castes attempting to adopt their customs.

Kumud Pawade's Journey

- Kumud Pawade, in her autobiography, recounts her experiences as a Dalit woman aspiring to become a Sanskrit teacher.
- She became interested in Sanskrit because it could help her enter a field that was usually closed to her due to rules about gender and caste.
- She was particularly motivated to explore how Sanskrit texts addressed issues concerning women and Dalits, seeking knowledge that could empower her community.
- Throughout her journey, she faced a spectrum of reactions from society, ranging from guarded acceptance to brutal rejection, highlighting the challenges faced by individuals breaking caste and gender barriers.

---

3 **Polygamy** It is a form of marriage in which one husband has many wives or one wife have many husbands.

4 **Modernisation** It refers to improvement in technology and production process.

Impact of Sanskritisation

- **Cultural Influence** Sanskritisation has significantly impacted various cultural domains, including language, literature, ideology, music, dance, drama, lifestyle and rituals.
- Its effects are observable not only within Hinduism but also in cultures outside of it, with regional variations across India.
- **Regional Dynamics** In regions dominated by highly sanskritised castes, the overall culture tends to undergo a degree of sanskritisation.
- Conversely, areas where non-Sanskritic castes are predominant experience a phenomenon known as **De-Sanskritisation**, where their cultural influences prevail. For example, in Punjab, Sanskritic influence has historically been weak, with Persian culture predominating until the late 19th century.

Criticism of Sanskritisation

- **Social Mobility** Critics argue that Sanskritisation overstates the social mobility and potential for lower castes to attain higher social status. Despite efforts, fundamental inequalities persist in society.
- **Reinforcement of Hierarchies** The process inherently accepts upper caste customs as superior, while viewing lower caste practices as inferior, fostering an environment where imitation of upper caste traditions is considered desirable and natural.
- **Justification of Inequality** Sanskritisation seems to support a system based on inequality and exclusion. It gives the impression that accepting ideas like purity and pollution among groups of people is acceptable.
- **Adoption of Upper Caste Practices** The adoption of upper caste rites and rituals can lead to negative consequences, such as increased seclusion of women and girls, the entrenchment of dowry practices and further caste discrimination.
- **Impact on Dalit Culture and Identity** The effect of this trend harms Dalit culture by making their work and skills less important. For example, the value of labour performed by 'lower castes' is degraded and seen as shameful. Identities based on work like craftsmanship, artisanal skills, and knowledge systems such as medicine, ecology, agriculture, and animal husbandry are regarded as useless in the industrial era.

Sanskritisation and Social Group Position

- **Improvement in Status** M.N. Srinivas noted that the sanskritisation of a social group typically enhances its position within the local caste hierarchy.
- **Economic and Political Context** This improvement often relies on either an elevation in the economic or political status of the group or a heightened self-awareness stemming from interactions with sources of Hinduism's 'Great Tradition', such as pilgrimage sites or monasteries.
- **Obstacles to Assimilation** In India's highly stratified society, significant barriers still exist that prevent lower castes from easily adopting the customs of higher castes. Traditionally, dominant castes would punish lower castes attempting to assimilate upper caste practices, illustrating the complexities and challenges of sanskritisation.

Quick Test 2

1. Name any two social evils that plagued Indian society.
2. In which language Vishnu Shastri translated Vidyasagar's book Indu Prakash?
3. Name the organisation which opposed the practice of polygamy among Muslims.
4. Did sanskritisation exist before colonial rule?
5. Who coined the term sanskritisation?

2.3 Westernisation

- M.N. Srinivas defines westernisation as the changes in Indian society and culture resulting from over 150 years of British rule, encompassing changes in technology, institutions, ideology and values.
- Westernisation in India is often associated with adopting British customs, but in recent times, American influences have also become prominent, especially in writing, speech and accents.

Kinds of Westernisation

- **Adoption by Intellectuals** Some Indian intellectuals embraced Western ways of thinking and lifestyles, supporting the expansion of Western culture. Reformers from the early 19th century fall into this category.
- **Cultural Adoption Without Values** Some Indians adopted Western clothing and appearances but lacked democratic and egalitarian values. For instance, Western-educated Indians may hold biassed views against various ethnic or religious communities.
- **Spread of Cultural Traits** There has been a general dissemination of Western cultural traits, including new technologies, styles of dress, food and changes in people's habits and lifestyles.

Impact of Westernisation

- **Middle-Class Homes** The initial impact of westernisation is visible in middle-class households, where furniture and electronic items reflect a Western style of living, such as sofa sets, dining tables, refrigerators and TVs.
- **Art and Literature** Indian art and literature have been influenced by Western styles. Notable artists like Ravi Varma, Abanindranath Tagore, Chandu Menon and Bankim Chandra Chattopadhyay engaged with colonial influences in their work.
- **Cultural Conflicts** Generational conflicts in modern times often manifest as cultural conflicts resulting from Westernisation.
- **Opportunities in Education** Western education has opened new opportunities for various groups, particularly in the North-East region. There are also instances of lower castes adopting a cosmopolitan lifestyle reflective of Western customs instead of those of upper castes.
- Srinivas observed that while lower castes aimed to adopt Sanskritic traditions, upper castes leaned toward Westernisation.
- This idea doesn't apply universally in India. For example, the Thiyyas in Kerala, not considered an upper caste, embraced British culture to lead a cosmopolitan life and challenge caste practices. Similarly, Western education created new opportunities for various groups, such as those in the North-East.

2.4 Modernisation

- The term modernisation was viewed positively in the 19th and 20th centuries, initially associated with advancements in technology and production. Today, it reflects the developmental paths taken by Western Europe and North America.

Characteristics of Modernisation

- Modernisation involves a shift from local ties and narrow thinking towards universal values and commitments.
- It favours rationality and science over emotions and religious tendencies.
- The individual is prioritised over the group in social and political contexts.
- Work is based on choice rather than birth, promoting personal agency.
- People emphasise their efforts and hard work rather than relying on fate and destiny.

- Relationships among people are based on personal choices rather than family background.
- Individual identity in society is defined by work and achievements rather than caste, community or religion.
- Work is separated from family and community in bureaucratic organisations.

Modernisation in India

Modernisation in India is distinct due to its colonial history, resulting in unique features as following

- India has a scientific tradition and a vibrant, secular, democratic political system.
- Caste and community-based identities are still prevalent.
- Jobs in India are often assigned by birth, rather than personal choice.
- Marriages are frequently arranged based on caste and community.
- India has a rich tradition of plurality and argumentation, which continues to evolve.

2.5 Secularisation

Secularisation refers to the decline in the influence of religion in society, indicating an increasing secular nature. The level of secularisation is measured by people's involvement in religious organisations and their religious beliefs.

Secularisation and Modernisation

- Secularisation is closely linked to modernisation and **Westernisation**[5]. While it was once believed that modern practices led to secularisation, this is not always the case. In India, exposure to modern ideas during the colonial period fostered the emergence of religious reform organisations.
- Rituals within religions can also have secular dimensions, providing opportunities for socialising among peers and superiors, while also holding economic and political significance.

Secularisation of Caste

- The caste system operates within a religious framework, historically tied to beliefs of purity and pollution. Today, caste functions more as a pressure group, with increasing influence from caste associations and caste-based political parties.
- Caste is a major organisational cluster for much of the population and politics aims to capture power for specific goals, manipulating **social structures**[6] to gain mass support.
- Consequently, politics can alter the form of caste relations, reflecting the dynamic interplay between social and political influences.

Some Social Reformers

- **Raja Ram Mohun Roy** Founder of the Brahmo Samaj in 1828, influential in politics, public administration, education and religion. He campaigned for the abolition of Sati, utilising humanitarian and natural rights arguments alongside Hindu scriptures. Known as the Father of the Indian Renaissance.

Raja Ram Mohun Roy

- **Pandita Ramabai** A social reformer and advocate for women's empowerment and education. She was recognised as a Sanskrit scholar and made significant contributions to women's rights.
- **Sir Syed Ahmed Khan** An Islamic reformist and philosopher who emphasised free inquiry (ijtihad) to foster social change. He sought to reconcile Quranic teachings with modern scientific principles.

---

5 **Westernisation** It includes changes that occur at different levels such as technology, institutions, ideology and values.
6 **Social Structure** It refers to arrangement of persons in relationships that are defined or controlled by institutions.

- **Viresalingam** He is known as the **Father of the Renaissance Movement** in Telugu, he championed women's education, widow remarriage and fought against the dowry system. He founded schools and wrote significant literary works.
- **Vidyasagar** A key figure in the Bengal Renaissance, he contributed to modernising Bengali prose and was instrumental in passing the Widow Remarriage Act. His efforts in education and social reform were profound.
- **Jotiba Phule** He was an anti-caste activist and social reformer from Maharashtra. He worked towards eradicating untouchability, promoting women's rights and reforming Hindu family life. He founded the **Satyashodhak Samaj** to advocate for equal rights for lower castes.

Jotiba Phule

- **Raja Ravi Varma** A renowned Indian painter, he is celebrated for merging European artistic techniques with Indian themes. His affordable lithographs greatly enhanced his reach and influence as a painter and public figure.

Quick Test 3

1. Who has defined Westernisation as the changes brought about in Indian society and culture as a result of over 150 years of British rule?
2. Name any two famous artists who struggled with colonial encounters.
3. On what factor the work of men is based?
4. What is one of the organisational clusters along which the bulk of the population live?

NCERT Folder

Exercise Questions

1. Write a critical essay on Sanskritisation.
Or **Critically examine the concept of Sanskritisation.**

Ans. The term 'Sanskritisation' was coined by M.N. Srinivas. It may be defined as the process by which a low caste or tribe or other group takes over the customs, ritual, beliefs, ideology and style of life of a high and in particular, a 'twice-born (dwija) caste'.

Impact of Sanskritisation

- Its influence can be seen in language, literature, ideology, music, dance, drama, style of life and ritual.
- It is primarily a process that takes place in the Hindu space though Srinivas argued that it was visible even in sects and religious groups outside Hinduism.
- It operated differently in different regions. In those areas where a highly sanskritised caste was dominant, the entire region underwent a certain amount of sanskritisation. In the areas, where non-sanskritic castes were dominant, non-sanskritic influence was stronger; this can be termed as the process of 'de-sanskritisation'.
- Sanskritisation allows people to improve their status through adoption of names and customs of culturally high-placed groups.

Criticisms of Sanskritisation

- It has been criticised for exaggerating social mobility or the scope of lower castes to move up the social ladder.
- It leads to no structural change but only positional change of some individuals.
- Inequality continues to persist though some individuals may be able to improve their position within the unequal structure.
- The ideology of sanskritisation accepts the ways of the upper caste as superior and that of the lower caste as inferior. Thus, the desire to imitate the upper caste is seen as natural and desirable.

- Sanskritisation seems to justify a model that rests on inequality and exclusion. The notion of upper caste and lower caste strengthens the discrimination and undemocratic vision in the society.
- Since sanskritisation results in the adoption of upper caste rites and rituals it leads to practices of secluding girls and women, adopting dowry practices instead of bride-price and practising caste-discrimination against other groups.
- The effect of such a culture is that it erodes characteristics of Dalit culture and society. Identities based on the basis of work, crafts, artisanal ability are regarded useless.

2. Westernisation is often just about adoption of Western attire and lifestyle. Are there other aspects to being westernised? Or is that about modernisation? Discuss.

Or **Westernisation does not involve the imitation of external forms of culture. Illustrate the process of westernisation.** **CBSE 2025**

Ans. Westernisation in general refers to the spread of Western culture and its traits such as use of new technology, cuisine, dress, habits and lifestyles among the people. In India, it was also a result of long rule of Britishers and brought changes in the fields of technology, institutions, ideology and values.

There were different kinds of westernisation as follows

- One kind refers to the emergence of a westernised sub-cultural pattern through a minority section of Indian who first came in contact with the Western culture. This included the sub-culture of Indian intellectuals, who not only adopted many cognitive patterns or ways of thinking but also styles of life and supported its expansion.
- There has been a general spread of Western cultural traits such as the use of new technology, dress, food and changes in general.
- Westernisation does involve the imitation of external forms of culture. It does not necessarily mean that people adopt modern values of democracy and equality.
- Apart from Western ways of life and thinking, the West influenced Indian art and literature.

Modernisation

- Modernity as opposed to westernisation assumes that local ties and parochial perspectives give way to universal commitments and cosmopolitan attitudes.
- That the truths of utility, calculation, and science take precedence over those of the emotions, the sacred and the non-rational.
- That the individual rather that the group is the primary unity of society and politics.
- That the associations in which men live and work be based on choice and not birth.
- That mastery rather than fatalism orient their attitude toward the material and human environment.
- That the identity is chosen and achieved not assigned and accepted.
- That work is separated from family, residence and community in bureaucratic organisation.

It would be simplistic to say that westernisation is often just about Western attire and lifestyle. Westernisation pervades many aspects and shares a complex relation with modernisation.

3. Write short notes on

(i) Rites and Secularisation

(ii) Caste and Secularisation

(iii) Gender and Sanskritisation

Ans. **(i) Rites and Secularisation**

The customs and the activities associated with a religion are categorised as rites or rituals. Securalism means a process of decline in the influence of religion. With society becoming secularised, it had been believed by many, people will leave the traditions of rites or rituals. However, that is not entirely true.

A considerable part of ritual in India has direct reference to the pursuit of secular ends. Rituals have secular dimensions i.e. they provide men and women occasions for socialising with their peers and superiors. They get an opportunity to show off family's wealth, clothing and jewellery. During the last few decades in particular, the economic, political and status dimensions of ritual have become increasingly conspicuous.

(ii) Caste and Secularisation

Caste system operates within a religious framework in India. Belief systems of purity and pollution were central to its practice. However, presently caste is functioning as a pressure group. Many caste based associations and parties are increasingly joining Indian politics, thus resulting in secularisation of caste.

Today politicians mobilise caste groupings and identities in order to organise their power. Where there are other types of groups and other bases of associations, politicians approach them as well. And as they change the form of such organisations, they change the form of caste as well.

(iii) Gender and Sanskritisation

Sanskritisation refers to the adoption of customs, culture, beliefs, and lifestyle of high caste people by the lower caste or other groups of people.

It affects men and women differently, as men belonging to lower caste can uplift their position but women will be more disempowered. The women face more discrimination and also is faced with evils of dowry to become part of high caste people. The position of women is weaker among high caste groups of people.

Exam Pattern Questions

Objective Type Questions

Multiple Choice Questions (MCQs)

1. Sociologist ……….. elaborates upon the modern context by sketching three aspects to the modern framework of change in colonial India: modes of communication, forms of organisation and the nature of ideas. New technologies have speeded up various forms of communication.

(a) Satish Saberwal (b) Max Weber
(c) Raja Ram Mohun Roy (d) Jotiba Phule

2. Which social reformer was a philosopher, printer, writer, publisher, entrepreneur, etc.?

(a) Jotiba Phule (b) Raja Ravi Varma
(c) Vidyasagar (d) Viresalingam

3. Which of the following statements is not true about the role of communication in the social reform movements of the 19th century? Competency Based Que.

(a) New technologies like the printing press and telegraph played a significant role in the spread of reform ideas.
(b) Reformers communicated exclusively through traditional methods like word-of-mouth.
(c) Railways and steamships facilitated the movement of people and ideas across the country.
(d) Social reformers from different regions exchanged ideas through public media like newspapers and journals.

4. In the context of the social reform movements, which of the following best describes the nature of debates regarding polygamy?

(a) The debates were centered around the preservation of traditional practices.
(b) There was unanimous support for polygamy among the reformers.
(c) Social reformers like Jahanara Shah Nawas argued that polygamy went against the true spirit of the Quran.
(d) Polygamy was only debated within the Hindu community.

5. Which of the following was a common theme in the social reform movements of 19th century India?

(a) Upholding the dominance of the caste system
(b) Addressing the plight of the upper-caste, middle-class individuals
(c) Combating social evils like child marriage, sati and caste discrimination
(d) Reaffirming the belief in colonial rule as a means of progress

6. Which of the following best describes the essence of Sanskritisation? Competency Based Que.

(a) The attempt of lower castes to reject their identity and adopt the ways of upper castes.
(b) The process of improving social status through the adoption of customs of higher castes.
(c) The creation of new caste-based political parties.
(d) The pursuit of political power by lower castes without changing their customs.

7. Which of the following statements is not true about the concept of sanskritisation? Competency Based Que.

(a) It involves the adoption of customs and rituals of higher castes by lower castes.
(b) Sanskritisation leads to significant structural changes in the caste system.
(c) It can result in the improvement of a group's social status.
(d) Sanskritisation is primarily a process within the Hindu space, although it can be seen in other religious groups as well.

8. The impact of sanskritisation is many sided. Its influence can be seen in CBSE 2024

(a) Language only
(b) Literature only
(c) Drama only
(d) Language, Literature, Drama

9. Which of the following concepts involves the imitation of external forms of culture? It does not necessarily mean that people adopt modern values of democracy and equality. CBSE 2024 C

(a) Modernisation (b) Sanskritisation
(c) Secularisation (d) Westernisation

10. "The result is that although I try to forget my caste, it is impossible to forget. And then I remember an expression I heard somewhere: "What comes by birth, but can't be cast off by dying - that is caste." The above mentioned views were represented in whose autobiography?

(a) Kumud Pawade (b) Savitri Phule
(c) Pandita Ramabai (d) Sarojini Naidu

11. Who is known as the Father of Indian Renaissance?

(a) Sir Syed Ahmed Khan (b) Jotiba Phule
(c) Raja Ravi Varma (d) Raja Ram Mohun Roy

12. Which of the following statements is true for westernisation? **CBSE 2025**

(a) The changes brought about in Indian society and culture is a result of over 150 years of British rule.
(b) Westernisation does not involve the imitation of external forms of culture.
(c) The West did not influence Indian art and literature.
(d) Westernisation did not include the sub-culture of Indian intellectuals.

13. Put the following social reformers and their contributions in the correct order. **Competency Based Que.**

I. Raja Ram Mohun Roy attacked the practice of sati based on humanitarian principles and Hindu scriptures.
II. Jotiba Phule opened the first school for women in Pune, advocating for female education.
III. Sir Syed Ahmed Khan emphasised the validity of free inquiry and the compatibility of Islam with modern science.
IV. Pandita Ramabai travelled across India to promote women's rights and education.

Codes
(a) IV, III, II and I (b) I, II, III and IV
(c) II, IV, I and III (d) III, I, IV and II

14. Which of the following is the correct order for the statements about Social Movements? **Competency Based Que.**

I. These protests were perceived by elites as a major threat to the established order of society.
II. 'Crowd' and the 'mob' were not made up of anarchic hooligans out to destroy society. Instead, they too had a 'moral economy'.
III. The public resorted to protest because they had no other way of expressing their anger and resentment against deprivation.
IV. There was an anxiety among people to maintain the prevailing social order.

Codes
(a) I and IV (b) III and IV
(c) II, IV and III (d) I, II and III

15. The attempts made to fight social discrimination in pre colonial India were based on which ideology? **Competency Based Que.**

I. Buddhism II. Sufi Movement
III. Bhakti Movement

Codes
(a) I and II (b) II and III (c) I and III (d) I, II and III

16. How has development of railways helped reformers in the movement of new ideas? **Competency Based Que.**

I. Social reformers from Punjab and Bengal communicated with reformers of Madras and Maharashtra.
II. Pandita Ramabai travelled to different corners of the country.
III. Christian missionaries reached many parts of present Nagaland, Mizoram and Meghalaya.

Codes
(a) I and II (b) II and III
(c) I and III (d) I, II and III

17. Which of the following concepts involves the imitation of external forms of culture? It does not necessarily mean that people adopt modern values of democracy and equality. **CBSE 2024**

(a) Modernisation
(b) Sanskritisation
(c) Secularisation
(d) Westernisation

Assertion-Reason Questions

Direction (Q. Nos. 18-20) Two statement are given in the question below as Assertion (A) and Reason (R). Read the statements and choose the appropriate option.

(a) Both A and R are true and R is the correct explanation of A
(b) Both A and R are true, but R is not the correct explanation of A
(c) A is true, but R is false
(d) A is false, but R is true

18. **Assertion** (A) It was the social reformer Jotiba Phule who opened the first school for women in Pune.
Reason (R) Reformers argued that for a society to progress women have to be educated.

19. **Assertion** (A) The process of sanskritisation affects both men and women differently.
Reason (R) In the case of women, the adoption of upper-caste customs leads to practices that further restrict their social mobility, such as seclusion and dowry practices.

20. **Assertion** (A) The Backward Classes Movement emphasised secular factors as key to the upward mobility of caste groups.
Reason (R) The movement advocated for the removal of the desire to imitate Brahminical or upper-caste traditions, focusing instead on the pride of belonging to one's own caste.

Case Based Questions

Read the passage given below and answer the questions that follow by choosing the correct option.

21. New technologies speeded up various forms of communication. The printing press, telegraph and later the microphone, movement of people and goods through steamship and railways helped quick movement of new ideas. Within India, social reformers from Punjab and Bengal exchanged ideas with reformers from Madras and Maharashtra. Keshav Chandra Sen of Bengal visited Madras in 1864. Pandita Ramabai travelled to different corners of the country. Some of them went to other countries. Christian missionaries reached remote corners of present day Nagaland, Mizoram and Meghalaya.

(i) Which technology helped in the quick movement of new ideas in India?

(a) Television (b) Printing press
(c) Radio (d) Telephone

(ii) Which reformer from Bengal visited Madras in 1864?

(a) Pandita Ramabai (b) Keshav Chandra Sen
(c) Vishnu Shastri (d) Dayanand Saraswati

(iii) Which of the following social organisations was set up in Bengal?

(a) Brahmo Samaj
(b) Arya Samaj
(c) Anjuman-e-Khawatn-e-Islam
(d) All of the above

(iv) Which missionary group reached remote corners of Nagaland, Mizoram and Meghalaya?

(a) Christian missionaries (b) Arya Samaj
(c) Brahmo Samaj (d) Theosophical Society

Answers

1. (a) Satish Saberwal
2. (c) Vidyasagar
3. (b) Reformers communicated exclusively through traditional methods like word-of-mouth.
4. (c) Social reformers like Jahanara Shah Nawas argued that polygamy went against the true spirit of the Quran.
5. (c) Combating social evils like child marriage, sati and caste discrimination
6. (b) The process of improving social status through the adoption of customs of higher castes.
7. (b) Sanskritisation leads to significant structural changes in the caste system.
8. (d) Language, Literature, Drama
9. (d) Westernisation
10. (a) Kumud Pawade
11. (d) Raja Ram Mohun Roy
12. (a) The changes brought about in Indian society and culture is a result of over 150 years of British rule.
13. (a) IV, III, II and I
14. (d) I, II and III
15. (d) I, II and III
16. (d) I, II and III
17. (d) Westernisation
18. (a) Both A and R is true and R is the correct explanation of A
19. (a) Both A and R are true and R is the correct explanation of A
20. (a) Both A and R are true and R is the correct explanation of A
21. (i) (b) Printing press
 (ii) (b) Keshav Chandra Sen
 (iii) (a) Brahmo Samaj
 (iv) (a) Christian missionaries

Subjective Questions

Very Short Answer Type Questions

1. What were the two of the issues or themes taken up by the social reform movements of the 19th and early 20th centuries?

Ans. Social reforms of the 19th century and early 20th century wanted to bring changes in the social practices that discriminated against women and lower castes. The issues of *Sati*, child marriage, widow remarriage and caste discrimination concerned them.

2. In colonial India what were the new technologies which speeded up the various forms of communication?

Ans. The technologies like telegraph, printing press and microphone speeded up the various forms of communication in colonial India.

3. What was unique about the social reform movements of the 19th century? **CBSE SQP 2023**

Ans. The social reform movements of the 19th century were unique in several ways. Some of the important features are as follows

- It challenged the colonial rule in India and brought changes in social practices that discriminated against women and lower castes.
- The social reforms of the 19th century were characterised by modernity and mixed ideas. It was a creative combination of modern liberal ideas of the West and the new perceived traditional literature.
- These movements were to purify and rediscover an Indian civilisation that would be conformant with the European ideals of rationalism, monotheism and individualism.

4. Orthodox members of the Hindu community in Bengal formed an organisation called Dharma Sabha. Why was Dharma Sabha formed?

Or **What ideas of society did the Dharma Sabha Project?** **Competency Based Que.**

Ans. Dharma Sabha was formed by the orthodox Hindu community of Bengal to oppose and petition the British arguing that reformers had no right to interpret sacred texts.

5. Mention the contribution of Jotiba Phule in social reforms?

Ans. Jotiba Phule advocated female education in India. He opened the first school for women in Pune and also supported the glory of pre-Aryan age.

6. What is cultural change?

Ans. Cultural change refers to the change in customs, traditions, beliefs, lifestyle, behaviour etc. Cultural change is any impact or change on the cultural side. It also means when changes start to occur in the culture of any society. Cultural change is also change in aspects of daily life.

7. New ideas of liberalism and freedom emerged in colonial India as stated by sociologist Satish Saberwal. Identify them. **CBSE 2019**

Ans. The nature of new ideas were as following

- New ideas of homemaking and marriage.
- New roles for mothers and daughters.
- New ideas of self-conscious pride in culture and tradition.
- The value of education.
- Crucial for a nation to become modern but also retain its ancient heritage.

8. The term sanskritisation was coined by M.N. Srinivas. Explain the meaning of sanskritisation.

Ans. Sanskritisation is a process by which a low caste or tribe or other group adopts the customs, rituals, beliefs, ideology and style of life of a high caste people.

9. What did M.N. Srinivas means by sanskritisation and de-sanskritisation?

Or **Give the meaning of the term 'de-sanskritisation'.**

Or **What is de-sanskritisation?**

Ans. The term sanskritisation was coined by M.N. Srinivas. It is defined as the process by which a low caste or tribe or other group takes over the custom, ritual, beliefs, ideology and style of life of a high and a twice-born (dwija) caste.

De-sanskritisation refers to the strong influence of the non-Sanskritic castes in the areas where they are dominant.

10. "Sanskritisation in India often encounters significant obstacles due to the deeply entrenched caste system and social inequalities. While the process involves lower castes adopting the customs of higher castes to improve their social status, the dominant castes have historically resisted such changes, maintaining rigid social hierarchies."

Elaborate on the obstacles faced by lower castes in the process of sanskritisation. **Competency Based Que.**

Ans. Lower castes face resistance from dominant castes when attempting Sanskritisation, as higher castes often view their adoption of customs as a threat to social order. This leads to hostility and punishment, preventing lower castes from improving their social position.

11. Explain sanskritisation as a process of change.

Or **How is sanskritisation a process of social change?**

Or **"Sanskritisation seems to justify a model that rests on inequality and exclusion." Give two reasons to support this statement.** CBSE 2022 Term II

Ans. Sanskritisation is a process by which a low caste or tribe takes to the customs, rituals, beliefs, ideology and the style of life of a high and in particular a 'twice born caste'.

(i) Its influence can be seen in language, literature, ideology, music, dance, drama, style of life and rituals.

(ii) Practices like adopting vegetarianism, wearing of Sanskrit thread, performance of specific prayers and religious ceremonies and so on were suggested by people so that they could improve their status.

12. Kumudtai's journey into Sanskrit began with great interest and eagerness with Gokhale Guruji, her teacher at school…At the University, the Head of the Department was a well known scholar and he took great pleasure in taunting Kumudtai…Despite the adverse comments she successfully completed her Masters in Sanskrit…. Source: Kumud Pawade (1938)

Read the source and answer the following question.

Do you think sanskritisation is a gendered process? Give a reason for your answer.

Or **Using the example of Kumud Pawade, show how the process of sanskritisation is gendered.** CBSE SQP 2023

Ans Yes, I think sanskritisation is a gendered process. According to passage Kumud Pawade felt that the study of Sanskrit can help her break into a field that was not possible for her to enter on grounds of gender and caste. As she proceeds with her studies, she meets with varied reactions ranging from surprise to hostility, from guarded acceptance to brutal rejection.

13. According to M.N. Srinivas what does Westernisation means?

Ans. M.N. Srinivas defines Westernisation as the changes brought about in Indian society and culture as a result of over 150 years of British rule. It includes changes that occur at different levels such as technology, institutions, ideology and values.

14. Westernisation does involve the imitation of external forms of culture. It does not necessarily mean that people adopt modern values of democracy and equality.

What do you mean by Westernisation?

Ans. Westernisation refers to the general spread of western cultural traits, such as the use of new technology, dress, cuisine and changes in the habits and living styles of people.

15. The term modernisation has a long history. From the 19th and more so the 20th century, the term began to be associated with positive and desirable values.

Explain the term modernisation.

Ans. The term modernisation was associated with positive and desirable values in the 19th and 20th century. In the earlier period, modernisation referred to improvement in technology and production process but now it refers to the path of development that much of the West Europe or North America has taken.

16. What is the meaning of modernity?

Or **What does the term modernity assume?**

Ans. Modernity assumes that local ties and parochial perspective give way to universal commitments and cosmopolitan attitudes. The truths of utility, calculation and science take precedence over those of emotions. Behaviour, thought and attitude are not decided by family, tribe, caste, community, etc.

17. What is meant by secularisation?

Ans. It is a process of decline in the influence of religion in the society. It assumes that society becomes increasingly secular. The extent of secularisation is measured through the involvement of people with religious organisations and holding of religious views of people.

18. In what way do rituals have secular dimensions?

Or **Rituals also have secular dimensions as distinct from secular goals. Explain.** Competency Based Que.

Ans. Rituals have secular dimensions. They provide opportunities to exhibit family's wealth, status and economy. They also provide occasions for socialising with peers and superiors.

19. Modernisation and secularisation are part of a set of modern ideas. How are the two processes linked?

Ans. Modernisation and secularisation are said to be a part of a set of modern ideas. The two processes are linked in the following ways

- Change in attitude towards religion and celebration of festivals, change in ceremonies, taboos and sacrifices.
- Modern ways lead to decline in traditional and religious ways.
- This leads to a scientific and rational outlook.

20. Modernisation and secularisation in India have taken unique paths, differing from Western experiences. Provide two examples to illustrate how. Competency Based Que.

Ans. Two examples to illustrate this are

(i) **Rituals with Secular Goals** Rituals, such as weddings, now emphasise economic and social status, with displays of wealth like cars and VIP attendance, highlighting their non-religious dimensions.

(ii) **Secularisation of Caste** Caste functions as political pressure groups, forming associations or parties to demand rights, shifting from religious to political roles.

Short Answer Type Questions

1. "The struggle for women's upliftment in the 19th and early 20th centuries was led by male reformers." Discuss with suitable examples. Competency Based Que.

Ans. The reform movements of the 19th and early 20th centuries tried to address the issues that discriminated against women. The struggle was led by male reformers in this regard. They are

- **Raja Ram Mohun Roy** He attacked the evil practice of *Sati* which was present in society. He opposed it on the basis of humanitarianism, natural rights doctrines and Hindu *shastras*.
- **Jotiba Phule** Female education was encouraged by him and he also opened the first school for women in Pune.
- **Ranade** His writings supported the remarriage of widows on the basis of Shastras. He wrote the book, 'The Texts of the Hindu Law' on the lawfulness of the remarriage of widows and vedic authorities for widow remarriage.

2. "What marked these 19th century social reform attempts was the modern context and mix of ideas." Interpret the given statement.

Ans. These 19th century social reform attempts was the modern context and mix of ideas as

- It was a creative combination of modern ideas of Western liberalism and a new look on traditional literature.
- Raja Ram Mohun Roy attacked the practice of Sati on the basis of both appeals to humanitarian and natural rights doctrines as well as Hindu Shastras.
- Ranade's writing entitled The Text of Hindu Laws on the lawfulness of the remarriage of widows and vedic authorities for widow marriage elaborated the shastric sanction for remarriage of widows.
- The content of new education was modernising and liberal. The literary content of the courses in the humanities and social sciences was drawn from the literature of the European Renaissance, Reformation and enlightenment. Its themes were humanistic, secular and liberal.
- Sir Syed Ahmed Khan's interpretation of Islam emphasised the validity of free enquiry (itjihad) and the alleged similarities between Koranic revelation and the laws of nature discovered by modern science.

3. "19th century reform initiated a period of questioning, reinterpretations and both intellectual and social growth." Using suitable examples, justify the given statement.

Ans. 19th century social reform initiated a period of questioning, reinterpretations and both intellectual and social growth as in following ways

- The idea of female education was debated intensely. Reformers argued that for a society to progress women have to be educated. Some of them believed that in pre-modern India, women were educated. Others contested this on the grounds that this was so only of a privileged few. Thus, attempts to justify female education were made by recourse to both modern and traditional ideas.
- They actively debated the meanings of tradition and modernity. Jotiba Phule thus recalled the glory of pre-Aryan age while others like Bal Gangadhar Tilak emphasised the glory of the Aryan period.
- Muslim social reformers actively debated the meaning of polygamy and purdah. For example, a resolution against the evils of polygamy was proposed by Jahanara Shah Nawas at the All India Muslim Ladies Conference.
- Debates within communities were common during this period. For instance, Sati was opposed by the Brahmo Samaj. Orthodox members of the Hindu community in Bengal formed an organisation called Dharma Sabha and petitioned the British arguing that reformers had no right to interpret sacred texts.

4. The varied social reform movements did have common themes. Yet there were also significant differences discuss. CBSE 2025

Ans. The social reform movements in India had both common themes and differences

- **Common Themes** Most reform movements aimed to modernise society, promote education, improve the status of women and reduce social evils like caste discrimination, polygamy and sati. Reformers used public meetings, media and translations to spread their ideas and inspire change.

- **Differences** These movements had varied focuses. For instance, some emphasised the problems of upper-caste women, while others addressed the discrimination faced by lower castes. Views also differed on tradition and modernity—some reformers wanted to revive ancient Indian heritage, while others criticised religious practices that perpetuated social injustices.

5. What was the contribution of Raja Ram Mohun Roy in the social reform of India?

Ans. Raja Ram Mohun Roy also known as the Father of the Indian Renaissances made a great contribution in initiating Socio Reform Movement in India.

- He is widely known for his role in the abolition of Sati.
- He propagated Western education among Indians.
- His influence was apparent in the field of politics, public administration, education as well as religion.
- He worked for the improvement in the position of women. He stressed on rational and modern scientific approach.
- He advocated widow remarriage and education of women.

6. What were the major women's issues taken up by various reformers in Indian history?

Or **Explain the role of social reformers in uplifting the status of women in India.**

Or **Discuss the role of social reformers in dealing with the women's issues during the colonial period.**

Or **The women's question arose in Modern India as part of 19th century middle-class social reform movements. These reformers used a mix of ideas. Explain these ideas.** **CBSE 2023**

Ans. Women's issues were taken up by various reformers in Indian history.

- The issues of practice of *Sati*, child marriage and widow remarriage were taken up by the reformers.
- Female education was also discussed intensively. Female education was promoted by the social reformers and new ideas of liberalism and freedom also brought new ideas of homemaking and marriage.
- New roles for mothers and daughters also emerged with the growth of new ideas and new consciousness. Jotiba Phule, the social reformer opened the first school for women in Pune.
- Muslim social reformers also debated the issues of polygamy and purdah. Jahanara Shah at the All India Muslim Ladies Conference proposed a resolution against the evils of polygamy in Islam. The resolution said that polygamy was against the true spirit of *Quran*.
- The social reformers tried to bring changes in the social practices that discriminated against women.
- Raja Ram Mohun Roy attacked the practice of *sati* on humanitarian grounds as well as on the writings of Hindu *shastras*. Similarly, Ranade's writings elaborated the *shastric* sanction for remarriage of widows.

7. Process of sanskritisation encourages inequalities and discrimination. Explain with examples.

Or **Sanskritisation seems to justify a model that rests on inequality and exclusion. Explain this model.** **CBSE 2023**

Ans. Sanskritisation is the process through which the low caste people try to uplift their political and economic status.

- The lower caste assume that upper caste is being superior hence to be imitated. Justification of the practice of inequality and exclusion as a marked privilege of upper caste makes it a discriminatory system.
- Process that is gendered though progressive for men, upper caste practices like Purdah system, low age of marriage, dowry in place of bride price are regressive as far as women are concerned.
- Erosion of Dalit culture would be an expected outcome. The work performed by the Dalits is also considered shameful and it leads to the erosion of Dalit culture and ethos.
- The upper castes look down upon the lower castes. It reflects the undemocratic vision in society. Thus, sanskritisation creates inequality and discrimination in society instead of erasing them.

8. Critically examine the concept of Sanskritisation. **CBSE 2024 C**

Ans. Sanskritisation has been criticised for making people think they can improve their social position by copying upper caste customs. This doesn't change the unfair system, it just helps some people move up. It also makes lower caste traditions less valuable and can lead to harmful practices like dowry and caste discrimination. Instead of breaking social barriers, sanskritisation keeps inequality alive by suggesting that upper caste ways are better, while ignoring the worth of lower caste cultures and work.

9. Which sociologist coined the term sanskritisation? Differentiate between sanskritisation and de-sanskritisation. **CBSE 2024**

Ans. The term sanskritisation was coined by sociologist M.N. Srinivas. Sanskritisation is when a lower caste or group adopts the customs, rituals, and ways of higher castes to improve their social status. On the other hand, de-sanskritisation is the opposite process, where regions or groups move away from Sanskrit-based practices.

For example, in some areas, people rejected the dominance of Sanskrit and embraced other cultural influences, like Persian in Punjab, leading to a change in cultural traditions and practices.

10. What do you mean by Westernisation? Explain its different aspects.

Ans. Westernisation is the spread of the Western cultural traits such as use of new gadgets and technology, cuisine, dress and changes in habits and styles of people. In India, Westernisation has been the result of long period of British colonialism in India.

Different aspects of westernisation are

- The impact and influence of Western culture is seen at different levels such as technology, institutions, ideologies, values, cuisine, clothing, etc. For example, many middle class homes in India have a television set, fridge, dining table, sofa set that are very much a part of Western living.
- There is a subculture of people and mainly intellectuals in India who not only adopt Western ways of thinking but also support its growth and expansion.
- There are also individuals who are Western in clothing and appearances but they do not process democratic, egalitarian and modern thinking of the West.
- Westernisation do involve the imitation of external forms of culture but not necessarily values of democracy and equality.

11. Do you think Westernisation is one of the reasons for generation conflict?

Ans. Westernisation is one of the reasons for generation conflict, as younger people are faster in adopting Western lifestyle, while older people believe more in Indian cultural ethos and practices.

It leads to differences between them. Old and young generation of people have many things uncommon to them due to westernisation.

Old people often love Indian classical music or spiritual songs but youth likes pop songs and Western songs. Mutuality between the old and the young is becoming difficult day-by-day.

Sometimes the parents and children become strangers in a family due to different tastes and likings in various areas of life. Therefore, Westernisation is one of the reasons for generation conflict.

12. "The term modernisation has a long history. From the 19th and more so the 20th century, the term began to be associated with positive and desirable values. People and societies wanted to be modern. In the early years, modernisation referred to improvement in technology and production processes. Increasingly, however, the term had a wider usage." What, according to sociologists, constitutes the modernisation process? CBSE 2024

Ans. According to sociologists, the modernisation process involves several key aspects. It includes the shift from local ties to universal commitments, the prioritisation of utility, science and rationality over emotions and the sacred, and the focus on individualism rather than group identity. Modernisation emphasises that work and social positions should be based on choice, not birth and that identity is achieved rather than ascribed. It promotes mastery over fatalism and encourages a scientific, calculated approach to material and human environments.

13. Explain the phenomenon of Modernity as given by Rudolph and Rudolph. CBSE 2023

Ans. The phenomenon of Modernity as given by Rudolph and Rudolph can be understood with help of following points

- Modernisation assumes that local ties and narrow thinking give way to universal values and commitments.
- The principles of rationality and science are favoured over emotions and religious tendencies.
- Individual rather than the group is favoured as unit of society and politics.
- The work of men is based on choice rather than birth.
- People believe in their own efforts and hard work rather than fate and destiny.
- The relations among people are based on personal choice and likings rather than birth in a particular family.
- The identity of man in society is based on his work and achievement rather than his caste, community or religion.
- The work is separated from family, residence and community in a bureaucratic organisation.

14. What is the relationship between modernisation and secularisation?

Ans. There is close relationship between modernisation and secularisation. They overlap with each other in many areas of human life. They are also closely linked with each other, as they both are part of a set of modern ideas.

Secularisation is the process of declining role of a religion in society but modernisation is the process whereby people adopt modern values of merit, knowledge, rationality and individuality.

Secularisation helps in the spread of modernity and modernity also helps in the process of secularisation. Both of them have a cause-effect relation in many areas of human activity.

Modern values of rationality, science and individuality help in loosening the grip of religion in people's lives. Secularisation helps to remove the discrimination which stem from the orthodox religious tradition. Similarly, modernisation focuses on choice and merit of the person rather than his birth in a particular family. Thus, secularisation and modernisation strengthen and support each other.

15. Rituals have also secular dimensions as distinct from secular goals. Explain. Competency Based Que.

Ans. Secularisation refers to the declining role of religion in society. Performance of rituals often hampers the process of secularisation in the society. However, rituals also have their secular dimensions apart from their religious purposes. Rituals do not have any direct secular goals but they have secular dimensions attached to them.

They provide opportunities to people to meet with their friends, relatives and elders. They have also become an occasion to show off one's wealth, clothing and jewellery.

The economic and political status are also reflected by the number of people attending a particular ceremony and the participation of VIPs.

The participation of people from various arenas of life in the ritual ceremony of a family also provides the opportunity to enhance the social status. Thus, rituals serve some unintended secular purposes besides the religious one.

16. "In traditional caste India system operated within a religious framework. Belief systems of purity and pollution were central to its practice. Today it often functions as political pressure groups."
Illustrate the process of secularisation of caste. CBSE 2024

Ans. The secularisation of caste refers to the shift from a religious framework, where caste was based on beliefs of purity and pollution, to a more political and social role. In contemporary India, caste no longer operates solely through religious rituals but functions as a political force. Caste-based associations and political parties have emerged, advocating for the rights and demands of specific caste groups. This transformation reflects caste's evolving role in influencing policies, social mobility and political representation, independent of religious beliefs.

Long Answer Type Questions

1. Elaborate on three aspects of change in colonial India as stated by Satish Saberwal. Competency Based Que.

Ans. Satish Saberwal highlighted three key aspects of social change in colonial India as following

- **Modes of Communication** The introduction of technologies like the printing press, telegraph and steamships allowed faster communication of ideas across regions. Reformers from different parts of India exchanged ideas, promoting social change.
- **Forms of Organisation** Various social reform movements formed organisations such as the Brahmo Samaj and Arya Samaj to spread their ideas through public meetings, media and translations of writings.
- **Nature of Ideas** New ideas emerged, focusing on liberalism, freedom and the importance of education, especially for women. Social reformers debated the roles of women and the importance of modern education in society.

2. Define sanskritisation. Why was it criticised at different levels?

Or **How has sanskritisation as a concept been criticised?**

Or **Enumerate different levels at which sanskritisation as a concept has been criticised.**

Ans. The sanskritisation term was coined by M.N. Srinivas. It refers to the process by which a lower caste, tribe or other social group adopts the customs, rituals, beliefs and lifestyle of a higher caste, usually a 'twice-born' caste, to improve their social status. This process often happens when the lower caste becomes wealthier or politically stronger.

Criticisms of sanskritisation are as follows

- **Exaggeration of Social Mobility** Sanskritisation gives the false impression that lower castes can easily improve their social status, but inequality persists in society.
- **Inferiority of Lower Castes** It accepts the customs of upper castes as superior and treats lower caste practices as inferior, promoting imitation rather than equality.
- **Reinforces Inequality** By justifying upper caste customs, sanskritisation strengthens social discrimination and exclusion.
- **Leads to Social Evils** The adoption of upper caste rituals may lead to practices like dowry, caste discrimination and the seclusion of women.

3. What was the impact of sanskritisation on lower castes?

Ans. The process of sanskritisation has greatly affected the caste system of Indian society. Its process has reduced the impact of caste system and lower castes tried to uplift their social status with this process.

The impact of sanskritisation is many sided. Its impacts are as follow

- The process of sanskritisation has increased mobility among lower castes. This process has improved the status of lower castes. People of lower castes adopt the traditions, rituals, ideals and lifestyle of higher castes as they start to call themselves as members of higher castes.
- The process of sanskritisation has brought many changes in occupational status of lower castes. They started to leave those occupations which were considered as impure and started to operate pure occupations.
- The process of sanskritisation also brought about many changes in their culture-folk ways, traditions, customs, beliefs, values, etc. They started to do yagyas, puja etc. They started to celebrate Hindu festival as well.
- The economic status of the lower caste was affected due to sanskritisation. They entered the industrial sector and government jobs with which their income improved. They started to receive technical and occupational education and achieved higher posts. Their incomes increased due to modern occupations with which their economic status improved.
- Social life of lower caste also changed with the process of sanskritisation. Members of lower castes started to receive education to improve their social status. They got jobs in offices and administration.
- Now, they started to interact with the people of higher castes which resulted in reduction of caste differences. Their ways of living also changed with economic status. We take it for granted that as we are modernising we are becoming more secular.

4. Read the passage and answer the following questions.

With the advent of progress and the influences of modernisation, attitudes have changed to religion and to the celebration of many festivals. Rituals, procedures of ceremonies, taboos associated with these ceremonies, the value and amount of sacrifices to be made are now all subjects of constant change, especially in the mushrooming urban areas.

These new pressures on the concept of tribal identity have meant that traditional practices and their preservation have become almost a necessary expression of being tribal. Festivals have emerged as an emphatic projection of sense of a unified tribe identity. It is as if the collective celebration of the festival has become a fitting response to the clarion call of 'Loss of Culture, Loss of Identity' that is doing the rounds in today's tribal society.

(a) What do you mean by modernisation? Why the attitude to religion have changed?

(b) Why are the festivals important for tribal groups?

Ans. (a) Improvements in technology and manufacturing methods is referred to as modernisation. However, the word began to be used in a broader sense. It was a reference to the development direction taken by most of Western Europe and North America. Local relations and parochial viewpoints give way to universal commitments and cosmopolitan attitudes; utilitarian, calculative and scientific truths take precedence over emotional, sacred, and non-rational truths; and the person, rather than the community, is the primary unit of society and politics.

The attitudes to religion have changed due to the progress and the influences of modernisation.

(b) Festivals are important for tribal groups because festivals are the means to preserve the tribal culture and identity. The collective celebration of festivals is response to the concern of 'Loss of Culture and Loss of Identity' among the tribal people. Lot of changes are taking place in rituals i.e. procedures of ceremonies, sacrifices and taboos of tribal society. These changes have made the issue of tribal identity a central concern and festivals are expressions to preserve tribal culture.

5. Explain the concept of secularisation and its indicators in society. How does the process of secularisation in India differ from that of the modern West?

Competency Based Que.

Ans. Secularisation refers to the decline of religious influence in society. It involves a shift away from religious beliefs and practices, with social and political systems becoming less influenced by religious institutions.

In the modern West, secularisation has often meant a decrease in religious involvement and the diminishing role of religious organisations in governance and social life. Indicators of secularisation include lower participation in religious activities, a reduced role of religious institutions in societal matters and the rise of secular beliefs over religious ones.

In India, however, the process of secularisation has followed a different path. While religion still plays a significant role in many aspects of Indian life, secularisation is seen in the transformation of traditional practices, like rituals, which now also serve social, political and economic functions. For example, weddings and rituals have become occasions to display wealth and status, rather than purely religious events.

Additionally, caste, once deeply tied to religious beliefs, now functions more as a political tool, with caste-based associations and political parties pressing for state recognition and rights, thus reflecting a form of secularisation.

6. Read the passage and answer the following questions.

Those in India who complain of 'casteism in politics' are really looking for a sort of politics, which has no basis in society… Politics is a competitive enterprise, its purpose is the acquisition of power for the realisation of certain goals and its process is one of identifying and manipulating existing and emerging allegiances in order to mobilise and consolidate positions.

The important thing is organisation and articulation of support and where politics is mass-based. The point is to articulate support through the organisations in which the masses are to be found. It follows that where the caste structure provides one of the principal organisational clusters along which the bulk of the population is found to live, politics must strive to organise through such a structure.

Politicians mobilise caste groupings and identities in order to organise their power… Where there are other types of groups and other bases of association, politicians approach them as well. And as they everywhere change the form of such organisations, they change the form of caste as well.

(i) Explain the term 'casteism in politics'. What is the purpose of politics? Why caste is important for politics?

(ii) Why politicians' mobilises caste groupings?

Ans. (i) Those who complain about 'casteism in politics' in India are really looking for a type of politics that has no foundation in society. Politics is a competitive activity whose aim is to gain control in order to achieve specific objectives. Its mechanism entails defining and exploiting current and new allegiances in order to mobilise and consolidate positions. The main thing is organisation and articulation of support and in mass-based politics, the point is to express support through the organisations where the masses can be found.

(ii) The purpose of politics is to acquire power, realise certain goals and identify as well as manipulate existing and emerging allegiances in order to mobilise and consolidate positions.

Politics articulate, supports and mobilises the masses in order to organise their power. Caste is one of the organisations in society in which large population lives and it is easy for the politicians to seek the support on the basis of caste.

To capture power and realise its certain goals, politics strive to organise the support on the basis of caste of people. Therefore, caste is important for politics.

Politicians mobilises caste groupings in order to organise their power, where there are other basis of associations politicians approach then as well.

SELF ASSESSMENT TEST

Objective Type Questions

1. Which of the following is an example of the co-existence of traditional and modern ideas in the 19th century reform movements?

(a) The complete rejection of all traditional practices.
(b) The reformers' efforts to justify female education by drawing on both modern and traditional ideas.
(c) The universal acceptance of Western cultural norms.
(d) The decline of caste-based discrimination without reference to traditional Hindu texts.

2. Which of the following statements is true about the social reformers of 19th-century India?

(a) They all focused solely on the issues affecting women in the society.
(b) They were united in their approach, with no ideological differences.
(c) They used both traditional and modern ideas to address societal issues.
(d) Their efforts were concentrated only in urban areas, without any impact on rural society.

3. Which of the following correctly describes the impact of new communication technologies on social reform movements in India?

I. They facilitated the rapid dissemination of reform ideas across regions.
II. They primarily benefited only the educated elite in urban areas.
III. They enabled collaboration among reformers from different parts of India.
IV. They had no significant effect on traditional practices and beliefs.

Codes

(a) I and II (b) I and III (c) II and IV (d) I, III and IV

4. **Assertion** (A) Raja Ram Mohun Roy is known as the Father of the Indian Renaissance.

Reason (R) He advocated for the abolition of the practice of Sati based on humanitarian principles and Hindu texts.

(a) Both A and R are true and R is the correct explanation of A
(b) Both A and R are true, but R is not the correct explanation of A
(c) A is true, but R is false
(d) A is false, but R is true

Case Based Questions

The idea of female education was debated intensely. Significantly, it was the social reformer Jotiba Phule who opened the first school for women in Pune. Reformers argued that for a society to progress women have to be educated. Some of them believed that in pre-modern India, women were educated. Others contested this on the grounds that this was so only of a privileged few. Thus attempts to justify female education were made by recourse to both modern and traditional ideas. They actively debated the meanings of tradition and modernity.

(i) Who opened the first school for women in Pune?

(a) Bal Gangadhar Tilak (b) Raja Ram Mohun Roy
(c) Jotiba Phule (d) Pandita Ramabai

(ii) What was the primary focus of the debates on female education in the 19th century?

(a) The need for men's education.
(b) The difference between modern and traditional ideas.
(c) The importance of maintaining caste purity.
(d) The promotion of male education over female education.

Very Short Answer Type Questions

1. Modernisation has historically been linked with technological advancement and societal progress, often drawing from Western Europe and North America's paths of development. In India, however, modernisation took place within the colonial context and had unique characteristics. For instance, while education became a key to upward mobility for many, it was also influenced by local cultures and traditions.
   What factors made the process of modernisation in India distinct from that in Western societies?
2. "The concept of modernity involves a shift from traditional ties and perspectives to more universal commitments, prioritising science and individual choice over inherited roles and beliefs. In the case of the Naga community, education became a key to upward mobility and communication with the wider world. Despite the presence of modern values, traditional beliefs still held sway in many parts of India."
   What role did education play in this process of change?
3. Give the meaning of secularisation of caste.
4. How do you think the adoption of Western culture in India reflects a contradiction between external appearances and internal values?

Short Answer Type Questions

1. "The 19th-century social reform movements in India were a mix of modern Western liberal ideas and traditional Indian thoughts. These movements sought to address social issues like sati, child marriage, and caste discrimination, often using both traditional and modern arguments. The idea of female education, for instance, was debated intensely, with reformers drawing from both ancient traditions and modern liberalism."
   Do you think the 19th-century social reform movements were successful in creating a balance between tradition and modernity? Provide reasons for your answer.
2. Westernisation has impacted almost every aspect of life in India. Explain.
3. Rituals help in the process of secularisation in India. Discuss.
4. "The term 'modernisation' has evolved over time. Initially, it was linked to improvements in technology and production. Over the years, however, it came to represent a broader concept of development, often tied to Western ideals."
   What, according to sociologists, are the key elements that define the process of modernisation?

Long Answer Type Questions

1. It is primarily a process that takes place within the Hindu space though Srinivas argued that it was visible even in sects and religious groups outside Hinduism. Studies of different areas, however, show that it operated differently in different parts of the country. In those areas where a highly sanskritised caste was dominant, the culture of the entire region underwent a certain amount of sanskritisation. In regions where the non-Sanskritic castes were dominant, it was their influence that was stronger. This can be termed the process of 'de-Sanskritisation'. There were other regional variations too. In Punjab culturally Sanskritic influence was never very strong. For many centuries until the third quarter of the 19th century, the Persian influence was the dominant one.
   (a) According to Srinivas, what is the process of Sanskritisation, and how does it affect the position of a group in the caste hierarchy?
   (b) How does the process of 'de-Sanskritisation' differ from Sanskritisation in terms of regional cultural influences?
2. There was difference of opinion in approaching and operationalising the social reforms in India. Discuss.
3. Modernisation is not an isolated process and it is linked to secularisation and westernisation. Discuss.
4. Discuss the criticism of sanskritisation. Has sanskritisation been able to lift the condition of Dalits in India?

03 CHAPTER

Changes and development in rural society are closely linked to agriculture, which remains the primary livelihood for most rural populations.

YOUR STUDY GOALS

YOUR PRACTICE GOAL

- Objective Type Questions (25 Qs ; MCQs, A-R, Case Based Questions)
- Subjective Questions (26 VSAs, 10 SAs, 8 LAs)

Change and Development in Rural Society

3.1 Indian Society: A Primarily Rural Society

Indian society is primarily rural, with 69% of the total population living in rural areas, as reported by the 2011 Census. Rural inhabitants rely on agriculture or related occupations, making agricultural land the most crucial productive resource.

Agriculture and Culture

- A close connection exists between agriculture and culture in rural India, where social structure is tied to agricultural practices.
- The nature of agriculture varies from region to region, reflected in local cultures and festivals, such as Pongal in Tamil Nadu, Bihu in Assam, Baisakhi in Punjab and Ugadi in Karnataka.
- These festivals celebrate the new harvest season, marking the start of the main agricultural cycle.

Rural Life

- Agriculture is the primary source of livelihood for the majority of the rural population.
- In addition to agriculture, many activities that support agricultural and village life provide livelihoods, including various artisans such as potters, carpenters, weavers, ironsmiths and goldsmiths.

- Rural life also includes specialists and craftsmen, including story-tellers, astrologers, priests, water distributors and oil makers.
- The diversity of occupations in rural India is reflected in the caste system, which includes specialist and service castes like washermen and potters.
- While some traditional occupations have declined, the growing connections between rural and urban economies have led to diverse employment opportunities.
- Many rural residents engage in non-farm activities, such as working in government services, factories or the military.

3.2 Agrarian Structure: Caste and Class in Rural India

- Agrarian structure refers to the distribution of landholdings in rural society, where agricultural land is the most vital resource.
- Land distribution is unequal; some individuals own large areas, while others have only small plots and some own no land at all.
- Access to land significantly shapes the rural class structure and determines individuals' roles in agricultural production.

Types of Landholdings

Type of landholdings in the rural areas are as following

- **Medium and Large Landowners** They own sufficient land to generate substantial income through cultivation.
- **Agricultural Labourers** They lack land ownership and work for others, often receiving wages below the statutory minimum and experiencing job insecurity.
- **Tenants** These cultivators lease land from landowners, earning less than owner-cultivators as they must pay a significant portion of their profits, typically 50% to 75% as rent.
- **Women** They are usually excluded from land ownership in most regions due to patrilineal kinship systems. Despite legal provisions for equal property rights, women's access to land remains limited.

Caste and Class Structure in Rural India

- The agrarian caste-based rural society can be understood through class structure, with caste and class intermingling in complex relationships.
- It is not always straightforward to equate higher caste status with greater land ownership or income; for example, Brahmins, who are considered higher castes, are often not major landowners.
- Rural society typically includes dominant castes, which are economically and politically powerful landowning groups.

Dominant Caste

- Every rural region usually has one or two dominant landowning castes, defined by **M.N. Srinivas**. They are the economically and politically influential groups in the rural areas.
  Some dominant castes include
  - Jats and Rajputs in Uttar Pradesh
  - Vokkaligas and Lingayats in Karnataka
  - Kammas and Reddis in Andhra Pradesh
  - Jat Sikhs in Punjab
  - Bhumihars in Northern Bihar
- These dominant groups generally belong to middle or upper castes.

Scheduled Caste or Tribes or Other Backward Castes

- Rural society also comprises marginal farmers and landless individuals from lower caste groups, including Scheduled Castes, Tribes or Other Backward Classes.
- These individuals, including former 'untouchables' or 'dalits,' provide agricultural labour to dominant landowning groups, facilitating intensive cultivation and higher returns.

Proprietary Caste

- In many areas, 'proprietary castes' own most resources and can command labour. Practices like 'begar' (free labour) have historically required lower caste members to work without pay for local zamindars or landlords.
- The lack of resources and dependence on the landed class for economic and social support have tied many poor labourers into hereditary labour relationships, such as the Halpati System in Gujarat and the Jeeta System in Karnataka.
- Although these practices are legally banned, they persist in many regions.
- The correlation between caste and class means that typically, upper and middle castes have the best access to land and resources, leading to power and privilege.

Quick Test 1

1. Which group of landowners owns a large amount of land?
2. Which cultivator leases their land from landowners?
3. Which section of the society is usually excluded from ownership of land?
4. Which caste group owns most of the resources and can command the labour to work from them?

3.3 The Impact of Land Reforms

- The agrarian structure in India has evolved significantly from the pre-colonial era to the colonial period and after independence.
- In the pre-colonial period, while the dominant castes were cultivators, they did not directly own the land.
- Local kings or zamindars, typically from Kshatriya or other high castes, controlled cultivated land.
- Peasants[1] had to pay a substantial portion of their produce as rent to these ruling groups.

Land Reforms in the Colonial Period

- The British colonial administration ruled India through local zamindars, granting them property rights and increased control over land.
- Heavy land revenue taxes imposed by the British on the farming, zamindars pressured to extract maximum produce or money from cultivators.
- One effect of the Zamindari system was that agricultural production either stopped growing or decreased during British rule. This happened because peasants ran away from harsh landlords, and present famines and wars reduced the population.
- Two systems were prominent: the zamindari system, where the zamindars used to collect taxes and the other was the raiyatwari system[2], where cultivators paid taxes directly. The raiyatwari system had a lower tax burden, encouraging cultivators to invest in agriculture, resulting in more productive and prosperous areas.

1 Peasants It refers to those small farmers which are unable to produce for market but primarily produce for themselves.
2 Raiyatwari System It is a system of land settlement in which the actual cultivators were responsible for paying the tax.

Land Reforms in Independent India

- After independence, policymakers, led by Nehru, focused on agrarian reforms and industrialisation to improve the agriculture sector.
- Agriculture sector was facing low productivity, reliance on imported food grains and widespread poverty.
- A major reform in the agrarian structure, particularly in landholding and distribution, was necessary for agricultural progress.
- Land reforms were introduced to address these issues and promote social justice, implemented from the **1950s** to the **1970s**, including
  - **Abolition of the Zamindari System** This reform eliminated Intermediaries[3] between cultivators and the state, improving the status of actual landholders and reducing the zamindars' economic and political power.
  - **Tenancy Reforms** Acts were passed to abolish tenancy or regulate rents, providing security to tenants. While these laws were not effectively implemented in most states, areas like West Bengal and Kerala saw significant restructuring, granting land rights to tenants.
  - **Land Ceiling Acts[4]** These laws established an upper limit on land ownership per family, with ceilings varying by region based on land productivity. The state was to identify and redistribute surplus land (beyond the ceiling) to landless families, including Scheduled Castes (SCs) and Scheduled Tribes (STs).
  - The success of these acts varied; many loopholes allowed landlords to retain surplus land. Some wealthy farmers even divorced their wives to avoid regulations but kept living with them to retaining control over land.
- Overall, while the agrarian structure has changed substantially since colonial times, it remains highly unequal. This inequality constraints agricultural productivity, making land reforms essential for enhancing agricultural output, alleviating poverty and achieving social justice in rural areas.

Quick Test 2

1. Who controlled the cultivated land in the Pre-colonial period?
2. The zamindars belonged mostly to which caste?
3. What were the problems faced by the agricultural sector after independence?
4. Which reform in the 1950's to 1970's removed the layer of intermediaries?
5. According to which act, the state is supposed to identify and take possession of surplus land?

3.4 Green Revolution and its Social Consequences

- The Green Revolution was a government programme aimed at modernising agriculture.
- It was funded by international agencies and focused on providing High-Yielding Variety (HYV) or hybrid seeds, along with pesticides, fertilisers and other inputs to farmers.
- In India, the initiative was led by the Indian agricultural scientist **M.S. Swaminathan.**

First Phase of Green Revolution

- The Green Revolution began in the 1960s and 1970s, targeting areas with assured irrigation, as the new seeds and cultivation methods required sufficient water.
- It mainly focused on wheat and rice-growing regions.

---

3 **Intermediaries** It is the middleman between the zamindars and the actual tillers of the land who exploited the poor peasants for their own interests.
4 **Land Ceiling** It refers to fix a specific area of land to be acquired by the landowners.

- Regions such as Punjab, Western Uttar Pradesh, coastal Andhra Pradesh and parts of Tamil Nadu primarily benefited from this initiative.

Positive Consequences of First Phase

- There was a sharp increase in agricultural productivity due to the introduction of new technology.
- India achieved self-sufficiency in food grain production for the first time.
- The crops from the Green Revolution were highly profitable, allowing farmers to earn more money.
- Employment and wages for agricultural workers increased in many regions due to the higher demand for labor.

Negative Consequences of First Phase

- Small and marginal farmers could not benefit from the Green Revolution, as they could not afford the expensive new seeds and technology. Mainly medium and large farmers benefited.
- Only those farmers who could produce surplus for the market gained from the Green Revolution. Farmers involved in **subsistence agriculture**[5] did not benefit from it.
- The Green Revolution created and increased inequalities in rural society.
- Many tenant cultivators were displaced as land was reclaimed by landowners when agriculture became more profitable.
- Several service caste groups were displaced due to the introduction of machinery in agriculture, such as tractors, threshers, and harvesters.
- The migration from rural to urban areas increased as many people became unemployed.
- Differentiation in Indian rural society occurred in which the rich grew richer while the poor became poorer.

Second Phase of Green Revolution

- The second phase of the Green Revolution began in the 1980s, when farmers in India's dry and semi-arid regions started adopting Green Revolution farming techniques.
- This phase involves a significant shift from dry to wet (irrigated) cultivation and changes in cropping patterns and types of crops grown.
- The second phase supported the positive effects of the first phase but also added to its negative outcomes, such as
  - Instead of enhancing livelihood security, increased commercialisation and dependence on markets led to greater livelihood insecurity for farmers.
  - Farmers faced increased risks by switching from a multi-crop system to a **mono-crop system**[6].
  - Regional inequalities existed, as the Green Revolution mainly helped states like Punjab, Haryana and Western Uttar Pradesh to grow while leaving other regions poor.
  - Some regions continue to have a feudal **agrarian structure**[7], where landowners maintained power over lower castes, landless workers and small cultivators.
  - There has been an increase in various kinds of violence, including inter-caste violence, due to sharp caste and class inequalities and exploitative labour relations.
  - Despite the introduction of **scientific farming methods**, the conditions of Indian farmers have not necessarily improved.

---

5 **Subsistence Agriculture** It is a form of agriculture where agriculturalists produced primarily for themselves and are unable to produce for the market.

6 **Mono-crop System** It is a farming method where a single crop is grown in the same field year after year.

7 **Agrarian Structure** It refers to the structure of distribution of land holdings among the people.

- Farmers have cultivated the land for centuries and possess deep traditional knowledge about their crops and land. Much of this traditional knowledge and many traditional seed varieties have been lost due to the promotion of hybrid, high-yielding, and genetically modified seeds.
- Many rural people believe that hybrid varieties are less healthy than traditional ones.
- Due to the negative environmental and social impacts observed from modern cultivation methods, both scientists and farmers suggest a return to traditional, more organic seeds and cultivation practices.

Quick Test 3

1. What was the objective of the Green Revolution?
2. Who led the Green Revolution in India?
3. What were the negative impacts of the Green Revolution?
4. In which regions of India was the second phase of the Green Revolution introduced?
5. Which type of problems visible in the market increases insecurity of farmers?

3.5 Transformations in Rural Society after Independence

- After independence, rural social relations underwent significant changes due to the Green Revolution.
- The changes included, an increase in agricultural labour as cultivation intensified, a shift from grain payments to cash payments and the erosion of traditional bonds between landowners and agricultural workers.
- The rise of 'free' wage labourers became evident, with sociologist Jan Breman characterising these shifts as a transition from 'patronage to exploitation', which reflected the emergence of capitalist agriculture.
- As agriculture commercialised, rural areas began integrating into a broader economy, leading to increased cash flow and expanded business opportunities.

▲ *Cultivation in different parts of the country*

- The 19th century, large parts of Maharashtra were dedicated to cotton farming, linking farmers directly to the global market.
- After independence, the government worked to accelerate changes in rural areas. They promoted modern farming methods and introduced various strategies to modernise agriculture and the rural economy.

- The government focused on building rural infrastructure, such as irrigation systems, roads and electricity. Additionally, they provided agricultural inputs like credit through banks and cooperatives to support farmers.
- Uninterrupted electricity is vital for continuous agricultural growth. To address this need, the Deen Dayal Upadhyaya Gram Jyoti Yojana was launched in 2014, ensuring better power supply in rural areas.
- These initiatives helped transform agriculture and modernise the rural economy. Improved infrastructure and new strategies contributed significantly to the development of rural India.

Alterations in Rural Social Structure

- Agricultural development during the 1960s and 1970s significantly altered rural social structures.
- Medium and large farmers who adopted new technologies experienced enrichment, while **dominant caste**[8] farmers invested profits into diverse business ventures.
- This investment led to the emergence of new entrepreneurial groups and regional elites, facilitating the spread of higher education, which enabled new rural elites to pursue professional occupations.
- Conversely, regions like Eastern Uttar Pradesh and Bihar saw limited changes due to ineffective land reforms and lack of political mobilisation.

3.6 Circulation of Labour

- The commercialisation of agriculture resulted in large-scale seasonal labour migration.
- This migration was driven by the breaking of traditional bonds of patronage between labourers and landlords, increased demand for labour and higher wages.
- Inequalities in rural areas since the mid-1990s forced individuals to combine multiple occupations for sustenance.
- Migrant workers, described by Breman as **footloose labour,** often lack rights and security, facing exploitation in low-wage environments.
- Local labourers often seek work outside their villages, while migrant workers fill roles in local farms, especially during peak agricultural seasons.

Effects of Large Scale Circulation of Labour

- The large-scale circulation of labour has profoundly affected rural society in both receiving and supplying regions.
- As male family members work outside villages, cultivation increasingly becomes a female task.
- Women have emerged as the main source of agricultural labour, resulting in the feminisation of the agricultural labour force.
- However, women face insecurity as they receive lower wages compared to men for similar work.
- Additionally, women are often excluded from official statistics as earners and workers despite their significant contributions to agricultural labour.

▲ *Changing technologies in agriculture*

8 **Dominant Caste** It is that group of rural society which is the most powerful group economically and that politically dominates the local society.

3.7 Globalisation, Liberalisation and Rural Society

- Since the 1980s, liberalisation policies have significantly impacted rural society by integrating Indian agriculture into global markets.
- Policy of liberalisation entails participation in the World Trade Organisation (WTO), which brought about a free international trading system.
- For many years, Indian farmers received support from the government, including subsidies and protection from foreign competition through controlled markets.
- Over time, this protective environment changed, and Indian farmers were gradually exposed to the challenges of competing in the global market.
- Farmers now compete with foreign products and many have entered contracts with Multinational Companies (MNCs) to grow specific crops.
- In this contract farming system, companies provide seeds, inputs and guarantee purchase at fixed prices, offering financial security but increasing dependence on these companies for livelihoods.
- This reliance leads to disengagement from traditional production processes and diminishes the relevance of farmers' traditional agricultural knowledge.
- Additionally, contract farming[9] focuses on export-oriented products, often diverting agricultural land away from food grain production and compromising ecological sustainability.

MNCs as Agents

- The entry of multinationals into agriculture has increased as they sell agricultural inputs such as seeds, pesticides and fertilisers.
- Over the past decade, the government has scaled down agricultural development programmes, replacing traditional agricultural extension agents with agents from MNCs.
- These MNC agents have become the primary source of information for farmers regarding new seeds and cultivation practices, often prioritising sales over farmers' best interests.
- This situation has led to increased dependence on costly inputs, ultimately reducing profits and escalating debt, contributing to an ecological crisis in rural areas.

Farmers' Suicide

- Many farmer suicides are linked to debt accumulation, particularly among marginal farmers who implemented Green Revolution methods.
- Contributing factors include a decrease in agricultural subsidies, which has raised production costs and market instability, forcing farmers to borrow heavily to invest in inputs.
- Suicides among farmers are often associated with debt and natural disasters that result in crop failures.
- To combat this issue, government schemes such as the Pradhan Mantri Fasal Bima Yojana, Gram Uday Se Bharat Uday Abhiyan and the National Urban Mission, National Mission for Sustainable Agriculture and Kisan Credit Card etc., aim to provide assistance and improve the quality of life in rural India.

Quick Test 4

1. Who describes the change in relations between landlords and agricultural workers as a shift from patronage to exploitation?
2. Which areas have witnessed few changes in agrarian structure due to lack of effective land reforms and redistributive measures?
3. What term did Jan Breman give to migrant labourers?
4. What is the main reason for the large scale suicide among farmers?

9 **Contract Farming** It is method of agriculture in which the company identifies the crop to be grown provides the seeds and other inputs and also the working capital on contract basis.

NCERT Folder

Activity 3.2

1. Think about what you have learnt about the caste system. Outline the various linkages between agrarian or rural class structure and caste. Discuss in terms of different access to resources, labour, occupation.

Ans. Caste system is unique to Indian conditions. Caste is decided by the birth of a person into a particular family which has already been assigned a lower or higher social status in the society.

In rural societies, caste and class of a person are generally inter-related.

Class and caste show relationships in terms of resources, labour, occupation, etc.

- **Resources** These are not evenly distributed in villages. Land is the most important resource in rural societies since most of the people are engaged in agriculture. In most regions of India, major landowning groups belong to upper castes of society. Lower caste groups have very less land or no land in their possession.
- **Labour** Most of the agricultural labourers or *begar* belong to lower castes. They are mostly dependent on the higher castes or the landlords for their work. Many of them work as tenants and have lower incomes than owner-cultivators.
- **Occupation** Caste system is often reflected in various occupations in villages such as that of washerman, potters, goldsmiths, etc. But in recent times due to linkage with urban areas, people in rural areas are getting employed in factories, education sector and other non-farm activities.

Exercise Questions

1. Read the passage given and answer the questions

"The harsh working conditions suffered by labourers in Aghanbigha were an outcome of the combined effect of the economic power of the maliks as a class and their overwhelming power as members of a dominant caste. A significant aspect of the social power of the maliks was their ability to secure the intervention of various arms of the state to advance their interests. Thus, political factors decissively contributed to widening the gulf between the dominant class and the underclass."

(i) Why do you think the maliks were able to use the power of the state to advance their own interests?

(ii) Why did labourers have harsh working conditions?

Ans. (i) The maliks were able to use the power of state to advance their own interests as they had the economic power and they belonged to the upper class.

(ii) The labourers had harsh working conditions because they belonged to the lower class and were exploited by upper castes or dominant sections of the society.

2. What measures do you think the government has taken or should taken to protect the rights of landless agricultural labourers and migrant workers?

Ans. The condition of agricultural labourers and migrant workers is very poor in India. The government has taken following measures to protect them, such as

- The zamindari system has been abolished such as *Halpati* system in Gujarat an *Jeeta* system in Karnataka.
- The tenancy abolition and regulation acts were introduced, either to outlaw tenancy altogether or to regulate rents to give some security to the tenants.
- Land Ceiling Acts were passed to put an upper limit on the amount of land that can be owned by a particular family.
  These acts aimed to distribute the surplus land among the landless SCs and STs population.

The above steps taken by the government could not improve the condition of landless and migrant workers in India. The government can take more steps in this regard such as

- They should be provided alternative employment opportunities to improve their life.
- Skill development should become an integral part of their overall development.
- Land reforms should be carried out as per the specific requirements and needs of a particular region of the country.
- They should be given all the rights and social security benefits that are given to workers in the organised sectors.
- The government should introduce laws to safeguard the occupational rights of migrant workers regarding the eviction scenarios.

3. There are direct linkages between the situation of agricultural workers and their lack of upward socio-economic mobility. Name some of them.

Ans. It is a correct statement that there are direct linkages between the situation of agricultural workers and their lack of upward socio-economic mobility.

Some of them are as follows

- The aspect of land, as the land decides the economical and social position of the individual in society.
- The poor working conditions and poor wages leading to low economic standards of agricultural workers and low status in terms of economic power dynamics.
- The exploitative nature and decreasing level of women participation, leading to decrease in their social position and more exploitation. Women workers in most of the regions of our country are usually excluded from ownership of land because of the prevailing patrilineal kinship system and mode of inheritance.

4. What are the different factors that have enabled certain groups to transform themselves into new wealthy, entrepreneurial, dominant classes? Can you think of an example of this transformation in your state?

Ans. There are various factors that have enabled certain groups to transform themselves into new, wealthy, entrepreneurial and dominant classes.

These factors are being discussed below

(i) **Commercialised Agriculture** One of the important factors that brought changes in many areas is that the agriculture was becoming more commercialised, i.e. where the crops were being grown primarily for sale in the market.

As the cultivation becomes more commercialised, these rural areas were also becoming integrated to the wider economy. This process increased the flow of money into villages and expanding the opportunities for business and employment.

(ii) **Emergence of New Regional Elite Group** It is considered one of the major factors which had enabled certain groups to transfer themselves in new wealthy entrepreneur and dominant classes in the society.

In several agriculturally rich regions, such as the coastal Andhra Pradesh, Western Uttar Pradesh and Central Gujarat, well-to-do farmers belonging to the dominant castes began to invest their profits from agriculture in other types of ventures.

This process of diversification gave rise to new entrepreneurial groups that moved out of rural areas into the growing towns of these developing regions, giving rise to new regional elites that become politically and economically dominant.

Exam Pattern Questions

Objective Type Questions

Multiple Choice Questions (MCQs)

1. ……… is a term that refers to the structure or distribution of landholdings. Access to land forms the rural class structure because agricultural land is the most valuable productive resource in rural areas. What role one plays in the agricultural production process is largely determined by one's access to land?

Competency Based Que.

(a) Industrial structure (b) Agrarian structure
(c) Infrastructure (d) Urbanisation

2. The redistribution of property rights on the land for the benefit of small farmers and agricultural labourers. It includes two types of institutional changes one relates to agrarian relation and the other to the size of the unit of cultivation. It is necessary not only to boost agricultural growth but also to eradicate poverty in rural areas and bring about social justice. The phenomenon talked about in above passage is known as ……… .

(a) Agriculture
(b) Land Reforms
(c) Green Revolution
(d) Globalisation

3. ……… are essentially the government's declared minimum procuring prices for agricultural products for a given year. It is primarily done to protect farmers from potential losses and to maintain a consistent price level.

(a) Support prices
(b) Subsidies
(c) Wages
(d) None of the above

4. The laws that imposed an upper limit on the amount of land that can be owned by a particular family is known as

(a) Abolition of Zamindari system
(b) Tenancy Abolition and Regulation Act
(c) Land Ceiling Act
(d) Rayatwari system

5. Name the sociologist who coined the term 'footloose labour'?

(a) Verrier Elwin (b) Jan Breman
(c) Auguste Comte (d) Herbert Spencer

6. Women are also emerging as the main source of agricultural labour leading to .... labour force. CBSE SQP 2023

(a) Feminisation of agriculture
(b) Womanisation of agriculture
(c) Reformation of agriculture
(d) Restoration of agriculture

7. The sociological importance of contract farming does not include which of the following? CBSE 2023

(a) It disengages people from the production process.
(b) Indigenous knowledge of agriculture becomes irrelevant.
(c) It caters primarily to the production of elite items.
(d) It is ecologically sustainable.

8. Which of the following is not true about land reforms in Independent India? CBSE 2024

(a) Abolition of the Zamindari System
(b) Tenancy Abolition
(c) Raiyatwari System
(d) Land Ceiling Acts

9. Which of the following statements is not true for Green Revolution? CBSE 2024

(a) Green Revolution was a government programme of agricultural modernisation.
(b) It was largely funded by international agencies.
(c) The first wave of the Green Revolution package was received by Bihar, Eastern Uttar Pradesh and Telangana.
(d) Green Revolution was targeted mainly at the wheat and rice growing areas.

10. The policy of liberalisation entails the participation in the ...., which aims to bring about a more free international trading system. CBSE 2024

(a) WTO (b) EPC
(c) WHO (d) UNCTAD

11. What is not true for globalisation and liberalisation in the rural society? CBSE 2023

(a) Non-participation in WTO
(b) Free international trade
(c) Opening of Indian markets to imports
(d) Competition from the global market

12. "The spate of farmer's suicides that has been occurring in different parts of the country since 1997–98 can be linked to the 'agrarian distress' caused by structural changes in agriculture and changes in economic and agricultural policies."

Which of the following is not a reason for agrarian distress? CBSE SQP 2023

(a) Changed cropping pattern
(b) Changing patterns of landholdings
(c) Heavy migration to cities
(d) Shift to cash crops

13. Which yojana was initiated by the government regarding the transformation of rural development?

(a) Deen Dayal Upadhayaya Gram Jyoti Yojana
(b) Pradhan Mantri Fasal Bima Yojana
(c) Gram Uday Se Bharat Uday Abhiyan
(d) National Rurban Mission

14. In which among the following states farmer suicides have become very common?

(a) Maharashtra and Karnataka
(b) Kerala and Andhra Pradesh
(c) Different parts of India
(d) All of the above

15. Which of the following is/are the characteristics of agricultural labour? Competency Based Que.

I. They own no land of their own.
II. They work for others.
III. They are more often paid less wages i.e. below the statutory minimum wages.

Codes

(a) I and II (b) II and III
(c) I and III (d) I, II and III

16. Which statement is in correct regarding the positive consequences of first phase of Green Revolution? Competency Based Que.

I. Many farmers shifted from multi-crop system to mono-crop system.
II. Migration from rural and urban areas increased.
III. The employment and wages of agricultural workers increased in many areas.
IV. It brought regional inequalities in India.

Codes

(a) I, II and III (b) I, II and IV
(c) II, III and IV (d) I, III and IV

17. Put the following statements in the correct order. **CBSE SQP 2024**

I. The worker works without wages until the loan is repaid.
II. The contractor will provide loan of some money.
III. The contractor goes to villages and asks if people want work.
IV. They can break the contract and find another employer.

Codes
(a) III, II, I and IV
(b) I, II, III and IV
(c) IV, III, II and I
(d) I, II, IV and III

18. Which of the following is not true for 'footloose labour'? **CBSE 2024**

I. Migration does not have any relations with footloose labour.
II. It implies freedom.
III. They are exploited.

Codes
(a) I and II
(b) II and III
(c) I and III
(d) I, II and III

Assertion-Reason Questions

Direction (Q. Nos. 19-21) Two statement are given in the question below as Assertion (A) and Reason (R). Read the statements and choose the appropriate option.

(a) Both A and R are true and R is the correct explanation of A
(b) Both A and R are true, but R is not the correct explanation of A
(c) A is true, but R is false
(d) A is false, but R is true

19. **Assertion** (A) Members of low ranked caste groups had to provide labour for a fixed number of days per year to the village zamindars.

Reason (R) Lack of resources and dependence on the landed caste for economic and social support meant that many working poor were tied to landowners in hereditary labour relationships

20. **Assertion** (A) Often it is thought that imparting knowledge of 'scientific' farming methods will improve the conditions of Indian farmers.

Reason (R) The Indian farmers have been cultivating the land for centuries, much before the advent of the Green Revolution. **CBSE 2025**

21. **Assertion** (A) Agriculture is the single most important source of livelihood for the majority of the rural population.

Reason (R) The rural is not just agriculture. Many activities that support agriculture and village life are also sources of livelihood. **CBSE 2025**

Case Based Questions

Read the passages given below and answer the questions that follow.

22. Many districts of colonial India were administered through the zamindari system. In other areas that were under direct British rule had what was called the raiyatwari system of land settlement (raiyat means cultivator in Telugu). In this system, the 'actual cultivators' (who were themselves often landlords and not cultivators) rather than the zamindars were responsible for paying the tax. Because the colonial government dealt directly with the farmers or landlords, rather than through the overlords, the burden of taxation was less and cultivators had more incentive to invest in agriculture. As a result, these areas became relatively more productive and prosperous.

(i) **During the British rule, the zamindari system caused .... to stagnate and decline.**
(a) industrial production
(b) agricultural production
(c) Both (a) and (b)
(d) Neither (a) nor (b)

(ii) **Which areas became more prosperous?**
(a) Where zamindari system was imposed
(b) Where raiyatwari system was imposed
(c) Both (a) and (b)
(d) None of the above

23. The Green Revolution, was a government programme of agricultural modernisation. It was largely funded by international agencies that was based on providing High-Yielding Variety (HYV) or hybrid seeds along with pesticides, fertilisers, and other inputs, to farmers. Green Revolution programmes were introduced only in areas that had assured irrigation, because sufficient water was necessary for the new seeds and methods of cultivation. It was also targeted mainly at the wheat and rice-growing areas. As a result, only certain regions such as the Punjab, Western UP, coastal Andhra Pradesh and parts of Tamil Nadu, received the first wave of the Green Revolution package.

(i) **In which areas the Green Revolution programmes were introduced?**
(a) Availability of raw materials
(b) Industrial location
(c) Assured irrigation
(d) Sanitation facilities

(ii) **What was the main focus of the Green Revolution.**
(a) Industrial growth
(b) Urbanisation
(c) Agricultural modernisation
(d) Education reforms

24. The change in the nature of the relationship between landlords (who usually belonged to the dominant castes) and agricultural workers (usually low caste), was described by the sociologist Jan Breman as a shift from 'patronage to exploitation' (Breman, 1974). Such changes took place in many areas where agriculture was becoming more commercialised, that is, where crops were being grown primarily for sale in the market. The transformation in labour relations is regarded by some scholars as indicative of a transition to capitalist agriculture. Because the capitalist mode of production is based on the separation of the workers from the means of production (in this case, land), and the use of 'free' wage labour.

(i) Which of the following sociologist describes the change in the nature of the relationship between landlords and agricultural workers?

(a) Karl Marx (b) Jan Breman
(c) Max Weber (d) Adam Smith

(ii) Deen Dayal Upadhyaya Gram Jyoti Yojana launched by Indian Government aims at which as the following.

(a) Increase in agriculture
(b) Uninterrupted power supply to rural India
(c) Both (a) and (b)
(d) Neither (a) nor (b)

Answers

1. (b) Agrarian structure
2. (b) Land Reforms
3. (a) Support prices
4. (c) Land Ceiling Act
5. (b) Jan Breman
6. (a) feminisation of agriculture
7. (d) It is ecologically sustainable.
8. (c) Raiyatwari System
9. (c) The first wave of the Green Revolution package was received by Bihar, Eastern Uttar Pradesh and Telangana.
10. (a) WTO
11. (a) Non-participation in WTO
12. (c) Heavy migration to cities
13. (a) Deen Dayal Upadhayaya Gram Jyoti Yojana
14. (d) All of the above
15. (d) I, II and III
16. (b) I, II and IV
17. (a) III, II, I and IV
18. (a) I and II
19. (a) Both A and R are true and R is the correct explanation of A
20. (a) Both A and R are true and R is the correct explanation of A
21. (b) Both A and R are true but R is not the correct explanation of A
22. (i) (b) agricultural production
(ii) (b) Where raiyatwari system was imposed
23. (i) (c) assured irrigation
(ii) (c) Agricultural modernisation.
24. (i) (b) Jan Breman
(ii) (c) Both (a) and (b)

Subjective Questions

Very Short Answer Type Questions

1. Indian society is primarily a rural society through urbanisation is growing. Explain what do you understand by rural society? Competency Based Que.

Ans. Rural society is one where agriculture is the single most important source of livelihood for the majority of the population. Also there are many activities indirectly related to agriculture that form a part of rural society.

2. There are rural residents employed in government services such as the postal and educational departments, factory workers, or in the army, who earn their living through non-agricultural activities.

Based on the above passage, answer the following question.

Why have traditional occupations declined in rural India? CBSE 2024 C

Ans. Traditional occupations in rural India have declined due to the shift towards non-agricultural jobs such as government services, factory work and the army. This change is driven by increasing education, economic diversification and better opportunities for stable incomes outside traditional agricultural activities.

3. In rural areas, the relationship between caste and class in the agrarian society is complex and not always straightforward.
Explain the main occupation of people in rural areas? Competency Based Que.

Ans. Primarily the people in rural areas are engaged in agriculture and the production through land is the main source of income for them. More than 2/3rds of the population of India resides in the rural areas and they are engaged mostly in agriculture related activities.

4. In what ways agriculture and culture are linked?

Ans. There are many cultural practices and patterns that are traced to the agrarian background of India. Baisakhi is one such example, whereby our cultural aspects have been shaped because of the fact that India was essentially a land of agricultural people.

5. Agriculture is the single most important source of livelihood for the majority of the rural population. But the rural is not just agriculture. Many activities that support agriculture and village life are also sources of livelihood for people in rural India.
Describe the meaning of agrarian society? Competency Based Que.

Ans. Agrarian society is a type of society where the maximum population is engaged in agriculture and allied activities. The main source of livelihood of an agrarian society is agriculture.

6. Agrarian society can be understood in terms of its class structure. But we must also remember the structure is itself through the caste system. In rural areas, there is a complex relationship between caste and class. This relationship is not always straightforward. Give two examples to prove that the relationship is not straightforward. CBSE SQP 2024

Ans. The relationship between caste and class in agrarian society is complex. For example, Brahmins, despite being the highest caste, are often not major landowners and fall outside the agrarian structure. Similarly, some wealthy individuals from lower castes have risen economically, breaking traditional caste-class hierarchies.

7. In most regions of the country, a 'proprietary caste' group owns most of the resources and can command labour to work for them.
What do you understand by proprietary caste group?

Ans. It is a type of caste group found in most of the regions of the country which controls most of the resources in a village and command labour to work in them.

8. The third major category of land reform laws were the Land Ceiling Acts. These laws imposed an upper limit on the amount of land that can be owned by a particular family.
Explain what are land reforms?

Ans. Land reform means the redistribution of property rights in land for the benefit of small farmers and agricultural laboures. It includes two types of institutional changes one relates to agrarian relation and the other to the size of the unit of cultivation.

9. Give reasons for the bringing of land reforms.

Ans. Land reforms were brought about because

- It was majorly done to increase the level of productivity in the agricultural sector.
- It was also brought about to stop the exploitation of the poor farmers by eliminating the intermediaries so that the farmers could get land.

10. Contract farming has sociological significance. Give two points to support this statement. CBSE 2024

Ans. Contract farming has sociological significance as it provides farmers with assured markets and stable incomes, reducing economic uncertainty. Additionally, it introduces modern agricultural practices and technology, transforming traditional farming methods and reshaping rural social structures by integrating small farmers into larger agribusiness networks.

11. Why were the Land Ceiling Acts 'toothless' in most of the states? Give two reasons. CBSE 2024 C

Ans. The Land Ceiling Acts were 'toothless' in most states due to widespread exploitation of loopholes and legal strategies by landowners to retain surplus land. Examples include *benami* transfers and sham divorces to divide landholdings, allowing landowners to evade redistribution mandated by the law.

12. What do you understand by support prices?

Ans. Support prices are basically the minimum procuring prices of the agricultural products declared by the government for a particular year. It is basically done to safeguard the farmers against the losses they may bear and provide a uniform level of price.

13. Many districts of colonial India were administered through the Zamindari system. What problems were faced by the peasants due to the Zamindari system? CBSE 2025

Ans. Peasants faced the following problems under the zamindari system in colonial India

- **Heavy Taxation and Exploitation** The zamindars extracted high taxes from peasants to meet British land revenue demands, often leaving cultivators in extreme poverty.
- **Land Alienation and Oppression** Peasants did not own land and were forced to hand over a large portion of their produce to landlords, leading to frequent displacement and economic hardship.

14. Differentiate between Zamindari system and Ryotwari system with regard to the consequence on agricultural prosperity. CBSE SQP 2023

Ans. With regard to the consequences on agricultural prosperity, the Zamindari and Ryotwari systems can be differentiated in the following ways

Zamindari System	Ryotwari System
Under this system, zamindars were recognised as the owner of the land and were given the rights to collect the rent from peasants.	Under this system, the ownership rights were handed over the peasants and the British Government collected taxes directly from the peasants.
Exploitation of land and labour, high taxes and no development in agricultural field led to an overall stagnation of agricultural produce and prosperity.	Cultivators had more incentive to invest in agriculture which resulted in the areas being relatively more productive as compared to those under zamindari system.

15. Write the meaning of the term 'circulation' in the concept of circulation of labour. CBSE 2023

Ans. The term 'circulation' in the concept of the circulations of labour refers to the movement of labour from rural to urban areas and back again. It describes the cyclical pattern of labour migration that occurs when rural workers leave their homes and families to work in urban areas and then return home periodically. This movement of labour is driven by economic factors such as the availability of jobs, wages and living conditions.

16. The ultimate outcome of the Green Revolution was a process of 'differentiation', in which the rich grew richer and many of the poor stagnated or grew poorer. Describe the process of differentiation?

Ans. Differentiation is a process by which the rich grew richer and the poor grew poorer. Rising prices reduced the wages or income from agriculture. This worsened the economic condition of poor people.

17. In the first phase of the Green Revolution, in the 1960s and 1970s, the introduction of new technology seemed to be increasing inequalities in rural society. Green Revolution crops were highly profitable, mainly because they yielded more produce.

Based on the above passage, answer the question given below.

How did the introduction of new technology increase inequalities in rural society? CBSE 2024 C

Or **One of the negative outcomes of the Green Revolution strategy was the worsening of regional inequalities. Give two reasons for your answer.** CBSE 2025

Ans. The introduction of new technology during the Green Revolution increased inequalities because only medium and large farmers, who could afford expensive inputs like hybrid seeds and fertilisers, benefited. Small farmers, unable to invest, remained disadvantaged, worsening the socio-economic divide in rural areas.

18. What were some of the notable changes that underwent due to Green Revolution?

Ans. The Green Revolution led to increased agricultural productivity, making India self-sufficient in food grains. However, it also widened inequalities, benefiting larger farmers while disadvantaging small ones. It caused displacement of tenant farmers, service castes and worsened regional disparities, especially in Eastern India.

19. Agricultural productivity increased sharply because of the new technology. India was able to become self-sufficient in food grain production for the first time in decades. It was primarily the medium and large farmers who were able to benefit from the new technology. CBSE SQP Term II, 2021

(a) What is subsistence agriculture?

(b) Who were able to reap the most benefits from Green Revolution and commercialisation of agriculture?

Ans. (a) Subsistence agriculture is practised to meet the needs of the farmer's family. Low level of technology and household labour are used to produce small output.

(b) It was the farmers who were able to produce a surplus for the market, they were able to reap the most benefits from the Green Revolution and from the commercialisation of agriculture that followed.

20. Read the passage and answer the following question.

The ultimate outcome of the Green Revolution was a process of 'differentiation', in which the rich grew richer and many of the poor stagnated or grew poorer. It should be noted that employment and wages for agricultural workers did increase in many areas, because the demand for labour increased.

What are negative outcomes of Green Revolution?

Ans. In most of the Green Revolution areas, farmers have switched from a multi-crop system, which allowed them to spread risks, to a mono-crop regime, which means that there is nothing to fall back on in case of crop failure. Another negative outcome of the Green Revolution strategy was the worsening of regional inequalities.

21. Several profound transformations in the nature of social relations in rural areas took place in the post-independence period, especially in those regions that underwent the Green Revolution. Name any two transformations happened due to Green Revolution. Competency Based Que.

Ans. The two transformations happened due to Green Revolution are as following

(i) Increase in the use of agricultural labour as cultivation became more intensive.

(ii) Shift in payment mode from kind (grain) to cash.

22. In the first phrase of the Green Revolution in the 1960s and 1970s the introduction of new technology seemed to be increasing inequalities in rural society.

Mention two ways by which inequalities increased. CBSE 2023

Ans. The two ways by which inequalities increased are

(i) Small and marginal farmers could not benefit from Green Revolution, as they could not buy expensive new seeds and technology. It was mainly medium or the large farmers who were able to benefit from new technology.

(ii) Many service caste groups were displaced due to introduction of machines in agriculture such as tractors, threshers, harvesters, etc.

23. Often it is thought that imparting knowledge of 'scientific' farming methods will improve the condition of Indian farmers. Is this statement true? Give one reason for your answer. CBSE SQP Term II, 2021

Ans. No, imparting knowledge of 'scientific' farming methods will not improve the condition of Indian farmer because much of traditional knowledge about the land they till and the crops they sow is being lost as hybrid, high-yielding, and genetically modified varieties of seeds are being promoted as more productive and 'scientific'.

24. Read the passage and answer the following question.

The state invested in the development of rural infrastructure, such as irrigation facilities, roads and electricity and on the provision of agricultural inputs. For regular agricultural growth, uninterrupted power supply to rural India is one of the necessities.

A recently launched scheme is an effort of the Indian Government in this direction. Name the scheme. State the overall result of this scheme. CBSE 2024

Ans. The scheme is the Deen Dayal Upadhyaya Gram Jyoti Yojna, launched in 2014. Its overall result is improved rural infrastructure, particularly uninterrupted power supply, which supports agricultural growth, modernises the rural economy and transforms rural society by enhancing economic opportunities and living standards.

25. Read the passage and answer the following question.

The more widespread aspect of the globalisation of agriculture is the entry of multinationals into this sector as sellers of agricultural inputs such as seeds, pesticides and fertilisers. Over the last decade or so, the government has scaled down its agricultural on been replaced in the villages by agents of seed, fertiliser and pesticide companies.

How is agriculture becoming more commercialised? CBSE 2024

Ans. Agriculture is becoming more commercialised through the entry of multinational companies selling seeds, fertilizers, and pesticides. Farmers increasingly rely on these expensive inputs, reducing profits and increasing debts. Government support has declined, replaced by company agents promoting products, driving dependency and ecological challenges.

26. India's liberalisation policies since the late 1980s, especially the participation in the World Trade Organisation (WTO), have brought significant changes to agriculture and rural society. With the opening of Indian markets to global competition, farmers have been exposed to both opportunities and challenges, such as the rise of contract farming and the entry of multinational companies in agriculture.
How has the process of globalisation impacted Indian farmers?

Ans. India's globalisation, driven by WTO participation, exposed farmers to both opportunities and challenges. While contract farming and multinational involvement provided financial security, they also increased farmers' dependency on global companies. This dependency, along with ecological and economic risks, has impacted farmers' livelihoods and sustainability.

Short Answer Type Questions

1. "A significant change in rural society that is linked to the commercialisation of agriculture has been the growth of migrant agricultural labour. As 'traditional' bonds of patronage between labourers or tenants and landlords broke down, and as the seasonal demand for agricultural labour increased in prosperous Green Revolution regions, a pattern of seasonal migration emerged."
Elaborate on this pattern of migration. CBSE SQP 2024

Ans. The pattern of migration linked to the commercialisation of agriculture involves landless labourers migrating seasonally from less productive, drought-prone areas to prosperous agricultural regions like Punjab and Haryana or urban construction sites. This migration occurs due to increased inequalities, seasonal demand for labour and better wages in Green Revolution regions. Men often migrate, leaving women and children behind to manage cultivation. Wealthy farmers prefer employing migrant labourers for intensive operations as they are paid lower wages, creating exploitative conditions. This pattern has also led to the feminisation of agricultural labour.

2. Several profound transformations in the nature of social relations in rural areas took place in the Post-Independence period.
Explain these transformations. CBSE 2024 C

Ans. Post-Independence, rural social relations underwent significant changes, especially in regions influenced by the Green Revolution. Agricultural labour became more intensive, shifting from payment in kind (grain) to cash. Traditional patronage bonds between landlords and workers weakened, giving rise to a class of 'free' wage labourers. These changes, termed a shift from 'patronage to exploitation' by sociologist Jan Breman, indicate the transition to capitalist agriculture. Commercialisation oriented farmers towards market-based production, increasing money flow and business opportunities in villages, transforming rural economies and integrating them into the wider economy.

3. Explain two land revenue administrative systems introduced by the British in colonial India. CBSE 2024

Ans. The British introduced two main land revenue administrative systems in colonial India zamindari and raiyatwari.

(i) Under the zamindari system, land was managed by zamindars, who collected taxes from peasants and paid a fixed amount to the British. This system often led to exploitation as zamindars extracted excessive taxes from farmers, causing widespread poverty and stagnation in agricultural production.

(ii) In the raiyatwari system, revenue was collected directly from individual cultivators, reducing intermediaries. This encouraged farmers to invest in agriculture, leading to better productivity in these regions.

4. Discuss some of the features of the zamindari system.

Ans. The features of the zamindari system are as follows

- In a zamindari system, the zamindar was the owner of the land and he used to give the land to marginal and landless farmers for tilling purposes.
- In return, the marginal farmer used to pay a heavy amount of tax to the zamindar and the zamindar used to pay the tax to the government.
- This system was majorly considered to be exploitative in nature and the farmers who were landless suffered at the hands of the zamindars who used to extort lot of money from these farmers.

5. From the 1950s to the 1970s, a series of land reforms laws were passed - at the national level as well as in the states. What were the reasons behind these reforms? CBSE 2025

Ans. The land reform laws from the 1950s to the 1970s were introduced to address issues of inequality and exploitation in rural India. The key reasons behind these reforms were:

(i) **Abolition of Zamindari System** To remove intermediaries who collected rent from farmers without cultivating the land themselves.

(ii) **Redistribution of Land** To provide land to landless farmers and reduce concentration of land in the hands of a few.

(iii) **Ceilings on Land Holdings** To prevent large landowners from holding excessive land and to distribute surplus land to the needy.

(iv) **Encouraging Agricultural Productivity** To make land ownership more equitable, ensuring better use of land for agricultural growth.

6. Explain meaning of land ceiling and what are the different reforms it brought about in India?

Ans. Land ceiling is a concept where an individual should possess cultivable land according to a prescribed limit. Previously, many people had lots of land in their ownership while there were many who were devoid of any land. This land ceiling was carried out to provide cultivable land to all and the fixing of the land came to be known as land ceiling.

It brought following reforms

- Redistribution of cultivable land.
- Ceiling of the upper limit of land holdings.

7. Mention the loopholes found in the implementation of the Land Ceiling Act. CBSE 2019

Or **How did the Land Ceiling Act prove to be toothless in most of the states?** CBSE SQP 2023

Ans. The loopholes found in the implementation of the Land Ceiling Act which proved it to be toothless are discussed below

- Land Ceiling Act imposed upper limit on the amount of land that can be owned by a particular family.
- Possession of surplus land (above the ceiling limit) held by each household and redistribute it to landless families.
- There were many loopholes and other strategies through which most landowners were able to escape from having their surplus land taken over by the state.
- In most cases landowners managed to divide the land among relatives and others, including servants, in so-called benamic transfers.
- In some places some rich farmers actually divorced their wives (but continued to live with them) in order to avoid the provisions of Land Ceiling Act, which allowed a separate share for unmarried women but not for wives.

8. Write briefly about Contract Farming.

Ans. Under the contract farming system the company identifies the crops to be grown, provide the seeds and other inputs as well as technical knowhow and also the working capital to a farmer. In this type of farming, the farmer is assured of the market because the company guarantees that it will purchase the product at a pre-determined fixed price.

It is very common now in the production of specialised items such as cut flowers, fruits like grapes, figs, etc. While contract farming appears to provide financial security, it can also lead to greater insecurity as farmers become dependent on these companies for their livelihoods. In contract farming the export-oriented products such as flowers and gherkins also means that agricultural land is diverted away from foodgrain production.

It caters mainly to the production of elite items because it usually requires high doses of fertilisers and pesticides and is often not ecologically sustainable.

9. What are the major positivities and negativities of contract farming? CBSE 2022 Term II

Ans. The major positivities of contract farming are as follows

- The company associated provides guarantee of purchase from the farmers just at the time of produce and that too at a pre-determined fixed price.
- All this provides financial security to the farmers who are assured of the revenue they get out of their produce.

On the other hand, there are many negativities associated with contract farming which are as follows

- It can lead to greater insecurity as farmers become dependent on companies for their livelihoods.
- The crops require high degree of fertilisers and pesticides which are not good for soil.
- Contract farming of export-oriented products also means that agricultural land is diverted away from foodgrain production. In addition, contract farming primarily caters to the production of elite items which is not ecologically sustainable.

10. Enumerate the indicators of the process of globalisation of agriculture. CBSE SQP 2024

Ans. The indicators of the globalisation of agriculture include the following

- **Increased imports** The opening of Indian markets to global imports, such as fruits and wheat, which were previously protected by import substitution policies.
- **Contract farming** Farmers in regions like Punjab and Karnataka enter into agreements with multinational companies to grow specific crops for processing or export.
- **Multinational involvement** The entry of multinational companies in selling agricultural inputs (seeds, pesticides, fertilisers) to farmers.
- **Ecological and economic challenges** The increased dependency on expensive inputs and ecological damage, along with financial insecurity for farmers.

Long Answer Type Questions

1. Discuss in detail about the land reforms that were introduced after independence in India.

Ans. India was an underdeveloped country at the time of independence where industries were not too developed and technology and science lagged behind to a great extent. The main source of income for the people of India was agriculture and more than 80 per cent of the population of India lived in rural India.

People who lived in the villages were in pitiable condition, so it followed certain non-governmental steps that had to be taken to bring fruitful reforms in the agricultural sector. Many land reforms that were initiated were as follows

- **Abolition of Intermediaries** Government had made certain types of laws that abolished the intermediaries between the farmers and the state after independence. The intermediaries used to extort money from the farmers and the system was very complex that had eventually caused complex set of problems for the farmers. There was absentee landlordism which was also a major problem within the agricultural set up.
- **Consolidation of Landholdings** Before independence, the landholdings of farmers were scattered in the country and the fields were at far off places. Consolidation of land in return provided for the increased productivity in agriculture.
- **Tenancy Reforms** Under the system of tenancy reforms, the actual tenants used to pay around half of their produce in the form of taxes. After the First Five Year Plan, it was fixed to 20 to 25 per cent after which the tenants were given the ownership and security of the land.
- **Land Ceiling Act** This law imposed an upper limit on the amount of land that a family could own. The ceiling varies region to region depending upon how fertile the land is. State is supposed to identify and take possession of surplus land need by each household and redistribute it among the landless families.

2. Discuss the consequences of commercialisation of agriculture.

Or **How did commercialisation of agriculture lead to circulation of labour?** **CBSE 2022 Term II**

Ans. The consequences of commercialisation of agriculture are as following

- The commercialisation of agriculture was beneficial to the British planters, traders and manufacturers, who were provided with opportunity to make huge profits.
- The poor peasants were forced to sell their produce just after harvest at whatever prices they could get as they had to meet in time the demands of the government, the landlord, the money lender and their family members.
- Indian money lenders advanced, cash advances to the farmers to cultivate the commercial crops and if the peasants failed to pay them back in time, the land of peasants came under the ownership of moneylenders.
- Commercialisation of agriculture did not encourage growth of land market because major profit of commercialisation went to company traders and mediators.
- Commercialisation effected traditional relations between agriculture and industry. In India, traditional relations acted as factors for each other's development which were hampered.

3. Show the relation between circulation of labour and feminisation of agricultural labour force. **CBSE SQP Term II, 2021**

Ans. The relation between circulation of labour and feminisation of agricultural labour force are as follows

- As 'traditional' bonds of patronage between labourers or tenants and landlords broke down and as the seasonal demand for agricultural labour increased in prosperous Green Revolution regions such as the Punjab, a pattern of seasonal migration emerged in which thousands of workers circulate between their home villages and more prosperous areas where there is more demand for labour and higher wages.
- Migrant workers come mainly from drought-prone and less productive regions and they go to work for part of the year on farms in the Punjab and Haryana, or on brick factories in UP or construction sites in cities such as New Delhi or Bangalore.
- Wealthy farmers often prefer to employ migrant workers for harvesting and other such intensive operations, rather than the local working class, because migrants are more easily exploited and can be paid lower wages.
- This preference has produced a peculiar pattern in some areas where the local landless labourers move out of the home villages in search of work during the peak agricultural seasons, while migrant workers are brought in from other areas to work on the local farms.
- The large scale circulation of labour has had several significant effects on rural society, in both the receiving and the supplying regions. For instance, in poor areas where male family members spend much of the year working outside of their villages, cultivation has become primarily a female task.

- Women are also emerging as the main source of agricultural labour, leading to the 'feminisation of agricultural labour force'.

4. The first important legislation was the abolition of the zamindari system, which removed the layer of intermediaries that stood between the cultivators and the state. Of all the land reform laws that were passed, this was probably the most effective, for in most areas it succeeded in taking away the superior rights of the zamindars over the land and weakening their economic and political power. This did not happen without a struggle, of course, but ultimately the effect was to strengthen the position of the actual landholders and cultivators at the local level. However, zamindari abolition did not wipe out landlordism or the tenancy or sharecropping systems, which continued in many areas. It only removed the top layer of landlords in the multi-layered agrarian structure.

(i) How was the end of zamindari system a benefit to mankind? In what way were the actual landholders and cultivators benefited by the abolition of the zamindari system?

(ii) What does the author think about the present system and what could be said about the nature of the author?

Ans. (i) The abolition and the end of zamindari system was a great service to the mankind in the sense that it helped to remove the intermediaries and stood for the cultivators of the state. It succeeded in taking away the rights of the zamindars over the land and also helped in weakening of their economic and political power.

The actual landholders and the cultivators got strengthed by the abolition and complete end of the zamindari system. They gained strength at the local level and were strengthened by this system. Hence, they were benefited to a large extent by the abolition of this system.

(ii) The author is not entirely satisfied by the system and the abolition of the zamindari system. It has not been able to wipe out the landlordism and the tenancy of the share cropping system. It had only removed the top level landlords in the multi-layered agrarian structure. The author is definitely a proactive and a thoughtful man who wants betterment of the society.

5. Migration and lack of job security create poor working and living conditions of migrant labour. Explain with reference to the circulation of labour in India. CBSE 2019

Ans. Migration and lack of job security created poor working and living conditions of migrant labour due to the following reasons

- Commercialisation of agriculture has led to the growth of migrant agricultural labour.
- The seasonal demand for agriculture labour increased in prosperous Green Revolution regions such as Punjab leading to seasonal migration.
- Labourers migrate due to the increasing inequalities in rural areas.
- Ten-twelve of them are housed in small rooms and sometimes one shift has to make way for another.
- Men migrate out periodically in search of work and better wages, while women and children are often left behind in their villages with elderly grandparents.
- Migrant workers come mainly from drought prone and less productive regions and they go to work for part of the year on farms or construction sites.
- Landless workers do not have many rights, they are usually not paid the minimum wage and can be easily exploited.

6. Explain Green Revolution and the social consequences associated with it?

Ans. The Green Revolution of the 1960's and 1970's introduced important changes. It was a government programme of agricultural modernisation and the programme of Green Revolution was funded by international agencies.

Green Revolution was mainly marked by High Yielding Variety (HYV) seeds alongwith pesticides, fertilisers and other inputs.

The programme of Green Revolution was introduced only in those areas that had abundant irrigation. But only some parts of the country could reap the benefits of Green Revolution like that of Punjab, Western Uttar Pradesh, Andhra Pradesh and some parts of Tamil Nadu. There were many social consequences of Green Revolution

- The agricultural productivity increased very rapidly and the medium and large farmers who produced a surplus for the market got the maximum benefit through Green Revolution.
- The service caste groups giving agriculture related services became jobless due to introduction of machinery thus worsening their economic condition.
- Small and marginal farmers could not benefit from Green Revolution as they could not buy new seeds and technology. It was only large farmers who were able to benefit from the new technology.
- Differentiation of Indian rural society took place due to it. The rich grew richer and poor became poorer.

- The excessive use of pesticides hybrid seeds etc. that needed assured irrigation also brought negative impacts. Many farmers shifted from multi-crop-system to mono crop system.
- Various kinds of violence such as inter-caste violence have risen due to sharp caste and class inequalities and exploitative labour relations.
- This satisfactory economic condition of farmers changed their social relationships. Their purchasing power increased and it made the rich farmers better off.

7. Read the passage and answer the following questions.

Another negative outcome of the Green Revolution strategy was the worsening of regional inequalities. The areas that underwent this technological transformation became more developed, while other areas stagnated. For instance, the Green Revolution was promoted more in the Western and Southern parts of the country and in Punjab, Haryana and Western UP, than in the Eastern parts of the country (Das, 1999). As a result, we find agriculture in states such as Bihar and in Eastern UP, and in dry regions such as Telangana, to be relatively undeveloped. These are also the regions that continue to have an entrenched 'feudal' agrarian structure, in which the landed castes and landlords maintain power over the lower castes, landless workers and small cultivators. The sharp caste and class inequalities together with exploitative labour relations in these regions has given rise to various kinds of violence (including inter-caste violence) in recent years.

(i) **What is the inhuman aspect that can be attributed to Green Revolution? What is the meaning of entrenched feudal agrarian structure?**

(ii) **What are the various reasons for the rise of violence in various areas?**

Ans. (i) The Green Revolution brought about increased regional inequalities. The effects of the Green Revolution did not spread evenly to all parts of the country. The areas where the technological benefits did not reach had been surrounded by high levels of inequalities. The technological evolution brought about a lot more changes that led to increase in the number of disparities within the people.

Entrenched feudal agrarian structure mentioned in the passage is a system whereby the castes and the landlords maintained dominance over the landless workers and the small cultivators. There was always the feeling of dominance of the landlords over their subjects. This always led to a certain degree of strife between the landless farmers and the landlords.

(ii) The sharp caste and class inequalities together with the exploitative labour relations have given rise to various kinds of violence especially in the rural areas. These inequalities have further created problems within different communities within the village.

8. The pattern of farmer's suicides point to the significant crises that the rural areas are experiencing. What do you understand by 'matrix event' and how are they responsible for farmer suicides? **CBSE 2019**

Ans. Farmers in India for centuries have periodically faced distress due to drought, crop failures or debt. Sociologists have attempted to explain this phenomenon by looking at the structural and social changes that have been occurring in agriculture and agrarian society. Such suicides have become 'matrix events' that is, a range of factors that come together to form an event. Some of the events or factors responsible for farmers' suicides are discussed below

- Agrarian distress caused by structural changes in agriculture and changes in economic and agriculture policies.
- The changed pattern of land holdings, changing cropping patterns especially due to the shift to cash crops.
- Liberalisation policies that have exposed Indian agriculture to the forces of globalisation.
- Farmers are heavily dependent on high cost inputs. Loss of crops due to pests or any natural disaster further leads to increase in suicides.
- There is a decline in state support in the form of subsidies for agriculture.
- They are unable to bear the debt burden as well as, natural disasters resulting in the failure of agricultural produce.
- The changing culture in rural areas in which increased incomes are required for marriages, dowries and to sustain new activities and expenses such as education and medical care.

SELF ASSESSMENT TEST

Objective Type Questions

1. Which of the following statements is true regarding the impact of liberalisation on Indian agriculture?

(a) Farmers are no longer exposed to competition from the global market.
(b) Contract farming has eliminated all financial risks for farmers.
(c) Multinational companies have contributed to a reduction in the use of pesticides and fertilisers.
(d) Liberalisation has increased farmers' dependence on expensive agricultural inputs and raised financial risks.

2. Which of the following statements is true regarding the globalisation of agriculture in India?

I. Contract farming guarantees financial security for farmers by assuring them of a fixed market for their produce.
II. Globalisation has led to the introduction of ecological farming practices, reducing dependency on chemical inputs.
III. Multinational companies play a major role in providing agricultural inputs such as seeds, pesticides, and fertilisers.
IV. The entry of multinational companies has made indigeneous knowledge of farming practices irrelevant.

Codes

(a) I and III (b) II and IV
(c) III and IV (d) I and II

3. Which of the following is not true regarding the agrarian structure in rural India?

(a) Agricultural land is equally distributed among all rural households.
(b) Women are generally excluded from ownership of land due to the prevailing patrilineal kinship system.
(c) Dominant landowning castes in rural areas are usually powerful both economically and politically.
(d) Agricultural labourers often face low incomes and insecure employment.

4. Which of the following statements correctly describes the consequences of the Green Revolution in India?

I. It increased agricultural productivity and self-sufficiency in food production.
II. It benefited only small and marginal farmers.
III. It led to greater regional inequalities in agricultural development.
IV. It contributed to the displacement of tenant-cultivators.

Codes

(a) I and II (b) I and III (c) II and IV (d) I, III and IV

5. **Assertion** (A) The introduction of hybrid seeds during the Green Revolution led to the loss of traditional agricultural knowledge among Indian farmers.

Reason (R) Hybrid varieties promoted by the Green Revolution were found to be less healthy than traditional seeds.

(a) Both A and R are true and R is the correct explanation of A
(b) Both A and R are true, but R is not the correct explanation of A
(c) A is true, but R is false
(d) A is false, but R is true

Case Based Questions

1. There are historical reasons why each region of India came to be dominated by just one or two major groups. But it is important to realise that this agrarian structure has changed enormously over time, from the pre-colonial to the colonial and after independence. While the same dominant castes were probably also cultivating castes in the pre-colonial period, they were not the direct owners of land. Instead, ruling groups such as the local kings or zamindars (landlords who were also politically powerful in their areas, and usually belonged to Kshatriya or other high castes) controlled the land.

(i) Which of the following is true regarding the agrarian structure in India?

(a) In regions with artificial irrigation, there was a higher proportion of landless labourers.
(b) The agrarian structure remained unchanged from the pre-colonial period to post-independence.
(c) Cultivators were the direct owners of land in pre-colonial India.
(d) The British granted property rights to the peasants, reducing the power of the zamindars.

(ii) In the context of the agrarian structure, which of the following best describes areas with assured irrigation?

(a) They had more landowners and fewer landless labourers.
(b) They had large numbers of bonded labourers, especially from the lowest castes.
(c) They were characterised by a lack of agricultural labor due to high rainfall.
(d) They were not affected by changes in the agrarian structure over time.

Very Short Answer Type Questions

1. "Access to agricultural land plays a crucial role in determining one's economic and social status in rural India."
Does this statement reflect social stratification? Give reasons for your answer.

2. "Access to land and control over resources determine one's position in the rural class structure, with some families owning large amounts of land while others remain landless and dependent on agricultural labour."
What are the reasons for this inequality in land distribution?

3. Define the term liberalisation.

4. "The abolition of the zamindari system aimed to weaken the power of landlords and improve the situation of actual cultivators."
How did the abolition of the zamindari system impact the agrarian structure in post-independence India?

Short Answer Type Questions

1. "The agrarian structure in India has been influenced by both the colonial legacy and post-independence reforms, with significant changes in land ownership and distribution over time."
How have land reforms affected the agrarian structure in India?

2. "Although land reform laws like tenancy abolition and land ceiling acts were introduced post-independence, their implementation has been inconsistent across different states." How has the uneven implementation of land reforms affected agricultural productivity and social justice in India?

3. The existence of caste and its dominance in the rural society forms a crucial point. Explain reference to relevant examples.

4. Give a detailed picture of the transformation of the rural society after India became independent.

Long Answer Type Questions

1. What is the need for land reforms? Discuss the impact of land reforms on Indian agriculture ever since India achieved independence.

2. There is a direct linkage between the situation of agricultural workers and their lack of upward socio-economic mobility. Name and explain some of them.

04 CHAPTER

Changes in technology and available jobs have transformed social relations, with social institutions such as caste, kinship networks, gender and religion playing significant roles in organising work and marketing products.

Change and Development in Industrial Society

YOUR STUDY GOALS

4.1 Industrial Society
4.2 Industrialisation in India
4.3 Globalisation, Liberalisation and Changes in Indian Industry
4.4 Employment Structure in India
4.5 Work Process
4.6 Working Conditions
4.7 Home-Based Work
4.8 Strikes and Unions

YOUR PRACTICE GOAL

- Objective Type Questions (24 Qs ; MCQs, A-R, Case Based Questions)
- Subjective Questions (22 VSAs, 15 SAs, 7 LAs)

4.1 Industrial Society

- An industrial society relies on technology for mass production and supports a large population with a high **division of labour**[1].
- Industrialisation often leads to greater equality, reducing disparities within societies that experience high levels of industrial development.
- The caste differences decrease in industrial settings, such as factories and public transportation, leading to improved economic conditions and rising income levels.
- A direct relationship exists between the decline of social evils and the growth of an industrial society.

Views of Theorists on Industrial Society

- Some social theorists like Karl Marx, Max Weber, and Emile Durkheim identified several features associated with industrialisation.
- These features include urbanisation and the shift from face-to-face relationships in rural areas to anonymous professional relationships in workplaces.

1 **Division of Labour** Division of labour is the process of separating a complex task into smaller tasks and assigning each task to a different person or group of people.

- They noted that industrialisation involves a detailed division of labour, where workers often focus on one small part of a product, leading to repetitive and exhausting work.
- Karl Marx described this situation as alienation, where workers feel disconnected from the products they produce, viewing work only as a means of survival.
- While industrialisation can reduce social inequalities but it can increase economic inequalities. In Industrial areas, upper-caste men dominate high-paying professions and women often receive lower wages than men for similar work.

4.2 Industrialisation in India

Specificity of Indian Industrialisation

- India, as a developing country, presents both similarities and differences compared to developed Western models.
- In developed countries, the majority of the workforce is in the service sector, with less than 10% in agriculture.
- In India, in 2018-19 approximately 43% of the workforce was employed in the primary sector (agriculture and mining), 17% in the secondary sector (manufacturing and construction), and 32% in the tertiary sector (trade and services).
- In India during 2018–19, 42.5% of people worked in agriculture. Only 0.4% worked in mining and quarrying, while 12.1% were in manufacturing. Jobs in trade, hotels and restaurants made up 12.6%, transport, storage and communication accounted for 5.9%, and 13.8% of people worked in community, social and personal services.
- Although the share of agriculture in economic growth has decreased, the sector employs a majority of the population while contributing relatively low income.
- In developed countries, most people are formally employed, whereas in India, over 52% of the population is self-employed, 24% engaged in casual labour, and only 24% in regular salaried jobs.

Organised or Formal Sector

- The organised sector consists of units employing ten or more people throughout the year. The companies in this sector need to be registered with the government to ensure employee benefits such as proper wages and job security.
- In India, government jobs are highly sought after due to their benefits and security.

Social Implications of Organised Sector

- A small portion of the Indian population works in the organised sector, leading to several issues, such as
  - Only few people experience employment in large firms, which promote interactions with diverse individuals.
  - Most Indian workers are employed in small-scale workplaces, where work is influenced by personal relationships rather than formal structures.
  - Access to secure jobs with benefits is limited, with a significant majority of secure positions in government.
  - The lack of union membership in the unorganised sector means workers often do not have experience advocating for better wages and working conditions.

Unorganised or Informal Sector

- The unorganised or informal sector comprises units that do not require government registration, with employees often lacking proper salaries, pensions, and benefits.
- Over 90% of the workforce in India is engaged in the unorganised or informal sector.

Quick Test 1

1. Who coined the term alienation?
2. What do you mean by organised sector?
3. India's economic growth primarily depends on which sector?
4. Which sector requires employees to be registered with the government?
5. What do you mean by Informal or unorganised sector?

4.3 Globalisation, Liberalisation and Changes in Indian Industry

- After 1990, the Government of India has implemented a policy of liberalisation, encouraging private companies, particularly foreign firms, to invest in sectors previously reserved for the government, such as telecom, civil aviation, and power.
- The requirement for licences to open industries has been eliminated, leading to many Indian companies being acquired by Multinational Corporations (MNCs) and some Indian firms becoming MNCs themselves.

After Effects of Liberalisation

- The government initiated the disinvestment process. It involves selling its shares in various public sector companies. The process of disinvestment raised concerns among government workers about potential job losses.
- Companies started to reduce their permanent workforce, outsourcing tasks to smaller companies or even home-based workers.
- MNCs often outsourced work globally, utilising cheap labour in developing countries like India. As smaller companies compete for contracts from larger firms, they tend to keep wages low, resulting in poor working conditions.
- The service sector, including shops, banks, IT industries, hotels, and other services, has seen increased employment, contributing to the growth of the urban middle class.
- However, access to secure jobs remains limited, and even those in regular salaried positions face increasing insecurity due to the rise of contract labour. Employment opportunities in the government sector have also diminished.
- Economists suggest that both liberalisation and privatisation have led to rising income inequality.
- With the decline of secure employment in large industries, the government is pursuing land acquisition policies for industrial development. These new industries do not necessarily create jobs for local communities and often contribute significantly to pollution.
- Many farmers, particularly adivasis, protest against low compensation rates and the forced transition to casual labour, resulting in their displacement and leading to lives of hardship in urban slums.

Quick Test 2

1. What was the impact of liberalisation on Indian industries?
2. How did disinvestment affect government workers?
3. What were the consequences of globalisation on employment opportunities in India?
4. How has liberalisation affected income inequality in India?
5. What are the challenges faced by farmers due to land acquisition for industrial development?

4.4 Employment Structure in India

- Job advertisements or employment exchanges are popular ways to find jobs, but they help only a small number of people.
- Most people find jobs through personal contacts, jobbers, or on a contract basis.

On the Basis of Personal Contacts

- Self-employed people, like plumbers, electricians, carpenters, and private tutors, rely on personal contacts for work.
- They hope that their work will be advertised through these connections.

Through Contractors or Jobbers

- Many factory workers used to get jobs through contractors or jobbers.
- In Kanpur textile mills, jobbers were known as mistris, and they were also workers from the same areas. Because they had the owner's support, they had control over the workers and put community pressure on them.
- Today, the role of jobbers has decreased, and both management and unions now help recruit workers.

Contract Basis

- Many factories employ badli workers to replace regular permanent workers when they are on leave.
- Some badli workers have worked for the same company for many years but do not have the same job security as permanent workers.
- This situation is called contract work in the organised sector.

Contractor System

- The contractor system is very visible in hiring casual labour for construction sites and brickyards.
- Contractors go to villages to hire people for different jobs.
- They give loans to workers, including the cost of transport to the work site.
- The loaned money is treated as an advance wage, and workers work without wages until they repay the loan.
- In the past, agricultural labourers were tied to their landlords by debt.
- Now, these labourers move to casual industrial work and, while still in debt, are no longer bound by other social responsibilities to the contractor.
- This means labourers have more freedom in industrial society; they can leave a contract and find another employer.

Employment Opportunities

- Employment opportunities include jobs in organisations and self-employment.
- Government schemes like 'Stand Up India' and 'Make in India' help create jobs and self-employment.
- These schemes aim to support marginalised groups in society, like SC/ST and other backward classes.
- There are positive signs for creating economic potential among India's demographic dividend.

4.5 Work Process

- In India, there is a wide range of work settings, from large companies with automated work to small home-based production.
- Companies increase production by extending working hours or increasing the amount produced in a given time.

Relationship Between Manager and Worker

- A manager's basic task is to control workers and make them work more.
- There are two ways to increase worker output: extending working hours and increasing production within a set time.

Mechanised Industry

- More machinery in industries means fewer people are employed. For example, in the Maruti Company, longer working hours and automation have increased production, but the number of permanent jobs has decreased.
- The firm has outsourced all services and security and the manufacture of parts to keep costs low.
- Outsourcing and 'just in time' methods keep costs down for the company, but workers feel tense because production can be delayed if supplies do not arrive.

'Time Slavery' in the IT Sector

- In the IT sector, professionals usually work 10-12 hours a day.
- It is common for them to work overtime to finish projects on time due to time differences with client locations.
- The structure of outsourced projects often underestimates the actual work time required, which is only 8 hours.
- Companies have changed their open and close times to adapt to these demands.
- The joint family system has re-emerged as parents need help with children.

Issues Related to Industrialisation

- A significant debate in sociology is whether industrialisation and the shift to service and knowledge-based work lead to greater skills in society.
- Sociologist Harry Braverman argues that using machinery actually deskills workers. For instance, architects and engineers used to be skilled draughtsmen, but now computers do much of this work.
- Both Marx and Mahatma Gandhi viewed mechanisation as a danger to employment.
- Even though machinery can increase production, it eventually replaces workers.

4.6 Working Conditions

- Working conditions for workers in India are very poor, despite many laws passed by the government to regulate them.
- The Mines Act of 1952, now part of the Occupational Safety, Health, and Working Conditions Code, 2020, sets rules about the maximum weekly working hours, requires overtime pay for extra work, and ensures safety regulations.
- While large mining companies may follow these laws, small mines and quarries often ignore them.
- Subcontracting means contractors do not keep proper records of workers, allowing them to avoid responsibility for accidents and benefits.
- After mining ends in an area, companies are supposed to cover open holes and restore the land, but this is rarely done.
- Workers in underground mines face dangerous conditions, including flooding, fire, roof collapses, gas emissions and ventilation failures.
- Many workers develop breathing problems and diseases like tuberculosis and silicosis.
- Workers in overground mines work in extreme weather and face injuries from mine blasting and falling objects.
- As a result, the rate of mining accidents in India is very high compared to other countries.

Migration of Workers

- In many industries, workers are migrants.
- Fish processing plants along the coast mostly employ single women from Tamil Nadu, Karnataka and Kerala. Ten to twelve of these workers live in small rooms, and often one shift must clear for another.
- These young and single migrants have little time to socialise, and whatever time and money they have is spent with other migrants.
- This situation leads to loneliness and vulnerability, but for many young women, it also means some independence and economic freedom.

Quick Test 3

1. What is the contractor system, and where is it most visible?
2. What are the working conditions like in coal mines in India?
3. Name two government schemes aimed at generating employment and self-employment.
4. How do migrant workers in fish processing plants experience life and work?
5. According to Gandhi, why is the craze for machinery dangerous for workers and society?

4.7 Home-Based Work

- Home-based work is another crucial part of the economy.
- This work includes making lace, zari, brocade, carpets, bidis, agarbattis, and other products.
- Women and children mainly do this work.
- Agents provide raw materials and collect finished products, paying home workers on a piece-rate basis for the number of items they make.

Bidi Industry

- The process of making bidis begins in forested villages where villagers pluck tendu leaves and sell them to the forest department or a private contractor.
- The government then auctions the leaves to bidi factory owners, who give them to contractors.
- Contractors supply tobacco and leaves to home-based workers.
- These workers, mostly women, roll bidis by dampening leaves, cutting them, filling them with tobacco, and tying them with thread.
- Contractors pick up the finished bidis and sell them to manufacturers, who roast them, brand them and distribute them to wholesalers, who sell them to local pan shops.

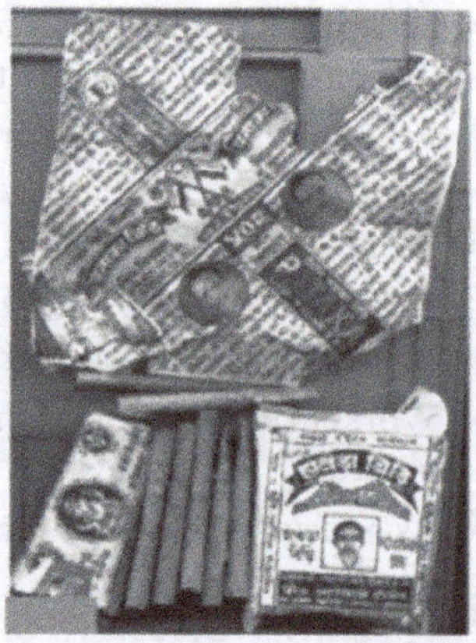

▲ *Different brands of bidi*

4.8 Strikes and Unions

- In response to poor working conditions, workers sometimes go on strike, meaning they do not go to work.
- In a lockout, management shuts the gates and prevents workers from entering.
- Calling a strike is a tough decision because managers may use substitute labour.
- Workers also find it challenging to survive without wages during a strike.
- The Bombay Textile Strike of 1982 was led by trade union leader Dr. Datta Samant and lasted nearly two years.
- Workers wanted better wages and the right to form their union.
- The government did not listen to the workers' demands.
- Eventually, people began working again out of desperation, and nearly one lakh workers lost their jobs, returning to their villages or taking up casual labour.
- Others sought work in powerloom sectors in towns like Bhiwandi, Malegaon, and Icchalkaranji.

Quick Test 4

1. By whom the Bombay Textile Strike of 1982 was led by?
2. Which were the two demands of the Bombay Textile Strike workers?
3. With what liberalisation and privatisation appears to be associated?
4. Name the two schemes of the Government of India which are helpful to the people of marginalised sections of society.
5. Who invented a new system of scientific management in the 1890s?

NCERT Folder

1. Choose any occupation you see around you and describe it along the following lines.

(a) **Social composition of the workforce – caste, gender, age, religion.**

(b) **Labour process – how the work takes place.**

(c) **Wages and other benefits.**

(d) **Working conditions – safety, rest times, working hours, etc.**

Ans. Occupation: Industrial Worker

(a) **Social Composition** The social composition plays a vital role in the industrial parameters. The stratification on the basis of caste, gender, etc. plays an imperative role in the formation of power dynamic structure within the working space. The inequalities within the employment structure faced by women is often hidden under professionalism. The upper caste dominates upon the lower caste as it leads to the exploitation of people belonging to the under privileged sections.

(b) **Labour Processes** The process of working also includes the primacy given to one class or primarily one gender over another. The functioning of occupations is subject to discriminative patterns.

(c) **Wages and other Benefits** The issue of equal pay has always been the primary force of movement of industrial workers against the exploitation against the sections of the society mainly dominated by males and upper caste.

(d) **Working Conditions** The terrible working conditions is the darkest reality of the contemporary world as it dominates the avenues of occupational and functioning parameters. The issues of maternity and paternity leaves are imperative to be recognised in the status quo.

2. How has liberalisation affected employment patterns in India?

Ans. The Indian Government has followed policy of liberalisation since 1990. The foreign companies are encouraged to invest in sectors earlier reserved for the government including telecom, civil aviation power etc. So government jobs and employment have come down and private especially MNCs jobs have increased in India.

- Licenses are no longer required to open industries. Definitely this policy has increased chances of self-employment.
- Due to liberalisation foreign products are now easily available in Indian market and shops.
- It increased the employment opportunities in Industries and MNC's.
- It increased the occupational mobility of people due to transportation facilities.
- It has also increased participation of women in occupational sector.
- It has increased Foreign Direct Investments and affected the corporate occupational opportunities of people.
- It led to occupational migration of village people to cities.

Exam Pattern Questions

Objective Type Questions

Multiple Choice Questions (MCQs)

1. ………… leads to greater equality, at least in some spheres. For example, caste distinctions do not matter anymore on trains, buses or in cyber cafes. On the other hand, older forms of discrimination may persist even in new factory or workplace settings. And even as social inequalities are reducing, economic or income inequality is growing in the world.

(a) Globalisation (b) Colonisation
(c) Industrialisation (d) Urbanisation

2. How does outsourcing in the context of modern factories, like Maruti Udyog, affect workers?

(a) It creates more job opportunities in the company.
(b) It leads to less dependency on suppliers.
(c) It reduces production costs but increases workers' wages.
(d) It decreases the number of permanent jobs and increases stress among workers.

3. In outsourcing, work is allocated by .... countries to .... countries. CBSE SQP 2023

(a) developed, developing
(b) underdeveloped, developed
(c) developing, underdeveloped
(d) developing, developed

4. Which of the following are the consequences of 'outsourcing'?

(a) Low wages
(b) Poor working conditions
(c) Permanent employees are reduced
(d) All of the above

5. In the context of casual labour in the construction industry, which of the following best describes the role of contractors?

(a) Contractors provide loans to workers, who work without immediate wages to repay the advance.
(b) Contractors always guarantee permanent employment for workers.
(c) Contractors are only responsible for organising transportation.
(d) Contractors help workers by paying them fair wages from the start.

6. Which of the following statements best describes the effect of mechanisation on the workforce?

(a) Mechanisation always leads to the betterment of workers' working conditions.
(b) Mechanisation leads to fewer jobs but increases productivity.
(c) Mechanisation has no impact on job availability.
(d) Mechanisation makes workers' tasks more creative and fulfilling.

7. What is the social effect of the shift to a globalised economy on workers?

(a) Workers enjoy more social interactions and support from family.
(b) Workers, especially migrants, experience loneliness and vulnerability.
(c) Migration leads to stronger community bonds among workers.
(d) The shift to a global economy has no impact on social life.

8. Who argued that the use of machinery actually deskills workers?

(a) Harry Braverman (b) Karl Marx
(c) Max Weber (d) Emile Durkheim

9. 'Stand Up India Scheme' and 'Make in India' are programmes that will help realise the CBSE SQP 2023

(a) benefits of high dependency ratio
(b) demographic dividend
(c) benefit of high death rate
(d) benefit of high fertility rate

10. The Bombay Textile Strike of 1982 was led which of the following trade union leader?

(a) Datta Samant (b) Jaiprakash Bhilare
(c) Kisan Salunka (d) Datta Ishwalkar

11. Which of the following is/are characteristic(s) of organised sector? Competency Based Que.

I. They have proper rules and regulations.
II. Modes of payment is transparent.
III. Employee cannot be removed from office without prior notice.

Codes

(a) I and II (b) II and III (c) I, II and III (d) I and III

12. How small scale industries are encouraged by the Government? Competency Based Que.

I. **Small scale industries are given loans on less rate of interest and on easy installments.**

II. **Things produced by these industries are kept in a tax-free zone.**

III. **Focal points in different cities are established to develop small scale industries.**

Codes

(a) I and II (b) II and III (c) I and III (d) I, II and III

13. Which of the following statements is not true for the Indian government's policy of liberalisation? CBSE SQP 2024

(a) Private companies, especially foreign firms, are encouraged to invest in sectors earlier reserved for the government.

(b) Foreign products are now easily available in Indian shops.

(c) Indian companies have ensured that they work within national boundaries.

(d) Licenses are no longer required to open industries.

14. Due to COVID-19 pandemic hundreds and thousands of workers worked from home. Which of the following can allow work from home? CBSE 2024

I. **IT sector** II. **Bidi Industry**

III. **Maruti factory** IV. **All Government firms**

Codes

(a) I and II (b) I and IV

(c) II and III (d) I, II, III and IV

15. Which of the following features is incorrect for alienation? CBSE 2024

(a) People do not enjoy their work.

(b) Work is repetitive and exhausting.

(c) People see the end result of their work.

(d) Survival depends on whether technology has room for any human labour.

16. Which of the following statements is incorrect with regard to professionals working in the service sector such as the software industry? CBSE 2024

(a) Software professionals are middle class and well educated.

(b) Their work is supposed to be self-motivated and creative.

(c) 10-12 hours is an average work day, and it's not uncommon for employees to stay overnight in the office.

(d) They do not want to show the boss that they are working hard.

17. The government of India implemented the policy of liberalisation after the year.

(a) 1980 (b) 1970 (c) 1990 (d) 2000

18. ……… coined the term alienation.

(a) Karl Marx (b) Emile Durkheim

(c) Max Weber (d) Harry Braverman

19. Karl Marx and ……… saw mechanisation as a danger to employment.

(a) Emile Durkheim (b) Mahatama Gandhi

(c) Dr. Datta Samant (d) Max Weber

20. In a ………, management shuts the door and prevent workers from entering

(a) strike (b) close-up

(c) shutdown (d) lockout

Assertion-Reason Questions

Direction (Q. Nos. 21-25) Two statement are given in the question below as Assertion (A) and Reason (R). Read the statements and choose the appropriate option.

(a) Both A and R are true and R is the correct explanation of A

(b) Both A and R are true, but R is not the correct explanation of A

(c) A is true, but R is false

(d) A is false, but R is true

21. Assertion (A) To call a strike is a difficult decision.

Reason (R) Managers may try to use substitute labour. Workers also find it hard to sustain themselves without wages. CBSE 2023

22. Assertion (A) Farmers who know how to grow crops based on their understanding of the weather, soil, and seeds are unskilled.

Reason (R) Machinery deskills workers. CBSE 2024

23. Assertion (A) Earlier architects and engineers had to be skilled draughtsmen, now the computer does a lot of the work for them.

Reason (R) The use of machinery deskills workers. CBSE SQP 2023

24. Assertion (A) The planters are in huge bungalows, set on sturdy wooden stills to save and guard the inmates against wild animals. They lived in luxury and comforts.

Reason (R) A number of bars his, malis and bearers were trained by the planters to serve them to perfection.

25. Assertion (A) The government has passed a number of laws to regulate the working conditions in coal mines.

Reason (R) Many contractors maintain proper register of workers and take responsibility for accidents giving all possible benefits. CBSE 2023

26. Assertion (A) Industrialisation leads to greater equality, at least in some spheres, such as, caste distinctions do not matter any more in trains, buses, etc.

Reason (R) Social inequalities are reducing in the wolrd. **CBSE 2025**

Case Based Questions

Read the passage given below and answer the questions that follow by choosing the correct option.

27. Job recruitment as a factory worker takes a different pattern. In the past, many workers got their jobs through contractors or jobbers. In the Kanpur textile mills, these jobbers were known as mistris, and were themselves workers. They came from the same regions and communities as the workers, but because they had the owner's backing, they bossed over the workers. On the other hand, the mistri also put community-related pressures on the worker. Now-a-days, the importance of the jobber has come down, and both management and unions play a role in recruiting their own people. Many workers also expect that they can pass on their jobs to their children. Many factories employ badli workers who substitute for regular permanent workers who are on leave.

(i) **Which sector employs the majority of people in India according to the 2018-19 data?**
(a) Secondary sector (manufacturing, construction, utilities)
(b) Primary sector (agriculture, mining)
(c) Tertiary sector (services)
(d) None of the above

(ii) **In India, the contribution of agriculture to economic growth has**
(a) increased sharply (b) stayed the same
(c) declined sharply (d) remained stable

28. In developed countries, the majority of people are in the services sector, followed by industry and less than 10% are in agriculture (ILO figures). In India, in 1999-2000, nearly 60% were employed in the primary sector (agriculture and mining), 17% in the secondary sector (manufacturing, construction and utilities), and 23% in the tertiary sector (trade, transport, financial services etc.). However, if we look at the contribution of these sectors to economic growth, the share of agriculture has declined sharply and services contribute approximately more than half. This is a very serious situation because it means that the sector where the maximum people are employed is not able to generate much income for them. (Government of India, Economic Survey 2001-2002).

(i) **Who were known as "mistris" in the Kanpur textile mills?**
(a) Factory managers
(b) Workers from other regions
(c) Jobbers with the owner's backing
(d) Union representatives

(ii) **What is the current trend in job recruitment in factories compared to the past?**
(a) Contractors and jobbers still play a major role.
(b) Management and unions recruit their own people.
(c) Workers are hired through community leaders.
(d) Factory jobs are mainly for casual laborers.

29. Gandhi on machinery, in Hind Swaraj 1924: "What I object to is the craze for machinery, not machinery as such. The craze is for what they call labour-saving machinery. Men go on 'saving labour' till thousands are without work and thrown on the open streets to die of starvation. I want to save time and labour, not for a fraction of mankind, but for all.
I want the concentration of wealth, not in the hands of the few, but in the hands of all." 1934: "When as a nation we adopt the spinning-wheel, we not only solve the question of unemployment but we declare that we have no intention of exploiting any nation, and we also end the exploitation of the poor by the rich."

(i) **What is Gandhi's primary objection to machinery in Hind Swaraj (1924)?**
(a) Machinery is too expensive to produce.
(b) The craze for machinery leads to unemployment.
(c) Machinery is harmful to the environment.
(d) Machinery makes workers less skilled .

(ii) **According to Gandhi, what is the consequence of the 'labour-saving machinery' craze?**
(a) It makes workers more productive.
(b) It creates opportunities for new types of jobs.
(c) It results in many people being unemployed and starving.
(d) It improves the working conditions for all workers.

Answers

1. (c) Industrialisation
2. (d) It decreases the number of permanent jobs and increases stress among workers.
3. (a) developed, developing
4. (d) All of the above
5. (a) Contractors provide loans to workers, who work without immediate wages to repay the advance.
6. (b) Mechanisation leads to fewer jobs but increases productivity.
7. (b) Workers, especially migrants, experience loneliness and vulnerability
8. (a) Harry Braverman
9. (b) demographic dividend
10. (a) Datta Samant
11. (c) I, II and III
12. (d) I, II and III
13. (c) Indian companies have ensured that they work within national boundaries.
14. (b) I and IV
15. (c) People see the end result of their work.
16. (d) They do not want to show the boss that they are working hard.
17. (c) 1990
18. (a) Karl Marx
19. (b) Mahatama Gandhi
20. (d) Lockout
21. (a) Both A and R are true and R is the correct explanation of A
22. (b) Both A and R are true, but R is not the correct explanation of A
23. (a) Both A and R are true and R is the correct explanation of A
24. (a) Both A and R are true and R is the correct explanation of A
25. (a) Both A and R are true and R is the correct explanation of A
26. (b) Both A and R are true, but R is not the correct explanation of A
27. (i) (b) Primary sector (agriculture, mining)
    (ii) (c) Declined sharply
28. (i) (c) Jobbers with the owner's backing
    (ii) (b) Management and unions recruit their own people
29. (i) (b) The craze for machinery leads to unemployment
    (ii) (c) It results in many people being unemployed and starving

Subjective Questions

Very Short Answer Type Questions

1. Describe the main field of interest for sociologists in the industry.

Ans. The sociologists are mainly interested in the questions about who produces what, who works where and what he sells. These are not only individual choices but are actually outcomes of social patterns. The choices that people make in turn influence the setup of the society.

2. Economists and others have often made a distinction between the organised or formal and the unorganised or informal sector. Justify. **CBSE 2019**

Ans. An organised sector consists of all units employing ten or more people throughout the year. These have to be registered with the government to ensure that their employees get proper salaries or wages, pension and other benefits.

While in an unorganised sector the employees do not get proper salaries or wages, pension and other benefits. Government has made laws to ensure that workers are benefitted but they are left to the decisions of the employer or contractor.

3. The formal sector in India is very small compared to the informal sector. What are the implications of having a small organised sector in India?

Ans. The small organised sector in India limits access to secure jobs with benefits, such as pensions and insurance. It also results in informal employment with inconsistent wages, poor working conditions, and a lack of job security, affecting workers' overall well-being and economic stability.

4. "By and large, work for most Indians is still in smallscale workplace. Here personal relationships determine many aspects of work."

In large organisations work is not determined by personal relationships. What inference can you draw from this statement? **CBSE 2025**

Ans. The statement highlights the difference between small-scale workplaces and large organisations in India. The key inference is that most Indian workers are in the informal sector, where personal relationships influence job security, promotions, and wages. In contrast, large organisations follow structured rules, ensuring transparency in recruitment and grievance redressal.

5. Differentiate between organised and unorganised sector. CBSE 2024 C

Ans.

Organised Sector	Unorganised Sector
It consists of all units employing 10 or more people throughout the year.	Personal relationships determine many aspects of work as opposed to organised sector which has well-defined rules.
These are registered with the government to ensure that their employees get proper salaries and wages.	The units need not be registered with the government.

6. Write a note on home based industry with the help of suitable examples.

Ans. Home based industry is a very significant part of the economy wherein the work is mainly done by the women and children. Workers in home based industries are generally paid on a piece rate basis depending on the number of pieces they make. For examples, in the agarbatti industry, the workers receive wages based on the number of agarbattis they make.

7. State, how can industrialisation contribute to reducing inequality?

Ans. In the process of industrialisation, the caste distinctions do not matter anymore because of work style and the culture of the work. In new types of factories and the workplaces, the social inequalities are greately reducing.

8. Give one advantage and one disadvantage of the policy of liberalisation. CBSE 2025

Ans. **Advantage** Liberalisation has led to economic growth by attracting foreign investment, increasing job opportunities, and expanding industries, improving the overall standard of living.

Disadvantage It has also increased economic inequality, as large corporations and wealthy individuals benefit more than small businesses and lower-income groups, widening the gap between rich and poor

9. How has liberalisation impacted the employment patterns in India? Mention any two ways? CBSE 2023

Ans. Liberalisation as impacted the employment patterns in India in following ways

(i) The service sector i.e. shops, banks, IT Industry, hotels and other services are employing more people and the urban middle class is growing.

(ii) Very few people in India have access to secure jobs and even the small number in regular salaried employed are becoming more insecure with incoming of contract labour. Now a days, employment opportunities under government is also reducing. According to economists, both liberalisation and privatisation is associated with rising income inequality.

10. How do people find jobs in an industrial society? CBSE 2019

Ans. In India, people find jobs through various means induding advertisements, employment exchange, personal contacts etc. Many workers also get their jobs through contractors or jobbers.

11. Define work in the organised sector. CBSE 2023

Ans. The organised sector consists of all units employing ten or more people throughout the year. These have to be registered with the government to ensure that their employees get proper salaries or wages, pensions and other benefits.

12. "You need energy. The eyes move, the neck, the legs and the hands, each part moves. Weaving is done under a continuous gaze - one cannot go anywhere, the focus must be on the machine. When four machines run all four must move together, they must not stop.

The more mechanised an industry gets; the fewer people are employed." What are the reasons for this? CBSE SQP 2024

Ans. The more mechanised an industry becomes, the fewer people are employed because machinery increases efficiency and production, reducing the need for manual labor. Automation allows machines to perform tasks previously done by workers, resulting in fewer workers being required for the same output.

13. To generate employment and self-employment the Government of India floated many schemes. Name any two schemes. What is the positive outcome of these schemes? CBSE 2024

Ans. Two schemes launched by the Government of India to generate employment and self-employment are 'MUDRA' and 'Aatmanirbhar Bharat.' The positive outcome of these schemes is the creation of economic opportunities, particularly for marginalised sections of society, including SC, ST, and other backward classes.

14. What are the social consequences of the long working hours in the IT sector? CBSE SQP Term II, 2021

Ans. Following are the social consequences of the long working hours in the IT sector

- If both husband-and-wife work, then children have to be put in creches. The joint family, which was supposed to have disappeared with industrialisation, seems to have re-emerged, as grandparents are roped in to help with children.

15. What is the basic task of a manager? CBSE 2023

Ans. The basic task of the worker in to control workers and get more work out of them.

16. "Many factories employ badli workers." Who are badli workers? CBSE 2024

Ans. Badli workers are the workers, who substitute for regular permanent workers who are on leave.

17. In what way does 'Time Slavery' influence the Industrial society.

Ans. Time slavery refers to employee working for more than 10-12 hours a day in order to meet the deadlines and complete the projects. Sometimes it leads to a condition where the employees work overnight and this might put extra stress on them.

18. Workers in underground mines face very dangerous conditions, due to flooding, fire, the collapse of roofs and sides, the emission of gases and ventilation failures. Many workers develop breathing problems and diseases like tuberculosis and silicosis.

Write about the conditions of overground mine workers?

Or **Workers in underground mines face very dangerous conditions. Give examples.** CBSE 2025

Ans. The conditions of overground mine workers is very poor. They have to work under harsh conditions. These workers have to work in both hot sun and rain and face injuries due to mine blasting, falling objects etc.

19. Compare the impact of just-in-time for the company vis-a-vis the worker. CBSE SQP Term II, 2021

Ans. Just-in-time keeps costs low for the company, but the workers are very tense, because if the supplies fail to arrive, their production targets get delayed, and when they do arrive they have to run to keep up which exhausts them.

20. Mention two features of The Mines Act, 1952. CBSE 2024

Ans. Two features of The Mines Act, 1952, include regulating the maximum number of working hours per week and ensuring overtime pay for extra hours worked. It also sets safety rules to protect workers from dangerous conditions like flooding, fire, and ventilation failures in mines.

21. In an industrial set-up, how can a manager make the workers produce more?

Ans. In an industrial set-up manager can make the workers produce more by providing them more than the prevailing wage rate and also by motivating them to work hard.

22. Differentiate between strike and lockout.

Or **In response to harsh working conditions workers have expressed anger through trade union. Differentiate between strike and lockout in the light of above statement.** CBSE 2019

Ans. Workers sometimes use a method in opposition to the harsh working conditions which is called a strike. In this, the workers express their anger by not going to work, so that their demands could be met.

Lockout is a counter method used by the management against the workers in which they prevent the workers from carrying any violent activity during a strike by locking up the gates.

Short Answer Type Questions

1. The Industrial Society is characterised by alienation. How? CBSE SQP 2023

Ans. According to Karl Marx, Alienation is a condition in industrial societies wherein a person is disconnected with the product he/she is producing. For them work is something that they have to do only in order to survive. For labours, industrialisation involves a detailed division of labour in which people do not see the end result of production process as they are producing only one small part of a product.

Also, their work is repetitive and exhausting. Yet for them, this work is better than being unemployed. This leads to alienation for people, don't enjoy their work and see it as something they have to do in order to survive and even that survival depends on whether the technology has room for any human labour.

2. Despite the increasing size of the services sector, India still is largely an agricultural country. Give reasons. CBSE 2024

Ans. India remains largely an agricultural country because a significant portion of its population, about 42.5% in 2018–19, is employed in the primary sector, which includes agriculture and mining. While the share of agriculture in the economy has declined, it still plays a crucial role in providing employment to a large number of people, especially in rural areas. The secondary and tertiary sectors, though growing, do not yet absorb enough workers from agriculture to make a significant shift in the employment structure, keeping India predominantly agricultural.

3. Discuss the main features of industrialisation in India.

Ans. Main features of industrialisation in India are as following

- The experience of industrialisation in India is in many ways similar to the Western model and in several different ways.
- In India, about 50% of the population is self-employed, only nearly 14% are in regular salaried employment, while approximately 30% are casual labour.
- The first modern industries in India were cotton, jute, coal mines and railways.

- After independence, the Central Government took over the commanding heights of the economy. This involved defence, transport and communication, power, mining and other projects which only government had the power to do and which was necessary for private industry to flourish.

4. Compare the experience of industrialisation in the West with that of the Indian experience.

Ans. The experience of industrialisation in the West and India differs significantly. In the West, industrialisation led to a shift from agriculture to services, with most people employed in regular salaried jobs in large organisations. In contrast, India's industrialisation is marked by a large agricultural workforce (43%), and a smaller proportion in manufacturing and services. India also faces a predominance of informal sector jobs, with over 90% of workers in unorganised sectors, unlike the West, where formal employment and labour rights are more established. This creates different social and economic challenges in India.

5. Discuss the impact of disinvestment on employees.

Ans. The impact of disinvestment on employees are as following

- Many government workers are scared that after disinvestment, they will lose their jobs. In the Modern Foods, which was set up by the government to make healthy bread available at cheap prices, and which was the first company to be privatised, 60% of the workers were forced to retire in the first five years.
- Indian agriculture as well as service sector such as shops, banks, the information and technology industries, hotels and other services, are employing more people on contract basis. This develops job insecurity.

6. "The more mechanised an industry gets, the fewer people are employed." Explain with a suitable example. **CBSE SQP 2023**

Ans. The more mechanised an industry gets, the fewer people are employed however they have to work at the pace of the machine. While production has gone up, the number of permanent jobs in the factory has gone down. The firm has outsourced all services like cleaning, and security, as well as the manufacture of parts. Outsourcing and just-in-time keeps costs low for the company, but the workers are very tense, because if the supplies fail to arrive, their production targets get delayed, and when they do arrive they have to run to keep up. Thus, they get exhausted and they leave their jobs.

For example, the fear of high mechanisation and low labour employment came to the front in the case of Maruti Udyog Ltd. In Maruti Udyog Ltd. two cars roll off the assembly line every minute. Workers get only 45 minutes rest in the entire day. Two tea breaks of 7.5 minutes each and one lunch break of half an hour. Most of them are exhausted by the age of 40 and take voluntary retirement.

7. Mahatma Gandhi saw mechanisation as a danger to employment. Explain. **CBSE SQP 2023**

Ans. Mahatma Gandhi saw mechanisation as a danger to employment because machines help to increase production but it also creates danger that eventually machines will replace workers. He was critical of machines because they left thousands of people without work. He wanted to use machine for the help of labour and not to make him unemployed. He opposed the craze of those industrialists who called labour-saving machinery. He objected to the craze for machinery, not machinery as such. The craze is for what they call labour-saving machinery.

8. What are some problems faced by the mine workers?

Ans. Some problems faced by the mine workers are as follows

- Rules are not followed in smaller mines and quarries. Labourers are kept under contractual system and are not given proper wages.
- Many contractors do not maintain proper register of workers, thus avoiding any responsibility for accident and benefits.
- Workers in underground mines face very dangerous conditions due to flooding, fire, the collapse of roofs and sides, emission of gases and ventilation failures. Many workers develop breathing problems and diseases like tuberculosis and silicoins.
- The mine workers working in underground mines have to work in both hot sun and rain and face injuries due to mine blasting falling objects etc.

9. What kind of work people do in the society?

Ans. In developed countries, majority of people work in the service sector and less than 10% in agriculture or agriculture related activities. In India in 1999-2000, nearly 60% people were employed in agriculture or mining, 17% in manufacturing, construction and utilities sector, and 23% in the trade, transport and financial services sector.

In India however, in terms of contribution to economic growth, the share of the agricultural sectors has reduced and share of the services sector has doubled. This is a cause for concern because the sector that employs the majority of people cannot generate much income for them.

10. Identify and discuss the plight of the various stakeholders in the Bombay Textile strike of 1982.

Ans. The plight of the various stakeholders in the Bombay Textile strike of 1982 were to be discussed

- The Bombay Textile strike of 1982, which was led by the trade union leader, Dr. Datta Samant, and affected nearly a quarter of a million workers and their families. The strike lasted nearly two years.
- Women workers participated actively in the strike. However, they experienced a conflict between their role as a participant in the strike and their responsibility towards their families and children.
- Nearly one lakh workers lost their jobs and went back to their village or took ujp casual labour.

11. Discuss the phenomenon of 'Time Slavery' in the IT Sector. CBSE 2023

Ans. The phenomenon of 'Time Slavery' in the IT Sector can be explained with and example of a service professionals who work on an average work day for 10-12 hours. But it is very common for them to work overtime to complete the project on time. This is due to the time difference between the client site and India. Further the structure of outsourced projects leads the underestimation in terms of mandays which is only 8 hours. Due to such working hours, many firms had changed their open and close time. In addition, the joint family system has reemerged as parents need them to help with children.

12. "In places like Bengaluru, Hyderabad and Gurugram, where many IT firms or call centres are located, shops and restaurants have also changed their opening hours and are open late."

Based upon the passage answer the following questions. Do you agree with the given statements? Give one reasons for your answer. CBSE SQP 2023

Ans. The late hours of IT cities such as Gurugram or Bengaluru and Hyderabad are due to several reasons. Some of them includes

(i) **Overtime as a Culture of IT Work** It is an inbuilt function of the industry which seeks to increase productivity with every minute of the day. In order to meet the deadlines and sometimes finish even before the deadline is expected out of employees and thus they end up extending their work hours.

(ii) **The Hoax of Flexible Time** Overtime is also normalised by creating an illusion of freedom to choose individual work hours, but the practice that workers end up working for as long as is needed to finish the assignment.

13. Explain the major forms of job recruitment in India.

Or **Job recruitment as a factory worker takes a different pattern. Explain this pattern** CBSE 2022 Term II

Ans. Job recruitment takes different forms in India Very few jobs are acquired through advertisements. In professions like plumbing and carpentry people are self-employed. Among the educated sections , tutors, writers and architects are self employed as their contacts play a dominant role in acquiring work for them. There is a lot of flexibility in their working hours.

A few workers are employed as permanent head worker and they get proper compensation, status and position for their work, whereas sometimes personnel are employed even on contract basis. Major forms of job recruitment are

(i) Newspaper
(ii) Employment Exchange
(iii) Contractors
(iv) Outsourcing
(v) Personal contacts

14. Explain the working conditions of workers working in coal mines. CBSE 2024

Ans. Working conditions of workers working in coal mines are as following

- Coal mines are often dark and are filled with dangerous gases, posing serious health risks to workers.
- Explosions are common threats due to the presence of combustible gases like methane.
- Workers are constantly exposed to coal dust, which can lead to respiratory issues, including black lung disease and chronic bronchitis.
- Mining is physically demanding work, requiring heavy lifting, bending, and long hours in awkward postures.
- Ventilation in mines is typically poor, leading to a buildup of harmful gases like carbon monoxide and methane, which can cause suffocation or poisoning.
- The workers working in underground mines face very dangerous conditions because of flooding, fire, the collapse of roofs and sides, the emission of gases and ventilation failures.

15. What does this strike reveal about the power dynamics between labour and management in industrial settings?

Ans. The Bombay Textile Strike of 1982 highlights the imbalance of power between labour and management in industrial settings. Workers, despite demanding better wages and the right to form unions, faced significant challenges as the management used substitute labour and resisted modernisation. The strike's prolonged duration resulted in job losses for many workers, forcing them into casual labour or migration. This power struggle underscores the vulnerability of workers in an unorganised sector and the difficulty in achieving fair labour rights against powerful industrial management.

Long Answer Type Questions

1. Discuss industrial society and different views of theorists on it. **Competency Based Que.**

Ans. Industrial society refers to a society that is driven by the use of technology to enable mass production. It generally supports a large population with a high capacity for division of labour.

Industrialisation often leads to greater equality and there are less disparities in societies with high levels of industrial development. The role of caste distinctions is reduced when people are working in factories or travelling in trains. With the decrease in the social inequalities, the economic condition is improving and the income level is rising.

There exists a direct relationship between the decline of the social evils and the growth of industrial society.

View of Theorists on Industrial Society

Social theorists like Karl Marx, Max Weber and Emile Durkheim associated a number of features with industrialisation such as urbanisation, loss of face to face relationships in rural areas and their substitution by anonymous professional relationships in modern workplaces. People did not see the end result of the production process, as they were only part of a small part of production. According to them, industrialisation involves a detailed division of labour and their work is often exhaustive and repetitive but it was much better from being unemployed.

Marx specifically emphasised upon his concept of alienation of labour, whereby he illustrated how a labour or a worker is disconnected with the product he is producing. A labour is working only for survival and to meet his needs.

There were eventually mixed views of the theorists on the effects of industrialisation. But eventually, they agreed upon the positive impact of industrialisation on modernisation and the benefit that industrialisation led to modernisation.

2. Discuss the main points of industrialisation in the early years of India's independence. **Competency Based Que.**

Ans. The initial modern industries in India were cotton, jute, coal mines and railways. After independence, the government took over the commanding heights of the economy. This involved defence, transport and communication power, mining and other projects which only government had the power to do and which was necessary for private industry also to flourish.

- In India's mixed economic policy some sectors were reserved for government, while other were open to private sectors. But within that, the government tried to ensure through its licensing policy that industries were spread over different regions.
- Before independence, industries were located mainly in the port cities like Madras, Calcutta and Bombay. But since, then we see that place like Vadodara, Coimbatore, Bengaluru, Pune, Faridabad and Rajkot have become industrial centres. The government also tried to encourage the small scale sector through special incentives.
- Many items like paper and wood products, stationary, glass and ceramics more reserved for small scale sector. In 1991, large scale industry employed only 28 per cent of the total workforce engaged in manufacture while the small scale and traditional industry employed 72 per cent.

3. Do you agree that all sections of people have benefitted from the liberalisation policies in India? Justify your answer with examples.

Ans. All sections of people are not benefited from the liberalisation policies in India. Effect of liberalisation is not uniform on across all sections.

- The service sector, such as banks, IT, hotels, and shops, has seen growth, leading to more job opportunities. The urban middle class has expanded as a result of these developments.
- Many people, especially in rural areas and among farmers, have not benefited. The disinvestment of public sector companies caused job insecurity, with fears of losing jobs. Moreover, as large industries decline, the government is acquiring land, displacing farmers, especially adivasis, who are offered low compensation and forced to work as casual labour in urban areas.
- Liberalisation and privatisation have led to rising income inequality. The rich have benefited, while the poor face insecure employment and poor working conditions.

4. "Employment by the government was a major avenue for increasing the well-being of the population, but now even that is coming down." Explain the statement in light of the graph shown above.
Describe how liberalisation and privatisation worldwide appear to be associated with rising income inequality. **Competency Based Que.**

Employment in Organised Sectors

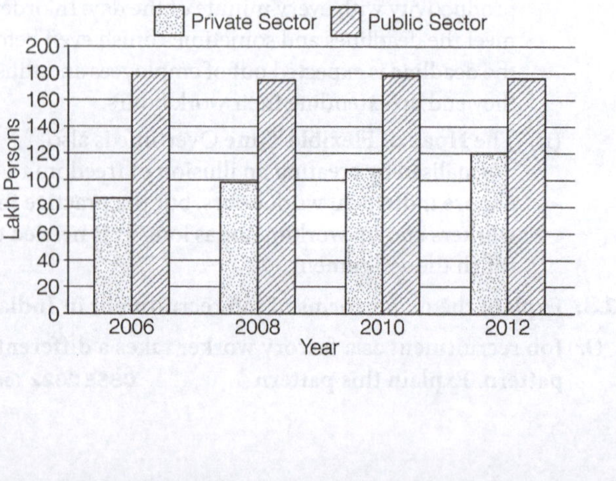

Ans. Employment by the government was a major avenue for increasing the well-being of the population, but now even that is coming down. India is still primarily a farming region. The service sector – stores, banks, the IT industry, hotels, and other services – is hiring more people, and the urban middle class is expanding, as are the ideals we see in television serials and films. However, we can see that very few citizens in India have secure jobs, and that even those who do have regular salaried jobs are becoming more precarious as contract labour becomes more prevalent.

Government jobs has previously been a significant source of growing the population's well-being, but even that is now dwindling. Some economists disagree, but global liberalisation and privatisation seem to be on the rise. While some economists disagree, liberalisation and privatisation tend to be linked to increasing income inequality across the world. The government is embarking on a programme of land acquisition for industry at the same time that secure jobs in large industry is declining. These companies do not actually provide jobs for the people in the surrounding areas, but they do pollute the environment significantly.

5. Explain the social impact of migration for work. How do migrants in industries like fish processing or bidi manufacturing experience loneliness and vulnerability, yet find independence and economic autonomy?

Ans. Migration for work, especially in industries like fish processing and bidi manufacturing, has significant social impacts on workers. Migrants, often from rural areas, leave their homes in search of better economic opportunities in urban settings.

In industries such as fish processing, young women, and in bidi manufacturing, both men and women, migrate to work in faraway cities. They live in cramped, shared spaces, often with little time for socialisation, and have limited contact with family. This leads to feelings of loneliness and isolation, as they are far from their support networks in their villages.

At the same time, migration for work offers a sense of economic autonomy. Many migrants, particularly young women, gain financial independence by earning wages that would not have been possible in their rural settings. This independence often empowers them to make decisions about their lives, such as contributing to their family's income or gaining some level of control over their future.

However, this autonomy comes with challenges, as migrants are vulnerable to exploitation due to their lack of legal protection and unstable living conditions. While they may achieve economic independence, the toll of loneliness and vulnerability highlights the complex, dual nature of migration for work in a globalised economy.

6. In the context of the construction industry, how does the contractor system exploit workers? Discuss the impact of debt and how workers are affected by this system.

Ans. In the construction industry, the contractor system often exploits workers by trapping them in cycles of debt and dependency. Contractors typically approach workers in rural areas, offering them work at construction sites in exchange for loans. These loans cover transport costs and sometimes basic living expenses, but they are treated as advance wages, meaning workers do not receive pay until the loan is repaid. This system places workers in a vulnerable position, as they work without wages for extended periods, essentially working to pay off their debt.

The impact of this debt is significant. Workers, many of whom come from economically marginalised backgrounds, are forced into a situation where they cannot easily escape the cycle. The contractors hold power over them, as workers are indebted and dependent on the job for survival. This creates a sense of forced loyalty to the contractor, limiting the workers' freedom to seek other employment opportunities.

Moreover, the workers' families are often involved, as entire families migrate together to fulfill labour needs, further intensifying their dependence on the contractor system.

This exploitation keeps wages low, denies workers basic rights like job security and social benefits, and traps them in a cycle of poverty and indebtedness, preventing them from achieving true economic freedom.

7. What is the difference between strike and a lockout? Discuss famous strike of Bombay Textile Mill of 1982. **CBSE 2022 Term II**

Or **"In response to harsh working conditions, sometimes workers went on strike." Justify taking the example of the famous Bombay Textile Strike 1982.** **CBSE 2025**

Ans. In response to harsh working conditions, sometimes workers go on strike. In a strike, workers do not go to work. In lockout the management shuts the gate and prevents workers from coming.

The Bombay Textile Strike of 1982, which was led by the trade union leader, Dr Datta Samant, is one of the prominent strikes. The strike lasted for nearly two years. The workers wanted better wages and also wanted the right to form their union. The government refused to listen to the workers' demands. After some time people started working as they were desperate and nearly one lakh workers lost their jobs and went back to village or took up casual labour, others worked in powerloom sectors in towns like Bhiwandi, Malegaon and Icchalkaranji etc.

SELF ASSESSMENT TEST

Objective Type Questions

1. According to 1999-2000 how many people were employed in tertiary sector?

(a) 17 per cent (b) 23 per cent (c) 20 per cent (d) 60 per cent

2. From which year the government has followed a policy of liberalisation?

(a) 1997 (b) 1990 (c) 1993 (d) 2000

3. What impact did the liberalisation policy post-1990 have on the Indian economy?

I. It encouraged foreign investment in previously restricted sectors.

II. It led to an increase in permanent employment in public sectors.

III. It contributed to the rise of outsourcing practices in various industries.

IV. It reduced the income inequality gap in society.

Codes

(a) I and III (b) II and IV (c) I and II (d) III and IV

4. **Assertion** (A) Outsourcing has become a popular practice among Indian companies.

Reason (R) Outsourcing provides Indian companies with access to cheaper labour and reduces production costs.

(a) Both A and R are true and R is the correct explanation of A

(b) Both A and R are true, but R is not the correct explanation of A

(c) A is true, but R is false

(d) A is false, but R is true

Case Based Questions

1. Many of the great works of sociology were written at a time when industrialisation was new and machinery was assuming great importance. Thinkers like Karl Marx, Max Weber and Emile Durkheim associated a number of social features with industry, such as urbanisation, the loss of face-to-face relationships that were found in rural areas where people worked on their own farms or for a landlord they knew, and their substitution by anonymous professional relationships in modern factories and workplaces. Industrialisation involves a detailed division of labour.

(i) Which thinkers associated social features like urbanisation and the loss of face-to-face relationships with industrialisation?

(a) Sigmund Freud, Charles Darwin, and John Locke

(b) Karl Marx, Max Weber, and Emile Durkheim

(c) Thomas Hobbes, Jean-Jacques Rousseau, and Auguste Comte

(d) Michel Foucault, Pierre Bourdieu, and Zygmunt Bauman

(ii) What is the main characteristic of work in modern factories and workplaces?

(a) Face-to-face relationships

(b) Division of labour and repetitive tasks

(c) High level of job satisfaction

(d) Freelance or self-employment opportunities.

Very Short Answer Type Questions

1. Mention any two features of an organised sector.
2. The contractor system is most visible in the hiring of casual labour for work at construction sites, brickyards, and so on. The contractor goes to villages and asks if people want work. How does the contractor system affect the lives of construction workers and their families?
3. India have access to secure jobs, with even the small number in regular salaried employment becoming more insecure due to the rise in contract labour. How has the rise of contract labour and outsourcing contributed to the increasing insecurity of jobs in India?
4. State any two points of images of Indian industrial society.

Short Answer Type Questions

1. The impact of liberalisation and privatisation has led to rising income inequality in India, especially with the decline in government jobs and the shift towards private sector employment. How has the rise of liberalisation in India contributed to increasing social and economic disparities?
2. Industrialisation leads to equality. Explain.
3. Discuss the role of home based work in Indian Economy.
4. Describe the *bidi* industry as a home based work in India.

Long Answer Type Questions

1. How has liberalisation influenced employment patterns of India?
2. Discuss the social and economic implications of the migration on both the workers and the cities they move to.

05 CHAPTER

Social movements have significantly shaped the world and continue to influence societies. They not only change societies but also inspire other movements.

Social Movements

YOUR STUDY GOALS

YOUR PRACTICE GOAL

- Objective Type Questions (23 Qs ; MCQs, A-R, Case Based Questions)
- Subjective Questions (12 VSAs, 8 SAs, 9 LAs)

5.1 Concept of Social Movements

A social movement occurs when a group of people comes together to bring about societal change regarding specific issues, aiming to alter public perspectives. For example, the 19th-century social reform movements against caste and gender discrimination, the Indian nationalist movement that led to independence from colonial rule in 1947, nationalist movements in Asia, Africa and America that ended colonial rule, the civil rights movement in the United States during the 1950s and 1960s advocating for equal rights for Black individuals, the anti-apartheid struggle in South Africa.

Features of a Social Movement

- **Sustained Collective Action** A social movement requires continuous collective action over time, often directed against the state to demand changes in policies or practices.
- **Organisation** Collective action must be organised, involving leadership and a structure that defines member relationships, decision-making and execution of plans.
- **Shared Objectives** Participants in social movements share common goals and ideologies.
- **General Orientation for Change** A social movement typically has a clear approach for achieving change.

- **Focus on Public Issues** Social movements often aim to address public issues, such as tribal rights to forest use or the rights of displaced individuals for settlement and compensation.

Counter Movements

- Social movements aim for change, whereas counter movements can arise to defend what was already existing (Status quo).
- Some examples of counter movements include
  - The Dharma Sabha, which opposed Raja Ram Mohun Roy's campaign against sati.
  - Protests against the education of girls, claiming it would harm society.
  - Social boycotts against reformers advocating for widow remarriage.
  - Withdrawal of upper caste children from schools when lower caste children enrolled.
- Peasant movements have often faced severe suppression and recent social movements for dalit rights have led to retaliatory actions.
- Proposals for extending educational reservations have sparked counter movements against such initiatives.

Challenges in Social Movements

- Social movements face challenges in effecting change as they oppose powerful, entrenched interests and values, leading to resistance and opposition.
- Over time, however, societal changes can occur as a result of sustained efforts.

Forms of Collective Action

- Protest is the most visible aspect of collective action, but social movements can operate in other significant ways.
- Social movement activists organise meetings to mobilise people around relevant issues, fostering shared understanding and agreement on collective agendas.
- Campaigns may involve lobbying the government, engaging with media and influencing public opinion.
- Different modes of protest can include the following
  - Candlelight vigils, use of black cloth, street theatre, songs and poetry.
  - In the Indian freedom movement, Gandhi used methods like Ahimsa and Satyagraha, promoting (Charkha) hand-spun clothing to support local producers and utilising symbols like salt during the Dandi March.

Breaking the Salt Laws, 1930
As part of civil disobedience Gandhi chose to break the Salt Laws as a mode of protest. In the first photograph, women are seen bearing pots containing brine on their way to the salt pans.

Photographs courtesy : Nehru Memorial Museum and Library, New Delhi

The Right to Vote

- Universal adult franchise, or the right of every adult to vote, is one of the foremost rights guaranteed by the Indian Constitution.
- It means that people cannot be governed by anyone other than those they have elected to represent them.
- It marks a radical departure from colonial rule when ordinary people had to submit to colonial officers representing the British Crown's interests.
- Even in Britain, not everyone had the right to vote; voting rights were limited to property-owning men.
- Chartism was a social movement in England advocating for parliamentary representation.
- In 1839, over 1.25 million people signed the People's Charter, which demanded
- Universal male suffrage.
- Voting by ballot.
- The right to stand for elections without property ownership.
- By 1842, the movement had collected 3.25 million signatures, a significant number for a small country.
- It was only after World War I, in 1918, that all men over 21, married women, women owning houses and women university graduates over 30 received the right to vote.
- The suffragettes, women activists advocating for all adult women's right to vote, faced bitter opposition and their movement was violently crushed.

Distinguishing Social Change and Social Movements

- Social change is continuous and ongoing. It consists of countless individual and collective actions gathered over time and space. Examples include Sanskritisation and Westernisation in India.
- On the other hand, social movements involve long and continuous social efforts and actions by people aimed at specific goals.
- The efforts of 19th-century social reformers to change society are regarded as social movements.

Quick Test 1

1. What are the main features of a social movement?
2. What did Chartism demand?
3. Why do social movements often face resistance?
4. How do social movements prepare for collective action?
5. What is a counter-movement?

5.2 Sociology and Social Movements

- Sociology has always been interested in social movements and society has witnessed many of them.
- The French Revolution was a violent culmination of several movements aimed at overthrowing the monarchy and establishing liberty, equality and fraternity.
- The Industrial Revolution in Britain was marked by social upheaval.
- Poor labourers and artisans protested against the inhuman living conditions in cities after leaving the countryside for work.
- Food riots in England were often suppressed by the government.
- Elites perceived these protests as a major threat to the established order.
- Sociologist Emile Durkheim reflected the elites' anxiety about maintaining social order in his work.
- Emile Durkheim believed that social movements could lead to disorder, which was more significant than individual actions.

- His works on division of labour, social facts, suicide and religion suggested that social structures enable integration. For him, social movements were forces leading to disorder.
- Scholars influenced by Karl Marx offered a different view of violent collective action.
- Historian E.P. Thompson argued that the 'crowd' and the 'mob' were not lawbreaking hooligans but had their own 'moral economy'–shared understandings of right and wrong that informed their actions.
- Research showed that poor urban residents had valid reasons for protesting and resorted to public protest due to a lack of other means to express their anger and resentment.

5.3 Types of Social Movements

Social movements can be classified in different ways based on their origin, causes, etc.

On the Basis of Purpose

Redemptive

- This type aims to change the personal consciousness and actions of individual members.
- For example, Narayana Guru led the Ezhava community in Kerala to change their social practices.

Reformist

- This movement strives to change existing social and political arrangements through gradual, incremental steps.
- Examples include the 1960s movement for reorganising Indian states based on language and the recent Right to Information campaign.

Revolutionary

- This type seeks to radically transform social relations, often by capturing state power.
- Examples include the Bolshevik Revolution in Russia, which deposed the Tsar to create a communist state, and the Naxalite movement in India, which aims to remove oppressive landlords and state officials.
- Most social movements contain a mix of redemptive, reformist and revolutionary elements.
- The orientation of a social movement may shift over time, starting with revolutionary objectives and later becoming reformist.
- A movement may transition from mass mobilisation and collective protest to become more institutionalised.
- Social scientists studying social movements observe that movements can evolve towards social movement organisations.
- The perception and classification of a social movement differ among various groups.
- For example, what was termed a **'mutiny'** or **'rebellion'** by British colonial rulers in 1857 was viewed as the first war of independence by Indian nationalists.
- This illustrates how people attach different meanings to social movements.

Distinguishing Old and New Social Movements

Social movements have evolved over time, from focusing on class-based issues to addressing broader concerns.

Old Social Movements

- Old social movements, like working-class movements in capitalist countries, fought for better wages, living conditions, social security, free education, and healthcare.

- Socialist movements during this period aimed to create new types of states and societies, with a strong focus on changing power structures.
- These movements were closely tied to political parties. For example, the Indian National Congress led India's independence movement, and the Communist Party led China's revolution.

New Social Movements

- In modern times, particularly in the affluent West with welfare states, class-based struggles have declined.
- New social movements focus more on improving the quality of life, such as protecting the environment, rather than redistributing power.
- These movements are not always led by political parties. Instead, they involve non-party groups like NGOs, women's organisations, environmental groups, and tribal activists.

Social Movement in India

- In India, political scientist Rajni Kothari argued that dissatisfaction with parliamentary democracy in the 1970s led to a rise in social movements.
- Many people felt that political parties were controlled by elites and did not represent the poor. As a result, they turned to social movements to put pressure on the government from outside formal political systems.

Globalisation and Social Movements

- Globalisation has significantly reshaped people's lives in various areas such as industry, agriculture, culture and media.
- Many businesses are now transnational, and international legal frameworks, like those of the World Trade Organisation (WTO), influence national policies. Global challenges, such as environmental and health risks or fears of nuclear warfare, affect everyone.
- Old and new social movements are forming alliances, such as the World Social Forum, to raise awareness about the risks and challenges posed by globalisation.

Identity and New Social Movements

- Unlike old movements, new social movements are not just about economic inequality. They often address identity, cultural issues, and aspirations.
- These movements unite people across class boundaries. For example
  - The women's movement includes both middle-class feminists and poor peasant women.
  - Regional movements for separate states bring together diverse groups with different backgrounds.

Quick Test 2

1. What are the key features of a social movement?
2. Which social evil Raja Ram Mohun Roy campaigned against?
3. What are the various forms of collective action used by social movements?
4. Who proposed the theory of collective action?
5. What are the different types of social movements based on their purpose?
6. What are the factors that contribute to the rise of social movements in India?

5.4 Ecological (Environmental) Movements

- The ecological or environmental movement is a diverse scientific, social and political effort aimed at addressing environmental issues.
- There is significant concern about the unchecked use of natural resources due to an emphasis on development.
- The dominant development model assumes all people benefit from it, but this has led to problems such as
  - Big dams displaced people from homes and livelihoods.
  - Industrial pollution negatively impacts communities.
- The ecological movement is interconnected with other social concerns.
- An example is the Chipko Movement, which occurred in the Himalayan foothills.
  - According to Ramachandra Guha in Uniquiet Woods, villagers united to protect oak and rhododendron forests from logging.
  - When government contractors aimed to cut trees, villagers, especially women, hugged the trees to prevent deforestation.
  - The trees were vital for their survival, providing firewood, fodder and other necessities.
- This movement highlighted the conflict between the livelihood needs of villagers and the government's desire to generate revenue from timber sales.
- The movement contrasted subsistence economies with profit-oriented ones.
- The Chipko Movement raised awareness about social inequality and ecological sustainability.
- Deforestation led to devastating floods and landslides in the region.
- Villagers valued forests not only for their survival but also as ecological wealth benefiting everyone.
- The movement also expressed resentment towards a distant government that seemed indifferent to villagers' concerns.

▲ *Chipko activists gather on World Environment Day at Saklana in 1986*

- Issues of economy, ecology, and political representation were significant in the Chipko Movement.
- Trees are essential for environmental conservation, just as clean water is for health.
- In response to ecological concerns, the Government of India launched initiatives like the Integrated Ganga Conservation Mission (Namami Gange) and Swachh Bharat Abhiyan to improve ecological balance and quality.

5.5 Class Based Movements

Peasant Movements

- Peasant movements, or agrarian struggles, have a long history in India, dating back to pre-colonial times.
- Movements from 1858 to 1914 were mostly localised, focusing on specific grievances
  - Notable movements included the Bengal Revolt (1859-62) against the indigo plantation system and the Deccan Riots (1857) against moneylenders.
- Many of these issues continued and under Mahatma Gandhi, they became linked to the independence movement.
  - The Bardoli Satyagraha (1928) was a non-tax campaign as part of the Non-Cooperative Movement.
  - The Champaran Satyagraha (1917-18) protested against indigo plantations.

- Between 1920 and 1940, peasant organisations began to emerge, with the Bihar Provincial Kisan Sabha (1929) being the first.
- In 1936, the All India Kisan Sabha was formed, demanding freedom from economic exploitation for peasants and workers.
- Two significant peasant movements at the time of Independence were the Tebhaga Movement (1946-47) in Bengal and the Telangana Movement (1946-51) in Hyderabad.
  - The Tebhaga Movement involved sharecroppers in Bengal and had support from the Kisan Sabha and Communist Party of India (CPI).
  - The Telangana Movement aimed to combat feudal conditions in Hyderabad and was also led by the CPI.

New Farmers Movements

- The so-called new farmer's movements began in the 1970s in Punjab and Tamil Nadu.
- These movements were regionally organised, non-party affiliated and focused on farmers rather than traditional peasants.
- The primary ideology of these movements were anti-state and anti-urban.
- Key demands included price-related issues such as
  - Price procurement
  - Remunerative prices
  - Prices for agricultural inputs
  - Taxation and non-repayment of loans
- Novel methods of agitation were employed, including blocking roads and railways and denying politicians entry to villages.
- The movements expanded their agendas to include environmental and women's issues, aligning with global trends in new social movements.

Workers' Movements

- Factory production in India began in the early 1860s, with colonial policies favouring raw material extraction from India and goods manufactured in the UK.
- Factories were set up in the port cities of Calcutta (Kolkata) and Bombay (Mumbai). Later, factories were also built in Madras (Chennai). Tea plantations in Assam started as early as 1839.
- Initially, labour was cheap and the colonial government did not regulate wages or working conditions.
- Over time, trade unions emerged and workers began to protest.
- Early worker protests were often spontaneous rather than sustained but increasingly aligned with anti-colonial sentiments.
- Economic hardships from wartime conditions led to food shortages and rising prices, resulting in numerous strikes.
  - In September and October 1917, about 30 strikes were recorded in textile mills in Bombay.
  - Jute workers in Calcutta also struck for better wages.
  - In Madras, the workers at Buchingham and Carnatic mills (Binny's) went on strike, asking for higher wages.
  - Textile workers in Ahmedabad demanded a 50% wage increase.
- The first trade union in India was established in April 1918 in Madras by B.P. Wadia, a member of the Theosophical Society.
- In the same year, Mahatma Gandhi founded the Textile Labour Association (TLA).

- The All India Trade Union Congress (AITUC) was formed in 1920 in Bombay, uniting diverse ideologies, including
  - Communists led by SA Dange and M.N. Roy.
  - Moderates led by M. Joshi and V.V. Giri.
  - Nationalists like Lala Lajpat Rai and Jawaharlal Nehru.
- The AITUC faced a split in 1947, leading to the formation of the Indian National Trade Union Congress (INTUC) by the Indian National Congress.
- The split in the AITUC paved the way for further divisions along political lines, with regional parties forming their unions.
- A major recession in 1966-67 led to decreased production and employment, heightening tensions between the state and trade unions.
- A significant railway workers' strike occurred in 1974, marking a critical point in state-union relations.

Quick Test 3

1. What is a reformist social movement?
2. Mention one example of a social change and a social movement.
3. What is the role of civil society in social movements?
4. How has globalisation influenced new social movements?

5.6 Caste Based Movements

The Dalit Movement

- The Dalit movement is characterised by its focus on addressing economic exploitation, political oppression, and the need for recognition as fellow human beings. It seeks to foster self-confidence, self-determination and aims to abolish the **stigmatisation**[1] associated with untouchability.
- The term 'Dalit', which means the poor and oppressed, refers to individuals who have historically been oppressed or marginalised by higher castes in society.
- It is important to note that there is no single unified Dalit movement; rather, various movements highlight different issues, although they share a common quest for equality, dignity and the eradication of untouchability.
- Examples of significant movements within this framework include the Satnami Movement in Chhattisgarh, the Adi Dharma Movement in Punjab, the Mahar Movement in Maharashtra, Jatava Mobilisation in Agra, and the Anti-Brahmin Movement in South India.
- The contemporary significance of the Dalit movement is evident in its growing visibility within the public sphere, accompanied by an expanding body of Dalit literature that reflects these struggles and aspirations.

Classification of Dalit Movements

- Dalit movements can be classified into three main types–reformative, redemptive and revolutionary.
- Historically, the anti-caste movement began in the 19th century under the leadership of Jotiba Phule, gained momentum in the 1920s through various non-Brahmin movements and was significantly shaped by the contributions of Dr. B.R. Ambedkar.
- The characteristics of these movements can be described as revolutionary in terms of societal change, redemptive for individuals seeking liberation from caste-based oppression and post-Ambedkar movements exhibit revolutionary practices that provide alternative lifestyles and advocate for social mobility.
- A general assessment indicates that while the Dalit movement has been reformist in nature, mobilising along caste lines, its efforts to dismantle the caste system have been limited. Nevertheless, it has achieved some societal changes, particularly for educated Dalits who have gained access to opportunities.

1 **Stigmatisation** The act of treating someone or something unfairly by publicly disapproving of them or it.

Dalit Literature

- Dalit literature plays a crucial role in opposing the Chaturvarna system and caste hierarchy. It calls for a social and cultural revolt while emphasising the importance of cultural struggles for dignity and identity.
- Additionally, it addresses the economic dimensions of these struggles, highlighting the intertwined nature of caste and class issues.

Backward Class/Castes Movements

- Backward class and caste movements emerged as political entities in both colonial and post-colonial contexts. The colonial state often distributed patronage based on caste, which led to significant political mobilisation among backward classes.
- It also encouraged similar caste groves to come together and form what is called a 'Horizontal stretch'.
- The term 'Backward Classes' gained traction in the late 19th century, particularly in various regions, including the Madras presidency, since 1872 in the Princely state of Mysore since 1918, and in Bombay presidency since 1925. As communities began to organise themselves for their rights and recognition.
- Numerous organisations were formed in the 1920s, such as the All-India Backward Classes Federation, advocating for the rights and welfare of backward castes. By 1954, as many as 88 organisations were actively working on these issues, reflecting the growing political consciousness among these groups.

5.7 Tribal Movements

Tribal movements are predominantly located in the tribal belt of central India, encompassing regions like Chota Nagpur and Santhal Parganas. These movements have a rich history that dates back over a century.

Tribal Movements in Jharkhand

- Jharkhand is a newly formed state in India, created in the year 2000 from the Southern part of Bihar. It was the culmination of over a century of resistance by tribal groups, significantly influenced by leaders like Birsa Munda, who led pivotal uprisings against colonial authorities.
- The presence of Christian missionaries played a crucial role in fostering literacy among the tribal population, enabling educated adivasis to document their history and culture. This contributed to the emergence of a shared identity as Jharkhandis.
- A middle-class adivasi leadership emerged during this period, advocating for a separate state to address the marginalisation caused by outside traders (dikus), who exploited local resources and undermined tribal livelihoods.
- Key issues that the movement has agitated against include land acquisition for development projects, survey operations, debt collections and the nationalisation of forest produce, all of which threaten the traditional rights and livelihoods of tribal communities.

Tribal Movements in the North-East

- After India gained independence, the process of forming states caused unrest in the hill districts of the North-Eastern region. Tribes, who valued their unique identity and traditional autonomy, were uneasy about being included in Assam's administrative system.

▲ *Struggles of the tribals continue*

- A major issue for tribal movements across the country is the loss of their forest lands. Ecological concerns, like the alienation from forests, are central to these movements, along with cultural identity and economic inequality.

5.8 The Women's Movement and Women Organisation

- In the early 20th century, women's organisations like the Women's India Association (WIA) in 1917, All India Women's Conference (AIWC) in 1926, and the National Council for Women in India (NCWI) in 1925 were formed.
- These groups focused on women's welfare, but their scope grew over time. For example, the AIWC started with the idea that women's welfare and politics were separate, but later emphasised that national freedom was essential for social reforms, including women's rights.
- This period may not have been a full social movement, it did bring attention to women's issues and created a space where these concerns could not be ignored.

Agrarian Struggles and Revolts

Women actively participated in various colonial struggles, including the Tebhaga movement in Bengal and the Telangana armed struggle, demonstrating their commitment to social change and national independence.

Post 1947

- Following India's independence in 1947, many women activists shifted their focus towards nation-building efforts. However, the mid-1970s marked a resurgence of the women's movement, characterised by the rise of autonomous movements that operated independently from political parties.
- The new focus areas for these movements included issues such as violence against women, which led to significant legal changes regarding land rights, employment opportunities and the dowry system.
- It is essential to recognise that women experience varying degrees of discrimination based on their class and caste and that both men and women are constrained by socially constructed gender identities.
- The concept of a gender-just society promotes equality and freedom for both genders, emphasising the importance of educating women and improving sex ratios. Initiatives like the Beti Bachao, Beti Padhao Yojana aim to foster a more equitable and gender-sensitive society.

Quick Test 4

1. Name one prominent Dalit movement in Maharashtra.
2. What role did Birsa Munda play in the Jharkhand movement?
3. What was the main aim of the anti-caste movements initiated by Jyotiba Phule and Dr. Ambedkar?
4. How has the women's movement in India contributed to legal changes regarding women's rights?
5. What did the early 20th-century women's organisations like WIA and AIWC focus on?

NCERT Folder

1. Imagine a society where there has been no social movement. Discuss. You can also describe how you imagine such a society to be.

Ans. A society where there is no social movement should have been an inclusive society where every section be it workers, women, tribals or dalits etc. will be enjoying benefits of development. The society will be based on egalitarian principles. This society will be free from exploitation of any kind and people will enjoy certain inalienable rights. This kind of society can also be referred to as one with continuous and ongoing social change but free from social movements.

This type of society can be imagined by choosing a welfare state approach in which society will be free from discrimination. The government should provide minimum basic amenities to the people. This type of approach will not allow the people to go for social movement as the interest of every group will be taken care of.

2. Write short notes on
 (i) Women's Movement
 (ii) Tribal Movements

Ans. (i) **Women's Movement** The early 20th century saw the growth of women's organisations at a national and local level. For example, the Women's India Association (WIA) (1917), All India Women's Conference (AIWC) (1926) and National Council for Women in India (NCWI) (1925). Women participated along with men in struggles and revolts originating in tribal and rural areas in the colonial period. For example, the Tebhaga movement in Bengal, the Telangana arms struggle and the Warli tribal's revolt.

In the mid 1970s, there was growth of autonomous women's movements. Apart from organisational changes, there were new issues that were focussed upon by women's movements. For example, violence against women, issues of land rights, employment for women and rights against sexual harassment and dowry.

(ii) **Tribal Movements** Most of the tribal movements have been largely located in the 'tribal belt' in middle India, such as the Santhals, Hos, Oraons, Mundas in Chota Nagpur and the Santhal Parganas. The region constitutes the main part of what has come to be called Jharkhand.

The social movement for Jharkhand had a charismatic leader as Birsa Munda, an Adivasi who led a major uprising against the British after his death. Some of the issues taken up by Jharkhand Tribal leaders include: nationalisation of forest produce which they boycotted, collection of loans, rent and cooperative dues, which were resisted, etc. One of the key issues that bind the tribal movements from different parts of the country is the alienation of tribals from forest lands.

3. Environmental movements often also contain economic and identity issues. Discuss.

Ans. Environmental movements now are questioning the modern view of development based on unchecked use of natural resources and greater exploitation of natural rerources. These movements are not just about the environmental protection, they are also about fight for the economic and identity issues.

For instance, in Chipko Movement, the local women who depended on the forests for their livelihood by getting firewood, fodder and other daily necessities, fought against government decision to cut down the forest for timber to generate greater revenue. In this case, we can see the economic dimension of this environmental movement.

Tribals in the present times are fighting government against mining, for forest rights, etc. Adivasis present in the forest are now trying to assert their identity and culture which is linked to the forest. For example, in Jharkhand movement, tribals opposed acquisition of land for large irrigation project and boycotted nationalisalion of forest produce. One of the key issues is alienation of tribals from forest lands. Thus in this case, environmental movements are associated with identity of tribals.

4. Distinguish between peasant and new farmer's movements.

Ans. **Peasant Movement** Peasant movements or agrarian struggles have taken place from pre-colonial days. The movements in the period between 1858 and 1914 tended to remain localised, disjointed and confined to particular grievances. Some well-known movement are the Bengal Revolt of 1859-62 against the indigo plantation system, the 'Deccan riots' of 1857 against moneylenders, Champaran Satyagraha (1917-18) was directed against indigo plantations, Bardoli Satyagraha (1928) and a non tax campaign.

New Farmer's Movement These movements began in the 1970s in Punjab and Tamil Nadu. These movements were regionally organised, were non-party and involved farmers rather than peasants. The basic ideology of the movement was strongly anti-state and anti-urban. The focus of demand were 'price related issues'. For example price procurement, remunerative prices, prices for agricultural inputs, etc. Newer methods of agitation were used like blocking of roads and railways, etc. It has been argued that the farmer's movements have broadened their agenda and ideology and include environment and women's issues.

Exam Pattern Questions

Objective Type Questions

Multiple Choice Questions (MCQs)

1. .... was a social movement for parliamentary representation in England. In 1839, more than 1.25 million people signed the people's charter asking for universal male suffrage, voting by ballot, and the right to stand for elections without owning property. In 1842, the movement managed to collect 3.25 million signatures, a huge number for a tiny country.

(a) Chartism (b) Fascism
(c) Communism (d) Regionalism

2. When Raja Ram Mohun Roy campaigned against sati and established the Brahmo Samaj, sati supporters formed the .... and petitioned the British not to legislate against it. Many people objected to reformers 'demands for girls' education, claiming that it would be devastating for society. Reformers who advocated for widow remarriage were socially shunned.

(a) Swatantra Sabha
(b) Dharma Sabha
(c) Arya Samaj
(d) None of the above

3. Which of the following is not a defining feature of a social movement?

(a) Sustained collective action over time.
(b) A shared ideology among participants.
(c) Spontaneous and disorganised protest.
(d) Demanding changes in state policy or practice.

4. Which of the following is/are true about the old social movements?

I. They aimed at reorganising power relations.
II. Political parties played a central role in them.
III. They focused on quality-of-life issues like the environment.
IV. They were mainly concerned with class-based exploitation.

Codes
(a) Only I and II (b) I, II, and IV
(c) II and III (d) I and IV

5. Which type of social movement aims to transform personal consciousness and actions?

(a) Reformist (b) Revolutionary
(c) Redemptive (d) Old social movement

6. New social movements differ from old social movements because

(a) they focus on class-based inequality.
(b) they aim to redistribute power in society.
(c) they address identity politics and quality of life issues.
(d) they are led by political parties.

7. Which of the following are the essential elements in creating social movements?

(a) Identity politics (b) Aspirations
(c) Cultural anxieties (d) All of these

8. Why is the study of Social Movements important in Sociology? **CBSE 2025**

(a) Social movements were about protests which were perceived by elites as a major threat to the established order of society.
(b) Social movements were not seen as forces that led to disorder.
(c) Participants of social movements do not have their own shared understanding of right and wrong.
(d) Participants did not often resort to public protest.

9. The New Farmer's Movement began in which period?

(a) 1960's (b) 1970's (c) 1980's (d) 1990's

10. Which of the following movements strive to change the existing social and political arrangements through gradual incremental steps.

(a) Reformist (b) Redemptive
(c) Revolutionary (d) Relative deprivation

11. Which of the following are features of social movement?

I. A social movement requires sustained collective action over time.

II. Social movements often arise with the aim of bringing about changes on a public issue.

III. There were no steps taken by reformers in past to bring about social change.

Codes

(a) I and II (b) II and III (c) I and III (d) I, II and III

12. Which of the following statements related to Tribal Identity is not true? CBSE 2025

(a) Assertions of tribal identity are on the rise.

(b) This can be laid at the door of the emergence of a middle class within the tribal society.

(c) Issues relating to matters of ethnic-cultural identity are becoming less important.

(d) Issues relating to control over vital economic resources like land and specially forests, are on the rise.

13. When Raja Ram Mohun Roy campaigned against Sati and formed the Brahmo Samaj, defenders of Sati formed Dharma Sabha and petitioned the British not to legislate against Sati. Which of the following movements does it highlight? CBSE 2024

(a) New Social Movement (b) Social Change

(c) Counter Movement (d) Revolutionary Movement

14. Which of the following statements is true for social movements? CBSE 2024

(a) A social movement requires sustained collective action over time.

(b) Collective action need not be marked by some degree of organisation.

(c) This organisation may not include a leadership and a structure.

(d) Those participating in a social movement may not have shared objectives and ideologies.

15. Which of the following is/are the characteristics of Ecological movements? CBSE 2024

I. Identity politics

II. Greater exploitation of natural resources

III. Cultural anxieties

IV. Social inequality

Codes

(a) Only I and II (b) Only II

(c) Only III (d) I, II, III and IV

16. Which of the following is/are true for New Movements? CBSE 2024

I. They are global in nature.

II. They are organised along class lines alone.

III. Identity politics, cultural anxieties and aspirations are essential elements for these movements.

IV. They are not within the framework of political parties.

Codes

(a) Only I (b) I and II

(c) I, III and IV (d) II and III

Assertion-Reason Questions

Direction (Q. Nos.17-20) Two statements are given in the question below as Assertion (A) and Reason (R). Read the statements and choose the appropriate option.

(a) Both A and R are true and R is the correct explanation of A

(b) Both A and R are true, but R is not the correct explanation of A

(c) A is true, but R is false

(d) A is false, but R is true

17. Assertion (A) The policy of protective discrimination adopted by Government of India, after independence, for Scheduled Castes/Tribes has become highly controversial today.

Reason (R) The reservations for SCs/STs in educational institutions and occupational fields have narrowed the gap between these castes on the one hand and higher castes on the other.

18. Assertion (A) Old social movements were class-based and focused on reorganisation of power relations.

Reason (R) They functioned primarily within the framework of political parties.

19. Assertion (A) Social movements are directed towards some broad goals.

Reason (R) It involves long and continuous social effort and action by people.

20. Assertion (A) Social movements are directed towards some broad goals.

Reason (R) It involves long and continuous social effort and action by people.

Case Based Questions

Read the passages given below and answer the questions that follow.

21. A great many students and office-workers around the world go to work only for five or six days and rest on the weekends. Yet, very few people who relax on their day off realise that this holiday is the outcome of a long struggle by workers. That the work-day should not exceed eight hours, that men and women should be paid equally for doing the same work, that workers are entitled to social security and pension — these and many other rights were gained through social movements. Social movements have shaped the world we live in and continue to do so. CBSE SQP 2024

(i) **Which of the following statements is incorrect?**
(a) The rights we enjoy just happened to exist.
(b) Social movements not only change societies; they also inspire other social movements.
(c) Movements are directed against the state and takes the form of demanding changes in state policy or practice.
(d) A social movement requires sustained collective action over time.

(ii) **Social Movements is an important subject matter of Sociology because-**
I. These protests were perceived by elites as a major threat to the established order of society.
II. 'crowd' and the 'mob' were not made up of anarchic hooligans out to destroy society. Instead, they too had a 'moral economy'.
III. Public resorted to protest because they had no other way of expressing their anger and resentment against deprivation.
IV. There was an anxiety among people to maintain the prevailing social order.
Codes
(a) I and IV (b) III and IV
(c) II, IV and III (d) I, II and III

22. There are different kinds of social movements. They can be classified as: (i) redemptive or transformatory; (ii) reformist; and (iii) revolutionary. A redemptive social movement aims to bring about a change in the personal consciousness and actions of its individual members. For instance, people in the Ezhava community in Kerala were led by Narayana Guru to change their social practices. Reformist social movements strive to change the existing social and political arrangements through gradual, incremental steps.

(i) **What is the primary aim of a redemptive social movement?**
(a) To radically transform social relations
(b) To bring gradual changes in social and political arrangements
(c) To change personal consciousness and actions of individuals
(d) To overthrow existing governments

(ii) **Which of the following is an example of a reformist social movement?**
(a) The Bolshevik Revolution in Russia
(b) The reorganisation of Indian states based on language
(c) The Naxalite movement in India
(d) The Ezhava community reforms in Kerala

23. The Chipko Movement, an example of the ecological movement, in the Himalayan foothills is a good example of such intermingled interests and ideologies. According to Ramachandra Guha in his book, Unquiet Woods, villagers rallied together to save the oak and rhododendron forests near their villages. When government forest contractors came to cut down the trees, villagers, including large number of women, stepped forward to hug the trees to prevent their being felled. At stake was the question of villagers' subsistence.

(i) **What was the main objective of the Chipko Movement?**
(a) To promote timber trade
(b) To save forests from being cut down
(c) To build roads in Himalayan regions
(d) To protest against industrial pollution

(ii) **What was the core conflict in the Chipko Movement?**
(a) Industrial development versus agricultural expansion
(b) Urbanisation versus rural development
(c) Villagers' subsistence needs versus government's revenue generation
(d) Scientific research versus traditional beliefs

Answers

1. (a) Chartism
2. (b) Dharma Sabha
3. (c) Spontaneous and disorganized protest
4. (b) I, II and IV
5. (c) Redemptive
6. (c) they address identity politics and quality-of-life issues.
7. (d) All of these
8. (a) Social movements were about protests which were perceived by elites as a major threat to the established order of society.
9. (b) 1970's
10. (a) Reformist
11. (a) I and II
12. (c) Issues relating to matters of ethnic- cultural identity are becoming less important.
13. (c) Counter Movement
14. (a) A social movement requires sustained collective action over time.
15. (b) Only II
16. (c) I, III and IV
17. (c) A is true, but R is false

18. (a) Both A and R are true and R is the correct explanation of A
19. (a) Both A and R are true and R is the correct explanation of A
20. (a) Both A and R are true and R is the correct explanation of A
21. (i) (a) The rights we enjoy just happened to exist.
(ii) (d) I, II and III
22. (i) (c) To change personal consciousness and actions of individuals
(ii) (b) The reorganisation of Indian states based on language
23. (i) (b) To save forests from being cut down
(ii) (c) Villagers' subsistence needs versus government's revenue generation

Subjective Questions

Very Short Answer Type Questions

1. What features mark or characterise a social movement?

Ans. Social movements often arise with the aim of bringing about changes on a public issue to bring in social change. A social movement requires sustained collective action over time. Such action is often directed against the state and takes the form of demanding changes in state policy or practice.

2. 'Social Movements also develop distinct modes of protests.' What are these? **CBSE 2019**

Ans. Social movements also develop distinct modes of protest. This could be in the form of

- Candle March
- Ahimsa
- Use of black cloth
- Torch light processions

3. Mention the four main features of social movements.

Ans. The four main features of social movements are as following

(i) Sustained collective mobilisation.
(ii) The organisational structure and leadership.
(iii) Shared objective and ideologies.
(iv) Change orientation i.e. aim of bringing about changes on a public issue.

4. Adivasis shared a common hatred for dikus. Why? Give two reasons. **CBSE 2025**

Ans. Adivasis shared a common hatred for dikus due to the following reasons

- **Exploitation and Land Alienation** Migrant traders and moneylenders took control of Adivasi lands and wealth, pushing the original residents into poverty.
- **Unequal Benefits from Industrial Projects** While the region was rich in minerals, the benefits of mining and industrial development mainly went to dikus, while Adivasis faced displacement and marginalisation.

5. Differentiate between a reformist and a revolutionary movement.

Or **What is meant by Reformist Social Movement? Give one example.** **CBSE 2022 Term II**

Ans. **Reformist Social Movements** These strive to change the existing social and political arrangements through gradual and incremental steps e.g. Right ot Information Campaign.

Revolutionary Social Movements These attempt to radically transform social relations, often by capturing state power e.g. Bolshevik Revolution in Russia.

6. What are Redemptive or Transformatory social movement? **CBSE 2022 Term II**

Ans. The Redemptive or Transformatory social movement aims to bring about a change in the personal consciousness and actions of its individual members. For example, people in the Ezhava communities in Kerala were led by Narayana Guru to change their social practices.

7. Define the concept of revolutionary movement with the help of an example. **CBSE 2024**

Ans. The revolutionary movement attempts to radically transform social relations, often by capturing state power. For example, the Bolshevik Revolution in Russia that deposed the Tsar to create a communist state and the Naxalite movement in India that seeks to remove oppressive landlords and state officials can be described as revolutionary movements.

8. In the old social movements, the role of political parties was central. Political scientist Rajni Kothari attributes the surge of social movements in India in the 1970s to people's growing dissatisfaction with parliamentary democracy. As a result of this people joined social movements or non-political party formations. What were the reasons for this growing dissatisfaction? **CBSE SQP 2024**

Ans. Rajni Kothari links the rise of India's 1970s social movements to dissatisfaction with parliamentary democracy and elite state control. Excluded groups formed social movements addressing issues like inequality, identity, and globalisation's impact. These movements transcend class lines, uniting diverse participants.

9. Differentiate between social change and social movement. CBSE 2024

Ans. Social change is a continuous and ongoing process. It indicates sum total of countless individual and collective actions gathered across time and space.

On the other hand, social movements are directed towards some specific goals. It involves long and continuous social effort and action by people.

10. With what objectives did new farmers movements begin in the 1970's? CBSE 2019

Or **Write the features of New Farmers Movement.**

Ans. The New Farmers Movement began in the 1970, in Punjab and Tamil Nadu. These movements were regionally organised, were non-party and involved farmers rather than peasants.

Objectives of New Farmers Movement were

- The basic ideology of the movement was strongly anti-state and anti-urban.
- The focus of demands were price and related issues. For example, price procurement, taxation, non-repayment of loans.
- Novel methods of agitation were used such as blocking of roads and railways refusing politicians and bureaucrats entry to villages.

11. The varied social reform movements did have common themes. Yet there were also significant differences. State any two differences. CBSE 2022 Term II

Ans. The varied social reform movements did have common themes yet there were also significant differences. This can be proved with the help of two points of differences as following

(i) For some, the concerns were confined to the problems that the upper caste, middle class women and men faced. For others, the injustices suffered by the discriminated castes were the central questions.

(ii) There was a movement for Muslim women. One group had argued against the practice of polygamy whereas other had fought for the abolishment of Triple Talaq.

12. At the time of Independence, we had the two classical cases of peasant movements. Write the names of the two peasant movements. CBSE 2023

Ans. At the time of Independence, there were two most classical cases of peasants movement, namely Tebhaga Movement (1946-47) and the Telangana Movement (1946-51). The first was the struggle of sharecroppers in Bengal. It had the support of Kisan Sabha and the Communist Party of India (CPI).
The second was directed against the feudal conditions in the princely state of Hyderabad and was led by the CPI.

Short Answer Type Questions

1. A social movement requires sustained collective action over time and is often directed against the state to demand changes in state policy or practice. In terms of defining features, explain the traits that characterise a social movement.

Ans. A social movement is characterised by sustained collective action over time, often aimed at changing state policies or practices.
It involves organised efforts with leadership, a clear structure, and shared objectives and ideologies. Members of a social movement collaborate to achieve a common goal, and the movement typically has a general approach to bring about or prevent change. These defining features may evolve as the movement progresses. Importantly, social movements often face resistance but can bring about long-term societal changes.

2. Name and define the three types of social movements.

Or **Discuss the Classification of Social movements.** CBSE 2025

Ans. The three types of social movement are as follows

(i) **Redemptive Social Movement** This movement aims to bring about a change in the personal consciousness and actions of its individual members. For instance, people in the Ezhava community in Kerala by Narayan Guru to change their social practice.

(ii) **Reformist Social Movements** The movement strive to change the existing social and political arrangements through gradual incremental steps. The 1960s movement for the reorganisation of Indian states on the basis of language and the recent Right to Information campaign are examples of reformist movements.

(iii) **Revolutionary Social Movements** This movement attempt to radically transform social relations, often by capturing state power. The Bolshevik Revolution in Russia that deposed the Tsar to capture a communist state and Naxalite movement in India that seeks to remove oppressive landlords and state officials are examples of revolutionary social movements.

3. Explain the 'ecological movement' with special reference to 'Chipko Movement'.

Ans. The ecological or environmental movement is a diverse scientific, social and a political movement for addressing environmental issues.

The Chipko Movement is an example of the ecological movement in the Himalayan foothills.

This conflict placed the livelihood needs of poor villagers against the government's desire to generate revenues from selling timber. The economy of subsistence was pitted against the economy of profit. The people used the method of hugging the trees to prevent them from felling down by the contractors. The Chipko Movement also raised the issue of ecological sustainability. Cutting down natural forests was a form of environmental destruction that had resulted in devastating floods and landslides in the region.

4. Evaluate worker's movement as class-based movement.

Ans. The first trade union was established in April 1918 in Madras by BP Wadia, Social worker and member of Theosophical Society. The All India Trade Union Congress (AITUC) was an organisation involving diverse ideologies.

The formation of the AITUC made the colonial government more cautious in dealing with labour.

It attempted to grant workers some concessions in order to contain unrest.

In 1922, the government passed the Fourth Factories Act, which reduced the working day to 10 hours. By the mid 1920s, the AITUC had nearly 200 unions affiliated to it and its membership stood at around 250,000.

After the British rule, the communist gained considerable control over the AITUC. The Indian National Congress chose to form another union called the Indian National Trade Union Congess in May 1947. In 1966-67, due to major recession, it led to a decrease in production and consequently employment.

In 1974, there was a major railway workers' strike.

The confrontation between the state and trade unions became acute. During the emergence in 1975-77, the government curbed all trade union activities. The workers movement was very much part of the wider struggle for civil liberties.

5. The women's question arose in modern India as part of the nineteenth century middle class social reform movements. The nature of these movements varied from region to region.

Explain any two social reform movements that addressed the women's question.

Ans. The Ezhava movement in Kerala, led by Narayana Guru, addressed the women's question by encouraging reforms in social practices, promoting equality, and uplifting marginalised groups, including women. Similarly, the women's movement that arose during the 19th-century middle class social reform era worked towards improving women's rights, focusing on education, social status and equality. These movements varied across regions but collectively aimed to challenge societal inequalities and empower women, uniting participants from diverse backgrounds to address critical issues affecting their lives.

6. Why are the new Farmers' Movement termed as new social movement?

Ans. In new Farmers' Movement certain issues which had dominated colonial times changed after independence. The so called new Farmer's Movement began in the 1970 in Punjab and Tamil Nadu. These movements were regionally organised.

These were non-party movements and involved farmers (farmers are said to be market-involved. They are both commodity producers and purchasers), rather than peasants. The basic ideology of the movement was strongly anti-state and anti-urban.

The focus of demand were price and related issues e.g. price procurement, remunerative prices, prices for agricultural inputs taxation, non-payment of loans. Novel methods of agitation were used i.e., blocking of roads and railways, refusing politicians and bureaucrats entry into village.

It has been argued that the farmers' movements have broadened their agenda and ideology and include environment and women's issues. So they can be seen as a part of worldwide new social movements.

7. Analyse the role of economic and ecological issues in shaping tribal movements in India.

Ans. Economic and ecological issues play a central role in shaping tribal movements in India. Tribals often face economic exploitation, such as land alienation due to industrial projects, and ecological marginalisation caused by the loss of forest resources critical to their livelihood. Movements like Jharkhand's demand for statehood highlight the struggle against land acquisition, unfair settlement practices, and forest nationalisation. Similarly, ecological concerns unite tribes across regions as they resist the loss of their traditional lands and resources, forming the foundation of their collective identity and resistance efforts.

8. Examine the significance of addressing violence against women as part of the women's movement in India.

Ans. Addressing violence against women has been central to the women's movement in India, as it highlights deep-rooted gender inequality and societal injustice. Campaigns against dowry, domestic violence, sexual harassment, and honour crimes have brought significant legal and social changes. These efforts led to reforms such as the Protection of Women from Domestic Violence Act (2005) and stronger laws against sexual harassment. Beyond legal measures, the movement has raised awareness, challenged patriarchal norms, and empowered women to seek justice, making it a pivotal step toward gender equality and a safer society.

Long Answers Type Questions

1. Discuss main features of social movements.

Ans. Following are the main features of social movements are

- **Sustained Collective Action** Social movements require ongoing efforts over time, often aimed at changing state policies or practices.
- **Organisation** A social movement needs structure and leadership to guide members, make decisions and carry out actions.
- **Shared Objectives and Ideologies** Participants in social movements share common goals and beliefs.
- **Orientation for Change** Social movements focus on bringing about change in society, often related to public issues like rights, education or environmental concerns.
- **Opposition and Resistance** Social movements face opposition from those with vested interests in maintaining the status quo. Despite resistance, change can occur over time.
- **Modes of Protest** Social movements use various methods such as protests, lobbying, street theatre, songs and peaceful resistance, as seen in the freedom movement led by Gandhi.
- **Counter Movements** Social movements may spark counter movements that defend traditional practices or oppose reforms.
- **Impact of Social Conflict** Social movements emerge from the recognition of oppression, but not all conflicts lead to collective action. Small acts of resistance, like those studied by James Scott, can also play a role.

2. Explain with suitable examples the class based movements in India.

Ans. Class-based movements in India focus on issues related to economic exploitation, social injustice, and rights of specific classes. Some key examples are

(i) Peasant Movements

- **Bengal Revolt** (1859-62) Peasants protested against the indigo plantation system.
- **Deccan Riots** (1857) Peasants protested against moneylenders.
- **Champaran Satyagraha** (1917-18) Mahatma Gandhi led peasants in Bihar against indigo plantations.
- **Bardoli Satyagraha** (1928) Peasants refused to pay land revenue in Surat under Gandhi's leadership.
- **Tebhaga Movement** (1946-47) Sharecroppers in Bengal demanded a larger share of the harvest.
- **Telangana Movement** (1946-51) Led by CPI, peasants fought against feudalism in Hyderabad.

(ii) New Farmers's Movements (1970s)

- These movements emerged in Punjab and Tamil Nadu, focusing on price issues, such as fair prices for agricultural produce and loan repayments. They were anti-state and anti-urban in ideology.
- They also addressed broader issues like environmental concerns and women's rights.

(iii) Worker's Movements

- **Early Worker's Protests** Factory workers in cities like Calcutta and Bombay protested poor wages and working conditions.
- **Trade Union Formation** The first trade union was formed in 1918, followed by the formation of the All India Trade Union Congress (AITUC) in 1920. Later, the Indian National Trade Union Congress (INTUC) was established.
- **Railway Worker's Strike** (1974) A major strike against poor conditions and pay.

3. Read the passage and answer the following question.

While protest is the most visible form of collective action, a social movement also acts in other, equally important ways. Social movement activists hold meetings to mobilise people around the issues that concern them. Such activities help shared understanding, and also prepare for a feeling of agreement or consensus about how to pursue the collective agenda. Social movements also chart out campaigns that include lobbying with the government, media and other important makers of public opinion.

CBSE 2024 C

(a) Name any two social movements and the issues that they fought for.

(b) Social movements also develop distinct modes of protest. Give examples.

Ans. (a) Two social movements and their issues are as follows

(i) **Chipko Movement** (1970s)

The Chipko Movement in India was initiated to protect forests and prevent deforestation in the

Himalayan region. Local villagers, especially women, hugged trees to stop loggers from cutting them, emphasising environmental conservation and the rights of forest-dependent communities.

(ii) **Dalit Movement**

The Dalit Movement fights against caste-based discrimination and for social justice, equality, and dignity for Dalits. It focuses on issues like access to education, land rights, and opposing untouchability practices.

(b) Social movements develop distinct modes of protest. Examples include Gandhi's novel methods like ahimsa, satyagraha, and the use of the charkha in the freedom movement.

During the colonial period, activists defied the salt ban and used picketing as innovative protest forms. Other forms include candlelight processions, black cloth protests, street theatre, songs, and poetry, which mobilise people and raise awareness.

4. Read the passage and answer the following question.

The fusion of foreign power and capital was the focus of social protest during India's nationalist struggle. Mahatma Gandhi wore khadi, hand-spun, hand-woven cloth, to support Indian cotton-growers, spinners and weavers whose livelihoods had been destroyed by the government policy of favouring mill-made cloth.

The legendary Dandi March to make salt was a protest against British taxation policies that placed a huge burden on consumers of basic commodities in order to benefit the empire. Gandhi took items of everyday mass consumption like cloth and salt and transformed them into symbols of resistance.

(a) What was the focus of social protest during India's nationalist struggle?

(b) What message did Gandhi want to spread through the legendary Dandi March? Competency Based Que.

Ans. (a) During India's nationalist struggle the focus of social protest was the fusion of foreign power and capital. The British rule had given too much importance to these two factors which India had suffered for a long time.

(b) The legendary Dandi March was a protest against British taxation policies. The British had placed a huge burden on consumers of basic commodities in order to benefit the empire. Gandhiji wanted that people should realise the value of freedom.

5. Using an example, explain an ecological movement.

Ans. The ecological or environmental movement is a diverse scientific, social and a political movement for addressing environmental issues.

- The Chipko Movement is an example of the ecological movement, started in the Himalayan foothills.
- When government forest contractors came to cut down the trees, villagers, including large number of women, stepped forward to hug the trees to prevent their being felled.
- All of them relied on the forest to get firewood, fodder and other daily necessities. This conflict placed the livelihood needs of poor villagers against the government's desire to generate revenues from selling timber.
- The economy of subsistence was pitted against the economy of profit. Along with this issue of social inequality (villagers versus a government that represented commercial, capitalist interests), the Chipko Movement also raised the issue of ecological sustainability.
- In addition, the Chipko Movement also expressed the resentment of hill villagers against a distant government headquartered in the plains that seemed indifferent and hostile to their concerns.
- So, concerns about economy, ecology and political representation underlay the Chipko Movement.

6. Read the passage and answer the following question.

"...The contractor's men who were travelling to Reni from Joshimath stopped the bus shortly before Reni. Skirting the village, they made for the forest. A small girl who spied the workers with their implements rushed to Gaura Devi, the head of the village Mahila Mandal (Women's Club). Gaura Devi quickly mobilised the other housewives and went to the forest. Pleading with the labourers not to start felling operations, the women initially met with abuse and threats. When the women refused to budge, the men were eventually forced to retire."

How are environmental movements also about economics and identity issues? Elaborate. CBSE SQP 2023

Ans. Environmental movements often also contain economic and identity issues because these are questioning the modern view of development based on unchecked use of natural resources and greater exploitation of natural resources. These movements are not just about the environmental protection, they are also about fight for the economic and identity issues. There are following examples that interlink both the economic and identity issues with the environmental movements as

In Jharkhand movement, tribals opposed acquisition of land for large irrigation project and boycotted nationalisation of forest produce. One of the key issues is alienation of tribals from forest lands.

Thus in this case, environmental movements are associated with identity of tribals.

7. Elucidate the history of peasant movements.

Ans. The term 'peasant movement' refers to all kinds of collective attempts of different strata of the peasantry either to change the system which they felt was exploitative, or to seek redress for particular grievances without necessarily aiming at overthrowing the system.

Peasant Movements between 1920 and 1940

The first organisation to be founded was the Bihar Provincial Kisan Sabha (1929) and in 1936 the All India Kisan Sabha. The peasants organised by the Sabhas demanded freedom from economic exploitation for peasants, workers and all other exploited classes.

Peasant Movements at the Time of Independence

The Tebhaga Movement (1946-47) Just before Independence, it was the Tebhaga struggle of 1946-47 in Bengal and North Bihar which was the most effective and widespread of all peasant movements. It was a struggle of share croppers (*bargadars*) to retain two-third share of the produce for themselves instead of the customary half.

The movement was the outcome of the politicisation of the peasantry which was made possible because of the efforts and support of the Communist Party of India (CPI) and the Kisan Sabha.

The Telangana Movement (1946-51) It was directed against the feudal conditions in the Princely State of Hyderabad and was led by the CPI. Certain issues which had dominated colonial times changed after independence. For land reforms, zamindari abolition, declining importance of land revenue and public credit system began to alter rural areas.

Peasant Movements After Independence

The New Farmer's Movements The so called 'New Farmers' Movements began in the 1970s in Punjab and Tamil Nadu. These movements were regionally organised, they were non-party and involved farmers rather than peasants.

The basic ideology of the movement was strongly anti-state and anti-urban. The focus of demand were on 'price related issues', e.g. price procurement, remunerative prices, prices for agricultural inputs, taxation and non-repayment of loans.

8. Read the passage and answer the following question.

There has not been a single, unified Dalit movement in the country, now or in the past. Different movements have highlighted different issues related to the Dalits, around different ideologies. Notwithstanding differences in the nature of Dalit movements and the meaning of identity, there has been a common quest for equality, self-dignity and eradication of untouchability. (Shah 2001 : 194).

(a) Write any two examples of Dalit Movement.

(b) Discuss the various issues highlighted by the Dalit Movements. CBSE 2024

Ans. (a) Examples are Satnami Movement of the Chamars in the Chhattisgarh plains in Eastern MP, or Adi Dharma Movement in Punjab, the Mahar Movement in Maharashtra, or the socio-political mobilisation among the Jatavas of Agra and the Anti Brahman Movement in South India.

(b) Different movements have highlighted different issues related to Dalits, around different ideologies.

- This is a struggle for recognition as fellow human beings. It is a struggle for self-confidence and a space for self-determination.
- It is a struggle for abolishment of stigmatisation, that untouchability implied. It has been called a struggle to be touched.
- However, all of them assert a Dalit identity though the meaning may not be identical or precise for everyone.
- There has been a common quest for equality, self-dignity and eradication of untouchability.

9. What were the goals and outcomes of the Anti-caste Movements initiated by Jotiba Phule and Dr. Ambedkar?

Ans. The Anti-caste Movements initiated by Jotiba Phule and Dr. BR Ambedkar aimed at dismantling caste-based discrimination and asserting the dignity and equality of dalits and marginalised communities. These movements combined elements of reformative, redemptive, and revolutionary struggles. Jotiba Phule's efforts in the 19th century laid the foundation for anti-caste ideologies, focusing on education and social awareness. Dr. Ambedkar expanded these efforts in the 20th century by advocating for the abolition of untouchability and the eradication of caste-based inequalities.

Key goals included achieving social equality, self-dignity, and economic mobility for Dalits. Dr. Ambedkar emphasised structural change, introducing measures like the abolition of caste through political and legal reforms, including drafting provisions for equality in the Indian Constitution. These movements sought not only to reform oppressive social norms but also to provide alternatives like religious conversion to Buddhism, as seen in the Neo-Buddhist Movement.

Outcomes of these movements were significant yet partial. They brought educational and social mobility for some Dalits, especially the educated sections, but failed to completely eliminate caste-based discrimination. While these movements achieved legal protections and societal reforms, the deep-rooted caste system and extreme poverty among Dalits continued to persist.

SELF ASSESSMENT TEST

Objective Type Questions

1. In which year, the Bihar Provinced Kisan Sabha was founded?

(a) 1940 (b) 1929 (c) 1936 (d) 1970

2. The term 'social movements' is best defined as

I. organised efforts by a group of people to promote or resist change in society.
II. spontaneous protests that lack a defined purpose or goal.
III. collective actions that aim to address social issues and promote social change.
IV. individual actions taken in isolation from others.

Codes

(a) I and III (b) II and IV (c) I, II and III (d) I, III and IV

3. The primary focus of the new farmer's movements in India is

I. To promote traditional farming practices without modernisation.
II. To address price-related issues such as procurement and agricultural input costs.
III. To demand greater political representation in state policies.
IV. To advocate for the establishment of large-scale corporate farming.

Codes

(a) I and IV (b) II and III (c) I and III (d) II and IV

4. **Assertion** (A) The Chipko Movement highlights the conflict between local livelihoods and government interests.

Reason (R) The movement was initiated by villagers to protect their forests from deforestation due to commercial logging.

(a) Both A and R are true and R is the correct explanation of A
(b) Both A and R are true, but R is not the correct explanation of A
(c) A is true, but R is false
(d) A is false, but R is true

Case Based Questions

1. In the old social movements, the role of political parties was central. Political scientist Rajni Kothari attributes the surge of social movements in India in the 1970s to people's growing dissatisfaction with parliamentary democracy. Kothari argues that the institutions of the state have been captured by elites. Due to this, electoral representation by political parties is no longer an effective way for the poor to get their voices heard.

(i) What was the main reason for the surge of social movements in India in the 1970s?

(a) The rise of new political parties
(b) People's dissatisfaction with parliamentary democracy
(c) The growth of industrialisation
(d) The influence of foreign governments

(ii) According to Rajni Kothari, why did the poor join social movements or non-party political formations?
   (a) To gain better wages
   (b) Because political parties were ineffective in representing their interests
   (c) To support the elites
   (d) To get access to government jobs

Very Short Answer Type Questions

1. What are some of the distinct modes of protest used by social movements?
2. The Dalit movement in India has been driven by a quest for equality, dignity and the eradication of untouchability. Discuss two key aspects of the Dalit movement that highlight its significance in modern India.
3. Social movements often aim to address issues related to the exploitation of natural resources and the rights of marginalised groups. One such movement focused on the rights of tribal populations to use forest resources. Discuss the significance of the tribal rights movement.

Short Answer Type Questions

1. Discuss what is an ecological movement by giving suitable examples.
2. In the Dalit movements, the struggle for recognition as fellow human beings, equality, and self-dignity has been central. These movements were not solely driven by economic exploitation or political oppression but also by a desire for identity and the abolition of untouchability. The Dalit movement has various movements that focus on different aspects of Dalit identity and social change, from cultural to economic dimensions.
   What do you think is the significance of identity in the Dalit movements, and how do these movements differ in their approaches to achieving social equality?

Long Answer Type Questions

1. Scholars influenced by the ideas of Karl Marx offered a different view of violent collective action. Historians like E.P. Thompson showed that the 'crowd' and the 'mob' were not made up of anarchic hooligans out to destroy society. Instead, they too had a 'moral economy'. In other words, they have their own shared understanding of right and wrong that informed their actions. Their research showed that poor people in urban areas had good reasons for protesting. They often resorted to public protest because they had no other way of expressing their anger and resentment against deprivation.
   (a) How did the French Revolution serve as an example of social movements aimed at overthrowing the monarchy?
   (b) What does the term 'moral economy' mean in the context of protests by poor people in urban areas?
2. Examine worker's movement as class-based movement.

Project Work

Meaning of Project

The word project comes from the Latin word 'Projectum' which means "before an action". At school level, a project is a research assignment given to a student which generally requires a larger amount of effort and more independent work that is involved in a normal assignment. It requires students to undertake their own fact finding endeavours, either from library, or from the internet or by means of primary data collection. A project report should

- be handwritten
- have diagrammatic presentation
- have topics with suitable headings
- be concise and clear
- have a length of 15 to 20 pages
- end up with conclusion

Utilities of Making a Project

Following points state the uses/utility of project work

(*i*) To provide information about the development and growth of institutions, business products, and government activities.

(*ii*) To provide information to the consumers about the price of commodities, quality and uses, etc of a product as per their interest.

(*iii*) It is helpful in estimating the preference of consumers for petrol car or diesel car, telephone or mobile phone, etc.

(*iv*) Project report is helpful for the shareholders, who may be interested in knowing the earning of an enterprise and possibility of getting dividend.

(*v*) To help in the policy formulation about the economic and social development of any country.

Thus, we can say that project work may help marketers, shareholders, economists, consumers and government in effective and efficient decision-making.

Elements of Project Report

A good project report should contain the following elements

Title Page

This should include the project title, name of the company on which you are conducting your research and name of the student. You can also list the name of your school, class and subject teacher.

Acknowledgement

It is usual to thank those individuals, who have provided particularly useful assistance, technical or otherwise, during your project.

Content Page

This should list the main sections and sub-sections of your report. Choose self-explanatory titles with their respective pages and use double spacing for clarity.

Introduction

This is one of the most important component of the project report. It should begin with a clear statement of what the project is about, so that the nature and scope of the project can be understood by a reader. It should summarise everything which you set out to achieve and provide a clear summary of the project's background, relevance and main contributions. The introduction should set the context for the project and should provide the reader with a summary of the key things to look out for in, the remainder of the report.

Background

The background section of the report should set the project into action, it specifies the problem of the company, what remedial actions were taken by the company and what are its effects.

Body of Report

The central part of the report usually consists of three or four sections detailing the technical work undertaken during the project. The structure of these sections is highly project dependent.They can reflect the chronological development of the project. It includes the detailed description regarding the matter of the project.

Evaluation

This might involve quantitative and qualitative evaluation such as expressibility, functionality, ease-of-use, etc of a product. At some point, you should also evaluate the strengths and weaknesses of what you have done. It includes certain questionnaires, sampling test which help in evaluating the result on the basis of truths and facts.

Conclusion

The conclusion should list the things, which have been learnt as a result of the work you have done. It shows the ultimate response of the project undertaken by a student. It should be expressive and impressive so that a reader would clearly evaluate the result and rated you on the basis of your presentation.

Bibliography

In this section, you should mention the details of all the secondary sources, *i.e.*, magazines, newspapers, reports, internet links, etc. used for developing the project.

Sample Project

ROLE OF COMMUNICATION MEDIA IN SOCIAL LIFE

Name : ....

Class : ....

Roll No. : ....

Subject : ....

School : ....

Submitted by .... *Submitted to* ....

Acknowledgement

I would like to extend my sincere and heartfelt obligation towards all those who have helped me in making this project. Without their active guidance, help, cooperation and encouragement, I would not have been able to present the project on time.

I am extremely thankful and pay my gratitude to my teacher Mr/Ms .... for his/her valuable guidance and support for completion of this project.

I extend my gratitude to my Principal Mr/Ms .... for the moral support extended during the tenure of the project.

I also acknowledge with a deep sense of reverence, my gratitude towards my parents, other faculty members of the school and friends for their valuable suggestions given to me in completing this project.

Date...........   ....

Name of Student

Certificate

Contents

Role of Communication Media in Social Life

Introduction

Communication media could include the mass media, like newspapers, television, films, internet and so on – i.e., media which convey information and are seen/accessed by large number of people. It could also include the media that people use for communicating with each other, such as the telephone, letters, mobile phones, e-mail and internet.

Statement of Purpose

This project aims to study the changing roll of mass media in social life, including print, audio and TV. It also explores the preferences of different groups (age, class, gender) for books, films, etc. and their views on new communication media (mobile phones, internet) and its impact.

The objective of this project work is to find out the changing place of mass media in social life and the shifts within major formats like print, radio, television, and so on. Learn about likes and dislikes of particular groups (classes, age groups, genders) regarding films, books etc. Perception of the new communication media (like mobile phones, or internet) and their impact.

Social Significance of Communication Media

Communication media is a tremendous source of information for individuals as well as society. They can help change people's attitude and habits. For instance, government has been extensively using communication media like newspapers, radio, television etc., to spread the schemes like "Swachh Bharat", "Beti Bachao, Beti Padhao" to bring changes in people's behaviour and attitudes in particular and society in general.

The communication media occupy a high proportion of our leisure time: people spend, on an average, 25 hours per week watching television, and they also find time for radio, cinema, magazines and newspapers. For children, watching television takes up a similar amount of time to that spent at school or with family and friends. In contemporary times, internet, and other social media applications are also playing an important role in shaping the behaviours of people in the society right from kids to elders.

TVs, Newspapers, Internet, Social Media nowadays have become prominent in modern people's lives. The speed of media has resulted in bringing people across the world closer. Mass media are used by the consumer industry to inform people about their products and services through advertising. Television, radio, internet are the best means of entertainment and extremely informative. Social media keeps us up to date with the happenings around the world.

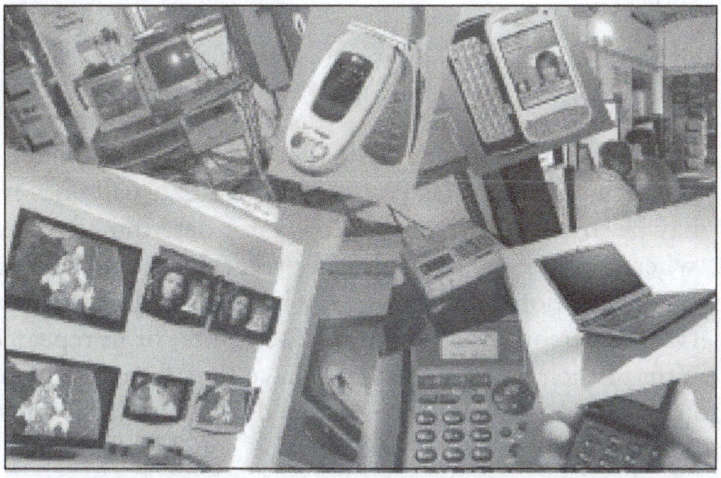

Research Method used in Project : Survey

The survey is probably the best known sociological method. It is now a part of modern public life. Today it is used all over the world in all sorts of contexts going well beyond the concerns of sociology alone. In India, too, we have seen the increasing use of surveys for various non-academic purposes, including the prediction of election results, the devising of marketing strategies for selling products, and for eliciting popular opinions on a wide variety of subjects.

Different Forms of Survey

Interviews

An interview is different from a survey in that it is always conducted in person and usually involves much fewer persons (as few as 5, 20, or 40, usually not much more than that). Interviews may be structured, that is, follow a pre-determined pattern of questions or unstructured, where only a set of topics is pre-decided, and the actual questions emerge as part of a conversation. Interviews may be more or less intensive, in the sense that one may interview a person for a long time (2-3 hours) or in repeated visits to get a really detailed version of their story. Interviews have the advantage of being flexible in that promising topics may be pursued in greater detail, questions may be refined or modified along the way, and clarifications may be sought. The disadvantage of the interview method is that it cannot cover a large number of people and is limited to presenting the views of a select group of individuals.

Observation

Observation is a method where the researcher must systematically watch and record what is happening in whatever context or situation that has been chosen for the research. This sounds simple but may not always be easy to do in practice. Careful attention has to be paid to what is happening without pre-judging what is relevant to the study and what is not. Sometimes, what is not happening is as important or interesting as what does actually happen. For example, if your research question is about how different classes of people use specific open spaces, then it is significant that a given class or group of people (say poor people, or middle class people for example) never enter the space, or are never seen in it.

Detailed Procedure for Implementation of Survey Method

As the word itself suggests, a survey is an attempt to provide an overview. It is a comprehensive or wide-ranging perspective on some subject based on information obtained from a carefully chosen representative set of people. Such people are usually referred to as 'respondents' — they respond to the questions asked to them by the researchers. Survey research is usually done by large teams consisting of those who plan and design the study (the researchers) and their associates and assistants (the latter are called 'investigators' or 'research assistants'). The survey questions may be asked and answered in various forms. Often, they are asked orally during personal visits by the investigator, and sometimes through telephone conversations. Responses may also be sought in writing, to 'questionnaires' brought by investigators or sent through the post. Finally, with the increasing presence of computers and telecommunication technology, these days it is also possible for surveys to be conducted electronically. In this format, the respondent receives and responds to questions by e-mail, the internet, or similar electronic medium.

The survey's main advantage as a social scientific method is that it allows us to generalise results for a large population while actually studying only a small portion of this population. Thus a survey makes it possible to study large populations with a manageable investment of time, effort and money. That is why it is such a popular method in the social sciences and other fields. The sample survey is able to provide a generalisable result despite being selective by taking advantage of the discoveries of a branch of statistics called sampling theory. The key element enabling this 'shortcut' is the representativeness of the sample.

The first principle is that all the relevant sub-groups in the population should be recognised and represented in the sample. Most large populations are not homogenous — they belong to distinct sub-categories. This is called stratification. The second principle of sample selection is that the actual unit — i.e., person or village or household — should be based purely on chance. This is referred to as randomisation, which itself depends on the concept of probability.

Research Questions (Questionnaire)

Name : XYZ

Age : ABC

Gender : MN

Profession : CBN

1. What kind of communication media do you use?
2. How much time do you spend on communication media?
3. Which is most influential communication media for you?
   (i) TV ☐
   (ii) Radio ☐
   (iii) Newspaper ☐
   (iv) Internet ☐
   (v) Movies ☐
4. What kind of news do you read in newspaper?
   (i) Political ☐
   (ii) Sports ☐
   (iii) Entertainment ☐
   (iv) Business ☐
   (v) Lifestyle ☐
5. What genre movies do you like to watch?
   (i) Cartoon/Animation ☐
   (ii) Action ☐
   (iii) Horror/Thriller ☐
   (iv) Drama ☐
   (v) Romcom/Comedy ☐
   (vi) Devotional ☐
6. Which TV channels do you prefer to watch?
   (i) NEWS ☐
   (ii) Entertainment ☐
   (iii) Educational ☐
   (iv) Sports ☐
   (v) Devotional ☐
   (vi) Cartoon ☐

7. How much time do you spend on watching TV?
8. What do you use internet for?
   (i) News and current issues ☐
   (ii) Science and technology ☐
   (iii) Social networking, e-mail ☐
   (iv) Play online games, watch videos etc., ☐
9. Do you use a smartphone?
10. How much time do you spend on smartphone?
11. Do you use social media?
12. What are the different social media apps you use?
   (i) Facebook ☐
   (ii) Instagram ☐
   (iii) Snapchat ☐
   (iv) Whatsapp ☐
   (v) Linkedin ☐
13. Do you get influenced by videos and messages present on the internet?
14. Are you afraid about children spending lot of time on communication media, especially social media?
15. What do you think, the age at which children should get mobiles in general and smartphones in particular?

Data Aanalysis

Sample Answers of different age groups

Age → Q. No. ↓	Children (6-12)	Teens (13-19)	Youth (20-30)	Adults (30-60)	Senior Citizens (60+)
1.	TV, Mobile, Movies	TV, Mobile, Newspaper, Movies	TV, Mobile, Newspaper, Movies	TV, Mobile, Newspaper	TV, Mobile, Newspaper
2.	2 - 4 hours	8 - 10 hours	6 -8 hours	4-6 hours	8-10 hours
3.	TV	Internet	Internet	TV	TV
4.	Do not read newspaper	Sports and Entertainment	Political, Sports, Entertainment	Political, Business, Lifestyle	Political, Business, Entertainment
5.	Animation	Action, Horror/Thriller, Animation	Romcom, Comedy, Action, Horror/Thriller	Romcom, Comedy, Drama	Devotional, Drama

Project Work

6.	Cartoon	Sports and Entertainment	NEWS, Sports, Educational(like Nat Geo), Entertainment	NEWS, Entertainment	NEWS and Devotional
7.	2 hours	4 hours	2 hours	2 hours	6 hours
8.	Play games	Social networking	News, Social networking, Science and technology	E-mail, Social networking	Do not use internet
9.	YES	YES	YES	YES	NO
10.	1 hour	4 hours	3 hours	2 hours	Do not use smartphone
11.	NO	YES	YES	YES	NO
12.	Do not use Social Media	Facebook, Instagram, Snapchat, Whatsapp	Facebook, Instagram, Snapchat, Whatsapp, Linkedin	Facebook, Whatsapp, Linkedin	Do not use social media
13.	Do not watch videos on internet	YES	YES	YES	Do not watch videos on internet
14.	-NA-	-NA-	YES	YES	YES
15.	10	13	16	18	21

Advantages of the Survey Method

- Survey research is relatively inexpensive.
- Survey research is useful in describing the characteristics of a large population, population structure based on age, and its emerging trends and patterns.
- Survey research can be administered from remote locations using mail, e-mail or telephone. Consequently, very large samples are feasible, making the results statistically significant even when analysing multiple variables.
- In survey research one can ask many questions about a given topic, which gives considerable flexibility to the analysis.
- We can choose different ways of administering a survey. From face- to-face interviews to telephones and emails one can use any mode of collecting data depending on one's requirements and limitations.

Limitations of Survey Method

- A preoccupation with standardisation results in designing questions in very general terms to make them minimally appropriate for all respondents. This could lead to simplification and one may end up missing what may be most appropriate to many respondents.
- Survey research is inflexible in the sense that it requires a precise study design. Everything must be worked out in advance, the tools to be used and the method of administering the tools. In order to make a survey methodologically sound, it should remain unchanged throughout the period of data collection.
- In order to make a survey viable and meaningful the researcher has to make sure that a large proportion of selected respondents agree to respond. This, however, may not always be an easy task to achieve. In such situations carrying out a survey becomes difficult.
- Surveys also demand a great deal of attention and honesty on the part of respondents, particularly when a questionnaire is being used and the survey is self-administered. Respondents may not always be willing to give such attention to filling the questionnaire. Sometimes, it may be hard for participants to recall certain information or to take a clear position on controversial issues.
- Another problem with survey research is that it is invariably context- blind. However, in the social world, context and the environment in which questions are being asked and answers given is very important. For example,the responses of a female respondent being asked questions about gender equality in her home, in the presence of her husband and other family members, may be very different from the same questions asked at her work place where she is employed. Survey research can rarely see the questions of "context".

Conclusion

Based on the answers given by different groups, we can observe that different age groups have different choices with regard to communication media. Children of age group 9 - 12 years do not use internet, mostly because of parental restrictions and they use it only under parental guidance. Senior citizens on the other hand do not use internet because of lack of knowledge about how to use it. We can also observe that different age groups are influenced by different kind of communication media. While children are enjoying cartoons and animated pictures, teens and youth like action and thrillers, while senior citizens like devotional pictures. The way different age groups use smartphone applications is also quite different.

Teens are more into social media applications like instagram and snapchat, while other age groups are limited to facebook and whatsapp.The time being spent on communication media by certain age groups like teens is alarming. Recent medical studies show that spending more time on smartphones, social media etc, would affect children physically and psychologically. There has been increasing obesity problems all over world, because children are hardly enjoying outdoor games. It is also affecting the interpersonal communications among family members. All this affects one's social life both directly and indirectly. From the questionnaire we can observe that senior citizens are feeling left out due to advance growth of communication media and there is a growing digital divide between present generation and senior citizens.

One more fall out is, because all the family members are busy in internet, tv and social media, senior citizens are feeling left out in the family and this is causing depression among senior citizens especially. Communication media is not just having negative effects on social life, it also has some positives. Educational videos on youtube have become useful to many children. Applications like Ola have made commuting easier and cheaper to many working men and women. Applications like Linkedin have made finding jobs easy for youth. Devotional TV channels have made senior citizens to spend their time qualitatively in home watching devotional genre programmes. Video calling, instant messaging has reduced the gap between parents, relatives and friends living in another city or country. We can conclude that, communication media has become a part and parcel of our lives. It should be used wisely and in moderation.

Viva Voce Questions

1. ***What is communication media?***

Ans. Communication media refers to the means of delivering and receiving data or information. It includes newspaper, TV, Radio, Mobile, Computer etc.

2. ***How does communication media influence social life?***

Ans. Communication media is a major source of information. Advertisements, movies, TV programmes etc. influence our lifestyle, choices, behaviours and ideologies, thus influencing our social life.

3. ***Which newspaper do you read? Give any two newspaper's names.***

Ans. I read The Hindu newspaper. The Indian Express and Mint are the other newspapers I am familiar with.

4. ***What will you do if the newspaper you read criticises your favourite leader?***

Ans. I would analyse whether the newspaper has presented the view point without any bias and based on facts. I would cross check the facts from other sources like internet also.

5. ***What is the importance of FM channels in our daily lives?***

Ans. FM channels provide us entertainment by playing songs. They are also helpful in knowing information about live traffic in cities.

6. ***Which is the movie that influenced you most? Why?***

Ans. Dangal. It gives a social message that, girls are no less than boys and if given a chance they will come out with flying colours. It also teaches about hardwork and dedication.

7. ***Do you think celebrities should be responsible while endorsing various brands through advertisements? Why?***

Ans. Yes. Celebrities are like role models to common people. So they should be cautious and promote brands which are genuine and credible.

8. ***Name some advertisements which are regressive and racist in nature.***

Ans. Advertisements like Fair and lovely are regressive and racist in nature. They are influencing people by telling that fair skin is better than darker skin.

9. ***Comment on recent TV news channels debates. Do you think they are acting like propaganda channels?***

Ans. Recent TV news channels debates have become illogical and irrational. Yes they are acting like propaganda tools for various vested interests.

10. ***How can we tackle problems like 'Blue Whale Challenge'?***

Ans. Parents should regularly interact with their children and know about their problems and try to solve them. Children should be encouraged to play outdoor games regularly.

11. ***Why should mobiles be not allowed in schools?***

Ans. Mobiles distract students. They are used by students for texting, watching videos etc which cause disturbance to other students also, affecting their studies.

12. ***What are the disadvantages of using too much of communication media?***

Ans. Main disadvantages are, information overload, inappropriate content and excessive advertising. It also makes people lose touch with real world and reduce social interaction with real people.

13. ***What is the use of outdoor games? How do they enhance one's personality?***

Ans. Outdoor games makes us physically fit. They help enhancing our leadership qualities and team work skills.

14. ***What are the challenges faced by senior citizens with the advancement of technology?***

Ans. Senior citizens face problems like digitally handicapped, alienated from present generation which in turn are causing depression problems.

15. ***Name a government programme which became successful, with the help of communication media.***

Ans. Polio programme is an example of using communication media in spreading awareness and making it successful.

16. ***Name some government programmes, for which government is using communication media extensively to bring awareness and bring behavioural changes in people.***

Ans. Bachao Beti Padao, Swachh Bharat are some of the government programmes which are using communication media extensively to bring awareness among people.

17. ***Name two advantages of survey method.***

Ans. Survey method is inexpensive and makes it possible to study large populations with a manageable investment of time, effort and money.

18. ***Name two other research methodologies.***

Ans. Participant observation and archival analysis are other research methodologies that can be used in sociological research.

19. ***How did communication media help in reducing distances between people?***

Ans. Instant messaging, e-mail, video calling etc., have decreased the distances between people. For instance, a son/daughter in USA can daily talk to his/her parents who are in India, on a video call.

20. ***Name some advantages of communication media.***

Ans. It educates people, acts as a good source of entertainment and diffusion of different cultures.

CBSE
Examination Paper 2025

SOCIOLOGY

Time : 3 Hours **Max. Marks : 80**

General Instructions

Read the following instructions very carefully and strictly follow them.

1. The question paper is divided into **four** sections.
2. There are 35 questions in all. **All** questions are **compulsory**.
3. **Section A** includes question No. **1-16**. These are MCQ type questions. As per the question there can be one answer.
4. **Section B** includes question No. **17-25**. These are very short answer type questions carrying 2 marks each. Answer to each question should not exceed 30 words.
5. **Section C** includes question No. **26-32**. They are short answer type questions carrying 4 marks each. Answer to each question should not exceed 80 words.
6. **Section D** includes question No. **33-35**. They are long answer type questions carrying 6 marks each. Answer to each question should not exceed 200 words each. Question no. 33 is to be answered with the help of the given graphics.

Section-A

1. Assertion (A) Industrialisation leads to greater equality, at least in some spheres, such as, caste distinctions do not matter any more in trains, buses, etc.
Reason (R) Social inequalities are reducing in the world. **(1)**
(a) Both (A) and (R) are true and (R) is the correct explanation of (A).
(b) Both (A) and (R) are true, but (R) is not the correct explanation of (A).
(c) (A) is true, but (R) is false.
(d) (A) is false, but (R) is true.

2. Assertion (A) The old social movements functioned within the frame of political parties.
Reason (R) Old social movements were national. **(1)**
(a) Both (A) and (R) are true, and (R) is the correct explanation of (A).
(b) Both (A) and (R) are true, but (R) is not the correct explanation of (A).
(c) (A) is true, but (R) is false.
(d) (A) is false, but (R) is true.

3. As per the theory of Demographic Transition, which of the following statements are correct? **(1)**
I. Population growth is linked to overall levels of economic development.
II. Every society follows a typical pattern of development.
III. The development is related to population growth.
IV. There are four stages of population growth.

Options
(a) I and II (b) II and IV (c) I and III (d) I, II and III

4. Assertion (A) Often it is thought that imparting knowledge of 'scientific' farming methods will improve the conditions of Indian farmers.
Reason (R) The Indian farmers have been cultivating the land for centuries, much before the advent of the Green Revolution. **(1)**
(a) Both (A) and (R) are true, and (R) is the correct explanation of (A).
(b) Both (A) and (R) are true, but (R) is not the correct explanation of (A).
(c) (A) is true, but (R) is false.
(d) (A) is false, but (R) is true.

5. Which of the following statements related to Tribal Identity is not true? **(1)**

(a) Assertions of tribal identity are on the rise.
(b) This can be laid at the door of the emergence of a middle class within the tribal society.
(c) Issues relating to matters of ethnic-cultural identity are becoming less important.
(d) Issues relating to control over vital economic resources like land and specially forests, are on the rise.

Based on the following passage, answer Q.No. 6 and 7.
Social inequality and exclusion are facts of life. Social inequality and exclusion are social because they are not about individuals but about groups. In every society, some people have a greater share of valued–resources money, property, education, health and power than others. People often face discrimination and exclusion because of their gender, religion, ethnicity, language, caste and disability.

6. Social inequality and exclusion are facts of life because **(1)**

I. this everydayness of social inequality and exclusion often makes them appear inevitable, almost natural.
II. we often think of them as being 'deserved' or 'justified' in some sense.
III. these are natural which can be changed.
IV. the poor and marginalised are not blamed for their own plight.

Which of the above statements are correct?

Options
(a) I and II (b) I and III (c) II and III (d) I and IV

7. Which of the following statements is not true related to Exclusion of Dalits? **(1)**

(a) The institution of untouchability does not refer to the avoidance or prohibition of physical contact.
(b) Untouchability refers to a much broader set of social sanctions.
(c) Untouchable castes are outside the caste hierarchy.
(d) They are considered to be so impure that their mere touch severely pollutes members of all other castes.

8. Assertion (A) The laws of a colonised country did not have to stick to the democratic norms that the British back home had to follow in Britain.

Reason (R) The colonial administrators were clear that harsh measures were taken against the labourers to make sure they benefitted the planters. **(1)**

(a) Both (A) and (R) are true and (R) is the correct explanation of (A).
(b) Both (A) and (R) are true, but (R) is not the correct explanation of (A).
(c) (A) is true, but (R) is false.
(d) (A) is false, but (R) is true.

Based on the following passage, answer Q.No. 9 and 10.
The socialisation process involves a continuous dialogue, negotiation and even struggle against significant others (those directly involved in our lives) like our parents, family, kin group and our community. Our community provides us the language (our mother tongue) and the cultural values through which we comprehend the world. It also anchors our self-identity.

9. Which of the following statements is incorrect? **(1)**

(a) We don't have to do anything to be born into a community.
(b) No one has any choice about which family they are born into.
(c) No one has any choice about which country they are born into.
(d) These types of identities are acquired.

10. Community conflicts are hard to deal with because **(1)**

I. each side in the conflict thinks of the other side as a hated enemy.
II. there is a tendency to exaggerate the virtues of one's own side.
III. there is a tendency not to exaggerate the vices of the other side.
IV. in such conflicts, they are constructing matching but reversed mirror images of each other.

Which of the above statements are correct?

Options
(a) I, III and IV (b) I, II and III
(c) I, II and IV (d) II, III and IV

11. Why is the study of Social Movements important in Sociology? **(1)**

(a) Social movements were about protests which were perceived by elites as a major threat to the established order of society.
(b) Social movements were not seen as forces that led to disorder.
(c) Participants of social movements do not have their own shared understanding of right and wrong.
(d) Participants did not often resort to public protest.

12. While urbanisation has been occurring at a rapid pace, it is the biggest cities - the metropolises - that have been growing the fastest.
Which of the following statements related to urbanisation is not true? **(1)**

(a) These metros attract migrants from the rural areas as well as from small towns.
(b) The larger cities in India are not growing at such a rapid rate.
(c) Urban infrastructure can hardly keep pace.
(d) With the mass media's primary focus on these cities, the public face of India is becoming more and more urban rather than rural.

13. **Assertion** (A) Agriculture is the single most important source of livelihood for the majority of the rural population.

Reason (R) The rural is not just agriculture. Many activities that support agriculture and village life are also sources of livelihood. **(1)**

(a) Both (A) and (R) are true and (R) is the correct explanation of (A).

(b) Both (A) and (R) are true, but (R) is not the correct explanation of (A).

(c) (A) is true, but (R) is false.

(d) (A) is false, but (R) is true.

14. **Assertion** (A) There is absorption of different tribal groups into caste Hindu society at varying levels of the hierarchy. **(1)**

Reason (R) Tribal lands were colonised and the forests cut down.

(a) Both (A) and (R) are true, and (R) is the correct explanation of (A).

(b) Both (A) and (R) are true, but (R) is not the correct explanation of (A).

(c) (A) is true, but (R) is false.

(d) (A) is false, but (R) is true.

15. Which of the following statements is true for westernisation? **(1)**

(a) The changes brought about in Indian society and culture is a result of over 150 years of British rule.

(b) Westernisation does not involve the imitation of external forms of culture.

(c) The West did not influence Indian art and literature.

(d) Westernisation did not include the sub-culture of Indian intellectuals.

16. Put the following statements in the correct order. **(1)**

I. Workers have to work at the pace of the machine.

II. The more mechanised an industry gets, the fewer people are employed.

III. Two tea breaks of 5-7 minutes each and one lunch break of half an hour.

IV. Workers get only 45 minutes rest in the entire day.

Options

(a) II, I, IV, III

(b) I, II, III, IV

(c) IV, I, III, II

(d) I, IV, III, II

Section-B

17. "By and large, work for most Indians is still in smallscale workplaces. Here personal relationships determine many aspects of work."

In large organisations work is not determined by personal relationships.

What inference can you draw from this statement? **(2)**

18. (a) "Cultural Diversity can present tough challenges." Support the statement with suitable examples. **(2)**

Or

(b) Give one argument each for and against secularism.

19. Adivasis shared a common hatred for dikus. Why? Give two reasons. **(2)**

20. (a) Workers in underground mines face very dangerous conditions. Give examples. **(2)**

Or

(b) Give one advantage and one disadvantage of the policy of liberalisation.

21. During the 1960s, scholars debated whether tribes should be seen as one end of a continuum with caste-based (Hindu) peasant society, or whether they were an altogether different kind of community.

What is the basis for the argument for tribe and caste distinction? **(2)**

22. Many districts of colonial India were administered through the Zamindari system.

What problems were faced by the peasants due to the Zamindari system? **(2)**

23. One of the negative outcomes of the Green Revolution strategy was the worsening of regional inequalities. Give two reasons for your answer. **(2)**

24. The major epidemic diseases in the past were fevers of various sorts, plague, smallpox and cholera. But the single largest epidemic was the influenza epidemic of 1918-19, which killed about 5% of the total population of India at that time.

Differentiate between epidemic and pandemic. **(2)**

25. "Theoretically, the caste can be understood as the combination of two sets of principles." Name them and define any one. **(2)**

Section-C

26. From the 1950s to the 1970s, a series of land reform laws were passed—at the national level as well as in the states. What were the reasons behind these reforms? **(4)**

27. Sociologists use the term 'Social Stratification' to refer to a system by which categories of people in a society are ranked in a hierarchy.

How does Social Stratification persist over generations? **(4)**

28. (a) Westernisation does involve the imitation of external forms of culture. Illustrate the process of westernisation. **(4)**

Or

(b) The varied Social Reform Movements did have common themes.

Yet there were also significant differences. Discuss.

29. Each one of us is born into a family, and most of us spend long years within it. Usually we feel very strongly about our family. The family is an integral part of lives. Elaborate. **(4)**

30. "In India, the impact of the very same British industrialisation led to de-industrialisation in some sectors."
Identify the impacts on the basis of the above statement. **(4)**

31. There is a close relationship between disability and poverty. Discuss. **(4)**

32. "In response to harsh working conditions, sometimes workers went on strike." Justify taking the example of the famous Bombay Textile strike of 1982. **(4)**

Section-D

33. The declining Sex Ratio in India 1901-2011 is given below.

Year	Sex Ratio all age group	Variation over previous decade	Child Sex Ratio (0-6 years)	Variation over previous decade
1901	972	–	–	–
1911	964	–8	–	–
1921	955	–9	–	–
1931	950	–5	–	–
1941	945	–5	–	–
1951	946	+1	–	–
1961	941	–5	976	–
1971	930	–11	964	–12
1981	934	+4	962	–2
1991	927	–7	945	–17
2001	933	+6	927	–18
2011	943	+10	919	–8

Based on the above data, answer the following questions.

(a) What are the reasons for the declining child sex ratio? **(2)**

Or (b) Based on the above data, compare the data of the 20th century with that of the 21st century and state your inferences. **(4)**

34. Discuss the classification of Social Movements. **(6)**

35. The Civil Society has been instrumental in taking many significant initiatives, the most recent being the campaign for the Right to Information. Discuss the initiative and its outcome. **(2 + 4 = 6)**

Answers

1. (b) Both (A) and (R) are true, but (R) is not the correct explanation of (A).

2. (b) Both (A) and (R) are true, but (R) is not the correct explanation of (A).

3. (d) I, II and III

4. (b) Both (A) and (R) are true, but (R) is not the correct explanation of (A).

5. (c) Issues relating to matters of ethnic-cultural identity are becoming less important.

6. (a) I and II

7. (a) The institution of untouchability does not refer to the avoidance or prohibition of physical contact.

8. (a) Both (A) and (R) are true and (R) is the correct explanation of (A).

9. (d) These types of identities are acquired.

10. (c) (I), (II) and (IV)

11. (a) Social movements were about protests which were perceived by elites as a major threat to the established order of society.

12. (b) The larger cities in India are not growing at such a rapid rate.

13. (a) Both (A) and (R) are true and (R) is the correct explanation of (A).

14. (b) Both (A) and (R) are true, but (R) is not the correct explanation of (A).

15. (b) Westernisation does not involve the imitation of external forms of culture.

16. (c) IV, I, III, II

17. The statement highlights the difference between small-scale workplaces and large organisations in India. The key inference is that most Indian workers are in the informal sector, where personal relationships influence job security, promotions, and wages. In contrast, large organisations follow structured rules, ensuring transparency in recruitment and grievance redressal.

18. (a) For answer refer to page no. 107 Question no. 5

Or

(b) **For Secularism** Secularism ensures equal treatment of all religions by the state and prevents religious discrimination. It promotes unity in a diverse country like India by allowing people of different faiths to coexist peacefully.

Against Secularism Some argue that secularism, when misinterpreted, can lead to unfair restrictions on religious practices. For example, policies that ban religious symbols in public spaces may be seen as suppressing religious freedom rather than ensuring neutrality.

19. Adivasis shared a common hatred for dikus due to the following reasons

- **Exploitation and Land Alienation** Migrant traders and moneylenders took control of Adivasi lands and wealth, pushing the original residents into poverty.
- **Unequal Benefits from Industrial Projects** While the region was rich in minerals, the benefits of mining and industrial development mainly went to dikus, while Adivasis faced displacement and marginalisation.

20. (a) For answer refer to page no. 191 Question no. 18.

Or

(b) **Advantage** Liberalisation has led to economic growth by attracting foreign investment, increasing job opportunities, and expanding industries, improving the overall standard of living.

Disadvantage It has also increased economic inequality, as large corporations and wealthy individuals benefit more than small businesses and lower-income groups, widening the gap between rich and poor.

21. The argument for distinguishing tribes from castes is based on the following factors

- **Distinct Cultural Identity** Tribes have their own unique customs, traditions, languages, and religious practices, which are often different from the caste-based Hindu society. They follow their own forms of worship and social organisation.
- **Social and Economic Differences** Unlike caste-based societies, which follow a hierarchical structure, tribal societies are generally egalitarian. They traditionally lived in forested or hilly areas, practicing shifting cultivation, hunting, or gathering, rather than being integrated into the settled agricultural economy of caste-based societies.

22. Peasants faced the following problems under the zamindari system in colonial India

- **Heavy Taxation and Exploitation** The zamindars extracted high taxes from peasants to meet British land revenue demands, often leaving cultivators in extreme poverty.
- **Land Alienation and Oppression** Peasants did not own land and were forced to hand over a large portion of their produce to landlords, leading to frequent displacement and economic hardship.

23. For answer refer to page no. 169 Question no. 17.

24.

Basis	Epidemic	Pandemic
Definition	An outbreak of a disease that spreads rapidly within a specific region or community.	A disease outbreak that spreads across multiple countries or continents, affecting a large number of people.
Geographical Spread	Limited to a particular area, city, or country.	Spreads across multiple countries or the entire world.
Example	Cholera outbreak in Bengal (19th century).	COVID-19 (2020-2022)
Impact	Affects a large population in a localised area.	Affects a much larger global population.

The Influenza Epidemic of 1918-19 was actually a pandemic, as it spread globally, affecting millions of people.

25. For answer refer to page no. 52 Question no. 2.

26. The land reform laws from the 1950s to the 1970s were introduced to address issues of inequality and exploitation in rural India. The key reasons behind these reforms were.

- **Abolition of Zamindari System** To remove intermediaries who collected rent from farmers without cultivating the land themselves.
- **Redistribution of Land** To provide land to landless farmers and reduce concentration of land in the hands of a few.

- **Ceilings on Land Holdings** To prevent large landowners from holding excessive land and to distribute surplus land to the needy.
- **Encouraging Agricultural Productivity** To make land ownership more equitable, ensuring better use of land for agricultural growth.

27. Social stratification continues over generations due to structural and cultural factors that maintain inequalities in wealth, power and social status.

The social stratification persist over generations in following ways

(i) **Inheritance of Wealth and Property** Economic disparities persist because wealth and assets are passed down within families, ensuring that privileged groups remain dominant.

(ii) **Access to Education** Children from higher social classes receive better educational opportunities, leading to better jobs and reinforcing class divisions.

(iii) **Socialisation and Cultural Norms** Families teach social values that sustain stratification, such as caste identity, racial superiority or class consciousness.

(iv) **Occupational Continuity** Professions often run in families, as access to certain jobs is influenced by family networks and social capital.

(v) **Discriminatory Practices** Social barriers like caste discrimination, racial segregation, and gender bias prevent mobility, which keeps social stratification intact across generations.

28. (a) For answer refer to page no. 141 Question no. 2.

Or

(b) For answer refer to page no. 147 Question no. 4.

29. Each one of us is born into a family, which plays a crucial role in shaping our identity, values, and emotional well-being. From childhood to adulthood, the family provides love, care, and security, making it an integral part of our lives.

Families offer emotional support during difficult times and celebrate our achievements, creating a sense of belonging. They are also the first source of socialisation, teaching us traditions, moral values, and life skills. The influence of family extends to education and career choices, as parents and elders often guide and support our decisions.

Additionally, the family acts as a safety net, providing financial and psychological security. Even as we grow older and become independent, the bond with our family remains strong. Whether in times of joy or hardship, the presence of family gives us strength and a sense of identity and makes it one of the most significant aspects of life.

30. For answer refer to page no. 130 question no. 3.

31. Disability and poverty are closely linked, often making each other worse. People with disabilities face many challenges that push them into poverty, while poverty increases the chances of disability due to poor healthcare, malnutrition, and unsafe living conditions.

One major issue is finding jobs. Many disabled people struggle to get good jobs because of discrimination, lack of skills, and workplaces that are not accessible. This makes them financially weak and dependent on others.

Another problem is high medical costs. Treatment, medicines and assistive devices are expensive, and poor families cannot afford proper care. This can make the disability worse over time.

Education is also a challenge. Many children with disabilities cannot go to school due to a lack of proper facilities. Without education, they get fewer job opportunities and remain stuck in poverty.

Poor areas also lack disabled-friendly infrastructure, making life harder. To break this cycle, we need better healthcare, education and equal job opportunities for disabled people.

32. For answer refer to page no. 195 Question no. 7.

33. (a) There could be several reasons for the decline in the sex ratio some of which includes

(i) Preference for sons.

(ii) Raising women is considered a wasteful investment as they have to get married ultimately.

(iii) Girl marriage is considered a burden due to the prevalence of the dowry system.

(b) The decline in the child sex ratio at the end of the 20th century indicates gender discrimination, female foeticide and societal preference for male children. However, its rise in the 21st century indicates improved awareness, government policies like Beti Bachao Beti Padhao, stricter laws against sex-selective abortions and changing social attitudes. This trend reflects progress toward gender equality and better opportunities for girl children in society.

34. For answer refer to page no. 213 Question no. 2.

35. For answer refer to page no. 111 Question no. 111.

SAMPLE QUESTION PAPER 1

A Highly Simulated Sample Question Paper for CBSE Class XII

SOCIOLOGY

Time : 3 hours | Max. Marks : 80

General Instructions

1. The question paper is divided into **four** sections.
2. There are 35 questions in all. **All** questions are **compulsory**.
3. **Section A** includes question No. **1-16**. These are MCQ type questions. As per the question there can be one answer.
4. **Section B** includes question No. **17-25**. These are very short answer type questions carrying 2 marks each. Answer to each question should not exceed 30 words.
5. **Section C** includes question No. **26-32**. They are short answer type questions carrying 4 marks each. Answer to each question should not exceed 80 words.
6. **Section D** includes question No. **33-35**. They are long answer type questions carrying 6 marks each. Answer to each question should not exceed 200 words each. Question no. 33 is to be answered with the help of the given graphics.

Section-A

1 The proportion of person in different age group relative to the total population is known as .... (1)

(a) Sex ratio (b) Age structure
(c) Occupation structure (d) Age composition

2 **Assertion** (A) Modernisation goes hand in hand with education, mass communication, urbanisation and political participation.
Reason (R) Dominance of the cultural influences from the West changes traditions elsewhere.
In the context which one of the following is correct? (1)

(a) Both A and R are true and R is the correct explanation of A
(b) Both A and R are true, but R is not the correct explanation of A
(c) A is true, but R is false
(d) A is false, but R is true

3 **Assertion** (A) Traditionally, a lower caste adopted the life-style of the dominant caste in the process of sanskritisation.
Reason (R) Adaption of the life-style of the dominant caste usually symbolised a caste of upward mobility within the caste system.
In the context which one of the following is correct? (1)

(a) Both A and R are true and R is the correct explanation of A
(b) Both A and R are true, but R is not the correct explanation of A
(c) A is true, but R is false
(d) A is false, but R is true

4 **Assertion** (A) Tribes are pristine societies uncontaminated by civilisation.
Reason (R) Tribes should really be seen as secondary phenomena arising out of the exploitative and colonialist contact between pre-existing states and non-state groups like the tribes.
In the context which one of the following is correct? (1)

(a) Both A and R are true and R is the correct explanation of A
(b) Both A and R are true, but R is not the correct explanation of A
(c) A is true, but R is false
(d) A is false, but R is true

5 **Assertion** (A) The Telangana Movement is one of the important militant peasant movements in India.
Reason (R) Indian National Congress gave it effective leadership.
In the context which one of the following is correct? (1)

(a) Both A and R are true and R is the correct explanation of A
(b) Both A and R are true, but R is not the correct explanation of A
(c) A is true, but R is false
(d) A is false, but R is true

6 **Assertion** (A) The culture of the dominant class controls the dominant meanings.
Reason (R) The structure of relations between classes perpetuates itself by reproducing its characteristics in the domain of culture.
In the context which one of the following is correct? (1)
(a) Both A and R are true and R is the correct explanation of A
(b) Both A and R are true, but R is not the correct explanation of A
(c) A is true, but R is false
(d) A is false, but R is true

7 **Assertion** (A) The principle of Nationalism assumes that any set of people have a right to be free and exercise sovereign power. It is an important part of the rise of democratic ideas.
Reason (R) Nation States are closely associated with the rise of nationalism.
In the context which one of the following is correct? (1)
(a) Both A and R are true and R is the correct explanation of (A)
(b) Both A and (R) are true, but R is not the correct explanation of A
(c) A is true, but R is false
(d) A is false, but R is true

8 Secularism refers to the principle of separation of the state from religious institutions. Which of the following is not a features of Indian secularism? (1)
(a) No discrimination by the state on the basis of religion.
(b) Non-interference in the functioning of any religion by the state.
(c) No official religion of India.
(d) Equal disrespect and unrecognition for all religious by the state.

9 The term Modernisation was associated with positive and desirable values in the 19th and 20th century. Choose the incorrect statement about Modernisation in India? (1)
(a) Caste and Community based Identify is prevalent in India.
(b) Job in India is often performed by choice.
(c) Marriage in India are done on the basis of caste and community.
(d) A scientific tradition and also have vibrant, secular and democratic political system.

10 Which of the following is true regarding Sir Syed Ahmed Khan's approach to women's education? (1)
(a) He opposed women's education completely due to religious beliefs.
(b) He supported girls' education, but with a curriculum that emphasised religious principles, handicrafts, and domestic skills within the confines of their homes.
(c) He was a vocal advocate for co-education in British-run schools for Muslim girls.
(d) He focused solely on modern, Western-style education for Muslim girls.

11 Which of the following is not a characteristic feature of Malthusian theory of population growth? (1)
I. Positive checks to population growth such as famines and diseases
II. The belief that poverty is caused by unequal resource distribution
III. Population grows in geometric progression while food supply grows in arithmetic progression
IV. Preventive checks include celibacy and postponing marriage

Codes
(a) Only II
(b) I and III
(c) II and IV
(d) I, II and III

12 Which of the following statements is correct about the First Phase of Green Revolution in India? (1)
I. It was initiated in the 1960s and 1970s and focused on regions with assured irrigation.
II. It primarily benefited small and marginal farmers who could easily adopt new technology.
III. The sharp increase in agricultural productivity led India to achieve self-sufficiency in foodgrain production for the first time.

IV. It caused an increase in rural inequalities and displacement of tenant-cultivators.

Codes
(a) I, II and III (b) II, III and IV
(c) I, III and IV (d) I, II, III and IV

Read the passage given below and answer the questions that follow.

The caste system in India is a distinct social institution that legitimises and enforces practices of discrimination against people born into particular castes. These practices are often humiliating, exclusionary, and exploitative. Historically, the caste system was closely linked to occupation and status. The Brahmins, the ritually highest caste, had significant religious authority but were subordinate to kings in secular matters. Over time, the rigidity of caste-based occupations has declined, but the correlation between caste and socio-economic status remains strong. Privileged sections of society are still predominantly from 'upper' castes, while disadvantaged groups belong to 'lower' castes.

13 Which of the following statements is correct based on the passage? (1)

I. Caste and occupation have always been completely unrelated.
II. The caste system continues to influence socio-economic status today.
III. The Brahmins held both secular and religious power in the caste hierarchy.
IV. The rigid link between caste and occupation remains unchanged.

Codes
(a) I and IV (b) Only II
(c) Only III (d) II and III

14 Which of the following is incorrect according to the passage? (1)

(a) Social movements have reduced caste-based discrimination over the past century.
(b) The privileged sections of society are overwhelmingly from 'upper' castes.
(c) The caste system no longer affects life chances in India.
(d) Disadvantaged groups often belong to 'lower' castes.

Read the passage given below and answer the questions that follow.

The working conditions of workers in India are very poor despite the presence of laws like the Mines Act of 1952. This act sets guidelines on working hours, overtime, and safety, but these are often overlooked, especially in small mines. Sub-contracting further weakens accountability, and post-mining restoration is rarely implemented. Workers in underground mines face severe hazards like floods, gas emissions, and ventilation failures, leading to health issues such as silicosis and tuberculosis. Overground workers are exposed to harsh weather and accidents. The rate of mining accidents in India is higher compared to other countries.

15 Which of the following statements is correct based on the passage? (1)

(a) The Mines Act of 1952 ensures perfect safety conditions for all mine workers.
(b) Small mining firms strictly follow government regulations.
(c) Sub-contracting leads to poor accountability for workers' conditions.
(d) The rate of mining accidents in India is comparable to global standards.

16 Which of the following is incorrect according to the passage? (1)

I. Underground mine workers face hazards such as gas emissions and ventilation failures.
II. Overground workers face risks of injuries from mine blasting and falling objects.
III. Mining companies consistently restore areas after mining is complete.
IV. Health problems like tuberculosis and silicosis are common among miners.

Codes
(a) I and II (b) II and III
(c) Only III (d) III and IV

Section-B

17 What does the term modernity assume? (2)

18 What do you understand by support prices? (2)

19 (a) What was drawback of Zamindari System? Which areas became more prosperous? (2)

Or

(b) How does industrialisation lead to greater inequality?

20 What rights does the Right to Information give to citizens? (2)

21 "A small size of population work in the organised section." Highlight any two features of an organised sector. (2)

FULLY SOLVED

22 Discuss briefly that tea plantation industry in India was governed by the colonial interest. (2)

23 What policies should be adopted in a multicultural nation to build a feeling of unity in diversity? (2)

24 "Social inequality is a universal phenomenon in all societies." What is social about social inequality? (2)

25 (a) Read the passage and answer the following question. (2)

The ultimate outcome of the Green Revolution was a process of 'differentiation', in which the rich grew richer and many of the poor stagnated or grew poorer. It should be noted that employment and wages for agricultural workers did increase in many areas, because the demand for labour increased.

What are negative outcomes of Green Revolution?

(b) Give reasons for the bringing of land reforms.

Section-C

26 OBC's are a much more diverse group than Dalits and Adivasis. Explain this statement. (4)

27 "The social movement also develop distinct modes of protests." Discuss the features of social movement. (4)

28 (a) "Encouraging cultural diversity is good policy from the practical and principled point of view." Justify the statement using India's case as a nation-state. (4)

Or

(b) "Women are the basic unit of the society." What were the major women's issues taken up by various reformers in Indian history?

29 "The practice of colonialism and the principle of nationalism are contradictory." Explain this given statement. Why?

30 Mention the loopholes found in the implementation of the Land Ceiling Act. (4)

31 "19th century reform initiated a period of questioning reinterpretations and both intellectual and social growth." Do you agree with given statement? Explain with a suitable example. (4)

32 If capitalism became the dominant economic system in the colonial period, nation-states became the dominant political form. Explain how this process took place. (4)

Section-D

33 "Employment by the government was a major avenue for increasing the well-being of the population, but now even that is coming down." (6)

(a) Explain the statement in light of the graph shown below.

(b) Describe how liberalisation and privatisation worldwide appear to be associated with rising income inequality.

Employment in Organised Sectors

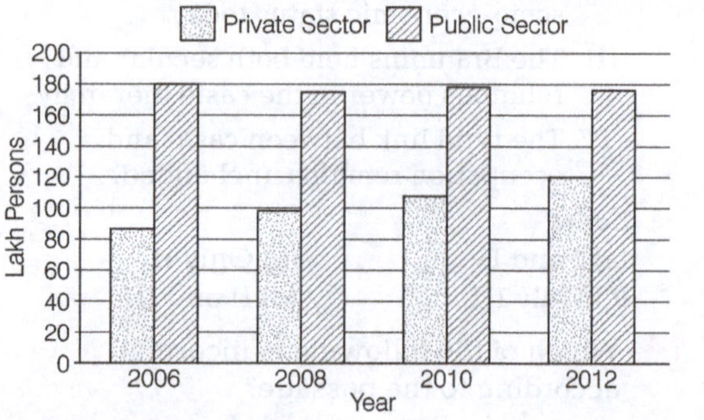

34 Explain the term 'casteism in politics'. What is the purpose of politics? Why caste is important for politics? Why politicians' mobiles caste groupings? (6)

35 Discuss the consequences of commercialisation of agriculture. (6)

Answers

1 (b) age structure

2 (b) Both A and R are true, but R is not the correct explanation of A

3 (b) Both A and R are true, but R is not the correct explanation of A

4 (d) A is false, but R is true

5 (a) Both A and R are true and R is the correct explanation of A

6 (c) A is true, but R is false

7 (b) Both A and R are true, but R is not the correct explanation of A

8 (d) Equal disrespect and unrecognition for all religious by the state.

9 (b) Jobs in India is often performed by choice.

10 (b) He supported girls' education, but with a curriculum that emphasised religious principles, handicrafts, and domestic skills within the confines of their homes.

11 (a) Only II

12 (c) I, III and II

13 (b) Only II

14 (c) The caste system no longer affects life chances in India.

15 (c) Sub-contracting leads to poor accountability for workers' conditions.

16 (c) Only III

17 Modernity assumes that local ties and parochial perspective give way to universal commitments and cosmopolitan attitudes. The truths of utility, calculation and science take precedence over those of emotions. Behaviour, thought and attitude are not decided by family, tribe, caste, community, etc.

18 Support prices are basically the minimum procuring prices of the agricultural products declared by the government for a particular year. It is basically done to safeguard the farmers against the losses they may bear and provide a uniform level of price.

19 (a) During British rule the Zamindari System caused agricultural production to stagnate and decline. The regions where Ryotwari system was imposed became more prosperous.

Or

(b) According to many sociologists, industrialisation leads to greater equality in certain sphere. It reduces the social inequality to a certain extent. However, it increases the economic or income inequality. Further,in many cases, older forms of discrimination persists even in new factory or workplace setting.

20 The Right to Information Act specifies that citizens have a right to

- Request any information.
- Take copies of document.
- Inspect documents, works and records.
- Take certified samples of materials of works.

21 The two features of an organised sector are

(i) Workers have job security.

(ii) Government rules are followed properly in terms of employment.

22 The British Government official reports show how the colonial government often used unfair means to hire and forcibly keep labourers and it clearly acted on behalf of the British planters.

So, through these aspects we get a glimpse of what life was for tea planters in this industry.

23 The policies that should be adopted are

- Enduring democracies can be established in politics that are multicultural.
- Explicit efforts are required to end the cultural exclusion of diverse groups and build multiple and complementary identities.

24 Social inequalities are social because they are not about individuals but about groups. They are social in the sense, that they are not only economic but also systematic and structured.

25 (a) In most of the Green Revolution areas, farmers have switched from a multi-crop system, which allowed them to spread risks, to a mono-crop regime, which means that there is nothing to fall back on in case of crop failure. Another negative outcome of the Green Revolution strategy was the worsening of regional inequalities.

Or

(b) Land reforms were brought about because

- It was majorly done to increase the level of productivity in the agricultural sector.
- It was also brought about to stop the exploitation of the poor farmers by eliminating the intermediaries so that the farmers could get land.

26 There were a large group of castes that were of low status and were also subjected to varying levels of discrimination but were not untouchables. These were the service and artisanal caste who occupied lower level in caste hierarchy.

The OBC's are defined negatively, they are neither part of the forward castes at the upper end of the status nor of the Dalits at the lower level. But since, caste has entered all the major Indian religions and is not confined to Hinduism alone, there are also members of other religions who belong to backward castes. They share the same traditional occupational identification and similar or worse socio-economic status. For these reasons, the OBCs are a much more diverse group than Dalits or Adivasis.

Or Community identity is based on birth and belonging rather than on some form of acquired qualifications of accomplishment. It is what we are rather than what we have become.

Our community provides us the language (our mother tongue) and the cultural values through which we comprehend the world. It also secures our self-identity. It is because of this accidental, unconditional and yet almost inescapable belonging that we can often be so emotionally attached to our community identity. Expanding and overlapping circles of community ties (family, kinship, caste, ethnicity, language, region or religion) give meaning to our world and give us a sense of identity of who we are. That is why people often react emotionally or even violently whenever there is a perceived threat to their community identity.

Scriptive identities and community feeling are universal. Everyone has a motherland, a mother tongue, a family and a faith and we are all equally committed and loyal to our respective identities.

27 The features of social movements are as follow

- A social movement requires sustained collective action over time. Such action is often directed against the state and takes the form of demanding changes in state policy or practice.
- Those people who participate in social movements have shared objectives and ideologies.
- Social movement activists hold meetings to mobilise people around the issues that concern them. Such activities help shared understanding.
- Social movements also plan out campaigns that include lobbying with the government, media and other important makers of public opinion.

28 (a) Nations are communities that have a state of their own, that is why the two are joined to form the term nation-state. The Indian nation-state is socially and culturally one of the most diverse countries of the world. This diverse population speak different languages.

In terms of religion, the population is diverse with Hindu, Muslim, Sikh, Christian, etc.

The Constitution declares the state to be a secular state, but religion, language and other such factors are not removed from the public sphere.

In fact, these communities are explicitly recognised by the state. By international standards, very strong constitutional protection is offered to minority religion, the tribal population, Scheduled Caste population linguistic minorities, etc. Therefore, comparative surveys of long-standing democracies show that India has been very cohesive, despite its diversity.

Or

(b) Women's issues were taken up by various reformers in Indian history.

The issues of practice of sati, child marriage and widow remarriage were taken up by the reformers.

Female education was also discussed intensively. Female education was promoted by the social reformers and new ideas of liberalism and freedom also brought new ideas of homemaking and marriage.

New roles for mothers and daughters also emerged with the growth of new ideas and new consciousness. Jotiba Phule, the social reformer opened the first school for women in Pune.

Muslim social reformers also debated the issues of polygamy and purdah. Jahanara Shah at the All India Muslim Ladies Conference proposed a resolution against the evils of polygamy in Islam. The resolution said that polygamy was against the true spirit of Quran.

The social reformers tried to bring changes in the social practices that discriminated against women.

Raja Ram Mohun Roy attacked the practice of sati on humanitarian grounds as well as on the writings of Hindu shastras. Similarly, Ranade's writings elaborated the shastric sanction for remarriage of widows.

29 The practice of colonialism and the basic principles of nationalism are opposite to each other. Nationalism assumes that a particular group of people have a right to be free and exercise sovereign power. On the other hand, colonialism is the control of one country by another.

The contradictory nature of nationalism and colonialism can be described as

- The nationalism gives rise to freedom and democratic rights, while colonialism tries to suppress the liberty of colonised people.
- British colonial masters strengthened their capitalistic tendencies and colonial interests

without caring for the welfare of colonised people. While colonialism changes the economic system of colonised people to extract maximum profit and gain.

- Nationalism promotes the economic development and industrialisation of one's own country, while colonialism tries to de-industrialise the colonies in order to promote its own colonial interests.
- Nationalism advocates the sovereignty of its own people, while colonialism denies it.

30 The loopholes found in the implementation of the Land Ceiling Act are discused below

- Land Ceiling Act imposed upper limit on the amount of land that can be owned by a particular family.
- Possession of surplus land (above the ceiling limit) held by each household, and redistribute it to landless families.
- There were many loopholes and other strategies through which most landowners were able to escape from having their surplus land taken over by the state.
- In most cases landowners managed to divide the land among relatives and others, including servants, in so-called benamic transfers.
- In some places some rich farmers actually divorced their wives (but continued to live with them) in order to avoid the provisions of Land Ceiling Act, which allowed a separate share for unmarried women but not for wives.

31 19th century social reform initiated a period of questioning, reinterpretations and both intellectual and social growth as in following ways

- The idea of female education was debated intensely. Reformers argued that for a society to progress women have to be educated. Some of them believed that in pre-modern India, women were educated. Others contested this on the grounds that this was so only of a privileged few. Thus, attempts to justify female education were made by recourse to both modern and traditional ideas.
- They actively debated the meanings of tradition and modernity. Jyotiba Phule thus recalled the glory of pre-Aryan age while others like Bal Gangadhar Tilak emphasised the glory of the Aryan period.
- Muslim social reformers actively debated the meaning of polygamy and purdah. For example, a resolution against the evils of polygamy was proposed by Jahanara Shah Nawas at the All India Muslim Ladies Conference.
- Debates within communities were common during this period. For instance, sati was opposed by the Brahmo Samaj. Orthodox members of the Hindu community in Bengal formed an organisation called Dharma Sabha and petitioned the British arguing that reformers had no right to interpret sacred texts.

32 Capitalism is an economic system in which the means of production are privately owned and organised to accumulate profits within a market system. The emergence of capitalism was a complicated process. It was an interplay of European exploration, growth in industrialisation, trade and science and technology.

With due course of time, capitalism became the dominant economic system. It was characterised by dynamism, growth, expansion, innovation and use of labour and technology.

Gradually, in Western countries it was found that if capitalism became the dominant economic system, then nation-state became the dominant political form. During the period before the First World War, people hardly had passports and these were not used in international travel. In the modern world, we see the nation-states. Nation-state is a particular type of state in which a government has supreme or sovereign power within a defined territorial area.

In this type of state, the people are citizens of a single nation. Therefore, nationalism is also closely related to nation-states. Nationalism advocates the right to freedom and sovereignty of a set of people living in a particular area. Thus, capitalism, nationalism and nation-states developed over the period of time.

33 (a) "Employment by the government was a major avenue for increasing the well-being of the population, but now even that is coming down." India is still primarily a farming region. The service sector – stores, banks, the IT industry, hotels, and other services – is hiring more people, and the urban middle class is expanding, as are the ideals we see in television serials and films. However, we can see that very few citizens in India have secure jobs, and that even those who do have regular salaried jobs are becoming more precarious as contract labour becomes more prevalent. Government jobs has previously been a significant source of growing the population's well-being, but even that is now dwindling.

(b) Some economists disagree, but global liberalisation and privatisation seem to be on the rise. While some economists disagree, liberalisation and privatisation tend to be linked to increasing income inequality across the world. The government is embarking on a programme of land acquisition for industry at the same time that secure jobs in large industry is declining. These companies do not actually provide jobs for the people in the surrounding areas, but they do pollute the environment significantly.

34 Those who complain about 'casteism in politics' in India are really looking for a type of politics that has no foundation in society. Politics is a competitive activity whose aim is to gain control in order to achieve specific objectives. Its mechanism entails defining and exploiting current and new allegiances in order to mobilise and consolidate positions. The main thing is organisation and articulation of support, and in mass-based politics, the point is to express support through the organisations where the masses can be found.

The purpose of politics is to acquire power, realise certain goals and identify as well as manipulate existing and emerging allegiances in order to mobilise and consolidate positions.

Politics articulate, supports and mobilises the masses in order to organise their power. Caste is one of the organisations in society in which large population lives and it is easy for the politicians to seek the support on the basis of caste.

To capture power and realise its certain goals, politics strive to organise the support on the basis of caste of people. Therefore, caste is important for politics. Politicians mobiles caste groupings in order to organise their power, where there are other basis of associations politicians approach then as well.

35 The consequences of commercialisation of agriculture are

- The commercialisation of agriculture was beneficial to the British planters, traders and manufacturers, who were provided with opportunity to make huge profits by getting the commercialised agricultural products at throw away prices.
- The poor peasants were forced to sell their produce just after harvest at whatever prices they could get as they had to meet in time the demands of the government, the landlord, the money lender and their family members' requirements.
- Indian money lenders advanced, cash advances to the farmers to cultivate the commercial crops and if the peasants failed to pay them back in time, the land of peasants came under ownership of moneylenders.
- Commercialisation of agriculture did not encourage growth of land market because major profit of commercialisation went to company traders and mediators.
- Commercialisation effected traditional relations between agriculture and industry. In India, traditional relations acted as factors for each other's development which were hampered.

FULLY SOLVED

SAMPLE QUESTION PAPER 2

A Highly Simulated Sample Question Paper for CBSE Class XII

SOCIOLOGY

Time : 3 hours | Max. Marks : 80

General Instructions

1. The question paper is divided into **four** sections.
2. There are 35 questions in all. **All** questions are **compulsory**.
3. **Section A** includes question No. **1-16**. These are MCQ type questions. As per the question there can be one answer.
4. **Section B** includes question No. **17-25**. These are very short answer type questions carrying 2 marks each. Answer to each question should not exceed 30 words.
5. **Section C** includes question No. **26-32**. They are short answer type questions carrying 4 marks each. Answer to each question should not exceed 80 words.
6. **Section D** includes question No. **33-35**. They are long answer type questions carrying 6 marks each. Answer to each question should not exceed 200 words each. Question no. 33 is to be answered with the help of the given graphics.

Section-A

1 Prolonged experience of discriminatory or insulting behaviour often produces a reaction on the past of the excluded who then stop trying for inclusion. In this context choose the incorrect statement. (1)

(a) Dalits may build their own temple
(b) Convert to another religion
(c) Social exclusion is involuntary
(d) They may no longer desire to be included in the Hindu temple or religious events

2 Parsis or Sikhs are examples of anomalous minority groups because of which of the following reasons? (1)

(a) They are religious minorities and economically well-off.
(b) They are not politically vulnerable
(c) They do not need any special protection because of their demographic dominance.
(d) They do not face any risk from majority community.

3 The caste system can be understood as the combination of two sets of principles, one is based on difference and separation and the other on wholism and hierarchy. Each caste is supposed to be different from other caste and is therefore strictly separated from every other caste.

Which of the following is not key principle of caste system? (1)

I. Competition II. Difference
III. Wholism IV. Competition

Codes

(a) Only I (b) I, II and IV
(c) II, III and IV (d) III and IV

4 **Assertion** (A) There is a close relationship between disability and poverty.

Reason (R) Malnutrition mothers weakend by frequent child birth, inadequate innunisation programmes, accidents in overcrowded homes, all contribute to an incidence of disability among poor people that is higher.

In the context which one of the following is correct? (1)

(a) Both A and R are true and R is correct explanation of A
(b) Both A and R are true, but R is not the correct explanation of A
(c) A is true, but R is false
(d) A is false, but R is true

UNSOLVED

5 **Assertion** (A) Sanskritisation usually accompanies or follows arise in the economic status of the caste attempting it.

Reason (R) Adopting the ritual, domestic and social practices of a caste (or castes) of higher status raises the social status of the members of middle or lower castes.

In the context which one of the following is correct? (1)

(a) Both A and R are true and R is the correct explanation of A

(b) Both A and R are true, but R is not the correct explanation of A

(c) A is true and R is false

(d) A is false and R is true

6 **Assertion** (A) Ritually highest caste - the Brahmins were subordinated to the secular power of kings and rulers belonging to the Kshatriya castes.

Reason (R) In strict scriptural terms, Brahmins were not supposed to a mass wealth.

In the context which one of the following is correct? (1)

(a) Both A and R are true and R is the correct explanation of A

(b) Both A and R are true, but R is not the correct explanation of A

(c) Both A and R are false

(d) A is true and R is false

7 **Assertion** (A) In the twentieth century, handloom cloth production expanded steadily.

Reason (R) This was partly because of technological changes.

In the context which one of the following is correct? (1)

(a) If both assertion and reason are true and reason is the correct explanation of assertion.

(b) If both assertion and reason are true, but reason is not the correct explanation of assertion.

(c) If assertion is true, but reason is false.

(d) If both assertion and reason are false.

8 The city offers anoymity which is an important reason for rural to urban migration. Who enjoys this anoymity? (1)

(a) Poor sections of the socially dominant rural groups

(b) Scheduled Castes and Scheduled Tribes

(c) Children

(d) Both (a) and (b)

9 **Assertion** (A) Prejudice is often grounded in stereotypes.

Reason (R) People do not face discrimination and exclusion on the basis of family system.

In the context which one of the following is correct? (1)

(a) Both A and R are true and R is the correct explanation of A

(b) Both A and R are true, but R is not correct explanation of A

(c) A is true and R is false

(d) A is false and R is true

10 **Assertion** (A) Matriarchy unlike Patriarchy has been a theoretical rather than an empirical concept.

Reason (R) There is no Historical or Anthropological evidence of matriarchy i.e. societies where women exercises dominance.

In the context which one of the following is correct? (1)

(a) Both A and R are true and R is the correct explanation of A

(b) Both A and R are true, but R is not the correct explanation of A

(c) A is true, but R is false

(d) A is false, but R is true

11 According to the theory of demographic transition, which of the following statements is incorrect? (1)

I. In the first stage, birth and death rates are both high, leading to low population growth.

II. The second stage is marked by a sharp decline in both birth and death rates, resulting in low population growth.

III. The third stage occurs in developed countries with low birth and death rates.

IV. Population explosion is caused by reduced death rates without a corresponding decline in birth rates.

Codes

(a) Only II (b) I and IV

(c) II and III (d) III and IV

12 Which of the following is not a form of capital that contributes to social inequality?
(a) Economic Capital (b) Cultural Capital
(c) Political Capital (d) Social Capital

Read the passage given below and answer the questions that follow.

Caste-based discrimination has not only social but also economic dimensions. Members of disadvantaged castes often face barriers in accessing education, employment, and resources. This perpetuates a cycle of poverty and inequality. Government initiatives such as reservation policies aim to address these disparities by providing affirmative action in education and jobs. However, debates persist over the effectiveness and scope of these measures, with some arguing for their expansion and others for their re-evaluation.

13 Which of the following statements is correct based on the passage? (1)
(a) Reservation policies have eliminated caste-based discrimination.
(b) Economic inequality is unrelated to caste-based discrimination.
(c) Reservation policies are a form of affirmative action.
(d) Education is accessible to all, irrespective of caste.

14 Which of the following is correct according to the passage? (1)
I. Disadvantaged castes face systemic barriers to upward mobility.
II. Some advocate for expanding reservation policies.
III. Reservation policies are universally accepted as effective.
IV. Economic inequality is the sole focus of caste-based discrimination.

Codes
(a) I and II (b) II and III
(c) I, II and III (d) III and IV

Read the passage given below and answer the questions that follow.

Migration in industries often involves workers moving from different regions. In fish processing plants along the coast, most workers are single women from Tamil Nadu, Karnataka, and Kerala. They live in crowded quarters and work in shifts. Migrant workers face loneliness and vulnerability in a globalised economy, but for some, this also represents economic independence. Similarly, home-based work is common, involving activities like making bidis, agarbattis, and carpets. These workers are paid on a piece-rate basis and primarily include women and children. The bidi industry heavily relies on women for rolling bidis, and this chain of production involves multiple intermediaries before reaching the end consumer.

15 Which of the following statements is incorrect based on the passage? (1)
I. Migrant workers in fish processing plants mostly live in luxurious accommodations.
II. Home-based work provides workers with regular salaries.
III. Women play a significant role in home-based industries like bidi making.
IV. Migrant workers do not face any challenges in globalised economies.

Codes
(a) I and III (b) III and IV
(c) II and IV (d) I, II and IV

16 Which of the following is incorrect according to the passage? (1)
(a) Migrant workers in the fish processing plants are often single women.
(b) The bidi production process involves no intermediaries.
(c) Home-based work includes the production of goods like carpets and agarbattis.
(d) Migrant workers experience both challenges and opportunities in globalised economies.

Section-B

17 What do you mean by the term 'Social Stratification'? (2)

18 How difference between endogamy and exogamy can be explained? (2)

19 Secularism is among the most complex terms in social and political theory. In the western context the main sense of these terms has to do with the separation of church and state. The separation of religious and political authority marked a major turning point in the social history of the west. (2)

Based on the given passage answer the following question.

Mention some differences between secularism followed in West as that in India.

20 State is indeed a very crucial institution when it comes to the management of cultural diversity in a nation. How? **(2)**

21 What changes have taken place due to marketisation? **(2)**

22 "Adivasi experiences of marginalisation and their sense of injustice were the mobilised to create shored Jharkhandi Identity".
Mention the issues against which leaders of Jharkhand agitated. **(2)**

23 (a) What is meant by secularisation? Mention any two feature of the secularism. **(2)**

Or

(b) How is Indian context of secularism different from the Western form of secularisation.

24 (a) Mention any two structural changes brought about by colonialism. **(2)**

Or

(b) What was the significant role of cities like Bombay during the British colonial period in India?

25 Colonialism led to considerable movement of people. Give examples. **(2)**

UNSOLVED

Section-C

26 (a) "Encouraging cultural diversity is good policy from the practical and principled point of view." Justify the statement using India's case as a nation-state. **(4)**

Or

(b) Examine the role of state's initiatives to address caste and tribe discrimination.

27 Untouchability is an extreme and vicious aspect of the caste system. Do you agree with the given statements. Give reasons for your answer. **(4)**

28 Colonialism in India introduced a wide array of change in every sphere. Explain this statement. **(4)**

29 "India has mixed economic policy." Explain with a suitable example. **(4)**

30 "Sociologists have tried to define what constitutes modernisation". Do you agree with the given statements. Explain this statements. **(4)**

31 How tribal people could be encouraged to get an education? **(4)**

32 The pattern of farmer's suicides point to the significant crises that the rural areas are experiencing. What do you understand by 'matrix event' and how are they responsible for farmer suicides? **(4)**

Section-D

33 What is urbanisation? What does the chart show in relation to percentage share of urban population? What does the industrialisation and urbanisation imply? **(6)**

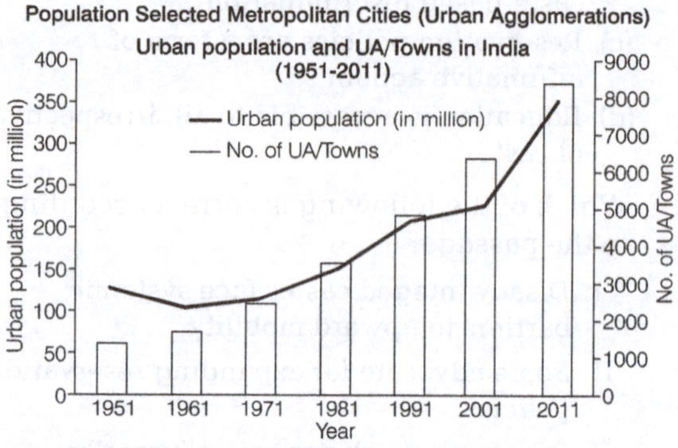

34 What are the major issues taken up by the women's movement over its history? **(6)**

35 What was the focus of social protest during India's nationalist struggle? What message did Gandhi want to spread through the legendary Dandi March? **(6)**

Answers

1 (c) Social exclusion is involuntary

2 (a) They are religious minorities and economically well-off.

3 (a) Only I

4 (a) Both A and R are true and R is correct explanation of A

5 (a) Both A and R are true and R is the correct explanation of A

6 (a) Both A and R are true and R is the correct explanation of A

7 (a) If both assertion and reason are true and reason is the correct explanation of assertion.

8 (d) Both (a) and (b)

9 (a) Both A and R are true and R is the correct explanation of A

10 (a) Both A and R are true and R is the correct explanation of A

11 (a) Only II

12 (c) Political capital

13 (c) Reservation policies are a form of affirmative action.

14 (c) I, II and III

15 (d) I, II and IV

16 (b) The bidi production process involves no intermediaries.

SAMPLE QUESTION PAPER 3

A Highly Simulated Sample Question Paper for CBSE Class XII

SOCIOLOGY

Time : 3 hours | Max. Marks : 80

General Instructions

1. The question paper is divided into **four** sections.
2. There are 35 questions in all. **All** questions are **compulsory**.
3. **Section A** includes question No. **1-16**. These are MCQ type questions. As per the question there can be one answer.
4. **Section B** includes question No. **17-25**. These are very short answer type questions carrying 2 marks each. Answer to each question should not exceed 30 words.
5. **Section C** includes question No. **26-32**. They are short answer type questions carrying 4 marks each. Answer to each question should not exceed 80 words.
6. **Section D** includes question No. **33-35**. They are long answer type questions carrying 6 marks each. Answer to each question should not exceed 200 words each. Question no. 33 is to be answered with the help of the given graphics.

Section-A

1 The laws that imposed an upper limit on the amount of land that can be owned by a particular family is known as **(1)**

(a) Abolition of Zamindari System
(b) Tenancy Abolition and Regulation Act
(c) Land Ceiling Act
(d) Ryotwari System

2 Language coupled with .... and .... have provided the most powerful instrument for the formation of ethno-national identity India. **(1)**

(a) region, religion
(b) regional, tribal identity
(c) religion, class
(d) class, gender

3 **Assertion** (A) To be effective, the ideas of inclusive nationalism had to be built into the constitution.

Reason (R) The Authoritarian states often limit or abolish civil liberties.

In the context which one of the following is correct? **(1)**

(a) Both A and R are true and R is correct explanation of A
(b) Both A and R are true, but R is not the correct explanation of A
(c) A is true, but R is false
(d) A is false, but R is true

4 Industralisation refers to the emergence of machine production, based on the use of inanimate power resource like steam or electricity. Choose the incorrect statement about industralisation in India? **(1)**

(a) It started much later in the 18th century
(b) It suffered a lot due to British monopoly of right to trade
(c) The First Cotton mill in Surat came UP in 1854.
(d) The colonial control over Indian trade stiffened the growth of Indian merchants.

5 **Assertion** (A) The planters are in huge bungalows, set on sturdy wooden stills to save and guard the inmates against wild animals. They lived in luxury and comforts.

Reason (R) A number of bars his mails and bearers were trained by the planters to serve them to perfection.

In the context which one of the following is correct? **(1)**

(a) Both A and R are true and R is correct explanation of A
(b) Both A and R are true, but R is not the correct explanation of A
(c) A is true, but R is false
(d) A is false, but R is true

6 **Assertion** (A) In order to survive, an authoritarian state resorts to repression, permanent mobilisation and manipulation.
Reason (R) In an authoritarian state, the bureaucratic apparatus becomes responsive to the needs of the masses.
In the context which one of the following is correct? (1)
(a) Both A and R are true and R is correct explanation of A
(b) Both A and R are true, but R is not the correct explanation of A
(c) A is true, but R is false
(d) A is false, but R is true

7 **Assertion** (A) In pre-independence India, backward classes movement was never strong enough to affect the whole country.
Reason (R) The various backward classes had serious internal differences and could never work together.
In the context which one of the following is correct? (1)
(a) Both A and R are true and R is correct explanation of A
(b) Both A and R are true, but R is not the correct explanation of A
(c) A is true, but R is false
(d) A is false, but R is true

8 **Assertion** (A) The higher the job opportunities for female population in the paid labour market, the higher the rate of acceptance of family planning.
Reason (R) Opportunity and cost of a child is directly proportional to the employment status of mother.
In the context which one of the following is corect? (1)
(a) Both A and R are true and R is correct explanation of A
(b) Both A and R are true, but R is not the correct explanation of A
(c) A is true, but R is false
(d) A is false, but R is true

9 **Assertion** (A) The inequalities in the literacy rate are especially important because they tend to reproduce inequality across generations.
Reason (R) Literacy rate also vary by social group. Historically disadvantaged communities like the scheduled castes and scheduled tribes have lower rate of literacy
In the context which one of the following is corect? (1)
(a) Both A and R are true and R is correct explanation of A
(b) Both A and R are true, but R is not the correct explanation of A
(c) A is true, but R is false
(d) A is false, but R is true

10 Which of the following are the negative consequences of the Second Phase of the Green Revolution? (1)
I. Increased livelihood insecurity due to dependence on the market for income.
II. Switching from multi-crop systems to mono-crop systems increased risks for farmers.
III. Significant reduction in regional inequalities across India.
IV. Loss of traditional agricultural knowledge and varieties of seeds.

Codes
(a) I, II and IV
(b) II, III and IV
(c) I, III and IV
(d) I, II, III and IV

11 Which of the following statements is correct about the Peasant Movements in India? (1)
I. The Bengal Revolt of 1859-62 was against the indigo plantation system.
II. The Deccan riots of 1857 were directed against feudal landlords.
III. The Tebhaga Movement (1946-47) was a struggle of sharecroppers in Bengal.

Codes
(a) I and II
(b) II and III
(c) I and III
(d) I, II and III

12 Which of the following movements was focused on 'price-related issues' and involved novel methods like blocking roads and railways?
(a) Telangana Movement
(b) New Farmers' Movement
(c) Tebhaga Movement
(d) Bardoli Satyagraha

UNSOLVED

UNSOLVED

Read the passage given below and answer the questions that follow.

Untouchability is an extreme and particularly vicious aspect of the caste system. It prescribes stringent social sanctions against those considered 'untouchables', who lie outside the caste hierarchy. Untouchables were historically excluded from shared resources like water and religious activities. This exclusion is coupled with economic exploitation, often involving forced or unpaid labour. The term 'Dalit', meaning 'downtrodden', became a rallying cry for empowerment, especially under leaders like Dr. Ambedkar and movements like the Dalit Panthers. Although untouchability is now a criminal offence, its vestiges persist in various forms.

13 Which of the following statements is correct based on the passage? (1)

(a) Untouchables historically held significant economic power.

(b) The term 'Harijan' was coined by Dr. Ambedkar.

(c) 'Dalit' conveys a sense of oppression and struggle.

(d) Untouchability is no longer relevant in Indian society.

14 Which of the following statements is incorrect according to the passage? (1)

I. Untouchability includes exclusion from shared resources and religious events.

II. 'Dalit Panthers' was a movement for the empowerment of oppressed groups.

III. The criminalisation of untouchability has eliminated all its forms.

IV. Dr. Ambedkar frequently used the term 'Dalit' in his writings.

Codes

(a) Only I (b) II and III

(c) Only III (d) I and IV

Read the passage given below and answer the questions that follow.

Apart from the untouchables, there were large groups of castes of low status subjected to discrimination. These were service and artisanal castes occupying lower ranks in the caste hierarchy.

The Constitution of India identifies such groups as "socially and educationally backward classes" (OBC). OBCs are distinct from the Scheduled Castes (SCs) and Scheduled Tribes (STs), representing diverse groups including members of other religions sharing socio-economic disadvantages. The First Backward Classes Commission, headed by Kaka Kalelkar, submitted its report in 1953. However, the OBC issue gained national prominence after the Mandal Commission report (1979) was implemented in 1990. Despite gaining political representation, OBCs face disparities, particularly between urban and rural sections.

15 Which of the following statements is correct? (1)

I. The Constitution of India recognises only caste-based disadvantages.

II. OBCs include members from multiple religions.

III. The Mandal Commission report was implemented in 1990.

IV. Disparities exist among upper and lower OBCs.

Codes

(a) I and III (b) II and IV

(c) I, II and III (d) II and III, IV

16 The politicisation of OBCs gained momentum after (1)

(a) the First Backward Classes Commission report in 1953.

(b) the implementation of the Mandal Commission report in 1990.

(c) early 20th-century southern caste movements.

(d) the Emergency period in the 1970s.

Section-B

17 (a) What does high infant mortality and maternal mortality rate indicate? (2)

Or

(b) What is the 'replacement level' of population growth?

18 What is Sanskritisation? (2)

19 Kumudtai's journey into Sanskrit began with great interest and eagerness with Gokhale Guruji, her teacher at school .... At the University, the Head of the Department was a well-known scholar and he took great pleasure in taunting Kumudtai .... .

Despite the adverse comments she successfully completed her Masters in Sanskit.

Read the source and answer the following question.

Do you think sanskritisation is a gendered process? Give a reason for your answer. (2)

20 Many factories employ badli workers who substitute for regular permanent workers who are on leave.
Who are badli workers? What kind of employment is adopted by them? (2)

21 Give reasons for bringing of land reforms. (2)

22 Matrilocal and patrilocal type of family is based on power. Given two characterstics of this type of family. (2)

23 "In Indian Nationalism, the dominant trend was marked by an Inclusive and a democratic vision." What do you mean by Inclusive and democrative in this statement. (2)

24 "Rituals have also secular dimensions as distinct from secular goals." Which social phenomena is reflected in this proverb? Give any two characteristics of this phenomena. (2)

25 (a) What are the constituents of social resources?

Or

(b) What are the various reasons of social exclusions and discrimination in the society?

Section-C

26 (a) Discuss the different aspects of mass media. (4)

Or

(b) ''Encouraging cultural diversity is good policy from the practical and principled point of view." Justify the statement using India's case as a nation-state.

27 "The struggle for women's upliftment in the 19th and early 20th centuries was led by male reformers." Discuss with suitable examples. (4)

28 "19th century reform initiated a period of questioning, reinterpretations and both intellectual and social growth." Explain with a suitable example. (4)

29 The varied social reform movement had common themes get were different. Do you agree with the given statement? Give reasons for your answer. (4)

30 (a) Identify and discuss the plight of the various stakholders in the Bombay Textile Strike of 1982. (4)

Or

(b) Discuss the role played by social reformers against the discrimination in the society.

31 Explain the concept of social exclusion with respect to Indian Society. (4)

32 "Tribal's have paid a disproportionate price for the development of the rest of Indian society.'' Highlight the sources of conflict between 'national development' and 'tribal development'. (4)

UNSOLVED

Section-D

33 The declining Sex Ratio in India, 1901-2011 **(6)**

Year	Sex ratio (all age groups)	Variation over previous decade	Child Sex ratio (0-6 years)	Variation over previous decade
1901	972	–	–	–
1911	964	–8	–	–
1921	955	–9	–	–
1931	950	–5	–	–
1941	945	–5	–	–
1951	946	+1	–	–
1961	941	–5	976	
1971	930	–11	964	–12
1981	934	+4	962	–2
1991	927	–7	945	–17
2001	933	+6	927	–18
2011	943	+10	919	–8

Note: *The sex ratio is defined as the number of females per 1000 males.*
Data on age-specific sex ratios is not available before 1961.

Source: *Census of India 2011. Government of India.*

(a) Give reasons for declining sex-ratio.

(b) In your opinion, what steps should be taken to deal with this bias against the girl-child?

34 How social stratification adversely impacts lower strata of the society? Discuss. **(6)**

35 What was the means of livelihood for the Dombari community? Why is their profession dying? In your opinion, what can be done to protect communities and occupations like Dombaris? **(6)**

Answers

1 (c) Land Ceiling act

2 (b) regional, tribal identity

3 (b) Both A and R are true, but R is not the correct explanation of A

4 (c) The First Cotton Mill in Surat came UP in 1854.

5 (a) Both A and R are true and R is the correct explanation of A

6 (a) Both A and R are true and R is the correct explanation of A

7 (a) Both A and R are true and R is the correct explanation of A

8 (a) Both A and R are true and R is the correct explanation of A

9 (a) Both A and R are true and R is the correct explanation of A

10 (a) I, II and IV

11 (c) I and III

12 (b) New Farmers' Movement

13 (c) 'Dalit' conveys a sense of oppression and struggle.

14 (c) Only III

15 (d) II, III and IV

16 (b) the implementation of the Mandal Commission report in 1990.